BACKWARDS
in High Heels

Also by Thomas J. Carty

A Catholic in the White House? Religion, Politics,
and John F. Kennedy's Presidential Campaign

BACKWARDS
in High Heels

Faith Whittlesey,
Reagan's Madam Ambassador
in Switzerland and the West Wing

THOMAS J. CARTY

CASEMATE
Philadelphia & Oxford

Published in the United States of America and Great Britain in 2012 by
CASEMATE PUBLISHERS
908 Darby Road, Havertown, PA 19083
and
10 Hythe Bridge Street, Oxford, OX1 2EW

ISBN 978-1-61200-159-3
Digital Edition: ISBN 978-1-61200-160-9

Cataloging-in-publication data is available from the Library of Congress
and the British Library.

10 9 8 7 6 5 4 3 2 1

Printed and bound in the United States of America.

For a complete list of Casemate titles please contact:

CASEMATE PUBLISHERS (US)
Telephone (610) 853-9131, Fax (610) 853-9146
E-mail: casemate@casematepublishing.com

CASEMATE PUBLISHERS (UK)
Telephone (01865) 241249, Fax (01865) 794449
E-mail: casemate-uk@casematepublishing.co.uk

Para Rosamaría

TABLE OF CONTENTS

FOREWORD

This fascinating and informative biography by Thomas J. Carty, Ph.D., brings back fond memories of a vibrant and challenging time. It also constitutes a valuable, even indispensable, contribution to the compelling history of the triumph of the free world led by the United States over the Soviet Empire.

Forty years ago, as my father emerged on to the national scene, he had already achieved prominence and made his mark in a number of areas—in state government, film, advertising, even organized labor. Political adversaries recognized in Dad's devotion to patriotism and principle an unprecedented threat to the power of the central government that had been expanding for several decades. Oh, the labels his opponents made up in their desperate attempts to prevent his efforts to restore confidence, security, and limited government as the United States approached the end of the 20th century! "Extremism" was a favorite epithet, followed closely by "divisive" and "ultraconservative." And what did "ultraconservative" mean? It meant "ultra–*anything that critics didn't like.*"

Dad laughed it all off, a talent which should not be misconstrued: he anchored his political views and his profound faith in God and the American dream, and that made him an optimist. He knew that what Jefferson called "the laws of nature and of nature's God" formed the firm foundation for his efforts to recover the spirit of liberty and peace that Americans were longing for after 35 years of living under the Soviet threat.

He asked a visitor in the late 1970s, "Would you like to hear my plan for ending the Cold War?"

"You bet, Governor," said his visitor, quite willing to miss his plane for that opportunity.

"We win," Dad said, with a grin. That was it. And that was Dad.

And how to win? Enter Faith Whittlesey. Like many other Americans, Faith recognized in Dad not only a proven leader but also a solid and very persuasive conservative. Well, Dad inspired people throughout the country, people in all walks of life who valued the virtues of hard work, thrift, self-reliance, family, church, and neighborhood. Like a ray of sunshine on a cloudy day, Dad's confident enthusiasm convinced millions of Americans that the restoration of limited government was not only possible but necessary as never before in the history of our beloved country.

Faith not only shared my father's goals, she pursued them with a unique combination of gifts. In the White House and as a diplomat in Switzerland, she represented Dad's desire to return government to its proper role of smaller government at home, and abroad a policy of resistance to continuous Soviet expansionism and human rights abuses. At home, that meant a government that is accountable, responsive, and, yes, conservative—because Dad and Faith Whittlesey fervently believed that there was much in America *worth* conserving. Abroad, that meant restoring America's mission as a beacon of hope to the world, not merely containing but defeating the Evil Empire.

This resurgence of confidence energized millions of Americans, many of whom had never voted for a Republican in their lives. For them, Faith opened the White House doors, offering countless educational programs designed to illuminate the truth about Dad's policies that were so opposed and derided by the "prestige" press. For the first time, Professor Carty's account painstakingly recounts the details of Faith's unprecedented network of information and energized action programs that spread the administration's message from the White House across America long before the days of the Internet.

And it didn't stop there. As Dad's two-time ambassador to Switzerland— the meeting point of international diplomacy and intrigue for countries all over the world—Faith tirelessly explained and advocated Dad's foreign policy to officials who covered a broad political spectrum, as well as to the Swiss people. And when I say tireless, I mean it. Faith paid attention to everything and everybody—nothing escaped her gaze, and no visitor escaped her cheerful advocacy of the virtues of a free market society and Ronald Reagan's strategies to win the Cold War. In that same spirit, the pages that follow reveal accounts of events and policies that will surprise many who have not read beyond the "received opinion" produced by historical establishment and mainstream sources from the media and the academy.

You will also be intrigued, as I was, by Faith's distinguished professional career in Pennsylvania politics and law before the 1980 elections. So many people who worked with Dad brought such rich and varied experience—records of extraordinary achievement—in their hometowns across America, experience that contributed so much to his administration's successes. They had honed those skills and long enacted that devotion to principle and the common good in communities across America.

Professor Carty's account is highly readable and often surprising. It constitutes a welcome new contribution to the historical literature of the period. His extensive research goes behind the scenes to seminal sources and materials that have never before appeared in print. Thus, his work contains new insights and documentation that previous accounts of the period had simply overlooked. Faith Whittlesey played a central role in the Reagan Administration, and Professor Carty deserves our gratitude for so ably bringing her contributions to light for the first time.

Whether in the White House or in the power centers of Europe, Faith never forgot where she came from. She was courageous because America was courageous. She was faithful because America's founders were faithful. She was loyal because Nathan Hale and Patrick Henry were loyal. She stood on solid rock because she knows the alternative is shifting sand. My Dad warmly admired her combination of tenacity and generosity, and was amazed at her endless capacity to take on new tasks of every kind—always devoted to ensuring that freedom would be secure for future generations.

Encino, California   MICHAEL REAGAN
July 3, 2012

ACKNOWLEDGMENTS

During the 2005 American Swiss Foundation's Young Leaders Conference, Steven Frick, M.D., of Charlotte, North Carolina, and I were speaking casually in Zürich with Ambassador Faith Whittlesey. At one point, Dr. Frick suggested, "Tom, you should write Ambassador Whittlesey's story." I responded enthusiastically, but the conversation soon moved to another topic.

Dr. Frick's words had planted a seed, however, in my mind. After the conference, I maintained a correspondence with Ambassador Whittlesey, and at some point we revived the idea. By the spring of 2009, we met at the Harvard Club, prior to an event of the Boston-based Friends of Switzerland, and she agreed to provide me with exceptional access for interviews as well as the names of several individuals who could comment in detail on her professional career. I appreciate both Dr. Frick's initial proposal and the consistent support of Ambassador Whittlesey, who demonstrated exceptional trust in my judgment by speaking openly and honestly with me about her life and career.

As important as this privileged contact was, I acquired an even more complete picture of Ambassador Whittlesey through the more than 100 people I interviewed. In every case, I was received respectfully by interviewees on the phone, in an office, or in their homes. These interviews proved important because each individual provided unique insights into Whittlesey's character, impact, and significance. The vast majority of these people highlighted particular accomplishments which she herself had never brought to my attention.

Most of the individuals I interviewed are mentioned within the text. But I would also like to acknowledge here a few people who provided insightful background information from which I did not quote directly in these pages. Dr. Hans Halbheer pointed me toward the individual who interviewed Whittlesey for her first posting as ambassador. Having known every U.S. ambassador to

Switzerland since 1962, Halbheer provided a rich context for my research, and he stated without reservation that he considered Faith Whittlesey the best among that group. At an early stage, Dr. Christopher Manion offered me his experience as a member of Senator Jesse Helms' staff, and this information helped me understand the interworking of the Republican Party in the 1980s. Ivan Pictet provided insights into the Swiss mindset and the complicated world of Geneva banking. Lifelong career government employee Marguerite Fry also generously shared her recollections with me.

George Norcross—a very successful entrepreneur, member of the Democratic National Committee, and co-owner of the *Philadelphia Inquirer*— helped me understand and appreciate Faith Whittlesey's ability to inspire the public and establish political connections with Democrats and labor unions. He called her the "Republican Hillary Clinton" in recognition of her achievements for a woman of her time, and told me a great story about how she helped create a friendship between his father, a powerful Democratic leader in New Jersey, and the Reverend Jerry Falwell, a committed Republican.

Several colleagues within the academy generously offered their knowledge to help me move this project forward. At an early stage, I received important advice about conducting oral history interviews from Dr. Bruce M. Stave, director of the Center for Oral History at the University of Connecticut. Dr. J. Garry Clifford, a professor and director of the graduate program in political science at the University of Connecticut, also pointed me in the direction of some very helpful resources, particularly the Library of Congress' Frontline Diplomacy project.

I want to thank several well-published scholars whose counsel proved valuable as I ventured into this project. Dr. Mark Rozell, professor of public policy at George Mason University, always provided a wealth of experience and knowledge in response to my queries. I benefited greatly from the thoughts of Dr. Paul Kengor, professor of political science at Grove City College in Pennsylvania, director of the college's Center for Vision and Values, and a prolific author of books about Ronald Reagan. I also appreciated the encouragement from one of the leading historians of contemporary American conservatism, Dr. Donald Critchlow, the Barry M. Goldwater chair of American institutions at Arizona State University.

I am also pleased to be able to express my great appreciation to a long-time friend, Dr. Gregory Witkowski, director of graduate studies and associate professor of philanthropic studies at The Center on Philanthropy at Indiana University. Greg read a late draft of the entire manuscript, and he offered useful comments which helped me in making important revisions.

In addition, several librarians helped me along the way. Alex Rankin and the staff at the Howard Gotlieb Archival Research Center of Boston University assisted me with the Whittlesey papers. I appreciated the assistance of the Ronald Reagan Presidential Library staff in Simi Valley, California, as well. I conducted a great deal of writing during the final stages of the manuscript's production at the University of Saint Joseph (West Hartford, Connecticut) library, where Antoinette Collins and Amber Monroe generously went out of their way to answer my questions.

At my home institution, Springfield College, I had many kind supporters. Professor Herb Zettl and Dean Mary Healey coordinated release time for my research and writing. Along with Vice President Jean Wyld and President Richard Flynn, they supported funding of my 2008–2009 academic sabbatical, during which my work on this project began. Several student workers—Amanda DiPaolo Wright, Jaclyn Novitzky, Matt Geanacopoulos, Christopher Malia, Connor Convery, and Brian Silva—transcribed interviews for me, and Matt read and commented on an early draft of the first chapter. Administrative assistant Christine Caster greatly eased the burden of preparing the manuscript by cheerfully responding to several of my requests for printing, faxing, or mailing drafts of chapters.

In the hectic final stages in particular, several individuals worked very hard to guarantee that this book was ready for publication by October 2012. Jeanne Marie Cella graciously read and commented on the entire book as well, Susan Graf assisted enormously with photoediting, and Sue Tomkin of Tomkin Design produced a nicely designed camera-ready copy. Kelly Waering provided very important editorial comments on the manuscript. Kelly's careful copyediting helped me produce a cleaner and more reader-friendly version.

Gene Waering coordinated communication with numerous people who participated in my research and provided valuable editing suggestions and fact checking from the earliest to the final stages. Gene's good judgment and grace in dealing with all involved with this book and his cordial manner and good humor contributed immensely to keeping the book on schedule. Both Waering brothers committed themselves to this project for long hours and multiple days. They took personal pride in ensuring the book presented an elegant and consistent style.

My family deserves special mention as well. In Lima, Peru, I worked several weeks each year from the home of my parents-in-law, Jorge León and Maruja León Gavonel. Along with my brothers-in-law Jorge (and his wife Luz Maria) and Roberto, they accommodated all of an author's needs—from office space to Internet connections to delicious coffee and the world-renowned Peruvian cuisine. I received the same generous support from my sister-in-law Anamaría León de la Torre (and her husband David), in whose home and study I often worked as well.

I can only recount here a few small examples of the innumerable acts of unconditional love my parents have shown me during my work on this book. Janice Carty, my mother, responded immediately and unreservedly (as she has for decades) to all my requests for help with challenges big and small. My father, Thomas J. Carty, Jr., functioned essentially as an ad hoc research assistant (bringing qualifications of a Ph.D. in biochemistry, no less!) during this project. He listened attentively to my ideas, researched newspaper databases, transcribed interviews, and even edited my earliest drafts of chapters.

My two children, Marisol Louise Carty and Thomas J. Carty, IV, provided me with many, many smiles and laughs during the past 3 years. Marisol's multiple talents and hobbies inspired me to a greater appreciation of classical piano (which helped me recognize the significance of Faith Whittlesey's dedication and extraordinary musical achievements at a young age) and contemporary literature, especially Harry Potter. Tommy's hard work and exponential progress in reading and language also inspired me to endeavor in a similar way to reach beyond what I thought I could reasonably achieve.

I dedicate this book to my wife, Rosamaría León, whose love and support were indispensable. She is my unfailing partner in each and every endeavor, and she helped me in many ways as I pursued this project. Besides reading and commenting on multiple drafts of my writing, she prodded me to take intellectual risks which I would otherwise have avoided. Rosamaría also shouldered many practical responsibilities for our family when I needed to focus single-mindedly on research and writing. I cannot imagine life without her, and her many years of love and support truly humble me and continue to surprise me as our marriage grows each year.

West Hartford, Connecticut   THOMAS J. CARTY
July 31, 2012

INTRODUCTION

"Ginger Rogers did everything Fred Astaire did, but she did it backwards in high heels." Faith Whittlesey popularized this quotation during the 1980s. The message resonated with many late-20th-century American women familiar with the Astaire-Rogers dancing duo in 1930s Hollywood musicals: society often expects women to mirror the moves of a male lead despite circumstances which distinctly increase the degree of difficulty.

This first book-length study of Faith Ryan Whittlesey relates a uniquely American story. I argue that Whittlesey deserves scholarly and popular recognition both as a pioneer for American women in politics and as an innovative advocate for U.S. interests at home and abroad. Most Americans, and the global public as well, are likely familiar with the stories of female public figures such as Eleanor Roosevelt, Hillary Clinton, and Nancy Pelosi. After careful analysis of Whittlesey's career, however, my research reveals a woman whose accomplishments deserve recognition within the same category as these other exceptional women.

Whittlesey's path to become ambassador to Switzerland and White House senior staff member came through a career of breaking new ground for women in politics. She entered law school in 1960 (10 years prior to Hillary Clinton) when women held only 3 percent of all professional graduate degrees in the United States.[1] She won election to the Pennsylvania House of Representatives in the early 1970s (a generation before Sarah Palin won election as mayor of Wasilla, Alaska) when women occupied less than 5 percent of seats in state legislatures nationwide.[2]

---

[1]   Rochelle Gatlin, *American Women Since 1945* (Jackson: University Press of Mississippi, 1987), p. 204.

[2]   Susan J. Carroll, "Women in State Government: Historical Overview and Current Trends," *The Book of the States, 2004* (Lexington, KY: The Council of State Governments, 2004), p. 4.

For the vast majority of her career, Whittlesey participated in politics without a powerful husband or father as a mentor and source of financial support. In addition to caring for three young children as a single mother—following her husband's sudden, tragic death in 1974—she made herself a significant factor in state, national, and international government service, and later in the private sector.

Perhaps authors have overlooked Whittlesey because she failed to fit the typical ideological profile of a woman politician. Neither did she conform strictly to Republican Party orthodoxy. Unlike many women (and men) in politics, Whittlesey often made her way by challenging conventional wisdom. In the early 1970s, she ascended the ladder within the Delaware County (Pennsylvania) Republican Party—one of the nation's most powerful, and all-male, political machines. She supported Ronald Reagan's pursuit of the Republican Party presidential nomination in 1976 when the party's leadership backed sitting President Gerald Ford. This audacious move was risky at the time, but it earned the trust of Reagan and his committed followers. When he campaigned again for the presidency in 1980, she worked even harder, and this time successfully, to ensure his election.

She and Reagan shared ideas which diverged widely from the dominant thinking of leaders in both the Republican and Democratic parties of the 1970s. Whittlesey might have conformed her views more closely to the establishment, or she could have used the political contacts she developed in Harrisburg, Pennsylvania, and Washington, DC, for a lucrative career as a lobbyist. Instead, she perceived public service in the manner of an American entrepreneur. When offered positions of responsibility—such as U.S. ambassador to Switzerland and director of the White House Office of Public Liaison—she looked to innovate and to challenge standard operating procedures. As president of the American Swiss Foundation, she leveraged her government experience to develop expanded private-sector diplomatic initiatives. As chairman of the Institute of World Politics for 6 years, and board member from its beginning, she played an active role in establishing a solid base for this new institution of statecraft in Washington, DC.

This inventive, contrarian mindset, coupled with her philosophy of diplomacy and government in general, deserves more serious consideration by academics and the general public. Perceiving herself as a "citizen ambassador," Whittlesey earned profound admiration from the Swiss by engaging with that country's decision makers and demonstrating appreciation of

Switzerland's heritage and constitutional legal system. As a result, Whittlesey earned credibility and discovered intersecting points where President Reagan's foreign policy goals coincided with Swiss interests. Scholars have categorized such skillful appeals to foreign nongovernmental actors as "public diplomacy," which has recently gained greater currency as a promising but underutilized tool of statecraft.

Whittlesey's confidence in public diplomacy derives primarily from her trust that individual American citizens will represent the United States abroad in a dignified and effective manner. Following her nearly 7 years of service in the Reagan administration, Whittlesey created private-sector initiatives to promote positive bilateral relations between the United States and Switzerland, China, and other nations. In particular, she revived the nonprofit American-Swiss Association primarily through an initiative known as the Young Leaders Conference. By careful selection of future decision makers from the United States and Switzerland and thought-provoking programs, Whittlesey generated open, serious, and substantive dialogue across national borders with a country that has been, for many years, one of the largest foreign direct investors in the United States and a valuable partner in various worldwide humanitarian efforts. During that time, Whittlesey urged Americans to engage foreign publics in positive ways by thinking beyond inflexible, rehearsed talking points.

This feature of Faith Whittlesey's career may prove her most important bequest to an increasingly interconnected world. Military and information technology has provided the U.S. government with awe-inspiring power to influence other nations. Whittlesey encouraged Americans to listen as well as speak. As a public servant, ambassador, and private citizen, she promoted a simple, traditional model of person-to-person diplomacy. From her perspective, each American must take responsibility for generating global goodwill—one individual at a time.

SOURCE MATERIAL AND THE HISTORICAL RECORD

This history relies primarily on personal interviews with Faith Whittlesey and more than 100 individuals—ranging in viewpoint from CEOs of multinational corporations to the U.S. embassy's household staff—who had professional and personal relationships with her. It differs from a memoir, however, in that I researched dates and facts to confirm or question the stories related to me.

I conducted most of these interviews in person, and with standards and methods endorsed by oral history professionals. For example, I researched the background of each interviewee. To avoid leading the interviewee in a direction predetermined by me, I crafted open-ended questions. By actively listening and encouraging interviewees to elaborate at times, I attempted to extract complete and detailed memories. Digital recordings, which were later transcribed, ensured the accuracy of quotations which appear in the book.

Owing primarily to my training and experience as a professional historian, I also incorporated written primary and secondary sources into the story. The interviews proved critical, however, because many records for this period remain classified. Furthermore, the nature of diplomatic secrecy (and fears of legal and political ramifications) often discouraged ambassadors and other diplomats from keeping diaries or other extensive written records. While memories may occasionally prove flawed, I cross-referenced stories with other interviews or with the written record whenever possible. Faith Whittlesey's manuscript collection at the Howard Gotlieb Archival Research Center at Boston University is yet to be fully organized, but I utilized this important resource as much as possible.

I believe that scholars will benefit from this assessment of Whittlesey's most important professional accomplishments and failures. Many of the participants in Whittlesey's story welcomed me into their homes and offices in Boston, New York City, Washington, San Francisco, Paris, and several Swiss cities—Vevey, Geneva, Bern, and Zürich. In these predominantly face-to-face meetings, I accumulated multiple eyewitness accounts which provided nuance and detail.

OUTLINE OF THE BOOK

In nine chapters, this book presents Faith Whittlesey's story, which intersected with many of the Reagan administration's pivotal actors and at times with world leaders such as the Soviet Union's Mikhail Gorbachev and China's Hu Jintao. Chapter 1 recounts the roots of her political values and management style from her Williamsville, New York, childhood to housewife and mother, and ultimately her appointment as U.S. ambassador by President Ronald Reagan. The next two chapters discuss her first tour in the U.S. embassy in Bern. Specifically, Chapter 2 describes how she persuaded U.S. and Swiss government officials to seek a diplomatic resolution of a contentious legal dispute between the American and Swiss governments related to Switzerland's banking privacy law. In Chapter 3, I address Whittlesey's use of "soft power" to engage with the Swiss public and leading decision makers and to represent the United States, and the Reagan administration's policies, in the most favorable light.

The next two chapters focus on Faith's return to the United States as the highest-ranking woman on President Reagan's White House senior staff. Chapter 4 treats in depth how Whittlesey became enmeshed in the internal administration debates about the potential existence of a "gender gap" unfavorable to the president. Chapter 5 explains how Whittlesey utilized her West Wing position to explain and advance the president's domestic and foreign policies, especially among the so-called Reagan Democrats during the lead-up to the 1984 election and beyond.

In the sixth and seventh chapters, I discuss Whittlesey's second tour as ambassador to Switzerland. Chapter 6 deals with her efforts to promote Reagan's foreign policy during the final stage of the Cold War. Chapter 7 recounts Faith's perseverance during a series of partisan and media attacks on her reputation as the Iran-Contra scandal threatened the Reagan presidency.

The final chapters present Whittlesey's continued public diplomacy after departing from her government posts. Chapter 8 focuses on her private-sector work in law and on corporate boards, as well as her revival of the nonprofit American-Swiss Association. As president and chairman of the (renamed) American Swiss Foundation, she envisioned and realized the highly successful annual Young Leaders conferences described above. Chapter 9 explains how she translated some of the techniques she developed in U.S.-Swiss relations to initiate new connections between the United States and the People's Republic of China.

Because of her unwavering advocacy of the president's agenda and commitment to the platform he was elected on, Faith Whittlesey was preeminently Reagan's "Madam Ambassador" during her tenure in Bern as U.S. ambassador and service on the White House senior staff. This book makes the case that both as a citizen diplomat of the Reagan administration and as a "diplomatic citizen" after she left government, Faith Whittlesey sought and still seeks to model her activities, employing sometimes novel and often ingenious means, and a unique combination of life experiences in a woman politician, to further a principled vision of the United States that she and President Reagan largely shared.

CHAPTER 1

From Williamsville, New York, to U.S. Embassy Bern

Martin Roy Ryan and Amy Jerusha Covell must surely have recognized some common characteristics when they met in the 1930s. Both had embraced habits of hard work and sacrifice for family. Martin's father Michael, an Irish immigrant, had died young. Due to financial necessity, Martin, the eldest of five siblings, had quit school after eighth grade and worked to help support his family. Similarly, Amy had risen daily at 4 A.M. to perform farm chores. In a family of 15 children, more than half of whom passed away due to illness, the Covells did not ask for government assistance. In the remote New York State "north country" near the Canadian border where Amy grew up, none would have been available anyway.

Martin had been raised as a Catholic in Maybrook, New York, and served as an altar boy. At that time, a marriage between a Catholic and Protestant (the Covells were Methodists) might well cause some family tension. This one was no exception. All but one of Amy's brothers shunned her after she decided to marry the less-educated, Irish Catholic Martin. Nevertheless, Martin and Amy wed, had two children, and were very happy together throughout their long lives, according to their first child, whom they named Faith Amy Ryan. Faith entered the world on February 21, 1939, at Margaret Hague Hospital in Jersey City, New Jersey. A brother named Thomas followed on December 25, 1941—just weeks following the Japanese attack on Pearl Harbor.

As the United States entered World War II, the Ryan family was urged to relocate to the outskirts of Buffalo, New York, where Faith's parents worked in war industries. Amy's mother, who had a college degree, tested airplane engines—the kind of occupation made famous by Norman Rockwell's popular *Rosie the Riveter* illustration. Martin, who exceeded the age limit for military service, worked as a middle manager in a private transportation company shipping war-related material. They first lived in a housing project for families working at war plants.

The Ryan family later moved to a neighborhood of beautifully manicured lawns and open fields in Williamsville—a small village at the time. Martin and Amy purchased a prefabricated home with one bathroom and two bedrooms—the dining room was converted into a third bedroom for Faith's brother Tom.[1] Faith recalled these childhood years as "very wholesome" without "fear of crime or predators." The Ryans had no television, listened to radio only on Saturdays, and each Sunday attended the Williamsville Methodist church, where Faith would sing in the choir. Faith and Tom frequently played outside, ice skating and sled riding in the winter.

Although both were working, Amy and Martin deliberately excused their children from household tasks so that Faith and Tom would focus on acquiring and developing academic and musical skills. "My parents knew instinctively that the world was a highly competitive place and every minute of preparation for that world counted." Faith and Tom dutifully learned through their parents' example to read widely and keep busy.

Martin and Amy Ryan lived a frugal, nuclear family lifestyle without ever employing a childcare worker, nor did they have any of the labor-saving devices increasingly available to Americans in the 1950s. For example, the Ryans had a clothes washing machine but no dryer. "They never purchased anything on credit, not even a car," Faith recalled. After boiling vegetables, Amy saved the vitamin-rich water for soups. "We were living what today would be described as an 'eco-friendly' life," Whittlesey observed in 2009.[2]

Many years later, Faith's friend and colleague James Shinn would suggest that her childhood experience could potentially explain her later respect for the Swiss. As deputy chief of mission (DCM) in Bern from 1982 to 1986, Shinn observed Faith on a near-daily basis in Switzerland. "She

---

[1]   Faith Whittlesey, interview by author, Cambridge, MA, September 8, 2009; Faith Whittlesey, interview by Ann Miller Morin, December 7, 1988. Frontline Diplomacy, Manuscript Division, Library of Congress, Washington, DC.
[2]   Faith Whittlesey, interview by author, Cambridge, MA, September 8, 2009.

was somebody who had accomplished a lot in her own life," Shinn noted, "and she recognized a country which, despite its limitations of almost zero resources, has nonetheless over the centuries accomplished a great deal as well. And I think the two respected each other."[3] Faith had grown up far from a major urban metropolis and the corridors of power.

FAITH'S DISCOVERY OF EUROPE

The Ryan household also provided Faith with an appreciation for European and American literature and music. Her mother, in particular, honored intellectual achievement. More than three decades prior to her appointment as U.S. ambassador to Switzerland, Faith's rigorous routine of classical piano practice—a full hour every morning, 7 days a week—began at age 5.

Her mother insisted that Faith learn to play expertly. Rather than rebel, she admired her mother's cultural understanding and especially her personal discipline, which Amy Ryan had demonstrated in her own life, working from very early morning until evening. Faith mastered works of Mozart, Chopin, Bach, and Beethoven. In Faith's later high school years, she taught piano to younger children in her home.

In addition to the piano, she participated in other extracurricular activities. Faith joined the large Williamsville High School Band, and played clarinet—first chair, first clarinet of 26 clarinets. She also performed most of the solos in the high school's elaborate water ballet productions. Practice for these events required 2 hours a day in the water. And she developed a love of books. The Ryans' small home had bookcases filled with the classics of European and American literature, which Faith—and especially her brother Tom—read, often several times. These books were supplemented by regular visits to the Williamsville Public Library for more books.[4]

At age 16, Faith had a formative experience which expanded her attraction to European culture. Her mother encouraged her—even to the point of sitting with her at the kitchen table while she filled out the application—to apply for an American Field Service Summer Exchange Program scholarship to live with a West German family during the summer of 1955. Faith was accepted.

Traveling in the years prior to inexpensive trans-Atlantic flights, she sailed for Europe from Montreal on a steam liner. Driving through Hamburg,

---

[3]   James Shinn, interview by author, Kensington, CA, March 16, 2010.
[4]   Faith Whittlesey, interview by author, Cambridge, MA, September 8, 2009.

West Germany, on her way to Flensburg, the town near the Danish border
where she would spend the summer, she was struck by the still clearly visible
massive rubble from Allied bombing of that city in World War II; she also
traveled to Denmark and Sweden. Europeans' personal code of behavior
impressed Faith. For example, she noted how European students immediately
rose from their chairs when a teacher entered their classroom, and how
young commuters routinely offered their seat on public transportation to
any approaching older adult—purely out of a learned respect.[5]

WELLS COLLEGE AND A CONTINUED CONNECTION TO EUROPE
Faith's appreciation for Western Civilization deepened in college. In 1956,
she earned a full-tuition scholarship as well as a New York State scholarship
at Wells College, an all-women's school near Cornell University, situated on
the shores of Cayuga Lake in upstate New York. (Henry Wells, the founder
of Wells Fargo & Company, established the institution in 1868.) She majored
in history and worked hard to excel.

Perceiving herself less prepared for college work than her private-school-
educated Wells College classmates, Faith dedicated herself to a "military-like
regimen" modeled, no doubt, on her mother's strict schedule. She continued
to practice the classical piano, now for two daily 1-hour sessions—once in
the morning and again in the afternoon. Prior to lunch, she spent a half-
hour reading the *New York Times*. While many of her classmates enjoyed
conversation and evening card games, such as bridge, Faith typically studied
in the main library from 7 until 11 P.M., Monday through Thursday. "I
wanted to keep my scholarship, and I really liked studying. I had come to
love history," she recalled. Faith found Wells to be intellectually stimulating.
On the weekends, she enjoyed dating and dancing with young men from
nearby Cornell University at various fraternity parties.[6]

During the summer of her sophomore year, Faith found a means of returning to Europe. In 1958, she earned a scholarship through the Experiment
in International Living program, which funded her travel to Austria where
she lived with a host family near Graz—that country's second-largest city
(after Vienna). During an eventful summer, she spent several weeks traveling by train through Italy, Yugoslavia, West Germany, and Austria with

5   Faith Whittlesey, interview by Ann Miller Morin, June 17, 1989. Frontline Diplomacy,
     Manuscript Division, Library of Congress, Washington, DC.
6   Faith Whittlesey, interview by author, Cambridge, MA, September 8, 2009.

other young Americans in the program. This opportunity to interact with people from outside her small town widened her perspectives on the world.

Faith's eyewitness experience of communism's impact on Yugoslavia also resulted in an immediate strong aversion to that system of government. Her Austrian host family's father, who had been forced to work as a medical doctor in Yugoslavia during the war, recounted vivid stories about the rigid imposition of Stalinist authority at the end of World War II and during its immediate aftermath as the Cold War period began. Entering into communist Yugoslavia, Faith perceived firsthand the stark contrast between the relative prosperity and freedom of Western Europe and the oppression and drab poverty of Belgrade and Sarajevo. A sense of constant police surveillance became her lasting memory of that communist nation. "I was never seduced, therefore—as so many others of my generation were—by the 'liberation of the people' arguments in favor of the communist ideology of so-called fairness and social justice," she later recalled.[7]

By contrast, she became enchanted with the natural beauty, art, music, and cuisine of central Europe. She traveled to the southeast of Switzerland to see beautiful Lake Lugano and in Italy, Lago Maggiore. In Austria, she improved her waltzing technique, German language skills, and personal appreciation of every Austrian bakery's signature desert, apple strudel.

During her senior year of college, Faith began to consider continuing her studies. Her mother had long regarded nursing as the most rewarding profession for a woman in the 1950s, and had so counseled her daughter. But when Faith mentioned to one Wells College English professor that she might pursue such a career, she instantly recognized his shocked and disappointed expression, which she never forgot. He clearly perceived such a choice as unfit for a young woman of her ability, especially one who had taken a strong interest in the world of ideas.

After reassessing her options based in part on her professor's expectations, Faith decided to apply for graduate programs in history and law. Intrigued intellectually by her European experience, and encouraged by her Wells College professors of German language and history, she applied first for graduate programs in history. In 1960, Faith graduated *cum laude* and Phi Beta Kappa—4th in her class of 72.[8]

---

[7] Ibid.
[8] Ibid.

"A COMPLETELY DIFFERENT WORLD"

Faith's limited finances and her parents' frugal ways significantly shaped her choice of postgraduate education. She applied to the graduate program in history at Stanford University, which accepted her and offered a small stipend. But this distant California institution's financial assistance package was less than the more proximate University of Pennsylvania Law School's, in Philadelphia (where she had applied as an alternative). Faith did not have great interest in pursuing a legal career, but Penn offered her a full scholarship, and her parents never considered applying for a bank loan. Without the economic means of subsidizing her education in California, the choice was clear.[9]

Law school would not prove an easy undertaking for Faith. Having come from a small town and a small college, she recalled being intimidated by the large, diverse student body at Penn. "I was frightened. ... I had the thought I could not make it." She perceived her classmates as much more sophisticated than she was. Philadelphia had a well-defined social hierarchy, she learned. Faith became more aware of people's responses to her commonly Irish Catholic surname, her limited knowledge of urbane fashion, and her lack of family connections in social circles of power and wealth.[10]

Compounding her sense of not belonging at Penn, she was 1 of only 6 women in her class of 142. This male-female ratio was typical for that period. In 1960, women held only 3 percent of all professional degrees in the United States.[11] Some of Faith's professors appeared to view the female students as oddities. One of them, she recalled, referred to the women in his class not by name but as Portia 1, 2, 3, and 4[12] (a reference to the quick-witted, articulate protagonist by that name in Shakespeare's *The Merchant of Venice*).[13]

Faith soon questioned her decision to attend law school. Upon arriving home in Williamsville after her first year, she broke down in tears and talked about not returning to Penn. But her parents insisted that she complete the two remaining years of graduate education. "My father was very sympathetic

---

[9]   Ibid.
[10] Faith Whittlesey, interview by Ann Miller Morin, June 17, 1989.
[11] Rochelle Gatlin, *American Women Since 1945* (Jackson: University Press of Mississippi, 1987), p. 204.
[12] Faith Whittlesey, interview by author, Cambridge, MA, September 8, 2009.
[13] John Adams addressed his wife Abigail as Portia in their correspondence, and Boston's Portia Law School was founded in 1908 as a women-only school (prior to being renamed the New England School of Law in 1969).

whenever he saw me cry but he said, ... 'It's absolutely out of the question. You're going back. You're not quitting.' "[14]

Although the law seemed overly technical and some professors appeared to relish humiliating students, she returned to Penn. Faith's writing skills served her well, and she studied just enough to remain in the top 50 percent of her class, enabling her to maintain her scholarship.[15]

While most of her male colleagues competed for high positions in the law review, Faith preferred the Philadelphia opera, even if she could find no one to join her. Faith sat in the highest, least expensive, balcony seats. To cover the cost of opera tickets and other spending, she worked as a substitute teacher in inner-city Philadelphia public schools, cutting a few of her law classes, as needed.[16]

Faith's fascination with Europe persisted during her time at Penn. In 1962, after completing her second year of law school, Faith applied for—and was awarded—a Ford Foundation grant to attend a summer session at The Academy of International Law in The Hague, Netherlands. She visited her brother, a junior at Yale who was studying at the University of Munich, and she extended the experience by hitchhiking and taking trains, buses, and boats with young friends through Holland, Italy, France, Greece, and Spain. (It was common and safe to hitchhike in Europe in those days.) Faith discovered "a goldmine of museums, castles, and cathedrals," and she relished the opportunity to attend the opera.[17]

Faith met many interesting people during her travels, including Dr. Robert Jastrow, who became a lifelong friend.[18] Having earned his Ph.D. in theoretical physics from Columbia University, Jastrow served as founding director of NASA's Goddard Institute for Space Studies from 1961 to 1981. He and Faith visited some of Greece's ancient ruins and other tourist attractions together. Years later, in Ronald Reagan's White House, Jastrow advocated actively for Reagan's Strategic Defense Initiative, publishing a book titled *How to Make Nuclear Weapons Obsolete* in 1985.[19]

---

[14] Faith Whittlesey, interview by Ann Miller Morin, June 17, 1989.
[15] Ibid.
[16] Faith Whittlesey, interview by author, Cambridge, MA, September 8, 2009.
[17] Faith Whittlesey, interview by Ann Miller Morin, June 17, 1989.
[18] Faith Whittlesey, interview by author, Cambridge, MA, September 8, 2009.
[19] John Schwartz, "Robert Jastrow, Who Made Space Understandable, Dies at 82," *New York Times*, February 12, 2008; Robert Jastrow, *How to Make Nuclear Weapons Obsolete* (New York: Little, Brown, 1985).

As Faith returned to Philadelphia for her last year of law school, opportunities for female lawyers appeared minimal. "We were advised by the law school administration not to even come to the interviews because we would not be hired," Faith remembered in 1989. "They were blunt. It was a completely different world."[20]

ROGER WHITTLESEY

Despite her lack of passion for the legal profession, Faith did find romantic love during her time at Penn. In April 1963, Faith's life changed in a dramatic way. While walking a law school classmate's Australian terrier in Center City (downtown) Philadelphia, she encountered a man dressed in work clothes who was renovating an historic old Trinity house (a 1700s-style home with three stories and only one room per floor) on a narrow cobblestone street. As Faith recalled, "He was tall and good-looking with striking features, curly brown hair, dark eyes, with a distinct twinkle."[21] He introduced himself as Roger and struck up a conversation with the young law student.

Roger and Faith quickly discovered that they shared two key passions—the opera and politics. Having graduated from William Penn Charter School in Philadelphia and Bowdoin College in Maine, Roger now worked as an advertising executive. "I was drawn to Roger because I saw immediately that he possessed the intelligence, social confidence, and grace I believed I lacked. I deeply wanted to possess as a woman the elegance, style, wit, and glamour he had as a man."[22]

Roger Weaver Whittlesey belonged to a prominent family which resided in Philadelphia's exclusive Huntingdon Valley suburbs. The family's history, with roots reaching deeply into premodern England, fascinated Faith. Roger's ancestors came from a town named Whittlesey, which lay less than 100 miles north of London in the county of Cambridgeshire. Roger's ancestry included William Whittlesey, who served as the 57th archbishop of Canterbury from 1368 to 1374.

Although Faith had rejected prior suitors—including one who traveled across the Atlantic Ocean to propose marriage to her at The Hague in 1962—she accepted Roger's proposal of marriage a mere 3 weeks after they had met. They found a church in the yellow pages of the telephone book. On

---

[20] Faith Whittlesey, interview by Ann Miller Morin, June 17, 1989.
[21] Faith Whittlesey, interview by author, Cambridge, MA, September 8, 2009.
[22] Ibid.

May 11, 1963—only days prior to her law school graduation—Faith Ryan and Roger Whittlesey exchanged nuptial vows in Old St. George's Methodist church in the old town of Philadelphia with only a few close friends and family in attendance.[23] Faith knew an expensive wedding would not have been possible for her parents.

While Faith initially worried about being accepted into a family whose social status contrasted strikingly with her own small-town background, she found the Whittleseys very welcoming. Barbara Weaver Whittlesey, Roger's mother, "gave me loving and specific lessons in proper decorum and dress, such as allowing older people to travel through doors first and placing soup spoons on the side of the plate while eating rather than leaving them submerged in the bowl." Barbara Whittlesey remained a "best friend for life." Faith also recalled listening with rapt attention to tales from Roger's father, Albert W. Whittlesey, who was born and raised in China by Presbyterian missionary parents, eventually becoming senior vice president of First Pennsylvania Bank. Faith also enjoyed visits by Roger's maternal uncle, William M. Weaver, Jr., a highly successful New York investment banker, who exuded charm, charisma, and generosity.

Whittlesey family history included stirring heroism and heart-wrenching tragedy, Faith discovered. One of Roger's distant relatives, Charles W. Whittlesey, a 1908 Harvard Law graduate, had earned a Congressional Medal of Honor after surviving battles in France's Argonne Forest during World War I.[24] After the war, Charles' despair at having commanded the "Lost Battalion," which had suffered such heavy casualties, prompted him to jump to his death from a cruise ship destined for Cuba.[25] Roger's uncle, Henry C. Whittlesey, was an officer during World War II attached to the "Dixie Mission," which traveled undercover behind enemy lines to gather intelligence for the United States, to coordinate anti-Japanese operations with China's communists, and to retrieve downed American airmen. He was killed on reconnaissance in Japanese-occupied China. Henry remained a celebrated American hero within the People's Republic of China long after the end of Japan's occupation.

---

[23] "Faith Amy Ryan Is Wed," *New York Times*, May 12, 1963, p. 89.
[24] Faith Whittlesey, interview by author, Cambridge, MA, September 8, 2009.
[25] Edward G. Lengel, *To Conquer Hell: The Meuse-Argonne, 1918* (New York: Henry Holt, 2008), p. 434; Richard Slotkin, *Lost Battalions: The Great War and the Crisis of American Nationality* (New York: Henry Holt, 2005), pp. 475–480; Alan Gaff, *Blood in the Argonne: The "Lost Battalion" of World War I* (Norman: University of Oklahoma Press, 2005), pp. 281–285.

Faith Whittlesey later described her 11 years of marriage to the tall, handsome, debonair Roger as romance sufficient to last a lifetime. She gave birth to three children—Henry, on December 18, 1965, Amy on September 19, 1967, and William on October 18, 1972. Roger and Faith enjoyed visiting the Caribbean and Europe—sometimes accompanied by the children but more frequently as a couple, normally leaving their children in the care of nannies (who were often Swiss).

Roger and Faith socialized actively in Philadelphia with his business and political friends. Roger, an active member of several social organizations—such as the Racquet Club, the Marion Golf Club, the Union League Club, and the Huntingdon Valley Country Club—attended many dinner parties. The Whittleseys hosted these functions in their home on occasion, as well.[26]

INTRODUCTION TO POLITICS 101

Since Roger devoted some of his time as an advertising executive to marketing Republican Party candidates, Faith quickly learned political lessons about the GOP ("Grand Old Party") which her college and law school curricula had not included. Although she had initially leaned toward the Democratic Party after the model of her Wells College and Penn Law School professors, Roger's family identified with the GOP. His creative advertising ideas proved effective in helping elect Republican politicians such as Arlen Specter, who won election as Philadelphia's district attorney in 1965 (and who would later serve as a U.S. senator from Pennsylvania for more than 30 years).

Faith witnessed up close the boom-and-bust political cycle through Roger's victories and defeats. In 1966, Roger campaigned for himself and won the Republican primary for the Pennsylvania State House of Representatives seat from Center City Philadelphia. But he lost to the Democratic candidate in a district dominated by Democrats. Roger succeeded in winning election as president of both the Young Republicans of Center City Philadelphia and the Center City Residents' Association.[27]

In 1968, Roger was selected as executive director of Richard Nixon's presidential campaign in Pennsylvania, which was one of the "big seven" states specifically targeted by the GOP nominee. Pennsylvania's size—it was one of the eight largest U.S. states—and the closely divided political party

---

26 Faith Whittlesey, interview by author, Cambridge, MA, September 8, 2009.
27 Ibid.

loyalties of its citizens made it a "battleground state." While Nixon failed
to win Pennsylvania in November, he prevailed nationally in that closely
fought election.[28] Roger served as master of ceremonies on election night
at the Sheraton Hotel in Philadelphia, and he announced Nixon's victory
to the large cheering crowd of assembled Republicans.[29]

Faith herself gained substantial legal experience during these years.
Her educational credentials and Whittlesey family connections helped her
secure appointments as, first, a law clerk to federal Judge Francis Van Dusen
in 1965, as a Pennsylvania special assistant attorney general from 1967 to
1970, and later as assistant United States attorney from 1970 to 1972.[30]

As a woman in the legal and law enforcement fields, Faith worked
in what was overwhelmingly a man's world. In 1970, men made up more
than 95 percent of all lawyers and judges in the United States.[31] Although
outnumbered, she worked hard not to be outsmarted. According to Jeanne
Marie Cella, who worked as Faith's assistant in the U.S. attorney's office,
"Faith was admired for her brilliance, work ethic, and ability to inspire
others to accomplish their very best work."[32]

THE "FAITH" POTHOLDER CAMPAIGN

While content to remain in the shadow of her husband's political activities
for several years, Faith herself entered the world of electoral politics in early
1972. Roger and Faith had moved to Haverford—a Republican township in
the Philadelphia suburbs that is part of what is called the "Main Line"—with
their two young children Henry and Amy. Local party members had invited
Roger to run for that district's (the 166th) seat in the Pennsylvania House
of Representatives. After he declined, Faith deliberated privately for 3 days
before finally proposing herself as a candidate whom Roger could market.
Despite Roger's initial reservations, he eventually agreed enthusiastically.

The clearest path to Faith's nomination went through the "War Board"—
the name by which people referred to the Republican organization in
Delaware County (which included Haverford and the 166th district).[33]

---

[28]   Faith Whittlesey, interview by Ann Miller Morin, June 17, 1989; Stephen Ambrose, *Nixon, Vol. 2: The Triumph of a Politician, 1962–1972* (New York: Simon & Schuster, 1989), pp. 179, 220; Conrad Black, *A Life in Full: Richard M. Nixon* (New York: PublicAffairs: 2007), p. 558.

[29]   Richard Nixon to Henry, Amy, and William Whittlesey, July 8, 1974. Letter in Faith Whittlesey's possession.

[30]   Faith Whittlesey, interview by author, Cambridge, MA, September 8, 2009.

[31]   Gatlin, *American Women Since 1945*, pp. 36, 205.

[32]   Jeanne Marie Cella, email to author, April 12, 2012.

[33]   Faith Whittlesey, interview by author, Cambridge, MA, September 8, 2009.

This "select, secret committee of 13 to 15 local supervisors" dominated the county. Through a well-run patronage network, these "bosses" had persuaded sizable majorities of voters to elect Republicans, who had held sway in Delaware County since 1920.[34] This oligarchy amounted to a powerful political "machine" which determined the choice of party candidates and appointments to political office in Delaware County. According to Pulitzer Prize-winning political reporter David Broder, the War Board "had built a reputation as one of the strongest (and most corrupt) surviving Republican machines in the country."[35]

The War Board had risen to power through many successful battles for the votes of a diverse ethnic and religious constituency of Irish, Italian, and African Americans of Catholic, Quaker, and other faiths. Delaware County was the largest Republican county in Pennsylvania and thus also of critical importance in Pennsylvania statewide politics.

Seeking to gain the War Board's endorsement—and thereby avoid a costly and divisive struggle for the party's nomination—Faith addressed a gathering of the party leaders as a total unknown. In a dark, smoke-filled room typical of these local "old boys' network" machines, she and several male candidates delivered speeches to sway these power brokers. After the War Board declined to endorse any candidate and declared an "open primary," Faith recalled succumbing to tears outside the building in response to the rejection. Much to her surprise, Roger rejoiced at the prospect of winning the nomination without having to adhere to the War Board rules: "This is the best thing that could have happened," he excitedly told Faith. "Now we owe them nothing, and we will beat the pants off them!"[36]

With her husband's strong encouragement and day-to-day guidance, Faith Whittlesey mounted a door-to-door campaign supplemented by strategic marketing. Each day—even during rain, cold, and snow—she visited households in an effort to meet as many of the district's 68,000 citizens as she possibly could. "Together, we worked at nothing else ... didn't have any social engagements; we did nothing but ring doorbells."[37] On six separate

---

[34] Paul B. Beers, *Pennsylvania Politics Today and Yesterday: The Tolerable Accommodation* (University Park: Pennsylvania State University Press, 1980), p. 137. John McClure, the original "boss" of Delaware County, created the War Board with four members in the 1920s. John Morrison McLarnon III, *Ruling Suburbia: John J. McClure and the Republican Machine in Delaware County, Pennsylvania* (Newark, DE: University of Delaware Press, 2003), p. 184.
[35] David Broder, *Changing of the Guard: Power and Leadership in America* (New York: Simon & Schuster, 1980), p. 270.
[36] Faith Whittlesey, interview by author, Cambridge, MA, September 8, 2009.
[37] Broder, *Changing of the Guard*, p. 269.

occasions, Faith suffered dog bites. Amidst all of these challenges, she tried to hide her expanding midsection, which held William, the third Whittlesey child. She believed that voters might disapprove of an expectant mother pursuing elected office.[38]

Faith's earnestness and intelligence impressed many voters. Evelyn Yancoskie, a real estate agent and mother of young children, recalled deciding to join her campaign. Yancoskie denied that she acted out of a desire to elevate a woman to the legislature. "I really have never been a woman's advocate. But Faith was very knowledgeable. She projected trust, commitment, and the capability of getting it done." Yancoskie approached Faith after hearing her speak, and asked if she could help Faith's campaign.[39] She became one of a large contingent of suburban housewives and energetic young men who campaigned door-to-door for Faith.

Roger's practiced skill and creativity in campaign advertising also contributed significantly to the cause, which Yancoskie dubbed "The Potholder Campaign." Potholders were custom designed and produced with patriotic red trim, white background, and blue letters. The text, on one side, reminded voters of the primary on "April 25, 1972." The opposite side contained the simple message, "FAITH," to impress the candidate's name on the public. Roger had conceived of the idea that a useful household gadget could simultaneously generate awareness of the primary's date and build Faith's name recognition.

Roger and Faith left no stone unturned in strategy. A big truck parked in the district's most trafficked intersection carried a sign designed in the same fashion as the potholders. Roger organized telephone banks and mailing appeals. Seeking to win a largely middle-class Irish Catholic district, Faith now introduced herself to voters as Faith *Ryan* Whittlesey—pointedly including her Irish maiden name.

On primary day, the 5-months pregnant Whittlesey won nearly 50 percent of the Republican primary votes against six male opponents. Roger had been right in his prediction of victory. With the help of Roger's marketing strategies, Faith's projection of ability, and their collective hard work, she had beaten the machine. They celebrated with a trip to London and Zürich. In Switzerland, Roger engaged in his hobby of buying and selling gold and

---

[38] Faith Whittlesey, interview by author, Cambridge, MA, September 8, 2009.
[39] Evelyn Yancoskie, interview by author, telephone, May 17, 2012.

silver coins on the Bahnhofstrasse, that city's "Fifth Avenue," which Faith experienced for the first time.[40]

CAMPAIGN BABY

The 1972 general election campaign remained ahead. Despite the Republican Party's strength in suburban Delaware County, Faith and Roger did not take the outcome for granted. As she recalled, "I took to heart Democratic President Lyndon Johnson's often quoted adage about campaigning: 'If you do everything, you win.'"

As Faith prepared for the November election, her expected child became an object of contention. Some Republican leaders cautioned Faith that tradition-bound Catholic and other voters might not vote for a pregnant candidate, and one Pennsylvania Republican leader predicted to her that she would lose the seat because of her pregnancy. Only weeks prior to giving birth, Faith needed to sit rather than stand during the formal debate between the two candidates. In early October, Faith underwent tests because doctors believed that she might have a prediabetic condition which would require a Caesarean section. After these examinations proved negative, Faith promptly returned to the work of winning votes.

Faith's campaigning only slowed down for the delivery of her third child. On October 18, during a routine examination less than 3 weeks prior to election day, doctors decided to induce the birth of Faith's third child. Five hours later, William Weaver Whittlesey was born, weighing nearly 10 pounds. Faith recovered quickly, to say the least. On November 7, from 7 A.M. to 7 P.M., she methodically visited each of the district's polling places for a last-minute appeal as voters cast their ballots. In the traditional election day exercise, she personally thanked the voters and her legion of volunteers.

Faith won handily. It was a good year for Republicans statewide and nationally. President Nixon won reelection with 61 percent of the vote against Democratic challenger George McGovern. Faith Whittlesey, mother of three young children, was heading for Harrisburg as a newly elected state legislator and part of the 10-member solidly Republican Delaware County House delegation.[41]

---

[40] Faith Whittlesey, interview by author, Cambridge, MA, September 8, 2009.
[41] Ibid.

"SISTER FAITH"

When Faith arrived in Harrisburg to assume her seat in 1973, she soon met Representative Matthew J. Ryan, also from Delaware County. Republicans had selected Ryan as the party's "whip," a reference to this official's responsibility to ensure that party members vote as a unit.

As a former Jersey shore lifeguard, U.S. Marine, and graduate of Villanova Law School, Ryan impressed Faith as "brainy and charming." Ryan's "intelligence and Irish wit" provided him with substantial authority to guide Republican legislators with a firm hand. But Faith's independence of judgment made her particularly unreceptive to being "whipped."

As a state representative, for example, she steadfastly opposed a bill that sought to increase pensions for public school teachers. The popular Pennsylvania auditor general—Democrat Robert Casey (the father of current U.S. Senator Robert Casey, Jr.)—also openly and strongly opposed the pension increase. Faith recalled Ryan literally running back to her desk in the chamber of the House of Representatives to talk her out of her vote, but she had already pressed the only red "no" button in an otherwise sea of Republican green "yes" votes.[42]

Whittlesey and Casey had taken a daring risk by defying the powerful teachers' union. Paul Beers, a reporter in Harrisburg since 1957, characterized Casey's stance as "politically courageous—or damn foolish—to fight a system that supports 110,000 state employees and their families."[43] As the sole Republican House member voting in opposition (there were also four Democrats opposed), Faith publicly defended her decision in a detailed letter to the editor published in the *Philadelphia Inquirer* along with her photo. In a 1980 book, the reporter Beers subsequently validated the legitimacy of one of her key objections by noting that, by 1977, "the system had an unfunded liability of $3.5 billion."[44]

Faith argued that this lobby's pressure on politicians contributed unacceptably to the "ballooning costs" of government payrolls. While she certainly valued the public education system, of which she was a product, Whittlesey also believed, however, that elected officials should demonstrate fiscal discipline with public funds.

---

[42] Faith Whittlesey, discussion with author, telephone, May 7, 2012.
[43] Beers, *Pennsylvania Politics*, p. 414.
[44] Ibid.

In Whittlesey's view, rapidly increasing government programs undermined the responsibility of family members to care for one another. Having worked part-time as a substitute high school teacher in inner-city Philadelphia during law school, she had witnessed a lack of respect for authority which she attributed to a more permissive society and the fracture of the traditional family structure. During her years as a state prosecutor, she handled family court cases brought by the Pennsylvania Department of Public Welfare. Rarely would she encounter the sacrifice of parents, spouses, and siblings for their families which she had experienced in her own family. She believed, too, that her predominantly Irish and Italian working-class district supported her efforts to keep important decisions at the local level and to resist the increasing centralization and cost of governmental power in Pennsylvania's capital in Harrisburg.

Faith's maverick stands on principle won her enemies, but her consistent adherence to conservative public policy also secured loyal supporters. After developing the habit of reading *Human Events* and William F. Buckley's *National Review*, Whittlesey came to espouse the emerging movement for a more limited governmental role in the economy, and uncompromising anticommunism.[45] She seemed to have completed a political migration from liberal Democrat in law school to a budding "movement conservative" Republican in the state legislature. Charles Gerow, a college student who worked in Republican Whip Matt Ryan's office, recalled the moment when he came to admire Faith: "I was a hard-core conservative and very distrustful of establishment Republicans. And, I remember the first time that I was in Faith's home. I spotted a copy of the *National Review*. [Faith had passed] my own personal litmus test."[46]

Faith and Matt Ryan soon achieved a mutual respect, according to Gerow and George Cordes, another young Republican at the time. Ryan's rapidly ascending career path would eventually make him the second-longest-serving speaker of the House in Pennsylvania history. In Cordes' view, Ryan served as Faith's "political godfather." Gerow also described the friendship as close. "He made sure that she was—I know it sounds condescending—politically cared for."[47] In the knock-down, drag-out world of Pennsylvania and Delaware County politics, their relationship

---

[45] Faith Whittlesey, interview by Ann Miller Morin, June 17, 1989.
[46] Charles Gerow, interview by author, telephone, October 5, 2010.
[47] George Cordes, interview by author, telephone, May 11, 2012.

was summarized and symbolized in Ryan's tongue-in-cheek reference to Whittlesey as "Sister Faith" (referring to her maiden name, although Ryan was a common Irish name and they had no known common ancestry).

PERSONAL TRAGEDY

Several crises descended on the United States, Delaware County, and Faith personally in 1973 and 1974. During this period, economic and military struggles challenged Americans' sense of national pride. The Republican Party suffered severe setbacks which threatened its very core. Amid this turmoil, Faith Whittlesey lost her husband.

Like many Americans, the Whittleseys experienced financial uncertainty as the U.S. economy floundered in 1973. Gas and oil became scarce as petroleum-exporting Arab countries placed an embargo on the United States for providing weapons to their enemy, Israel. The U.S. government continued to fund a costly war in Vietnam. Inflation threatened to undermine U.S. growth and prosperity. Roger's investments and business ventures suffered unexpected setbacks, and he became very discouraged.[48]

The Republican Party to which Faith belonged also received multiple wounds to its brand name. Locally, Delaware County's War Board encountered relentless charges of corruption in the *Delaware County Daily Times.* Compounded by internal divisions among its members, the War Board would subsequently disband after more than 50 years of existence, although vestiges of organizational power remained. On the national level, Republican President Richard M. Nixon resigned on August 8, 1974, after more than a year of investigations surrounding his former aides who had arranged for the theft of documents from Democratic National Committee offices at the Watergate building in Washington, DC.[49] In this challenging political climate for a GOP incumbent, Faith prepared for her 1974 reelection campaign.

Personal tragedy subsequently compounded these professional difficulties. Faith's husband Roger had entered into a personal spiral of negativity and depression in the wake of his financial misfortunes. In March 1974, he took his own life by asphyxiation.

Faith suddenly faced several unforeseen challenges in addition to her own personal grief. Having lost a husband under incomprehensible,

---

[48] Faith Whittlesey, interview by author, Cambridge, MA, September 8, 2009.
[49] McLarnon, *Ruling Suburbia*, pp. 243–247.

heartrending circumstances, she confronted the monumental responsibility of comforting three young children traumatized by their father's sudden death and having to become sole breadwinner. On top of these burdens, her husband had incurred financial debts. Her political friend Matt Ryan came to her aid, and traveled as far as Mexico in order to help settle Roger's debts and secure what assets he had left.

These financial and emotional pressures somehow reinforced Faith's habits of personal discipline and dedication to her family and her job that supported them. "I didn't have the luxury or time for collapse," Faith reflected years later. "I had three children who needed me now more than ever."[50]

THE "NEW LOOK"

Although Faith easily won her 1974 reelection campaign, Pennsylvania Republicans panicked in the wake of the party's self-inflicted wounds. Faith's personal organization and reputation for independence served her well as the War Board fragmented. Nixon's Watergate scandal contributed to factors which permitted Democrats to win numerous Delaware County elections that year.

In a striking reversal of fortune, the War Board approached Faith to ask for help. In the words of reporter Broder, "By 1975, the now-chastened machine knew that its only chance of surviving in power was to ask the onetime rebel to run for the key job—in terms of patronage and power—of county commissioner."[51] Matt Ryan had persuaded her that she could help rebuild Republican Party strength in Delaware County.[52] Many believed that the Democrats would win control of the once powerful Republican Delaware County stronghold in 1975. "I said 'yes' because it was my obligation to do what I could to save the party."[53]

Ryan convinced Faith to run for the Delaware County Commission in 1975.[54] With voters more actively questioning the character of Republicans at all levels of government, Ryan hoped Faith's intelligence, competence, youth, and charm would counteract voter doubts. George Cordes also recalled that Ryan's strategy included gender. "She's good for 5 to 8 [percentage] points because she's a woman," Ryan told him.[55] After a number of decades in which

---

[50]   Faith Whittlesey, interview by author, Cambridge, MA, September 8, 2009.
[51]   Broder, *Changing of the Guard*, p. 270.
[52]   Faith Whittlesey, interview by author, Cambridge, MA, September 8, 2009.
[53]   Broder, *Changing of the Guard*, p. 270.
[54]   Faith Whittlesey, interview by author, Cambridge, MA, September 8, 2009.
[55]   George Cordes, interview by author, telephone, May 11, 2012.

an oligarchy of secretive men had dominated the county, voters might well consider a woman and mother as more trustworthy and a welcome change.

Faith had also cultivated a strong following of women volunteers in the county. The potholders returned in force. "I heard that in Haverford Township and Delaware County, the mostly male political leaders of the time referred to me and my army of lady volunteers—behind our backs—as 'The Skirts'," Whittlesey recalled, "but I was not offended. Indeed, I thought it was funny."[56] In Faith's view, her cadres of well-dressed, attractive female supporters represented a key element of her appeal.

Whittlesey mobilized suburban women by stressing the need for competent and accountable limited government. Some organized women's groups opposed her candidacy because they were Democrats and disagreed with her policy positions. "While political feminists did not support me, ordinary women, mostly housewives and professional women, came out in droves to help me."[57] U.S. Congresswoman Bella Abzug from New York and other liberal women had created the National Women's Political Caucus for the defined purpose of increasing the number of women in political office,[58] but such organizations did not support Whittlesey. While defining their agenda as "women's issues," these women did not share the same objective of limiting and decentralizing government as did Faith and her female supporters. "They were really not 'for all women,' just for certain, mainly Democratic, bigger-government, women," Whittlesey commented.

Running on a ticket with two other young newcomers to politics— Charles Keeler and Frank Hazel—Faith was part of a triumvirate which became known as the "New Look." These three candidates attempted to outwork their opponents and thereby prove their worthiness for the commission and the district attorney's office. Keeler recalled campaigning "door to door throughout the county, 7 days a week. It was a very aggressive campaign—could not be more aggressive, in fact, at any level."[59]

Each member of the Whittlesey-Keeler-Hazel triumvirate deferred credit to the others. Keeler and Hazel both called Faith their leader. "Faith gave the campaign direction," said Hazel. "There was no question that she was the

---

[56] Faith Whittlesey, email message to author, May 18, 2012.

[57] Faith Whittlesey, interview by author, Cambridge, MA, September 8, 2009.

[58] Ellen Carol DuBois and Lynn Dumenil, *Through Women's Eyes: An American History with Documents,* 2nd ed. (Boston: Bedford/St. Martin's, 2009), p. 695.

[59] Charles Keeler, interview by author, telephone, November 23, 2010.

top of the ticket, in my mind."[60] Housewives and working mothers again rallied behind Faith. In Keeler's recollection, "She brought a large group of very enthusiastic women into the organization and into the campaign."[61] In Faith's view, however, their collective victory resulted from a combination of Keeler's "wise counsel and intellectual depth" and Hazel's "quick wit."[62]

Whittlesey, Keeler, and Hazel promised honesty and transparency. According to Hazel, "Openness was the underlining theme of the campaign."[63] Keeler recalled that the trio adopted a proactive policy with the media, as well. "The attitude of the old-time politicians was 'I won't talk to the press,' which is stupid—the easy way out. We were just the opposite and we'd take every opportunity to talk to them."[64]

The New Look candidates won big in 1975. Faith led the ticket. Matt Ryan and the rest of the Delaware County Republican leadership breathed a sigh of relief. They had saved the county from the threat of Democratic Party domination. Frank Hazel became Delaware County's district attorney, while Whittlesey and Keeler joined the county commission, overseeing some 600,000 citizens—more than in five individual U.S. states.[65] For the next 4 years, she would manage (with Keeler) 2,000 county employees and a $62 million budget.[66]

"BOSS FAITH"

While the Republicans maintained control of the county offices, Faith and her running mates did not submit to the party leaders' dictates. Many voters had chosen them based on the assumption that the New Look campaign was more than a catchy phrase. Although some party leaders resisted her independence of mind, Faith made her own decisions.[67]

Faith and Charlie Keeler encountered several challenges on the county commission. Their predecessors had not adopted a budget for 1976. Furthermore, as a panicked response to fears of losing control of the county to Democrats, the departing county government had agreed to permit collective bargaining for public employees—but had failed to agree

---

[60] Frank Hazel, interview by author, telephone, May 16, 2012.
[61] Charles Keeler, interview by author, telephone, November 23, 2010.
[62] Faith Whittlesey, email to author, June 16, 2012.
[63] Frank Hazel, interview by author, telephone, May 16, 2012.
[64] Charles Keeler, interview by author, telephone, November 23, 2010.
[65] Faith Whittlesey, interview by author, Cambridge, MA, September 8, 2009.
[66] Broder, *Changing of the Guard*, p. 270.
[67] Faith Whittlesey, interview by author, Cambridge, MA, September 8, 2009.

upon a contract with the union. As Keeler recalled, this uncertainty created tensions. "Not having a labor contract meant that we were going to have difficult relations with county employees as soon as we walked in the door."

The county's personnel practices had contributed to financial problems. Hiring and firing decisions were conducted by one of the members of the War Board without consideration of each candidate's qualifications, according to Keeler.[68] Predictably, given this careless oversight, the county had accumulated a substantial deficit and an underqualified staff in key posts.

In response to these challenges, Whittlesey and Keeler used their newly obtained authority to improve the quality of the county workforce. Critics suggested that "Boss Faith" mimicked the corrupt War Board's tactics. Whittlesey did not run away from that title. "In the sense that I believe in party discipline, I am [a boss]." Delaware County citizens needed to present a united front at times, she believed, to compete with other regional political forces. "In the legislature, the money goes flowing to the city of Philadelphia, and the suburban counties, who are glorifying the idea of independence, are on the short end of the stick, because we can't move our votes as a bloc."[69]

But Faith's supporters disagreed with the negative connotation of the term "boss." Jeanne Cella credited the Whittlesey-Keeler political organization with responsible use of their authority, saying, "They limited the political patronage to highly qualified individuals who improved the government for Delaware County citizens."[70] According to Keeler, he and Faith searched carefully for qualified individuals to assume government positions.[71]

FIGHTING FOR REAGAN IN KANSAS CITY

The year 1976 also brought the quadrennial contest for president, and Whittlesey clashed with leaders of the statewide Republican Party about the party's nomination process. President Gerald Ford, who assumed office following Nixon's resignation, had hoped Pennsylvania's Republicans would offer their support. But Faith's strong suspicion of Republican establishment "business as usual" practices and policies led her to join the insurgent movement behind California's former two-term Governor Ronald Reagan.

Governor Reagan was mounting a challenge to the official Republican Party leadership, which supported Ford's election. Faith viewed Reagan as

[68] Charles Keeler, interview by author, telephone, November 23, 2010.
[69] Broder, *Changing of the Guard*, p. 270.
[70] Jeanne Cella, email to author, April 12, 2012.
[71] Charles Keeler, interview by author, telephone, November 23, 2010.

an authentic and principled advocate of decentralization of political power and firm resistance to communism. He also appeared most likely to win, she believed. In the first presidential contest since President Nixon's resignation, Faith did not think voters trusted the GOP establishment. Within the powerful Republican Delaware County network, she was the only leader who openly supported and campaigned for Reagan in 1976.[72]

Faith won election as an alternate delegate to the Republican Party National Convention in August in Kansas City, Missouri. Pennsylvania remained a heavily populated large state with a substantial number of delegates and thus proved an important prize for candidates. In a demonstration of that state's importance, Reagan broke tradition by naming Pennsylvania's U.S. Senator Richard S. Schweiker as his intended running mate in the hope of winning delegates prior to the party convention.[73] When Faith persuaded all but one Delaware County convention delegate to support Reagan's bid for the party's nomination, many of the state's leading Republicans—especially Drew Lewis, the Republican leader of Montgomery County, and the powerful U.S. Congressman Bud Shuster—viewed her as disloyal and a troublemaker. Lewis and Shuster would not soon forget the embarrassment they suffered when Faith outmaneuvered them in their efforts to rally every Pennsylvania delegate behind Ford.[74]

But Faith behaved as a loyal party member after Ford won the Republican nomination, and she campaigned actively for the president against the Democratic nominee, Jimmy Carter. After Ford's defeat in November, however, Faith did regard the results as some vindication of her decision to resist the party establishment. Nonetheless, powerful Republicans did not like the fact that they could not dictate marching orders to this very independent-minded woman.[75]

"THE SON"

Faith continued to play her leadership role with passion, rigor, and enthusiasm. Other than her devotion to her three children, politics had become her vocation and an escape from continuing sorrow. She treated her campaign volunteers as family and earned their affection. Her closest supporters truly

---

[72] Faith Whittlesey, interview by author, Cambridge, MA, September 8, 2009.
[73] Craig Shirley, *Reagan's Revolution: The Untold Story of the Campaign That Started It All* (Nashville, TE: Nelson Current, 2005), pp. 274–276.
[74] Faith Whittlesey, interview by author, Cambridge, MA, September 8, 2009.
[75] Ibid.

believed that she reciprocated their loyalty, and she took genuine pleasure in having her friends around. Whittlesey opened her Haverford home to guests for dinner and sing-along parties. On these occasions, she would play the piano and encourage friends and family to provide voice accompaniment. Frank Hazel marveled at Faith's ability, as a single mother, to host people in her home so often, and in such a seemingly effortless way. "Her three children participated in her political and private activities, and they were always well dressed and acted appropriately. I don't know how she did it!"[76]

In 1978, Faith decided to run for the Republican Party's nomination for lieutenant governor. Drew Lewis and other establishment Republicans panicked, and sought out and convinced William Scranton III, the 30-year-old son of a former governor, to run against her.[77] They viewed Faith as simply too independent, i.e., "not controllable." This was the political price Faith paid for her support of Ronald Reagan in 1976.[78]

Whittlesey tried to contrast Scranton's life of privilege with her own small-town roots. "My father never made more than $100 a week in his life," she told Pennsylvanians. Appealing to working-class voters, Faith cited her struggles as a maverick and political outsider, saying "I came up the same way you did: up from the rough and tumble, up by the bootstraps."[79] Although one writer claimed that she "constantly dismissed young Scranton as 'The Son'" whose credentials included nothing more than birthright,[80] Whittlesey avoided criticizing her opponent's father, who was "revered across the state."[81]

Faith traveled to Pennsylvania's then 67 counties in her bid for the nomination, but Scranton won. She nonetheless received more primary votes than Arlen Specter—whom Richard Thornburgh defeated in the primary election for gubernatorial nominee. Among six candidates vying for the position, furthermore, she had finished second.[82]

---

[76] Frank Hazel, interview by author, telephone, May 16, 2012.
[77] Bill Peterson, "A Political Tradition: Following in Famous Footsteps," *Washington Post*, May 16, 1978, p. A4.
[78] Faith Whittlesey, interview by author, Cambridge, MA, September 8, 2009.
[79] Peterson, "A Political Tradition," p. A4.
[80] Vincent P. Carocci, *A Capitol Journey: Reflections on the Press, Politics, and the Making of Public Policy in Pennsylvania* (University Park: Pennsylvania State University Press, 2005), p. 188.
[81] Peterson, "A Political Tradition," p. A4.
[82] Faith Whittlesey, interview by author, Cambridge, MA, September 8, 2009.

THE "SMOKE-FILLED ROOMS"

Having established herself as a Republican power broker, Whittlesey resisted efforts to dismiss her on the basis of gender. In 1980, David Broder featured Faith in a chapter on women in his book *Changing of the Guard: Power and Leadership in America*. While characterizing her as "about as tough and outspoken a politician as one could meet," he also quoted Faith's aversion to this term. "To call a man tough, politically forceful and strong-minded is considered … praise," she noted. Whittlesey's comments highlighted the double standard in how people talked about men and women, saying "But if these same attributes are seen in a woman, she is called arrogant, ruthless and lacking in compassion."

In Whittlesey's view, many Americans could not accept a woman in such a position of power: "A woman is supposed to be submissive. I won't play that role. I wouldn't be where I am today if I did."[83] While some might criticize her persistence as toughness, Faith portrayed this strength of purpose as an essential ingredient of her political survival.

This perspective certainly distinguished Faith from male chauvinists; but neither did she share many of the standard feminist views of the 1970s. While she adopted no clear position on abortion rights at that time, she disagreed with feminists on the Equal Rights Amendment and the expansion of government-sponsored child care. "I don't buy their whole agenda, so that doesn't suit them."

In fact, Whittlesey believed that organized women's groups merely worked on the fringes of the political centers of power. "The smoke-filled rooms are filled with men. I was certainly not invited in. I fought my way in." Despite having broken through the proverbial glass ceiling, Faith earned no recognition from feminists—due to her policy views, she concluded. "I'm never invited to the women's movement's functions, because I am a conservative."[84]

FIGHTING FOR REAGAN, AGAIN

In 1979, Ronald Reagan decided to pursue the presidency again. Drew Lewis and Faith reconciled as they now joined in supporting Reagan's nomination. As Democratic President Jimmy Carter struggled with economic and foreign

---

[83] Broder, *Changing of the Guard*, p. 269.
[84] Ibid., p. 271.

policy challenges, Republicans united behind the prospect of returning one of their own to the Oval Office.

Predictably, given her earlier commitment to Reagan, Faith took a leadership role in his Pennsylvania campaign. Whittlesey became cochairman with Lewis of the state's Reagan-for-President Committee.[85] The day following Reagan's announcement that he would pursue the Republican presidential nomination in 1980, he made his first campaign stop in Folcroft, Pennsylvania, in Delaware County. Faith had personally arranged the venue, a fire hall, for Reagan's address to the citizens of this blue-collar factory town. Rather than bring the candidate to the posh Main Line, she purposely selected a middle-class location. These voters would respond well to Reagan's message, she believed, and they could help the candidate expand upon the Republicans' typically upper-class constituency.

At the party's national convention scheduled for July in Detroit, party leaders chose Faith as cochairman (with U.S. Congressman Jack Kemp) of the 1980 Republican Party Platform Subcommittee for National Security and Foreign Policy. Whittlesey claimed that both gender and ideology played a role in her selection. "I was asked because they thought I was reasonably intelligent and that I wasn't a wild woman," she said in 1989. "I was a known Reagan supporter and I could be counted on to do the right thing for Ronald Reagan in this area of the platform that was very important to him."[86]

On this subcommittee, Faith was given a leadership role. In particular, she became friendly with Senator John Tower of Texas. During the committee's deliberation about who would deliver the platform's national defense, she asked for Tower's support. "I made the argument to John Tower, which I've made since, that we need to have women as spokesmen on defense policy," she said in 1989. "We don't want overweight middle-aged men." On July 15, 1981, Whittlesey delivered the defense platform plank to the convention hall. Described as a "slender delegate from Haverford, Pa." in the *New York Times* coverage, she provided a strong delivery which prompted delegates to "really pay attention," according to the reporter.[87]

At the convention, Whittlesey worked closely with several other individuals who would soon emerge as major players in the Reagan presidency. Richard V. Allen (Reagan's national security advisor from 1981 to 1982),

---

[85] Faith Whittlesey, interview by author, Cambridge, MA, September 8, 2009.

[86] Faith Whittlesey, interview by Ann Miller Morin, June 17, 1989.

[87] Francis X. Clines, "Convention Journal: Goldwater Relives the Glory of '64," *New York Times*, July 16, 1981, p. A18.

Robert "Bud" McFarlane (Reagan's national security advisor from 1983 to 1985), Senator Jesse Helms of North Carolina, and future Secretary of the Navy John F. Lehman all served with her on the subcommittee.[88] As expected, Reagan won the party's nomination, and he prepared to challenge the sitting president.

Whittlesey campaigned for Reagan's election with dedication and perseverance. She traveled all over Pennsylvania to deliver speeches and lobby voters. Charles Gerow recalled flying to a campaign rally with Faith in Lewis' plane as election day approached. Air turbulence shook the aircraft violently. Since Pennsylvania had experienced several fatal crashes in which leading Pennsylvania politicians had been killed, Whittlesey was particularly terrified, thinking of her three children.[89]

In November, Reagan carried Delaware County and won all of Pennsylvania's 27 electoral votes (only California and New York had more electoral votes in 1980). The once marginal Reagan had surprised many so-called election experts by winning an election which signified the success of the conservative movement, and which some commentators now called a "revolution."[90] Faith and Drew Lewis were flooded with letters of application from individuals who knew they were close allies of the president-elect. These people each wanted help in securing one of the 600 jobs requiring presidential appointment.[91]

AVOIDING THE "RUBBER CHICKEN CIRCUIT"

Although she initially resisted the idea of accepting a federal appointment, Faith ultimately agreed to be considered for a few positions. Lewis accepted the offer of U.S. transportation secretary—a cabinet-level position—and he encouraged Whittlesey to join the administration.

When the subject of an ambassadorship came up, Faith knew the competition would be strong. Many powerful Republicans, such as U.S. senators and campaign donors, often held sway in the appointment to prestigious posts in U.S. embassies abroad. The Senate possessed the constitutional authority to confirm or reject presidential nominees, and financiers provided the life blood of campaigns.

---

[88]   Faith Whittlesey, interview by author, Cambridge, MA, September 8, 2009.
[89]   Charles Gerow, interview by author, telephone, October 5, 2010.
[90]   E.g., Rowland Evans and Robert Novak, *The Reagan Revolution* (New York: Dutton, 1981).
[91]   Gil Troy, *The Reagan Revolution: A Very Short Introduction* (Oxford, UK: Oxford University Press, 2009), p. 60.

But a position as an ambassador seemed the most beneficial and appealing career move, in Faith's assessment. She had just begun a new career in 1980 at a major Philadelphia law firm, Wolf, Block, Schorr, and Solis-Cohen. In the event she determined to accept a government post, the firm's partners urged her to seek a position that would have some relevance to business when she finished and returned to Philadelphia. Wanting to maintain her possibilities in the private sector, Faith viewed the idea of an ambassadorship as a position which might expand contacts outside of politics as well as giving her a chance to return to the Europe she loved.

Robert McFarlane—with whom she had worked on the foreign policy platform subcommittee—agreed to help argue her case with the incoming administration's decision makers. When he asked her "What country do you want?," she expressed her preference for Switzerland.[92] Proximity to the Swiss financial center would offer the potential to develop wider professional connections. On a personal level, she believed the post made the most sense as a mother of three young children. Swiss international schools and security appealed to her.[93]

She refused to travel to Washington and lobby for the job, but powerful Republicans rallied behind Whittlesey's candidacy for the Swiss post. Letters of support for Whittlesey's appointment arrived in the White House from many prominent figures who had served on the foreign policy platform subcommittee with Whittlesey. The newly appointed Secretary of the Navy John F. Lehman praised her knowledge, political skills, "industry, executive abilities and dedication."[94] Jack Kemp also wrote on her behalf.[95] McFarlane, Reagan's newly appointed assistant secretary of state, indicated his support for Whittlesey's appointment in a late July letter, saying, "I have been doing what I can here to foster your interests and so far so good."[96]

Whittlesey's candidacy had two major strengths—first, her long-standing commitment to Reagan's vision, and secondly, her knowledge of the German language and European culture. Wendy Borcherdt, who had worked on all of Reagan's campaigns since 1966, had the responsibility of reviewing

---

[92] Faith Whittlesey, interview by author, Cambridge, MA, September 8, 2009.
[93] Dick Kirschten, "The Switch from Dole to Whittlesey Means the Election Is Getting Closer," *National Journal*, April 30, 1983, p. 885.
[94] John F. Lehman, Secretary of Navy, to Richard V. Allen, April 3, 1981, Box 14 Folder 1. From the Faith Whittlesey Collection, Howard Gotlieb Archival Research Center at Boston University (hereafter referred to as FW).
[95] Jack Kemp to Faith, February 11, 1981, Whittlesey papers, Box 14 Folder 1. FW.
[96] Robert McFarlane to Faith, July 23, 1981, Whittlesey papers, Box 14 Folder 1. FW.

candidates for ambassadorial appointments in the Reagan transition. Reagan specifically asked Borcherdt to consider his core values when recommending candidates, telling her, "You know the people who really supported me, and you will know who didn't."

The president-elect also wanted ambassadors to be fluent in the language and familiar with the culture of the countries to which they were assigned. Whittlesey's experience traveling through Europe on scholarships and her undergraduate studies in German language and history contributed to her being seriously considered for the Bern post, Borcherdt remembered. After reviewing Whittlesey's resume and conducting an interview, Borcherdt recalled her as an "articulate, soft-spoken woman with strong opinions" and "totally in-sync with Reagan's philosophies and policies." After reviewing Borcherdt's recommendations of three candidates—with Whittlesey as the first choice—Reagan phoned Whittlesey to make a verbal offer of the posting.[97] The public announcement came on September 4, 1981.[98]

Faith invited a large contingent of Delaware County friends, acquaintances, and former political workers to her induction ceremony at the State Department. Bill Scranton III, her opponent in the 1978 Republican primary contest for lieutenant governor, with whom she was then fully reconciled, gave a speech to the large group. Scranton reminded the audience of the primary election when he beat Faith, saying, "Now Faith is going to beautiful Switzerland, and I'm stuck in Pennsylvania on the rubber chicken circuit. I'm not sure who really won that race after all."[99]

The U.S. ambassador's residence in Bern would indeed provide Whittlesey with a tranquil home for the next 15 months. Faith recognized this country as a stable, democratic, and free market-oriented "sister republic." As she told a *New York Times* reporter prior to her departure, "The importance of Switzerland far exceeds its size. It is a major financial center, at the crossroads of the world. The opinions of the Swiss are respected worldwide, and they travel all over the world."[100]

As she prepared for her mission to Switzerland, however, Faith discovered a very tense U.S.-Swiss disagreement related to U.S. stock markets and Swiss banks. As the U.S. government resisted the Soviet Union's expansion

---

[97] Wendy Borcherdt, interview by author, telephone, June 25, 2011.
[98] "Reagan Names Envoys to 3 Nations and U.N.," *New York Times*, September 5, 1981, p. 2.
[99] Faith Whittlesey, interview by author, Cambridge, MA, September 8, 2009.
[100] William Robbins, "Mother, Lawyer, Politician, Envoy: 'Like Some Kind of Fairyland' Hard Work Pays Off," *New York Times*, October 4, 1981, p. 78.

in Afghanistan while experiencing double-digit inflation and unemployment, America appeared to need good friends more than ever. The next chapter reveals how Whittlesey proactively determined to seek a diplomatic resolution to this acrimonious bilateral standoff.

CHAPTER 2

Reducing Tensions
Between the Sister Republics
The First Bern Tour (part 1)

Diplomacy is the management of international relations
by negotiation [and] the method by which these relations
are adjusted and managed by ambassadors and envoys.
                                      —Sir Harold Nicolson[1]

Christmas Eve would generally bring joy to Jean Zwahlen, a polished and experienced French Swiss diplomat with bright blue eyes and a broad, charming smile. On December 24, 1981, however, Zwahlen returned home with a distressed expression. He bore the full weight of an impending crisis with the U.S. government on his shoulders.

In the nearly 10 years he had served as the head of the finance and economics office of the Swiss Federal Department of Foreign Affairs, Zwahlen had never encountered so daunting a challenge. A looming crisis with the United States threatened the future of Switzerland's financial center. After looking into the case, Zwahlen concluded that the problem was technical, complex, and very contentious. "I didn't know if I was able to cope with this matter," Zwahlen recalled nearly 30 years later. "I had the feeling the world was collapsing."[2]

---

[1]   Sir Harold Nicolson, *Diplomacy* (New York: Oxford University Press, 1964), pp. 4–5.
[2]   Jean Zwahlen, interview by author, Geneva, August 17, 2009.

"WALKING INTO A MINEFIELD"

Several months earlier, Faith Whittlesey assiduously prepared for questioning by members of the U.S. Senate. Her appointment as President Reagan's ambassador to Switzerland depended upon the senators, who held the power to confirm or deny presidential selections. The executive branch prepared nominees for these hearings, and the U.S. State Department—which oversees the Foreign Service diplomatic corps—had assigned Ward Thompson, the officer who manned its "Swiss desk" in Washington, to brief Whittlesey on relevant subjects.

While knowledgeable and very friendly, Thompson particularly emphasized one issue—recent mass protests by Swiss youths who decried the cost of government-financed renovations to the opera house in Switzerland's financial capital, Zürich. From Whittlesey's perspective, the issue—public funding of elite entertainment—appeared inconsequential to U.S. foreign policy. But the sometimes violent demonstrations had attracted substantial press attention.[3] Whittlesey particularly remembered being told that young people had marched naked down Zürich's primary commercial thoroughfare—the Bahnhofstrasse. The protestors had also shattered priceless stained glass windows painted by the famous Russian artist Marc Chagall at an historic old church known as the Fraumünster.

Another source—one of her best friends, former University of Pennsylvania Law School classmate Albert Schultheis—informed Whittlesey of the more serious problem between the U.S. government and Switzerland. Schultheis, who worked as a lawyer in New York for the giant Swiss Bank Corporation, telephoned to alert Whittlesey of a fast-developing clash between the United States and Switzerland. In Schultheis' estimation, she was "walking into a minefield," Whittlesey recalled.[4]

CATCH-22: SWISS BANKING PRIVACY AND U.S. "INSIDER TRADING" LAWS

A bilateral crisis—which pitted U.S. law against Swiss law—appeared on the horizon. As Faith had listened to stories about naked youths running through Zürich's streets, no one had explained to her the implications of the U.S. government's taking legal action against Swiss banking institutions,

---

[3] E.g., Paul Hofmann, "Swiss Malaise," *New York Times*, February 8, 1981, p. SM9.
[4] Swiss Bank Corporation merged into the even larger Union Bank of Switzerland in 1998 to create an entity subsequently known as UBS. Faith Whittlesey, interview by author, Cambridge, MA, September 8, 2009.

which represented a sizable portion of the Swiss economy and provided large capital flows into U.S. markets.

When Schultheis reached Whittlesey by phone, he fully explained the U.S. government allegations, lawyer to lawyer. According to the United States, individuals had used Swiss banks to subvert U.S. law. On behalf of certain clients, Swiss banks had purchased U.S. stocks, or equities. These bank clients, however, stood accused of having engaged in financial transactions based on privileged, nonpublic, or "inside" information. The U.S. Congress had legislated against such exchanges of U.S. stocks or other corporate securities based on knowledge obtained privately by a person employed inside the company or close relatives and associates of such persons.

The bilateral disagreement emerged when the United States requested private client data from Swiss banks. U.S. government regulators and law enforcement officers did not consider the Swiss response timely. U.S. officials in the Securities and Exchange Commission (SEC) and Treasury Department had an obligation to implement U.S. law, they insisted. These U.S. officials requested the prompt release of information about Swiss bank account holders trading in the American equities markets. The Swiss Parliament, however, had required Swiss banks to guarantee the strict privacy of a client's financial information in Switzerland since 1934.[5]

Thus, a confrontation ensued between the U.S. demand for transparency and Swiss financial privacy requirements. An obligation to enforce U.S. law fell upon the SEC, which the U.S. Congress had created to regulate U.S. stock markets and investigate criminal activity in 1934. Switzerland's government also was committed to insist on Swiss law, which prohibited Swiss banks from divulging the names of clients unless evidence of a crime existed. Thus, if Swiss bank executives acceded to U.S. requests for client data, they faced the prospect of criminal prosecution in Switzerland.

SEC officials countered that they indeed possessed facts indicating criminal activity had occurred in the U.S. marketplace. Since the Swiss government had signed, in 1977, a bilateral treaty with the United States pledging mutual assistance in law enforcement, Switzerland had a duty to comply with the SEC's investigation, the Americans believed.[6]

---

[5]   Edward F. Greene, "U.S., Switzerland Agree to Prosecute Inside Traders," *Legal Times,* October 4, 1983, p. 12.

[6]   Ibid.

But in 1981, Switzerland had no criminal law against so-called insider trading. Under Swiss law, therefore, the financial exchanges in question did not constitute a crime, and the treaty would not apply to such a case. Switzerland's own duly elected Parliament, however, *had* legislated against divulging client information without evidence of criminal intent. Could Swiss bankers place the claims of an extraterritorial authority, such as the United States, above the client privacy laws enacted by their own Parliament? Could bank executives risk criminal indictment in their own country?

The U.S. government's claims of jurisdiction over Swiss banks doing business in U.S. markets created a seemingly intractable contest between U.S. and Swiss legal authorities. On one side, members of the U.S. Justice Department and the SEC argued that traders of U.S. securities exploited Swiss banking confidentiality to circumvent U.S. law. On the other side, Switzerland claimed that the United States could not impose its law within the borders of another sovereign country. The Swiss bankers faced a true quandary in which neither of two choices appeared to offer a favorable result, which some might characterize as a "Catch-22."[7]

"HOBNAILED BOOTS"

Whittlesey's life experience inspired her to investigate for herself. She had learned—at her piano bench at home, in her education from high school through law school, in multiple political campaigns, and in her various state and federal government jobs—that success in resolving a problem required thorough preparation and persistence. Furthermore, she believed the issue called for a political solution rather than one crafted by a U.S. judge. A resolution negotiated in good faith might avoid contentious relations or a hostile breach with an historically friendly, if formally neutral, nation such as Switzerland.

The consequences of a breakdown in U.S.-Swiss cooperation, Whittlesey also understood, might prove detrimental to the U.S. economy and U.S. security. American businesses benefited from substantial foreign direct investment in the United States by and through Switzerland.[8] Furthermore,

---

[7] In Joseph Heller's 1961 novel *Catch-22*, the protagonist Yossarian is constantly faced with dilemmas which leave him with no viable options.

[8] During the period 1975–1980, Swiss investment in the United States had increased by 1.7-fold. Switzerland had been one of the primary sources of foreign direct investment in the United States for several years. R.A. Ajami and R. BarNiv, "Utilizing Economic Indicators in Explaining Foreign Direct Investment in the U.S.," *Management International Review* 24, no. 4 (1984): 16–26.

the Reagan administration pursued enhanced harmony with other nations to achieve the president's goal of winning more friends in the world. Breaches of normal relationships with an economic powerhouse such as Switzerland did not serve Reagan's ultimate purpose of seeking to undermine the Soviet Union's worldwide expansionist empire.

Surprisingly, Whittlesey's immediate predecessor as ambassador, Richard Vine, showed little interest in negotiating a diplomatic solution to this problem. During a lunch meeting in Washington, prior to her departure for Bern, Ambassador Vine recommended that Whittlesey avoid the minefield altogether. This career Foreign Service officer—approaching retirement after decades of service—spoke his views plainly and confidently. Vine had concluded that the U.S. judges would likely rule that Swiss banks and those clients who traded through them had violated U.S. law. In Vine's view, the U.S. court system should resolve the dispute. Whittlesey disagreed, and his judgment did not impress her. She found him "very abrupt, almost rude."

Vine also appeared chauvinistic to Whittlesey. He opined that the Reagan administration erred in sending a woman to lead the Bern mission because the Swiss would not respect a female ambassador.[9] Ironically, this Foreign Service officer appeared uninformed about his department's own history of female American ambassadors in Bern. Frances Willis, the first female career officer appointed as an ambassador, had been assigned by President Dwight D. Eisenhower, in 1952, to Switzerland.[10]

Whittlesey recognized the broad-ranging power of the men and women who occupied the federal bench, having worked as a special assistant attorney general in Pennsylvania, an assistant U.S. attorney in the Eastern District of Pennsylvania, and a law clerk for a federal judge. If this issue went to court, she believed, government officials and diplomats from both nations would have lost the ability to bring the matter back into diplomatic channels and negotiate a mutually amicable solution.

In Whittlesey's view, active bilateral diplomatic negotiations in good faith offered the best potential for a mutually amicable solution. She believed that incentives for compromise existed. The citizens of both nations were

---

[9]   Faith Whittlesey, interview by author, Cambridge, MA, September 8, 2009; Faith Whittlesey, interview by Ann Miller Morin, June 21, 1989. Frontline Diplomacy, Manuscript Division, Library of Congress, Washington, DC.

[10] Ann Miller Morin, *Her Excellency: An Oral History of American Women Ambassadors* (New York: Twayne Publishers, 1995), p. 1.

firmly committed to free market principles, the rule of law, individual rights, and the ideals of limited government.[11]

Prior to her departure for Switzerland, therefore, Whittlesey made her own arrangements to discuss the subject with officials from the U.S. departments of Treasury and Justice and the SEC in Washington. She discovered that the Treasury Department's legal team had apparently abandoned the negotiation option and had prepared to file lawsuits against the Swiss banks in New York. Officials at the Justice Department "were visibly upset," Whittlesey recalled, "using very harsh language about the attitude of the Swiss toward law enforcement questions."[12] These officers believed that the Swiss sought to avoid prosecution based on technicalities or ambiguities of the law.

SEC officials also experienced domestic political pressure to prosecute the Swiss banks if they appeared to have facilitated violations of U.S. insider trading laws. Reagan SEC Chairman John Shad, who had assumed office in May 1981, asserted in one of his earliest official interviews that he would seek to stamp out insider trading "with hobnailed boots."[13] John Fedders, the SEC's new director of enforcement, recalled significant pressure from political leaders to police the U.S. marketplace. In Fedders' memory, "When I testified before Congress in my early days, I was put under the microscope there." Liberal Democrats especially suspected that the conservative Republican Reagan administration would go "soft" on corporate America.[14]

Whittlesey recognized that she would need a lot of time to persuade U.S. officials against pursuing federal litigation. In order to keep the matter on a "diplomatic track," therefore, she recalled deciding to make "a major selling effort" to all parties involved.[15]

A "TREMOR" IN THE SWISS BANKING ESTABLISHMENT

Upon arriving in Switzerland, Whittlesey inserted herself into the process as an honest broker. As a Pennsylvania politician, she had negotiated many deals with competing interest groups. She was, furthermore, the sole attorney on the embassy staff of 125. Her training and experience provided

---

[11]   Faith Whittlesey, interview by author, Sherborn, MA, July 12, 2010.
[12]   Faith Whittlesey, interview by author, Cambridge, MA, September 8, 2009.
[13]   Andrew L. Rothman, "John Shad Becomes 22nd SEC Chairman," *SEC Employee News* 5, no. 2 (April/May 1981): 1. On the "hobnail boots" quotation, see Leonard Sloane, "John S. R. Shad Dies at 71; SEC Chairman in the 80's," *New York Times*, July 9, 1994, p. 11.
[14]   John Fedders, interview by author, Washington, DC, September 15, 2010.
[15]   Faith Whittlesey, interview by Ann Miller Morin, June 21, 1989.

skill in the art of compromise and an intricate understanding of the U.S. justice system.

The new ambassador visited several leading Swiss bank executives, who did not appear particularly pleased to see her. "I assumed they were thinking, 'Who does she think she is?'," Whittlesey later noted.[16] "I can't really even imagine now how I had the courage to do that, but I did." The meetings were not always congenial.[17]

Perhaps remembering Ambassador Vine's warning that the Swiss would not welcome a female ambassador, Faith wondered if gender played a role in the bankers' cold response to her visit. In a 1989 interview, Whittlesey described her impression of the initial visits: "I remember going to the leadership of the Union Bank of Switzerland, the biggest bank, and trying to explain this to them in diplomatic, tactful language. I was there by myself, thinking, in their society there are no women in business. Hardly any at all."[18] Nearly 30 years later, the memory of this uncomfortable gender dynamic remained strong. "They were looking at me, a relatively young woman, with stern expressions. These big bankers were sitting around the table, very polite, but scowling."[19]

Court cases are very unpredictable, she warned, because of a judge's broad power in the U.S. legal system. "It would be outside the realm of any diplomacy if it ended up in a federal court," she concluded.[20] She explained why a diplomatic resolution would serve them better than a colossal court battle in New York.

Whittlesey offered numerous reasons why legal action would not benefit the bankers' best interests. Judges could possibly rule in a manner which might cause irreparable public relations injury to the banks. Trial in a U.S. court entailed the risk for the Swiss banks of multiple damage fines, contempt of court citations, and unpleasant headlines in the New York and international financial press. In Whittlesey's understated assessment, these outcomes "would be highly unattractive to them."[21] Investors might decide to avoid placing their money in banks which operated under a cloud of suspicion after being reprimanded by U.S. courts.

---

[16] Ibid.
[17] Faith Whittlesey, interview by author, Cambridge, MA, September 8, 2009.
[18] Faith Whittlesey, interview by Ann Miller Morin, June 21, 1989.
[19] Faith Whittlesey, interview by author, Cambridge, MA, September 8, 2009.
[20] Ibid.
[21] Faith Whittlesey, interview by author, Sherborn, MA, July 12, 2010.

But in her efforts to encourage the Swiss to choose diplomacy, Whittlesey encountered a powerful adversary. The Swiss banks had hired big American law firms which all recommended going to trial. She understood the financial incentive for lawyers at these firms to pursue the courtroom route, which would benefit their bottom line, as protracted litigation invariably does. In Whittlesey's view, "If this had gone to court [the Swiss banks] would have been the ATM machines for the law firms. It would have gone on forever. The lawyers would have generated huge legal fees."[22]

Drawing on her experience working for a big U.S. law firm, she could readily anticipate the bankers' argument for fighting this case in a U.S. court room. "I could do opposition analysis. I knew what [the U.S. lawyers] were saying to the banks to make the case."[23] Faith hoped that she had planted a seed which would convince the Swiss banks to seek a bilateral agreement through diplomatic means rather than follow the advice of their American lawyers.

Whittlesey's proactive approach proved important because trust between the two nations quickly deteriorated. In October, the SEC obtained court orders to seize the profits—worth about $5 billion—of transactions through several bank offices in Switzerland.[24] When the SEC asked U.S. District Judge Milton Pollack to issue sanctions against Swiss bank Banca della Svizzera Italiana (BSI) for refusing to provide client data, the judge authorized fines of $50,000 for each day of noncompliance, a total freeze of BSI's assets in the United States, and the arrest of all BSI officers on U.S. territory.[25] This ruling "sent a tremor through the Swiss banking establishment," recalled SEC official Michael Mann.[26]

"THE U.S. AMBASSADOR STEPPED IN"

Whittlesey recognized intransigence on the Swiss side, but she also disliked unilateral U.S. legal threats and demands. Each side appeared blind to the other's perspective. In her role as ambassador, Faith believed she needed

---

22 Faith Whittlesey, interview by author, Cambridge, MA, September 8, 2009.
23 Ibid.
24 The banks involved included Credit Suisse, Citibank, Chase Manhattan, and Swiss Bank Corporation. *Economist*, October 31, 1981, pp. 84, 87.
25 Jane E. Siegel, "United States Insider Trading Prohibition in Conflict with Swiss Bank Secrecy," *Journal of Comparative Corporate Law and Securities Regulation* 4 (1983): 362.
26 Michael Mann, interview by Wayne Carroll, June 13, 2005, p. 13. Securities and Exchange Commission Historical Society Oral Histories.

to remind the Americans about the larger importance of the bilateral relationship.

For Whittlesey, it was important that the U.S. law enforcement agencies understand Switzerland's significance for U.S. foreign policy. Due to that country's small size and low profile, Americans generally knew little about Swiss contributions to the U.S. economy. Few countries exceeded Switzerland in providing foreign direct investment to the United States. Such inflows of capital were highly beneficial to American prosperity. A major breach with Switzerland might also weaken U.S. security as well. Anti-American sentiment might reverberate throughout Europe, and could risk Swiss cooperation with the United States in a variety of policy areas, she explained to SEC Chairman Shad.[27]

Besides working to persuade the Swiss, therefore, Whittlesey also communicated the banks' grievances to the U.S. side. In a November 1981 letter to Shad, Whittlesey conveyed the complaints she heard during "informal conversations with Directors and Chief Operating Officers of Swiss banks." She had listened as the executives explained their impression that American officials employed bully tactics to require compliance with U.S. rules—even when such laws contradicted Switzerland's national legislation enacted through a rigorous democratic process. Proud of their sovereign rights as an independent nation, the Swiss viewed such acts as coercion by a foreign power and antithetical to their high regard for individual political and economic liberty.[28]

Whittlesey placed much of her hope for a resolution in John Fedders, the newly appointed SEC director of enforcement. The Swiss believed that Fedders' predecessor, Stanley Sporkin, had not treated them as equal partners in negotiations.[29] In 20 years at the SEC, Sporkin had built a favorable reputation in the United States as an aggressive prosecutor, and had now assumed the post of general counsel of the Central Intelligence Agency.[30] But Sporkin's brusque treatment of the issue clearly offended the Swiss. Thus, Faith stressed the importance of bringing the Swiss into contact with a new SEC representative, such as Fedders, who could establish trust and a more conciliatory attitude. In a letter to SEC Chairman Shad, Whittlesey

---

[27] Faith Whittlesey, interview with author, Sherborn, MA, July 12, 2010.
[28] Faith Whittlesey to John Shad, November 13, 1981. From the Faith Whittlesey Collection, Howard Gotlieb Archival Research Center at Boston University (hereafter referred to as FW).
[29] Faith Whittlesey, interview with author, Sherborn, MA, July 12, 2010.
[30] "Stan Sporkin to Leave Commission," *SEC Employee News* 5, no. 2 (April/May 1981): 3.

reported having told the Swiss that Fedders would bring a more open-minded approach to the job.[31]

Whittlesey believed that SEC Chairman Shad would welcome a diplomatic solution, which Fedders' presence in Switzerland might promote. "I do think it would be enormously helpful if John [Fedders] could be released to come to Switzerland, particularly Zürich," Whittlesey wrote to Shad. Faith placed confidence in the idea that the United States would persuade the Swiss rather than dictate its policies to them. In her letter to Shad, she suggested that Fedders could "participate in an informal briefing session with the Swiss financial community explaining present policies and enforcement procedures of the SEC with particular emphasis on 'insider trading.'" In Whittlesey's view, such an approach could avoid expensive and potentially explosive legal proceedings by encouraging the Swiss government to regulate its own financial center in a manner congruent with U.S. law.

Willing to defer credit for the idea of these negotiations, Whittlesey almost made it appear that the Fedders visit was Shad's idea. In her letter to Shad, she enclosed an *Economist* article which quoted the chairman expressing a desire to accomplish compliance through education and explanation. "You, of course, are the best judge of your allocation of John's scarce time resources," Whittlesey noted, in a deferential spirit, "but I urge you to consider this request favorably and make John available sometime after Christmas, if possible." Whittlesey's suggestions, while respectful, revealed the unique potential for a noncareer ambassador to bypass bureaucratic procedures and deal directly with the federal government's most powerful decision makers. As a longtime Reagan political ally with connections at the administration's highest levels, Whittlesey could accelerate the diplomatic process in a manner nearly impossible for a Foreign Service officer. To emphasize the urgency of this request, Whittlesey sent copies of this letter to Secretary of State Alexander Haig, Secretary of the Treasury Donald Regan, and White House Chief of Staff James Baker.[32]

Whittlesey's behind-the-scenes intervention proved critical in persuading the SEC to undertake face-to-face negotiations with the Swiss. As SEC General Counsel Edward Greene recalled, "The U.S. ambassador stepped

---

[31] Whittlesey also wrote that the bank leaders were "anxious to cooperate," but "unanimous … in their condemnation of the harsh tactics and manner of Mr. Fedders' predecessor, Mr. Sporkin." Faith Whittlesey to John Shad, November 13, 1981. FW.

[32] Faith Whittlesey to John Shad, November 13, 1981. FW.

in, and said, 'We've got to work out a way other than simply having assets frozen, and fingers pointed.'" In Greene's recollection, SEC Chairman Shad agreed with Whittlesey's assessment: "We talked with Shad, and there was a sense that this was creating tension between governments."[33]

A GRACE PERIOD

As Whittlesey worked behind the scenes, the standoff intensified. Some of Switzerland's government officials sought leverage through letters to U.S. officials and protests in the media. Swiss bankers remained resistant to diplomatic efforts to obtain a mutually acceptable solution to the crisis. And the U.S. courts and government officials showed no immediate signs of abandoning legal action against the banks.

Switzerland made some gestures for a diplomatic solution in late 1981. In a formal letter, an officer from the Swiss Department of Justice and Police urged the U.S. Justice Department to consider these issues with "thorough reflection and discussion."[34] BSI also appeared to have negotiated a short-term solution by obtaining certain clients' permission to release their names to the SEC. If BSI clients voluntarily disclosed their identity, the bank's executives reasoned, BSI would not have to violate the Swiss privacy statutes regarding accounts. When the SEC demanded more names, however, Swiss Ambassador to the United States Anton Hegner protested formally to the U.S. State Department's legal advisor, and an unnamed official from the Swiss embassy in Washington called this investigation a "fishing expedition." Nonetheless, a U.S. judge threatened further fines and a ban of BSI trades in U.S. securities markets if the bank failed to comply.[35]

This crisis in U.S.-Swiss relations crossed Jean Zwahlen's desk in late December 1981. As the representative of the Swiss government assigned to this problem, Zwahlen concluded—after an agonizing Christmas Eve—that the only viable path was to negotiate with the Americans. But he did not know any U.S. officials at the SEC, the U.S. Justice Department, or the U.S. Treasury Department. Zwahlen, therefore, approached the U.S. ambassador in Bern.

---

[33] Edward Greene, interview by Kenneth Durr, February 15, 2008, pp. 13, 14. Securities and Exchange Commission Historical Society Oral Histories.

[34] Pierre Schmid, Division of International Legal Assistance and Police Matters, to Michael Abbell, Office of International Affairs, November 26, 1981. FW.

[35] Fred Farris, "Swiss Object to Insider Probe Methods," *International Herald Tribune*, December 5–6, 1981, p. 12.

Zwahlen's message was simple. He needed time to resolve internal disputes among the Swiss themselves. "The circle of persons I had to bring under one single roof was very broad," he recalled. Zwahlen's plan also required that he gather information from several banks, small and large, in the diverse German-, French-, and Italian-speaking cantons of Switzerland. "Harmonizing internally a group of probably about 20 persons representing different circles, avenues of the Swiss Confederation—it was not easy at all," he recalled.[36] As a representative of the Swiss government, Zwahlen would have to convince many Swiss executives from these different organizations and regions that he would act in each of their interests.

Zwahlen needed to persuade the Swiss bankers to participate in a diplomatic solution. "I had some legal advisors telling me, 'We cannot go farther—this is Swiss legislation. We cannot break it,'" Zwahlen recalled. Many bankers seemed prepared to defy the U.S. court. Regarding the fines being threatened by a U.S. judge, in Zwahlen's recollection, "The banks were still saying, 'We cannot pay this—it's not fair.'"[37] Intense hostility toward the U.S. government was widespread in Switzerland's financial center. "As the U.S. administration struck without any preliminary diplomatic warning, the whole country felt bashed and reacted accordingly."[38]

Even if Zwahlen could persuade Switzerland's banks to support bilateral negotiations, he still needed to convince different entities within the Swiss government that a political rather than a legal solution best served his country's interests. "The legally minded ministries resented any negotiations,"[39] Zwahlen noted. From the perspective of law enforcement agencies, any concessions amounted to an unwarranted breach of the Swiss legislation protecting client privacy. But "the more economically oriented ministries" recognized financial benefits from pursuing discussion with the Americans.[40] Although Switzerland had not passed a law against insider trading, these officials generally accepted the principle that such regulations made financial markets more predictable and secure.

In the short term, therefore, Zwahlen's immediate goal was to avoid the U.S. court's impending $50,000-per-day fine. Zwahlen asked Whittlesey if the United States would grant a grace period to prepare for negotiations.

---

[36]   Jean Zwahlen, interview by author, Geneva, August 17, 2009.
[37]   Ibid.
[38]   Jean Zwahlen, email message to author, June 27, 2012.
[39]   Ibid.
[40]   Ibid.

"And so I told Faith Whittlesey, 'Can't we find a way to avoid—for a limited period—that the Swiss banks pay this fine? We promise to start negotiations in a very earnest way in about two or three months.' And she was very receptive to this message."[41]

Having discussed the issue with many Swiss bankers, Whittlesey could identify with Zwahlen's dilemma. She understood the strong passions and sophisticated arguments which Zwahlen was hearing. Whittlesey immediately brought this proposal to SEC Chairman Shad.

GETTING A PH.D. IN DIPLOMACY

Nearly 30 years after these events, John Fedders expressed surprise that Whittlesey identified him as a leader of the U.S. delegation which visited Switzerland in February 1982. In Fedders' view, "Nobody would ever have guessed in those early 1980s that I would have ever been charged with some diplomatic responsibilities."[42] But Faith seemed confident Fedders and the rest of the U.S. officials would appreciate the foreign policy implications of their words and actions.

In a January 6 telegram, Shad had informed Whittlesey of his decision to send Fedders as part of a U.S. delegation to Switzerland. Shad's missive demonstrated an appreciation for the two nations' contrary perspectives. Shad outlined a bilateral solution: the SEC's goal was to protect "the fairness and integrity of the United States securities markets" while being "sensitive to the sovereignty and secrecy laws" of Switzerland. Shad thus expressed his intention to enforce congressionally enacted laws against insider trading while supporting the efforts of Whittlesey and others "to improve nation-to-nation law enforcement cooperation." Specifically, Shad endorsed Whittlesey's judgment that Fedders' visit would serve this purpose.[43] In the meantime, the SEC agreed to delay prosecution and imposition of the fine.[44]

Fedders recalled arriving in Switzerland prepared with scripted "talking points." In Fedders' memory, he planned to lecture the Swiss that they must subject themselves to U.S. law if they wanted to trade in the U.S. stock market. "My buzz words were 'the integrity of a marketplace' and 'transparency,'" Fedders recalled.[45] He had given a lot of thought to the importance

---

[41] Jean Zwahlen, interview by author, Geneva, August 17, 2009.
[42] John Fedders, interview by author, Washington, DC, September 15, 2010.
[43] John Shad to Faith Whittlesey, January 6, 1982. FW.
[44] Jean Zwahlen, interview by author, Geneva, August 17, 2009.
[45] John Fedders, interview by author, Washington, DC, September 15, 2010.

of prosecuting insider trading. In a late 1981 interview with the *Wall Street Journal*, he argued that the emerging information technology revolution required regulatory regimes to guarantee fairness, decency, and law.[46]

While Fedders arrived in Switzerland fully prepared to talk in rational, abstract terms about market integrity, Faith opened his eyes to a broader view of the topic. Arriving at the end of the business week, Fedders had a weekend to discuss the issue in a relaxed setting with the ambassador and other embassy officials, such as James Shinn, the deputy chief of mission. Whittlesey had arranged for some informal leisure time prior to the negotiations. In Fedders' assessment, this schedule proved critical. "The best thing that happened is the minute we got there, we did not get thrown into the fire," he later observed.[47]

Whittlesey believed the Americans should know Switzerland through direct experience. For the first days of their arrival in February 1982, therefore, she arranged for the entire U.S. delegation to visit Lauterbrunnen and Schilthorn in the Bernese Alps. Whittlesey had prepared an outing to the breathtaking Jungfrau, a majestic Alpine peak where the popular 1975 action movie *The Eiger Sanction* (starring Clint Eastwood) was filmed.[48] Fedders had not brought hiking clothes, but he embraced the adventure as a learning opportunity. "We were going up to these mountains, and I was wearing Fifth Avenue Allen-Edmonds shoes and suit pants—and freezing my tail off," Fedders recalled. "But we were having fun!"[49]

Over the weekend, Whittlesey gently reviewed with Fedders and the U.S. delegation how they planned to resolve the bilateral standoff. She did not dictate to the Americans, but her questions helped the group clarify their goals. "We had one enormous benefit," Fedders recalled. "Faith's a lawyer. She is a smart lady and she understood prosecution." Fedders gradually recognized that Whittlesey's questions and comments had made a strong impression on him.[50]

Whittlesey articulated the subject to Fedders in more concrete terms of common interests. After conferring with Whittlesey and Shinn, he began to understand how seriously the Swiss valued their sovereignty. "So, the word wasn't 'integrity of the U.S. marketplace'." Fedders recalled, "It

---

[46] Stan Crock, "A Talk with the SEC's Enforcement Chief," *Wall Street Journal*, December 18, 1981.
[47] John Fedders, interview by author, Washington, DC, September 15, 2010.
[48] Faith Whittlesey, interview by author, Cambridge, MA, September 8, 2009.
[49] John Fedders, interview by author, Washington, DC, September 15, 2010.
[50] Ibid.

was 'mutuality'."[51] If the Americans treated the Swiss as equal partners, Whittlesey had reasoned, the Swiss might exhibit greater willingness to pursue a negotiated solution.

Fedders understood that Faith wanted the Americans to appreciate how the Swiss viewed the United States. America appeared to Switzerland, at times, as a giant which demanded, rather than asked for, their cooperation. Fedders' outlook began to change. "And my attitude is becoming international," Fedders recalled thinking. He began to consider the ultimate goal as preserving the bilateral friendship "as opposed to just the sovereignty of our marketplaces." In Fedders' assessment, "She was teaching me a skill—that you simply couldn't go over there and say to these people, 'If you do this, then we're gonna sue you.'" These informal conversations with Whittlesey provided Fedders with a crash course on how to negotiate with the Swiss. "I was getting a Ph.D. from a diplomatic scholar in Faith," Fedders later related.[52]

THE "OPERA SINGER"

On Monday, tension filled the air as the Swiss prepared to greet the U.S. delegation for the first time. Jean Zwahlen recalled being very intimidated when the American officials from the departments of State, Treasury, Justice, and the SEC exited their car.

Zwahlen's first impressions crystallized the Swiss perspective that the U.S. Goliath was bullying the smaller David. "They were all at least 2 meters [tall]," Zwahlen recalled thinking. Indeed, Fedders, a former basketball player at Marquette University, stood at 2 meters, 13 centimeters—or 6 feet, 10 inches—tall. Roger Olsen, representing the Justice Department, was 6'9". There were not many smiles. "They were very serious," Zwahlen recalled. The initial meeting stifled Zwahlen's hopes for a mutually amicable solution. In his view, the Americans appeared unwilling to engage in an extended dialogue.[53]

Whittlesey also perceived some members of the U.S. delegation as appearing to expect prompt compliance from the Swiss without much discussion. Upon encountering resistance, some Americans quickly soured on the talks, in Faith's view. They "were only there one day and said they

---

[51] Ibid.
[52] Ibid.
[53] Jean Zwahlen, interview by author, Geneva, August 17, 2009.

wanted to go home immediately because they didn't think the Swiss were
serious and were trying to circumvent," Whittlesey remembered in 1989.[54]
The Treasury Department officials, particularly angry at the Swiss reaction
in Bern, determined to resume legal action. "The Treasury guys just wanted
the discussion to be ended in 15 minutes," she remembered. "And the Swiss
were not prepared to do that; they had a whole laundry list that they wanted
to go over," Whittlesey recalled. "The Swiss had a certain dignity which
they wanted to preserve."[55]

Unwilling to accept a collapse of the discussions so quickly, Faith called
on the Americans to demonstrate some empathy for the Swiss position. "I
put my political influence on the line to make it clear that I wanted this to
go forward," she recalled. "I wanted this *negotiation* to go forward; I did
not want them packing up and going."[56] As SEC General Counsel Greene
recalled, "Our ambassador in Switzerland said, 'You've got to step down
and try to work out an accommodation.'" The SEC delegation, having
been encouraged by their chairman to find a diplomatic solution, aided
Whittlesey's efforts to work through the technicalities and subtleties which
required exceptional patience to discuss and analyze.[57]

As the Americans agreed to resume negotiations over the course of
several days, John Fedders began to assume a leadership role, and he recognized that Whittlesey had tactfully boosted his credibility with the Swiss.
At the many events which Faith organized, someone from the embassy
constantly stayed at Fedders' side. Like a chief of staff for a politician, this
aide would provide him with instant information about, and/or introductions
to, his Swiss counterparts.[58] This support enabled Fedders to speak with
greater confidence and sophistication when he addressed his negotiating
partners from Switzerland.

Faith helped Fedders in other ways. Several Swiss individuals and
groups asked him—either in person or in calls to his hotel room—to address
their various organizations. Faith advised him about which invitations he
should accept. "I could've given 15 speeches a day, I was getting so many
requests," Fedders recalled.[59] In fact, Whittlesey had already encouraged the

[54] Faith Whittlesey, interview by Ann Miller Morin, June 21, 1989. Faith Whittlesey, interview by author, Sherborn, MA, July 12, 2010.
[55] Faith Whittlesey, interview by author, Cambridge, MA, September 8, 2009.
[56] Ibid.
[57] Edward Greene, interview by Kenneth Durr, February 15, 2008, p. 14.
[58] John Fedders, interview by author, Washington, DC, September 15, 2010.
[59] Ibid.

Swiss-American Chamber of Commerce and the Swiss Bankers Association in Zürich to ask Fedders to address them in that city.[60]

Faith's warning about Swiss sensitivities paid dividends as Fedders decided to establish a working relationship with his audience. He knew his audience expected a pedantic lecture about the need to comply with U.S. laws. "I was meeting the senior banking community in Switzerland who wanted to look at me with skepticism," Fedders recalled. "I even believed they wanted to dislike me." Many in the Swiss public still viewed the U.S. government as overly hostile in this case. Zürich's widely respected German-language newspaper, the *Neue Zürcher Zeitung*, printed a front-page political cartoon with a large, predatory animal with bared teeth and a U.S. flag pursuing a smaller creature with the Swiss flag. The caption quoted Fedders, who had earlier declared, "We are the most aggressive law enforcement agency."[61] The Americans appeared too aggressive, clearly, for Swiss taste.

In an effort to offer an olive branch, Fedders began his chamber presentation with some humorous references to the Zürich Opera House—which had recently generated so much controversy related to its expensive proposed renovations. For much of the evening prior to his talk, Fedders had sat in his hotel room thinking about "something light" with which he could preface his more serious, technical, and detailed comments.[62]

Having read newspaper reports about the protests, he decided to invent a story. "I was an opera star as a much younger man," Fedders deadpanned, "and I sang at the Zürich Opera House. When I was finished, the audience just kept clapping and clapping and they kept yelling 'encore, encore!' and so I sang four or five encores." Invoking the name of Rainer Gut, a member of the executive board of the major Swiss bank Credit Suisse, and someone Whittlesey had assured him would be a recognized name to the guests at the chamber event, Fedders continued theatrically, "After so many encores, I leaned over the stage to address Rainer Gut in the audience in an offhanded manner, asking rhetorically, 'How many encores do I have to do?'" Without missing a beat, Fedders apocryphally reported that Gut responded, "Until you get it right!" The audience erupted in a spontaneous and long-lasting

---

60 Gerald Monroe, memorandum to file, February 12, 1982. FW
61 Mr. Fedders later purchased a copy of the cartoon and caption for posterity. John Fedders, interview by author, Washington, DC, September 15, 2010.
62 John Fedders, discussion with author, telephone, June 21, 2012.

burst of laughter. Fedders had willingly exposed himself to ridicule, and the Swiss appeared to appreciate the gesture.[63]

In Whittlesey's recollection, Fedders' self-deprecating manner proved critical to success. He presented his arguments "in a graceful, humorous, and nonoffensive tone."[64] This event helped create conditions for greater civility and mutual understanding. Fedders pointedly constructed arguments to show how Switzerland could benefit from more effective U.S. regulation of insider trading. As Fedders later recalled, "We went over there and showed great respect, [and] talked about why liquidity in our markets and integrity in our markets was important to the Swiss." American stock exchanges held the potential for profit, Fedders noted, but not without transparency, regulation, and swift prosecution of criminal activity. "If we weren't able to police our own markets because of impediments in jurisdictions of secrecy," Fedders had told the Swiss, "the markets would not have this liquidity, speed, integrity," which benefited Switzerland as well as the United States.[65]

The first round of negotiations in Bern subsequently advanced in a less contentious way. In Zwahlen's view, the U.S. representatives—Fedders, in particular—increasingly demonstrated good faith and understanding of the Swiss side. "I was progressively convinced that the American side was negotiating *bona fide*," Zwahlen believed. "The quality of John Fedders' arguments and human behavior contributed greatly to that conviction." In his recollection, this change in American attitude persuaded the Swiss Federal Council—the seven-member rotating executive which governed the nation—to pursue a political solution to this bilateral standoff.[66]

Whittlesey's assistance certainly appeared to have ensured Fedders' "arias" remained in tune with his audience, and negotiations had begun on the right note. The U.S. delegation had not gone home after that very first, very tense, day. As the Americans showed a willingness to pursue a diplomatic solution, the Swiss agreed to cooperate in moving toward that goal.

MONTREAL: "GUNS TO OUR HEAD"

Fedders, Greene, and Zwahlen proved supportive diplomatic partners. Negotiations in Bern had proceeded well, but the three men recognized a

---

[63] John Fedders, interview by author, Washington, DC, September 15, 2010.
[64] Faith Whittlesey, interview by author, Sherborn, MA, July 12, 2010.
[65] John Fedders, interview by Kenneth Durr, August 9, 2006, p. 11. Securities and Exchange Commission Historical Society Oral Histories.
[66] Jean Zwahlen, email to author, June 27, 2012.

need to meet again. In order to satisfy the multiple stakeholders within both nations, these men realized they would need many more hours of intense analysis and discussion. The three men decided to hold another round of talks at a place and time to be determined.

Through the next several months of 1982, Whittlesey intervened in an effort to help both sides understand the pressures which their counterparts faced in their countries. She continued to explain the Swiss perspective to SEC Chairman Shad, whom Fedders recalled as personally committed to the success of their work. Upon returning from Switzerland, Fedders and Greene noticed the particular responsiveness of the SEC commissioners when they explained what had been discussed at their meetings.[67]

On the Swiss side, Faith also endeavored to articulate the U.S. domestic demands on the SEC. She invited Zwahlen and Rudolf Wyss, legal advisor from the Department of Justice and Police, to a working luncheon meeting at her residence on April 15. According to an internal embassy memo dated April 14, Whittlesey planned to explain how Fedders faced "political pressure" from Congress to "show results," and would specifically cite a deadline of June 21 after which the SEC would return to court action.[68]

Fedders, Greene, and Zwahlen decided that they needed to meet at an undisclosed location. By keeping the negotiations out of the public eye, they hoped to alleviate some of the intense pressures these men faced from their respective governments. "[The issue] was *so* sensitive," Greene remembered.[69] If the media or multiple government agencies began to comment or demand participation in the process, they believed, negotiations might falter and die. Zwahlen recalled, "I was very aware of the fact that many doubted I could achieve a reasonable success which, eventually, could satisfy everybody."[70] Each man had to defend the integrity of his nation's sovereignty and constitutional legal process. In Fedders' words, "Both Jean Zwahlen and I felt we had guns to our head."[71] Representatives of each man's respective government, business community, media, and public would meticulously dissect their decisions.

Secret meetings in Montreal that followed allowed Fedders, Greene, and Zwahlen to clarify how far the U.S. and Swiss governments could reasonably

---

[67] John Fedders, interview by author, Washington, DC, September 15, 2010.
[68] Gerald Monroe, memorandum to Ambassador Whittlesey, April 14, 1982. FW.
[69] Edward Greene, interview by Kenneth Durr, February 15, 2008, p. 14.
[70] Jean Zwahlen, interview by author, Geneva, August 17, 2009.
[71] John Fedders, discussion with author, telephone, June 21, 2012.

compromise and how they might reconcile seemingly intractable differences. In Fedders' view, these private talks "created the give and take where each side said, 'I have to have this.'" In particular, Fedders praised Ed Greene's role in "drafting language which provided flexibility to both sides."

"EVERYTHING WOULD HAVE FAILED"

At great risk to his reputation, Zwahlen decided not to inform any Swiss bankers or government officials of his Montreal meetings with Fedders and Greene. The complexity of the issues under discussion, in Zwahlen's view, required the clarification which the three men finally achieved in Montreal.

During the negotiations, he contacted only Swiss Minister of Justice Kurt Furgler, who was a member of the Swiss Federal Council since 1971, head of the Federal Department of Justice and Police since 1972, and President of the Swiss Confederation in 1981. These consultations allowed Zwahlen to gauge what concessions the Swiss government would accept: "[Furgler] gave me some instruction as to how far I could go."

When Zwahlen eventually revealed his secret negotiations to the Swiss bankers and ministers, they expressed anger. "When I told my working group, they felt betrayed," he later related.[72] He recognized that his compatriots might consider him a traitor. But he insisted upon the importance of having continued discussions without public scrutiny. "I told them we had to go ahead, otherwise everything would have failed."[73] Despite the complaints, Zwahlen had reached a resolution with the United States on behalf of the Swiss government, and he had avoided a protracted legal battle with the powerful U.S. government.

Fedders, who had frequent and candid contact with many leading Swiss government and business leaders during the negotiations, recalled Zwahlen's role with exceptional respect. "I learned that he faced monumental pressures within the Swiss financial center, government, and general public," Fedders recalled. "In retrospect, I characterize Zwahlen as essential, and indeed, heroic in the way he navigated those treacherous waters."[74]

---

[72] Jean Zwahlen, email to author, June 27, 2012.
[73] Jean Zwahlen, interview by author, Geneva, August 17, 2009.
[74] John Fedders, discussion with author, telephone, June 21, 2012.

"A BREATH OF FRESH AIR"

These extensive and laborious negotiations eventually resulted in Switzerland permitting its banks to cooperate with the SEC investigations of insider trading. The United States decided to respect the Swiss law guaranteeing the privacy of bank accounts, but within new parameters.

The Swiss Banking Association agreed to require clients to accept that their privacy would no longer be unlimited. According to Ed Greene, "It was a quite clever way of saying that the Swiss Banking Association would go back to the banks and clients and say that 'If you want to maintain your account, you're going to have to consent that under these circumstances we may provide information.'" This data would be "filtered in Switzerland" prior to its release to U.S. authorities, Greene noted. "So there would be some oversight to it." The American government thus had agreed "not to assault bank secrecy" while simultaneously ensuring Swiss cooperation with U.S. courts through "the idea of consent," in Greene's words.[75]

A Memorandum of Understanding (MOU) signed by John Shad and Jean Zwahlen on August 31, 1982, in Washington outlined the terms of this accord between the two governments. This MOU clarified America's 1977 Treaty with the Swiss Confederation on Mutual Assistance in Criminal Matters. Specifically, SEC requests for client information would be passed from the U.S. Justice Department to the Swiss Federal Office for Police Matters.

A three-member commission organized by the Swiss Bankers Association would receive the information. Under certain conditions, the Swiss bank would be asked to report details about a transaction and freeze the account of a criminally suspect client. The editors of the *Journal of Comparative Corporate Law and Securities Regulation* characterized the MOU as "a giant step toward ... comprehensive international cooperation."[76]

Zwahlen believed that the negotiations and resulting MOU accomplished several objectives for Switzerland. First, both countries had demonstrated mutual respect for the other as an "equal sovereign" partner. Second, the Swiss had "preserved the substance" and integrity of that nation's national "legal framework." Third, the agreement had alleviated the potential for one or more Swiss banks to suffer damaging fines—which might have forced

---

[75] Edward Greene, interview by Kenneth Durr, February 15, 2008, p. 14.
[76] Editors' postscript, "United States Insider Trading Prohibition in Conflict with Swiss Bank Secrecy," *Journal of Comparative Corporate Law and Securities Regulation* 4 (1983): 368.

these institutions into financial default and harmed Switzerland's national economy. Fourth, and finally, Switzerland had salvaged "amicable bilateral relations with the USA." In Zwahlen's opinion, these benefits relied "greatly" on Ambassador Whittlesey's intervention and her willingness to utilize her "close contacts" at the highest levels of the U.S. government.[77]

Swiss bankers appreciated Whittlesey's delicate handling of the bilateral relationship. Rainer Gut (whose name Fedders had playfully invoked in his *opera buffa* performance in Zürich) believed that Whittlesey's role as ambassador was crucial in resolving disputes between the United States and Switzerland: "She tried to understand the Swiss peculiarities, and to see if you could bring the two [countries] close to each other without clashing."[78]

Whittlesey's achievement also earned praise from the highest levels of the U.S. government. The United States had achieved, through negotiation, a result which U.S. officials had originally hoped to secure through the court system. The diplomacy proved fortuitous, according to Fedders, because the legal route would have entailed many potential pitfalls. "The progress of the litigation would have been unpredictable for the U.S., the SEC, and the Swiss." No matter which side won the case, an appeal was more than likely, he surmised. In summary, Fedders believed that a courtroom battle would have been "unpredictable, time consuming and expensive, ... and the publicity would have been negative for all concerned."[79]

For these reasons, Fedders praised Zwahlen and Whittlesey for choosing a politically negotiated solution. "The SEC and U.S. were fortunate that Ambassador Whittlesey was at her post in Bern, and that the Swiss officials led by Jean Zwahlen were receptive to meeting and conferring," Fedders concluded.[80]

Other high-ranking SEC leaders also recognized Faith's key role. Chairman John Shad congratulated her in a January 1983 letter to Faith, writing, "You have achieved remarkable results in such a short time."[81] That same month, SEC Commissioner Bevis Longstreth, a Democrat, wrote to White House Chief of Staff Baker in praise of the ambassador, saying, "Faith Whittlesey is simply one of the most effective political professionals

---

[77]   Jean Zwahlen, email to author, June 27, 2012.
[78]   Rainer Gut, interview by author, Zürich, August 21, 2009.
[79]   John Fedders, email to author, June 7, 2012.
[80]   Ibid.
[81]   John Shad to Faith Whittlesey, January 6, 1983. Box 29, folder 16. FW.

around. She demonstrated this by her brilliant work on securities matters with the Swiss, and, of course, her Pennsylvania record is well known."[82]

Ward Thompson, the officer whom the State Department had assigned to prepare Whittlesey for her Senate confirmation hearings in 1981, extolled her successful ambassadorship nearly two decades later. In a 1999 interview, he described Whittlesey's arrival in Bern as "a breath of fresh air." In Thompson's perspective, she had contributed significantly to U.S.-Swiss cooperation. "Dick Vine obviously was a competent professional," Thompson noted, "but I think the contrast was helpful in our relationship with Switzerland."[83]

Whittlesey's status as a noncareer ambassador appeared of vital importance to the success of these negotiations. Political appointees typically have more high-level connections with a presidential administration than a career ambassador. Faith's prior political relationship with SEC Chairman Shad clearly played a critical role in moving this bilateral standoff from a legal to a diplomatic track. A Foreign Service officer can rarely, if ever, make substantive, direct contact with heads of other federal departments.

In Whittlesey's interpretation, however, the true benefit of a political appointee is a predisposition to implement—with profound understanding and authentic enthusiasm—the incumbent administration's foreign policy. The next chapter will discuss how Whittlesey sought to market Reagan's foreign policy agenda to the Swiss.

---

[82] Bevis Longstreth to James A. Baker III, January 7, 1983. Box 29, Folder 16. FW.
[83] Ward Thompson, interview by Thomas Dunnigan, February 4, 1999. Frontline Diplomacy, Manuscript Division, Library of Congress, Washington, DC.

CHAPTER 3

Advocating Reagan's Policies to the Swiss People
The First Bern Tour (part 2)

The priceless asset of the diplomat is that he is there.
He is in the foreign country, on the spot.
—Ambassador Livingston T. Merchant[1]

In the early 1980s, Christoph Schaer was a tall, intense, blond-haired Swiss university student in his late teens. Nearly three decades later, he recalled his frustration at the angry, and sometimes violent, protests against the United States and President Ronald Reagan on many Saturdays in the Zürich of his university years. "It was a riot-like atmosphere with people throwing stones at bank windows," Schaer remembered. Paint balls were used to leave deep, long-lasting stains on the walls of government buildings and commercial establishments.[2] When Schaer and his group of friends expressed support for Reagan's foreign policy, the crowd attacked them. "We were beaten up at a peace demonstration," he noted ironically.[3]

Behind closed doors, Ambassador Faith Whittlesey had quietly helped resolve the standoff between the U.S. Securities and Exchange Commission and Justice Department on the one hand, and Swiss banks on the other.

---

[1] Quoted in Brandon Grove, *Behind Embassy Walls: The Life and Times of an American Diplomat* (Columbia: University of Missouri Press, 2005), p. 256.

[2] Christoph Schaer, interview by author, Zürich, August 24, 2009. Similar accounts were reported by other Swiss who studied in Bern and Zürich at the time. Peter Meyer Losenegger and Urs Steiner, interview by author, Lima, Peru, August 12, 2010.

[3] Christoph Schaer, interview by author, Zürich, August 24, 2009.

At the same time, she adopted a very public campaign to explain Reagan's foreign policy to the Swiss. In her first tour as ambassador, Whittlesey implemented a strategy of building relationships with Switzerland's non-governmental opinion leaders in addition to establishing contacts with traditional diplomatic sources in the Swiss government in Bern.

Faith recognized a pressing need for more "public diplomacy" in the embassy and in U.S. foreign affairs in general. She sought to extend diplomatic relations beyond conversations with foreign officials and to engage more actively with foreign publics. In later years, Harvard political scientist Joseph Nye popularized the term "soft power" to suggest that persuasion rather than coercion works best in defending national interests abroad.[4] Two decades earlier, starting in 1981, Whittlesey made public diplomacy a priority of the U.S. mission in Switzerland.

"THE WESTERN VOICE WAS MUTE"

"Public diplomacy is one of soft power's key instruments," wrote Jan Melissen, the founding coeditor of *The Hague Journal of Diplomacy*, in 2005. Melissen noted that America's diplomatic corps marginalized the idea of crafting messages for foreign publics. In Melissen's view, "It has always been difficult to give public diplomacy priority on the [U.S.] State Department's agenda (and few flashy careers were therefore built on diplomatic jobs in the field of information and cultural work)."[5]

Nearly 25 years earlier, Faith discovered that few embassy personnel had the aptitude or interest in the kind of public information strategies which she envisioned for advocating U.S. foreign policy in Switzerland. In Melissen's words, "Market-oriented thinking was anathema and even a vulgarization to traditional diplomacy, but is slowly but surely entering today's [2005's] diplomatic services."[6] Whittlesey certainly did her part to mobilize the U.S. embassy in Bern for a public diplomacy mission which would promote President Ronald Reagan's foreign policy goals among the Swiss.

President Reagan assuredly believed in the power of ideas to move nations, and he had outlined a clear, ambitious foreign policy agenda in his

---

[4] Joseph S. Nye, Jr., *Soft Power: The Means to Success in World Politics* (New York: PublicAffairs, 2004).

[5] Jan Melissen, "The New Public Diplomacy: Between Theory and Practice," in *The New Public Diplomacy: Soft Power in International Relations*, ed. Jan Melissen (New York: Palgrave Macmillan, 2005), p. 6.

[6] Ibid., p. 8.

earliest presidential addresses. Speaking at Notre Dame University in May 1981, he asserted that "the West won't contain communism, it will transcend communism."[7] A month later, as Poland's Solidarity movement challenged communist rule in that nation, Reagan told a press conference that "I think we are seeing the first, beginning cracks [in communism], the beginning of the end."[8] The new president had wasted no time in telegraphing a significant shift in U.S. policy—away from the 1970s notion of *détente*, which encouraged the relaxation of tensions with the Soviet Union.

Such words appeared shockingly prophetic after the Soviet Union's 1991 collapse, but 10 years earlier, many Europeans feared Reagan's rhetoric. Reagan had proposed placing U.S. nuclear-armed intermediate-range missiles in Western Europe to counter similar Soviet installations in Eastern Europe. The Soviet Union encouraged Europeans to view Reagan's actions as aggressive and dangerous provocations which might lead to another European war.

Charles Wick, the president's first and only director of the United States International Communication Agency (USICA),[9] traveled to Europe in the summer of 1981. Nearly immediately—"within six minutes of landing and every six minutes thereafter"—Wick encountered anti-Americanism and despair about America's failure of leadership in the Cold War.[10]

In Switzerland, Christoph Schaer harbored a similar frustration. While many Swiss military, businessmen, farmers, and tradesmen were entirely sympathetic to Reagan, they were not out on the streets. Schaer recalled protestors burning U.S. flags and raising the Soviet banner depicting the traditional hammer and sickle. U.S. and Western European governments might have mounted a strong, sustained rebuttal to these anti-Western attitudes, but from his vantage point, "The Western voice was mute."[11]

Wick's USICA mobilized the Reagan administration for action. Writing to National Security Advisor Richard V. Allen, Wick proposed that the United States confront Soviet propaganda "with wartime urgency." Diplomats, not

---

[7]   Paul Kengor, *The Crusader: Ronald Reagan and the Fall of Communism* (New York: Harper Perennial, 2006), p. 77.

[8]   Ibid., p. 78.

[9]   In August 1982, Congress approved the request to change USICA's name to the United States Information Agency. Nicholas J. Cull, *The Cold War and the United States Information Agency: American Propaganda and Public Diplomacy, 1945–1989* (Cambridge, UK: Cambridge University Press, 2008), p. 420.

[10]   Cull, *The Cold War*, p. 408.

[11]   Christoph Schaer, interview by author, Zürich, August 24, 2009.

soldiers, would occupy the front lines, in his view: "The administration's best speakers and thinkers should assemble to urgently shape a coordinated strategy to enable the United States *to speak with one voice* persuasively and with sensitivity to Soviet engendered disinformation."[12]

Wick believed that Europeans, if properly informed, would support Reagan's plan. In October 1981, he delivered USICA reports which revealed a decline in opposition to the U.S. missiles after respondents were asked to consider Soviet missile strength and U.S. willingness to participate in arms reduction talks.[13]

Likewise, Faith Whittlesey brought a public diplomacy plan to Bern. Her initiative to engage Swiss citizens took two forms. As a first step, she determined to travel through Switzerland and personally meet the people in the various regions of this small but highly sophisticated, diverse country. Second, she reviewed the 125-member embassy staff to learn who among them would most effectively present and explain U.S. foreign policy objectives.

ENGAGING SWITZERLAND'S "MOVERS AND SHAKERS"

Whittlesey's decision to meet the Swiss people in their own environment became a signature feature of her ambassadorship. Few U.S. ambassadors engaged with the Swiss public as effectively. She reached beyond the obligatory duties of the diplomatic circuit in Bern. In the process, Faith built relationships with private-sector leaders and average citizens across Switzerland.

For example, Whittlesey visited each of the 28 Swiss cantons—comparable to America's 50 states. This travel always had a purpose: she attended local fairs and cultural events, met with regional politicians, and granted interviews to many local Swiss newspaper reporters and television commentators. Since Switzerland has three official languages—Swiss German, French, and Italian—and distinct local cultures, Faith's ambitious schedule exposed her to a variety of the country's traditions.

This decision to go out into the Swiss countryside and cities outside the capital diverged dramatically from most ambassadors' habits. "A lot of the diplomats in Switzerland were close to retirement," Whittlesey recalled, "because this country was seen as a very posh assignment, as a kind of

---

[12] Cull, *The Cold War,* p. 408 (emphasis in original).
[13] Ibid., p. 412.

reward at the end of their careers."[14] During her initial months in Bern, Faith quickly recognized that an ambassador could fill his or her time almost entirely with social events among the diplomatic corps. But she did not perceive this lunch and dinner circuit in Bern, the capital, as politically productive. Whittlesey believed that the president and the United States needed her to connect with the Swiss people in a serious way.

While the population at large greatly appreciated meeting the U.S. ambassador, Faith soon realized that many Swiss looked to the leadership of Switzerland's financial and industrial institutions as opinion makers. The average Swiss understood that "the chief executive officers were the people who ensured their prosperity as a nation, so they paid a lot of attention," Whittlesey noted. In order to advocate for Reagan in Switzerland, therefore, she determined to meet the decision makers in those sectors of Swiss society. "I went out to the financial centers, the Big Pharma center in Basel, the private bankers in Geneva, and the industrial plants," she recalled. "That's where I spent my time."[15] By engaging with Switzerland's business leaders, she built credibility for the United States and created opportunities to advocate for Reagan's policies with the nation's private-sector leadership.

In the United States, some people might find this high regard for corporate executives a little odd. But Whittlesey noted that Americans also appeared mesmerized at times by the lifestyles and political views of the country's most wealthy and celebrated personalities. The U.S. Congress, in fact, occasionally asked Hollywood actors to testify about national topics which they may have only learned about through reading a movie script. Popular music personalities became American icons, or "idols." In Whittlesey's words, "In the United States, we all know Whitney Houston and Michael Jackson. In Switzerland, everybody knows the name of the chairman of [food packaging multinational] Nestlé and the chairman of [pharmaceutical multinational] Hoffmann-La Roche. They are the rock stars."[16] This widespread admiration for the creators of Swiss jobs and national wealth benefited Switzerland, Whittlesey believed, by promoting a less adversarial relationship between the business community and the rest of the country than often exists in the United States.

---

[14] Faith Whittlesey, discussion with author, telephone, February 21, 2012.
[15] Ibid.
[16] Ibid.

EXPLAINING THE "COWBOY" TO THE SWISS

The Swiss-American Chamber of Commerce provided one venue for Whittlesey to meet Switzerland's business community. Invited to deliver one of her first major speeches in Zürich, Whittlesey successfully created positive relationships with several Swiss corporate leaders. Entrepreneur Egon Zehnder, who organized the event as chairman of the chamber's program committee, recalled that she established an instant rapport with the audience. "Faith came across as very down-to-earth. She was interested in people, interested to exchange opinions."[17]

Whittlesey impressed the Swiss by demonstrating a genuine curiosity about their very successful business strategies and a wide range of knowledge about both their companies and Switzerland's culture. Chamber President Rainer Gut, who had served on the Credit Suisse executive board since 1973, recalled that she "came across sincerely—not phony."[18] Henry Bodmer, who served on several corporate boards of directors in Switzerland, was impressed with Whittlesey's ability to discuss finance, pharmaceuticals, engineering, history, geography, and opera in a sophisticated manner.[19] Whittlesey also found the Swiss held a great respect for America's entrepreneurial spirit, and she embraced the opportunity to explain her opinions about why the U.S. produced so many innovators.

While the Swiss-American chamber welcomed every incoming U.S. ambassador at a celebratory meeting, Swiss executives took particular interest in Whittlesey because of her prominence within the Reagan coalition. In Whittlesey's view, "They figured out pretty early that I could tell them information that they were not getting from other sources."[20] Whittlesey had joined the conservative movement in support of Ronald Reagan several years earlier than most U.S. political leaders, and therefore she had extensive contacts at the administration's highest levels and remained well informed about the policy process and decisions within the White House.

Many Swiss CEOs had extensive responsibility for investments and employees within the United States, so they naturally wished to know how the new president would alter the U.S. economy in particular. In 1980, Reagan's election came as a shock to many Europeans, who viewed him, at best, as a mere actor, or at worst, as a dangerous "cowboy" who might

---

[17] Egon Zehnder, interview by author, Zürich, August 20, 2009.
[18] Rainer Gut, interview by author, Zürich, August 21, 2009.
[19] Henry Bodmer, interview by author, Zürich, August 22, 2009.
[20] Faith Whittlesey, discussion with author, telephone, February 21, 2012.

inadvertently incite the Soviet Union into nuclear war. Since mainstream news sources sometimes indulged in propagating caricatures of Reagan, Faith possessed an inside track into the president's true character. Swiss business leaders recognized her as someone who might better explain why so many Americans had voted for him, and what the consequences might be for Switzerland and the world.

Whittlesey cautioned the Swiss against accepting the theory that Reagan's popularity merely reflected a cult of personality. "For Europe's liberal media, in particular," she recalled, "the U.S. conservative movement was as foreign as the map of Afghanistan."[21] Hindsight later revealed what she believed (but few people considered at the time to be true)—that an intellectual shift was occurring in Americans' conception of the federal government's proper role. Faith held valuable clues, therefore, about which priorities Reagan would advance, and she was more than happy to articulate the administration's agenda for change to Swiss audiences.

EMOTIONAL INTELLIGENCE

Swiss executives especially appreciated Whittlesey's earnestness in seeking to understand their nation's underlying motivations and goals. She valued Switzerland's importance to the United States as a key foreign investor and provider of many U.S. jobs. "I knew that aspects of the American economy depended on them continuing to like us, trust us, and invest in us," Faith recalled.[22]

Whittlesey's empathy for the Swiss perspective especially endeared her to the Swiss. In Zehnder's recollection, "She had an enormous confidence in this country and in its political institutions." Faith frequently spoke in Switzerland about the ties which bound that country with the United States. She emphasized that Swiss and Americans shared values—such as a commitment to limited government and the rule of law—which made them "sister republics," if not formal allies.[23] Despite Swiss neutrality, noted Zehnder, "She knew that our government was on the same side as the Americans."[24]

She also genuinely enjoyed hiking and skiing in the Alps, and Swiss high culture. This enthusiasm for Switzerland's physical beauty and national

---

[21] Ibid.

[22] Ibid.

[23] Faith Whittlesey, "Foreword," in *Switzerland Under Siege, 1939–1945: A Neutral Nation's Struggle for Survival,* ed. Leo Schelbert (Rockport, ME: Picton Press, 2000), p. vii.

[24] Egon Zehnder, interview by author, Zürich, August 20, 2009.

traditions provided the Swiss with opportunities to establish stronger ties. Within months of their arrival in Switzerland, Whittlesey and her children received an invitation to ski with Rainer Gut's wife Margot and children at the well-known Klosters resort near Davos.[25] She attended the opera with Henry Bodmer and his wife, who served on the board of the Zürich Opera House. According to Gut, Whittlesey formed lasting relationships with many of Switzerland's private-sector decision makers. "In most major Swiss corporations she had good friends up to the highest level."[26]

Egon Zehnder credited Whittlesey's skill with people for her success as an ambassador: "It's her outgoing, open personality."[27] Zehnder's assessment deserves special consideration because he led one of the foremost global companies dedicated to evaluating leadership skills. In 1964, he founded the executive search firm Egon Zehnder International, which connects corporate executives with companies and other large organizations, such as the World Bank.[28]

Recalling Whittlesey's qualities in 2009, Zehnder described her as having "enormous emotional intelligence." Zehnder's use of this phrase for Whittlesey appears especially meaningful because Daniel Goleman (who brought "emotional intelligence" into the lexicon with a best-selling book by that name in 1995) called Zehnder "a pioneer in creating an emotionally intelligent organization."[29] In Goleman's estimation, Zehnder had demonstrated a concrete appreciation for emotional intelligence as evidenced by the model of team building and cooperation on a global scale he created at Egon Zehnder International.[30]

By extending herself to meet corporate leaders on equal terms, Whittlesey earned their admiration. She displayed none of the mistakes typical of the characters in the 1958 best-selling novel *The Ugly American*. In particular, she consciously determined to avoid the appearance of dictating to Swiss business leaders, but carefully attempted to cultivate their goodwill.

[25] Rainer E. Gut to Faith Whittlesey, January 25, 1982, Box 44, Folder 10. From the Faith Whittlesey Collection, Howard Gotlieb Archival Research Center at Boston University (hereafter referred to as FW).
[26] Rainer Gut, interview by author, Zürich, August 21, 2009.
[27] Egon Zehnder, interview by author, Zürich, August 20, 2009.
[28] Daniel Goleman, *Working with Emotional Intelligence* (New York: Bantam Books, 1998), pp. 302–303.
[29] Ibid., p. x.
[30] Ibid., pp. 302–309.

James Shinn, deputy chief of mission (DCM) in Bern from 1982 to 1986, witnessed Whittlesey's popularity among the Swiss, which enabled her to address controversial issues without alienating her audience. For example, Whittlesey urged the Swiss government not to give agricultural aid to Nicaragua's pro-Soviet regime in Central America. "I don't think that the Swiss were terribly sympathetic to the message that she was conveying," Shinn recalled, "[but] she was able to make speeches about Reagan foreign policy to a Swiss audience and still be invited back."[31]

Zehnder called Faith "a very courageous person" for continuing to articulate the administration's agenda in the face of the loud and insistent protests.[32] In Zehnder's view, left-wing protestors had begun to set the public agenda in the 1980s. "I sometimes felt they almost monopolized the medi[a]."[33]

"PINK TOILET PAPER"

While endeavoring to meet Switzerland's corporate, government, and cultural leaders in person, Whittlesey also identified embassy staff members who could assist her in implementing public diplomacy. As head of the U.S. mission in Bern, Whittlesey sought out embassy officials who could engage with the Swiss population and actively promote Reagan's foreign policy to the Swiss.

An ambassador constantly confronts multiple challenges while trying to run an embassy efficiently. Brandon Grove, a career Foreign Service officer who served as ambassador to Zaire from 1984 to 1987, claimed that no career experience prepared a person to become an ambassador. "Being an ambassador is different from anything done before, whether one has been a career diplomat, a college president, or the CEO of a corporation," he wrote in the 2005 book *Behind Embassy Walls*.[34]

Similarly, John Kenneth Galbraith, longtime public servant for Democratic administrations and President John F. Kennedy's ambassador to India from 1961 to 1963, described the direction of an embassy as a unique challenge. In Galbraith's 1969 book *Ambassador's Journal*, he stated that performing his job "would have been inconceivable" without his wife.

---

[31] James Shinn, interview by author, Kensington, CA, March 16, 2010.
[32] Egon Zehnder, interview by author, Zürich, August 20, 2009.
[33] Ibid.
[34] Brandon Grove, *Behind Embassy Walls: The Life and Times of an American Diplomat* (Columbia: University of Missouri Press, 2005), p. 255.

Mrs. Galbraith managed the large staff (including "butler, assistant bearers, cook and assistant cooks, sweepers, gardeners, guards, drivers, laundry-men and more").[35] She also arranged "household entertainment, a wide range of protocol activities, concern for the problems of the American community, association with wives and families of my Indian and diplomatic associates, cultivation of the arts and representation of the Ambassador at a succession of functions during my absence."[36]

Faith Whittlesey, of course, encountered similar obligations. But, as a widow since 1974, she had no such spousal support. She would have to supervise the 125 embassy employees—including her many household staff members—on her own. Social, cultural, and political responsibilities would all fall under her direct purview. This scenario meant that she would rely heavily on her colleagues in the U.S. government for support. She thus determined to assess personnel very carefully.

Another Galbraith observation—that the large size of the State Department bureaucracy discouraged innovation—augured poorly for Whittlesey's plan to mobilize the embassy behind a public diplomacy initiative. In Galbraith's view, "One cannot get agreement on anything new."[37] Galbraith lamented the difficulty in reaching consensus among the various "counselors and attachés and their staffs—commercial, consular, press, agricultural, scientific and military—[who] deal with their special subjects and, on occasion, have trouble keeping busy."[38] Since so many Foreign Service officers sought to participate in implementing government policy, Galbraith found it was difficult to overcome "inflexibility."[39] Rather than engage the host country's citizens, Galbraith observed, embassy officers focused excessively on government-to-government "high level representation."[40] He even admitted to having deleted sections of his journal in which he recommended firing several State Department officials.[41]

Whittlesey sought out U.S. government officials whom she could trust to improve America's image. If embassy staff effectively explained the policies of the newly elected President Reagan to the Swiss, Faith could generate a

---

[35] John Kenneth Galbraith, *Ambassador's Journal: A Personal Account of the Kennedy Years* (Boston: Houghton Mifflin, 1969), p. xvii.
[36] Ibid., p. xx.
[37] Ibid., p. 212.
[38] Ibid., p. xix.
[39] Ibid., p. 212.
[40] Ibid., p. 244.
[41] Ibid., p. xv.

multiplier effect to her own efforts to advocate for the administration with Swiss opinion leaders and the general public.

In summary, Faith sought diplomats who "could sell a carton of pink toilet paper to a corner grocer who was already 10 cartons overstocked." Anyone who could succeed in that mission, she assumed, "could sell American foreign policy to the most difficult adversaries."[42] As she met and came to know the U.S. embassy team members in Bern, Whittlesey looked for every opportunity to find her best "toilet paper" salespeople.

"IF YOU DON'T SKI IN SWITZERLAND, YOU CAN'T DO ANYTHING"

On February 21, 1982, Ambassador Whittlesey's 43rd birthday, she ascended the Alps for an embassy staff ski outing. Instead of staying at home to celebrate, she was determined not to miss this event. Her young son William participated as well. Whittlesey believed that Americans could best connect with their Swiss counterparts by joining in Switzerland's favorite pastimes, such as skiing and hiking. She also hoped to become better acquainted with embassy personnel in order to identify those individuals best suited to represent the United States on a person-to-person basis with the Swiss.

Few people knew the ambassador well, as she had arrived only 5 months earlier. Since the days when all diplomats belonged to elite families, most people approached an ambassador reluctantly. One Foreign Service officer recalled State Department training which taught that an ambassador is "half way to God."[43] Many people addressed her as "Madam Ambassador." It was no surprise, therefore, that no one immediately stepped forward to ride up with her as she approached the two-person chair lift.

Susan Graf, a young, slim, energetic blond-haired woman, saw an opportunity and joined Whittlesey on the metal chair lift which would transport them up the mountain. Although Graf was a U.S. citizen, she had lived in Switzerland since 1980 with her Swiss husband. Working in the embassy as a "local"—rather than an American national—she believed that the State Department staff viewed her as second-class in the bureaucratic hierarchy. The fact that Graf's desk was located in a corridor of the embassy reinforced this impression in her mind. As an employee of the

[42] Faith Whittlesey, interview by Ann Miller Morin, December 7, 1989. Frontline Diplomacy, Manuscript Division, Library of Congress, Washington, DC.
[43] Douglas Sears, interview by author, Boston, July 9, 2009.

United States International Communication Agency, Graf typed President Reagan's speeches for distribution to Swiss media outlets.[44]

Given this unanticipated opportunity to speak one-on-one with the ambassador, she seized the moment. As they rose into the Alps, Graf made conversation by talking about a subject she knew well—the president's formal addresses, which she had been dutifully recording with her typewriter. Graf's ability to recite Reagan's opinions in detail impressed the ambassador, who quickly recognized Graf as someone who could effectively articulate the administration's policy agenda.

The more they talked, the more Whittlesey viewed Graf as a valuable resource, and a charming personality. Graf's intimate knowledge of Swiss customs through her husband also caught Whittlesey's attention. She had displayed personal initiative by engaging the ambassador in conversation. In Whittlesey's recollection, "She was bubbling over with enthusiasm; she was very socially graceful and everybody liked her. She was pretty, very well dressed and groomed at all times."[45] Furthermore, Whittlesey recognized in Graf the very characteristics she sought in order to make the embassy more accessible to the Swiss public. She asked, "Where are you working right now?" When Graf admitted to her entry-level clerical-typist position, Whittlesey interjected, "No, tomorrow you're on *my* staff."[46]

Graf soon emerged as one of Whittlesey's most trusted assistants in the embassy, and later on in the White House as well. Her close connections with the Swiss helped Whittlesey in conducting many tasks such as providing suggestions for a celebratory toast, remembering birthdays and anniversaries, managing the ambassador's social calendar, and selecting appropriate dresses for formal and less formal diplomatic functions.[47] As a widow, Whittlesey especially appreciated this assistance because the public presentation of the U.S. ambassador directly affected the image of the United States.

Colonel Justin LaPorte, the U.S. Army attaché, also attended this ski excursion, and he recalled Whittlesey's enthusiasm. "'This is great,' I remember her saying. 'We're going to do this every year.'" In LaPorte's view,

---

[44] Susan Graf, interview by author, New York, August 2, 2009.
[45] Faith Whittlesey, interview by author, Cambridge, MA, September 8, 2009.
[46] Susan Graf, interview by author, New York, August 2, 2009.
[47] Ibid.

Faith had found a useful means of relating to embassy personnel. "She was bonding with the staff," he believed.[48]

Skiing also provided U.S. nationals with an important entrée into Swiss culture. In LaPorte's opinion, communicating with the Swiss began with skiing. "If you don't ski in Switzerland, you can't do anything," LaPorte observed, half humorously. "You have no conversation in the winter with other people, because that's all they ask, 'Where did you ski last Sunday?'"

Whittlesey soon recognized LaPorte as a trusted colleague. She brought him with her when she traveled to promote the sale of the U.S.-made M1 Abrams tank to the Swiss government. She also valued LaPorte's presence as a uniformed officer during her speeches about the tank because he enhanced her credibility. At least one Swiss editor reportedly complained about her advocacy for U.S. military sales, saying "We were ... somewhat shocked by the idea of a woman, who is also a mother, selling a tank."[49]

In LaPorte's opinion, Whittlesey distinguished herself from other ambassadors for whom he had worked. "She had you working 24 hours a day, thinking about projects," he recalled. While some heads of mission appeared self-serving, LaPorte recognized Faith as always representing the president and the U.S. government with her primary loyalty. "She was there for the administration," he believed.[50]

LaPorte admired Whittlesey's public relations savvy and her command of the nuances of international relations and Cold War strategy. "Anything I know about politics, I learned from her," he said.[51]

CHANGING THE LEADERSHIP

An ambassador typically relies most heavily on the deputy chief of mission. The DCM serves as the ambassador's chief advisor, the senior manager of embassy staff, and—whenever the ambassador is out of the country—as the head of mission, or *chargé d'affaires*. Although Whittlesey arrived at the embassy in September 1981 without a clear choice for DCM, she decided to give the incumbent, Charles Stout, a chance to prove himself.

Faith perceived Stout as uncomfortable with her status as a Reagan Republican and her gender. "I did feel that he resented very much the fact that he was reporting to me, number one, a political appointee, number

[48] Justin LaPorte, interview by author, Madison, CT, June 8, 2009.
[49] Quoted in Beth Gillen, "Tough as Males," *Philadelphia Inquirer Magazine*, October 2, 1983, p. 13.
[50] Ibid.
[51] Ibid.

two, a woman younger than he," she recalled in 1989.[52] Stout's protests to the contrary did not convince her. He "made a great point of telling me that he was a Republican, ... and how open he was to the idea of women and minorities—that was a kind of *leitmotif* in his conversation."[53]

Most importantly to Whittlesey, Stout showed little interest in her effort to engage with the Swiss public. She asked him and the embassy's political and economic officers to devote more of their time to speaking engagements with Swiss opinion leaders, but they demurred. "I didn't want them to ... completely reorient their whole lives," Faith recalled, "but I wanted them to take 10 percent of their time and use it in public diplomacy." According to her, Stout and the others stonewalled. "They would say, 'Nobody asks us. We go if we're asked.'"[54]

Whittlesey wanted to establish relationships with Swiss opinion leaders outside the Foreign Ministry, but Stout "didn't have any contacts. He really wasn't in a position to tell me what was important, who was important, because he apparently didn't know."[55] Since she traveled frequently to Geneva, Basel, and Zürich to engage with industry, academic, cultural, and banking leaders in these cities, Whittlesey expected her deputy to represent the United States and promote the administration's agenda in her absence.

As she struggled to improve the president's image, Faith became extremely frustrated with Stout's judgment. When she asked him to distribute to members of the Swiss Parliament the text of President Reagan's "zero option" proposal for removing all nuclear weapons from Europe, he discouraged her, saying "Oh, no, we don't do that sort of thing." But she soon discovered that the Soviets had already sent the Swiss lawmakers their counterproposal.[56]

During the winter of 1982, Whittlesey began to consider a soft-spoken, bearded political officer in Bern as a replacement. James Shinn, a mid-career officer in the State Department hierarchy, as well as his wife Patricia, impressed Faith as cosmopolitan and sophisticated. Shinn had graduated from prestigious U.S. schools—Andover Academy in Massachusetts and the University of California at Berkeley. After serving in the U.S. Navy as

---

[52] Faith Whittlesey, interview by Ann Miller Morin, June 17, 1989. Frontline Diplomacy, Manuscript Division, Library of Congress, Washington, DC.
[53] Ibid.
[54] Ibid.
[55] Faith Whittlesey, interview by author, Cambridge, MA, September 8, 2009.
[56] Faith Whittlesey, interview by Ann Miller Morin, December 7, 1989.

an officer, he applied for, and was accepted into, the Foreign Service. Prior to his assignment in Bern, Shinn headed the U.S. consular establishment for northeast Italy in Trieste, where he had engaged in the kind of public outreach which Whittlesey appreciated. He spoke Italian and French, and Patricia also spoke both these languages.

James Shinn never imagined that the ambassador was considering him for this promotion. A colleague informed him of her thinking only a very short time before she asked him.[57] Whittlesey recalled looking for a husband and wife team that would present U.S. interests and policies in a manner appealing to the Swiss. James and Patricia both impressed her as intelligent and engaging.[58]

In early 1982, Whittlesey decided to elevate Shinn as her DCM, but the State Department procedures presented major challenges. By elevating Shinn, the ambassador would bypass many other State Department officers—members with "Senior Foreign Service Officer" rank—in the bureaucratic hierarchy.

Although the ambassador's title "plenipotentiary" theoretically implied boundless power, Whittlesey enlisted outside help to orchestrate Shinn's promotion. To navigate the State Department's power structure, she asked her friend, Michael Smith, a Foreign Service officer and U.S. trade representative in Geneva with the rank of ambassador, to come to her residence in Bern. Faith followed Smith's script word for word as she presented her choice of the much junior Shinn to Joan Clark, the director general of the Foreign Service in Washington, over the phone. Smith sat with her while she made the call. Whittlesey was successful.[59]

Gerald Monroe, economics officer in the Bern embassy, would have been in line for such a promotion, and he chafed at this elevation of a junior officer to the DCM role. In a 1999 interview, Monroe admitted feeling resentful of Shinn's rapid rise to DCM.[60] However, the rules at the time (they were later changed) allowed Whittlesey to choose any officer from the career service as her DCM regardless of rank.

But Faith was not insensitive to the strains of life in the Foreign Service, and she helped Monroe in a personal way. On Whittlesey's first tour,

---

[57] James Shinn, interview by author, Kensington, CA, March 16, 2010.
[58] Faith Whittlesey, interview by author, Cambridge, MA, September 8, 2009.
[59] Ibid.
[60] Gerald J. Monroe, interview by Raymond Ewing, March 22, 1999. Frontline Diplomacy, Manuscript Division, Library of Congress, Washington, DC.

Monroe's wife—consular officer Evangeline Monroe—required emergency evacuation to Yale University hospital following complications during minor surgery in Switzerland.[61] Whittlesey extended herself to assist the couple by contacting a former Wells College classmate who had a home in nearby Old Lyme, Connecticut. "Because of the kindness of my longtime friend, Charlotte Boline, the Monroes stayed at her house during Evangeline's recovery period."[62] As a result, Gerald Monroe recalled these 4 to 5 weeks as "delightful"—once Yale doctors had resolved Evangeline's medical problems successfully.[63]

Despite the bureaucratic infighting and damaged egos which resulted from Shinn's appointment, Whittlesey viewed this promotion as critical to her public diplomacy vision. Faith believed that most other possible candidates lacked Shinn's inclination, as well as his superior personal and professional skills, for presenting current U.S. policy to the Swiss in a favorable light. Based on the Shinns' openness to Swiss culture, personable manners, and conservative worldview, she believed that this couple would represent the United States and the Reagan administration in the way she expected.[64]

With a more trusted deputy in place, Whittlesey could travel more freely throughout Switzerland. Since she continued to meet frequently with industry, academic, cultural, and parliamentary leaders in Geneva, Basel, Zürich, and other Swiss cities, she occasionally asked Shinn to stand in for her on the diplomatic circuit. As Whittlesey recalled, "If I wanted to go to Zürich and there was a big dinner for the diplomatic corps in Bern, he and Pat Shinn could go and I would know that the United States that had elected Ronald Reagan would be well represented."[65]

OUTSIDE THE EMBASSY WALLS

Whittlesey urged embassy personnel to participate in local Swiss activities and address Swiss audiences on Reagan policy. Formal evaluations of career employees did not systematically reward State Department officers for public diplomacy, so some were less enthusiastic about this change in their duties. As ambassador, however, Whittlesey strove to create such person-to-person networking whenever she could.

---

[61] Ibid.
[62] Faith Whittlesey, discussion with author, telephone, February 22, 2010.
[63] Gerald J. Monroe, interview by Raymond Ewing, March 22, 1999.
[64] James Shinn, interview by author, Kensington, CA, March 16, 2010.
[65] Faith Whittlesey, interview by author, Cambridge, MA, September 8, 2009.

The Shinns, for example, had immersed themselves—quite literally—in the local culture. Shortly after they arrived in Bern, Patricia Shinn witnessed "heads bobbing down the stream" of the city's rapidly flowing Aare River. James and Patricia decided to join the crowds of local Bernese who congregated at numerous swimming clubs, known as *Schwimmbads*, and the green parks on the river banks. As Patricia recalled, "Very few people at the embassy had ever joined in that." Swimming in Swiss rivers was not for the faint of heart, they learned. "We found out why not many people indulged. The water was literally in the 50s!"[66]

Such openness to Swiss traditions pleased Whittlesey, who also embraced Swiss outdoor traditions with her children. Faith organized an outing in which embassy personnel, the Marines, and their families would load as many as five rafts into the Marine Corps van and drive up to a launching point near the Lake of Thun. Passengers would then "all go barreling down the river very fast on the rafts." Patricia Shinn recalled joining these excursions with enthusiasm. She and a few other embassy staff, who had become "addicted to the swimming," courageously disembarked from the rafts into the freezing cold river. Following the current, these adventurous souls would "just float back down to Bern ... at least as long as we could stay warm enough to not lose motion in our limbs—that was always a hazard."[67]

Christoph Schaer, the Swiss university student who had suffered physical attacks in 1981 for speaking in favor of U.S. policy, provided Whittlesey with another opportunity for outreach. He solicited help from the U.S. embassy in coordinating a response to anti-American protests at the German-speaking universities in Zürich, St. Gallen, and Bern.[68] Whittlesey, upon hearing of this request, arranged for American speakers to represent the administration. Since her arrival, she had actively sought such direct access to future leaders in Switzerland.

Under Ambassador Whittlesey, the embassy staff cooperated fully with Schaer's requests. "When we organized a speech and needed someone with credentials to talk about disarmament and the vast amount of money that the Soviet Union invested in their army, there were very few people who

---

[66] Patricia Shinn, interview by author, Kensington, CA, March 16, 2010.
[67] Ibid.
[68] Christoph Schaer, interview by author, Zürich, August 24, 2009.

had the know-how," Schaer remembered. "But the call to Faith Whittlesey brought you the speakers."[69]

Faith arranged for visits by American experts on a variety of topical issues. Schaer excitedly recalled the thrill he and his friends experienced upon having access to U.S. embassy officials and visiting dignitaries. Because of Schaer's fascination with U.S. technology and space exploration, he most enjoyed the opportunity she provided for him and his friends to meet a U.S. astronaut, who spoke to the Swiss university students. They even received invitations to events at the embassy.[70]

Whittlesey's outreach to Schaer embodied the spirit of President Reagan's public diplomacy initiatives. Director Wick's USICA (after 1982, known as the United States Information Agency) had developed a "successor generation" strategy to establish connections with Western Europe's young people.[71] On the ground in Bern, Faith was implementing such ideas.

"WE NEED ALL OARS IN THE WATER"

Faith Whittlesey enjoyed the elegant appearance of the U.S. ambassador's residence in Bern—one of the most beautiful U.S. embassy residences in Europe. She could view the highest Alpine peaks, the Eiger, the Mönch, and the Jungfrau, from every window at the rear of the 19th-century home. Sheep helped manicure the rear lawn (too steep for a lawnmower) while sustaining themselves by munching on the grass. (Whittlesey dispensed with the alarm system—two "attack" geese—which her predecessor had acquired.) A steep footpath descended behind the villa and along the "bright turquoise, rushing" Aare River. Whittlesey frequently walked this route alone or with friends.

Faith would employ this magnificent home frequently as a means of generating greater goodwill between the United States and Switzerland. "Invitations to residences are always the coin of the realm in diplomatic society," she later explained.[72] Whittlesey viewed social entertainment as a necessary component of her public diplomacy vision.

Although Shinn represented the ambassador on some formal occasions, Whittlesey took very seriously the ambassador's traditional duty of hosting guests at her residence in Bern. Eager to portray the United States in a

---

[69]   Ibid.
[70]   Ibid.
[71]   Cull, *Cold War*, p. 492.
[72]   Margo Hammond, "Faith Ryan Whittlesey," *TWA Ambassador*, January 1988, p. 62.

positive manner, Whittlesey hosted guests often and impressively. The high profile of her guests and the relaxed, welcoming atmosphere contributed to her success. She attempted to persuade the embassy staff to support this mission unreservedly.

For example, embassy dinners provided Whittlesey with an opportunity to solicit the aid of her staff in influencing opinions. Whittlesey beseeched U.S. diplomats to avoid congregating in Americans-only cliques and to engage their Swiss guests in meaningful conversations. "With everything she did, there was a purpose," noted U.S. Army attaché LaPorte. "There was nothing just totally social."[73] Several former embassy officials recalled that Whittlesey always reminded embassy staff to facilitate interaction by promptly introducing people to one another and to make every effort to put guests—especially the Swiss—at ease.[74]

From that perspective, Faith expected that members of each embassy department could explain the Reagan administration's policies at all times. When an agricultural attaché unapologetically recounted his inability to discuss Reagan's foreign policy agenda to a leading citizen of Zürich at an event there, Whittlesey was aghast. In order to improve knowledge of U.S. policy and to coordinate the embassy's message to the Swiss, therefore, she instituted additional briefings at weekly staff meetings in which each department's leaders—army attaché, commercial attaché, etc.—would educate the group on the administration's initiatives in their respective government agency. In this manner, she believed, each American embassy official would be better prepared to contribute to the overall mission of representing the United States. As she often commented, in a metaphor drawn from her childhood days on an upstate New York lake, "We need all oars in the water."[75]

"BANJO ON MY KNEE"

Soon enough, Whittlesey's social functions—the true "coin" of her "realm"—came to be a celebrated and coveted commodity. Having established friendships with many significant Swiss decision makers, Whittlesey could readily attract many of Switzerland's "rock stars" to her dinners.

---

[73] Justin LaPorte, interview by author, Madison, CT, June 8, 2009.

[74] E.g., DeLynn Henry, interview by author, Washington, May 29, 2009; Douglas Sears, interview by author, Boston, July 9, 2009.

[75] Faith Whittlesey, interview by author, Cambridge, MA, September 8, 2009.

Rainer Gut, who became chairman of the board of directors for the major bank Credit Suisse in 1983, was a prestigious and frequent guest. Both Swiss and Americans who attended Whittlesey's parties recalled seeing many Swiss captains of industry and finance at her residence and embassy events.[76]

Ardeshir Zahedi, former Iranian ambassador to the United States and son of the Shah's most loyal general, appeared on occasion as well. As a single man who lived in Switzerland and enjoyed social interaction with diplomats, Zahedi often invited Faith and her children to lunch, and lavished expensive culinary delicacies on the ambassador.

Zahedi's friendship with Whittlesey contributed to an event which symbolized the unpredictable and surprising character of her embassy events. During one of Whittlesey's Christmas parties for young children at the ambassador's residence, a Zahedi gift became an impromptu prize. Suddenly realizing that she had run out of awards for the winner of a musical chairs game, Faith quickly grabbed a beautifully wrapped gift from under her Christmas tree, and handed the child a box which she assumed to be chocolates. The next day, Whittlesey received a call from a surprised mother whose daughter had unwrapped a 5-pound glass container of caviar—Zahedi's Christmas present for the Whittlesey family. "The mother offered to return it," Faith recalled. "But of course, I told her to keep it."[77]

Whittlesey's extensive U.S. political network of contacts also enabled her to recruit interesting American personalities to her embassy events. She persuaded the highest officials of the Reagan administration and U.S. Congress to come to Bern. During her two tours as ambassador, more prominent visitors from the United States came than at any other time since World War II, one member of the Swiss Foreign Ministry related to James Shinn.[78] Vice President George H. W. Bush, Secretary of State George Shultz, Secretary of Defense Frank Carlucci, and Republican and Democratic senators and congressmen such as Al Gore, Bill Bradley, Jesse Helms, Charles Grassley, and Jack Kemp all passed through Bern at her invitation. Several prominent conservatives, such as William F. Buckley,

---

[76] E.g., Susan Graf, interview by author, New York, August 2, 2009; Jean-Vital de Muralt, interview by author, Geneva, August 15, 2009. See also Rainer Gut to Faith Whittlesey, August 31, 1982, Box 36, Folder 3, FW. On Gut, see Steven Greenhouse, "Reviving a Humbled First Boston," *New York Times,* March 11, 1991, p. D1.

[77] Faith Whittlesey, interview by author, Sherborn, MA, March 25, 2010.

[78] James Shinn, interview by author, Kensington, CA, March 16, 2010.

Jr., Mona Charen, James Dobson (head of Focus on the Family), and Edwin Feulner (president of the Heritage Foundation), came to the residence.

Beyond the political world, Faith also hosted events in honor of leaders from the academic and literary worlds. On two occasions, she invited college presidents—Dr. Norman Lamm of Yeshiva University (New York City) and Dr. John Silber of Boston University—as special guests.[79] James Baldwin, author of the 1953 novel *Go Tell It on the Mountain*, also attended an embassy dinner during her second tour.[80]

These visits were of great significance, especially since the Swiss capital was not a regular stop on the itinerary of most prominent U.S. visitors to Europe. As Shinn noted, "There was just a constant stream of notable people. She enticed them to come to Bern, which is not usually the place people go to in Switzerland—you go to Zürich or Geneva but not to Bern."[81] Whittlesey's ability to procure high-profile visitors enhanced the attraction of embassy events for prominent Swiss guests.

The style of Whittlesey's embassy dinners also proved effective in enhancing her public diplomacy efforts. Several participants reported that she eased social restraints which might otherwise have complicated U.S. efforts to connect with the Swiss. According to Shinn, strong bilateral bonds and relations resulted directly from Whittlesey's high standards for the quality of social events. "Her ability to entertain—her insistence that we entertain at a certain level—was able to draw people to her parties, which reinforced those contacts and channels of communication."[82]

Whittlesey personally helped relax cultural barriers to participate in meaningful cross-cultural dialogue. Having spent hours on daily piano practice from age 5 to age 21, Whittlesey encouraged guests to join her in playing and singing American Broadway tunes and folk songs. She soon learned traditional Swiss folk songs as well. More than a mere exhibition of her ability on the piano, Whittlesey's musical sing-alongs incorporated extensive audience participation. Whittlesey created a songbook so that the Swiss knew the lyrics, and she progressively added Swiss folk tunes to her repertoire and to the songbook.[83]

---

[79] Norman Lamm to Ambassador Faith Whittlesey, May 25, 1999, letter in Faith Whittlesey's possession; Faith Whittlesey, email to author, June 16, 2012.

[80] James Shinn, interview by author, Kensington, CA, March 16, 2010.

[81] Ibid.

[82] Ibid.

[83] Susan Graf, interview by author, New York, August 2, 2009; John McCarthy, interview by author, New York, August 11, 2009.

Faith's daughter Amy recalled these events as spontaneous. Her mother simply wanted to share her love of music with others. "There was no entertainment strategy," in Amy's words. "After a dinner gathering with Swiss guests, Mother would simply move to the piano room and I would start singing as she played." Music played a central role in the Whittlesey household, in Pennsylvania and in Bern, Amy explained.[84]

Several Swiss recalled her entertainment with fondness. Patricia Schramm, whose father Ulrich Meyer-Schoellkopf directed Lucerne's music festival in the 1980s, remembered how Whittlesey's parties overcame regional differences which—even in a small country such as Switzerland—tended to divide Swiss guests into discrete cliques.[85] Philibert Frick, a young Swiss entrepreneur, recalled his surprise at how Faith brought together "the top bosses from a variety of Swiss institutions—such as the army, banking, and political establishment, the Federal Council—and they all linked arms and swayed back and forth while singing along with the ambassador."[86]

Although they were quite reserved and formal in public, the Swiss truly appeared to appreciate her efforts. According to Susan Graf, Whittlesey could not have engaged the Swiss without extending herself in this personal manner: "You have to understand—and I married a Swiss, so I can say this with all honesty and candor—they are very shy. And they are very dry at first, until you get to know them. So, it took a certain amount of charm to win them over." Graf recalled the president of Switzerland singing "Banjo on my Knee" while standing behind Whittlesey, who was sitting at the piano bench, playing and singing along.[87]

"RADIO SILENCE" AND SOFT POWER

As ambassador from late 1981 to early 1983, Whittlesey helped generate genuine affection for the United States in Switzerland. Through her personal travel and leadership of the embassy staff, she effectively advocated for Reagan's policies.

Some members of the State Department criticized her, she recalled, for "wasting miles going out into the countryside with a car."[88] According to several Swiss friends, however, these trips partially explain the continued

---

[84]   Amy Whittlesey O'Neill, email to author, May 1, 2012.
[85]   Patricia Schramm, discussion with author, New York, May 5, 2010.
[86]   Philibert Frick, interview by author, Geneva, August 14, 2009.
[87]   Susan Graf, interview by author, New York, August 2, 2009.
[88]   Faith Whittlesey, interview by Ann Miller Morin, December 7, 1989.

respect for Whittlesey in Switzerland. For example, Rainer Gut noted: "The fact that she visited every canton was very positively noted. I mean, if you go to the canton of Appenzell as an American ambassador, that's a great honor for the people of Appenzell and the local government there." These efforts paid dividends, Gut concluded: "She represented the United States with dignity, but put herself on our level, and that's why she had access to everybody. She was integrated here."[89]

Christoph Schaer, who had so admired Reagan and Whittlesey in his youth, served in New York City for the Swiss diplomatic service during the 1990s. In Schaer's view, Faith's efforts made a strong, positive impact for the United States. "U.S. interests are not promoted solely inside the embassy," Schaer believed, but ultimately require outreach to the Swiss public. The Soviet embassy had provided a "huge amount of information" to student groups, Schaer recalled, and he had wanted to challenge this anti-American message.

Whittlesey's support bolstered the courage of pro-American Swiss students, such as Schaer, who faced real risks for speaking out. Schaer and other pro-American students gained confidence from knowing that the U.S. government would supply intellectual ammunition for his anticommunist arguments. But following Whittlesey's departure in early 1983, and until her return in 1985, Schaer summarized communication with the U.S. embassy as "radio silence."[90]

Nearly three decades after Whittlesey's arrival as ambassador, many Swiss continued to appreciate her public diplomacy. Whittlesey extended this idea beyond mere propaganda, according to Herbert Oberhaensli, vice president for economics and international relations at Nestlé Corporation. She effectively represented U.S. national interests in Switzerland, in Oberhaensli's view, by creating strong and enduring relationships with the Swiss.

In characterizing Whittlesey's success, Oberhaensli referred to Professor Joseph Nye's theory that the United States should emphasize "soft power," the art of persuasion rather than coercion. In Oberhaensli's view, Whittlesey did more than merely present U.S. ideas as cogent and convincing. Faith engaged in a true dialogue by listening to the Swiss. Whittlesey's public diplomacy, he believed, amounted to "building up a relationship where you really know how to work together, and also, in difficult times, support each

---

[89]   Rainer Gut, interview by author, Zürich, August 21, 2009.
[90]   Christoph Schaer, interview by author, Zürich, August 24, 2009.

other." This emphasis on strengthening bilateral ties required more than "bringing one's values to other societies, but also listening and learning from your friends."[91]

Maintaining this cordial relationship between the two liberal democracies was critical in sustaining and expanding goodwill for the United States. Oberhaensli noted that Whittlesey's style complemented military, or "hard," power. "I think the U.S. leadership can only work long-term if it comes with the values, with the kind of approach that Ambassador Whittlesey brought along. I'm not saying it doesn't need an army. I'm not naïve. But in the long term it does not work with an army alone. It works with the kind of relations that she is able to build up." If the relationships between diplomats break down, the mutual interests of two nations may also be damaged beyond repair.[92]

Faith Whittlesey's first tour as ambassador achieved significant private and public diplomacy milestones from 1981 to 1983. In many formal speeches and informal remarks, Whittlesey defended Ronald Reagan. In one example, on December 4, 1981, Whittlesey delivered a speech at a luncheon sponsored by the American Club of Zürich to explain the president's proposal—which had inspired vocal protests in the United States and Europe—to place intermediate-range nuclear missiles in Europe.[93]

These consistent public diplomacy efforts appeared to pay dividends after Whittlesey left Switzerland. University of Southern California scholar Nicholas Cull credited the Reagan administration's public diplomacy as "critical in bringing European opinion to the point at which it became possible to deploy the intermediate [range] nuclear forces necessary to bring Russia to the table for the final round of Cold War negotiation."[94] In Cull's view, the missiles "compelled the Soviets to return to the negotiating table," and Reagan's policy "looks like a critical winning move in the Cold War confrontation."[95] As anti-Reagan and anti-American protests captured headlines during the early 1980s, Faith offered an alternative opinion. While the impact of public diplomacy is hard to measure, Whittlesey's promotion

---

[91] Herbert Oberhaensli, interview with author, Vevey, Switzerland, August 17, 2009.
[92] Ibid.
[93] A copy of the speech is available at Faith Whittlesey's archives at Boston University, Box 23, Folder 11, FW.
[94] Cull, *The Cold War*, p. 495.
[95] Ibid., p. 427.

of this cause in Switzerland may have played some small role in Reagan's ultimate victory.

White House officials noted Whittlesey's effective diplomacy with the Swiss Foreign Ministry and the Swiss public. In January 1983, she would receive a call from Reagan Chief of Staff James Baker, who would ask her to leave her post in Bern. Whittlesey would be offered a position as the only woman on the White House senior staff, and she was asked to return to Washington "immediately."

CHAPTER 4

Resisting the "Gender Gap" in the West Wing
The White House Years (part 1)

"William, stand up—here comes the vice president!" Faith Whittlesey urgently called out to her 10-year-old son as Vice President George H. W. Bush approached her office. As had become her custom, she brought William for an early breakfast to her new workplace's restaurant—known affectionately as "the White House mess"—in the West Wing.[1] In early January 1983, Whittlesey had accepted a position on President Ronald Reagan's senior staff. Her office—on the second floor—provided her with exceptional proximity to the president. In order to prepare for her 8 A.M. meetings with President Reagan's chief of staff, James Baker, and other members of the White House senior staff, she needed to arrive early. As a widow and single mother, she resolved to spend quality time with William by bringing him with her to the mess where they could have breakfast together prior to her early-morning senior staff meeting. Then she would take him to the parking lot and drive him to school.

Faith struggled with the adjustment from ambassador in tranquil Bern to White House staff person. "It was like jumping on board a train going 90 miles an hour," she recalled. Physically drained from the move, she caught a bad flu, which lingered the entire winter. Little sympathy came from her new colleagues. "Nobody understands sickness there. You're not allowed to be

---

[1] Faith Whittlesey, interview by Ann Miller Morin, December 7, 1989. Frontline Diplomacy, Manuscript Division, Library of Congress, Washington, DC.

sick. The pace of life is so fast, working from seven or eight in the morning until late at night."[2] On several of those nights in the White House, she would receive a call from William at home. He would ask, "Mommy, when are you coming home?" When she did return home, she often continued to work and fell asleep in her clothes. "William would plead plaintively, 'Mommy, tune in, tune in!'"[3]

This chapter examines how Faith Whittlesey managed the obstacles confronting her as a female executive in the White House—one of the nation's best-known and predominantly male government organizations. From March 1983 to March 1985, Whittlesey was the only woman among Reagan's 18-member senior staff. At that time, few cases existed of a widowed, single mother of three young children in a high-ranking management position. While political observers have written extensively about Geraldine Ferraro— who in 1984 became the first female nominated for the vice presidency—no comprehensive study exists of Faith Whittlesey's pioneer-like impact on women's participation in the U.S. government at a high level.

Whittlesey's case reveals the perils confronting a woman with wide-ranging skills but no trusted mentor or sponsor within or outside the government bureaucracy. When asked to head the White House Office of Public Liaison (OPL), Whittlesey believed she could perform the same role of advocate for Reagan's programs in the United States as she had done in Switzerland and in Pennsylvania. Since the 1970s, presidents had come to rely on OPL to improve communications with an ever expanding number of organized voluntary organizations. In Whittlesey's first year as director of Public Liaison, however, she encountered mainstream media coverage which focused to a large degree on her gender and her approach to issues associated with women. Faith strongly resisted efforts by her superiors to assign her to a role primarily focused on "women's issues." Since her political experience included the full portfolio of policy areas, such as the economy and national security, she recoiled at such limitations on her responsibility and thought it demeaning that she would be regarded as assigned only "women's issues."

Some White House advisors also appeared to expect that a woman with Whittlesey's high level of education would sympathize with more liberal feminist policies. Analysis of public opinion polling data at the time suggested

---

[2]   Ibid.
[3]   Ibid.

that women would prefer that Reagan modify several of his stated policies. In particular, these analysts thought females wanted Reagan to retract his pledges to increase military spending, to limit the growth of social services and federal education spending, and to oppose laws allowing abortion. Reagan's Democratic opponents advanced the theory of a "gender gap" as a road map for defeating the Republican president. Even several senior White House staffers argued that Reagan should adjust his agenda in response to these survey results. But Whittlesey counseled Reagan to remain fully committed to the principles of the Republican Party platform on which he had run and won in 1980. In Whittlesey's view, economic growth and the creation of jobs for men and women would ensure Reagan's popularity with all Americans, regardless of gender.

At a time when the media and politicians focused so frequently on gender, Whittlesey often found herself at the center of this debate about how to gain and maintain women's support. Whittlesey's willingness and ability to articulate and defend Reagan's policies earned attention and respect from those Republicans who shared her views. But she also attracted opponents through her unwillingness to support administration officials who called upon Reagan to modify his agenda in response to the gender gap theory.

Members of this overwhelmingly male administration must have recognized, moreover, the symbolic power of Whittlesey's position. As the highest-ranking woman on the White House staff, Faith served as visible proof that women did not monolithically oppose Reagan's policies. In her view, the whole notion of treating women as a separate group seemed foolish and demeaning: "In my experience, women were clearly not a uniform voting bloc." By rejecting the notion that Reagan should adopt feminist—or "soft feminist"—policy stances, however, Whittlesey represented a threat to individuals who had a vested interest in changing the president's mind. As a result, some of Faith's White House senior staff colleagues and media allies mounted a stealth campaign to discredit her.

As a female professional and widow raising three children as a single mother, Whittlesey understood that women faced unique pressures in politics. No one needed to lecture her on working-women's challenges. To her surprise, she came to recognize the irony that, in Washington, her opponents expected her to think based on contemporary stereotypes. Faith refused to conform to these notions of how a woman in a position of power should view policy. As a result, high-ranking administration officials viewed her as insubordinate and sought to limit her authority.

TRANSITION IN THE OFFICE OF PUBLIC LIAISON: DECEMBER 1982

OPL had emerged during the 1970s in response to the expansion of federal government programs that targeted groups of individuals. In the 1960s and 1970s, national advocacy organizations had surged in number and importance. Citizens increasingly mobilized around common goals based on their gender, age, race, religious affiliation, business and professional membership, physical disability, and countless other differences. Presidents struggled to formalize communication with this multiplicity of interest groups until President Gerald Ford created the OPL in 1974.[4]

Since 1977, presidents had consistently appointed a woman as OPL director, and Helene von Damm, Reagan's assistant for presidential personnel in 1982, asserted that she searched carefully to find female candidates for administration posts. In von Damm's view, Reagan "was not a sexist" but adopted a "somewhat laissez-faire" approach to "women's status within his administration." Upon her arrival at the personnel office, she had created a task force—"with the president's vigorous approval"—to recruit women for Executive Office jobs. In her experience, most "politically active and interested" women embraced liberal views. Whittlesey's name thus arose in this context of von Damm's search to identify women who shared the president's conservative agenda. Von Damm also respected Faith's efforts to help advance females in government. "Faith Whittlesey was always on the lookout for qualified women."[5]

Beyond gender, Whittlesey had qualities which appealed to various members of Reagan's administration. She had earned her reputation as, in von Damm's words, a "very bright, outspoken Reaganite." Her longtime support for Reagan's core values pleased other California veterans, such as National Security Advisor William Clark and Special Counsel Edwin Meese, who both had served as chief of staff to Governor Reagan. In fact, Wendy Borcherdt, who had worked in Reagan's campaigns and offices for

---

[4]   Thomas L. Gais, Mark A. Peterson, and Jack L. Walker, "Interest Groups, Iron Triangles and Representative Institutions in American National Government," *British Journal of Political Science* 14, no. 2 (April 1984): 161–185. Roland Evans and Robert Novak, "Public Liaison Politicking," *Washington Post*, February 20, 1985. p. A21.

[5]   Helene von Damm, *At Reagan's Side: Twenty Years in the Political Mainstream* (New York: Doubleday, 1989), p. 267.

decades (including a year at OPL), denied that gender played any role in the selection of Faith.

Several individuals might have first suggested Whittlesey's appointment. Von Damm claimed that the choice of Faith came "at my suggestion, and urging."[6] Having worked for Reagan during his time as governor in the 1960s, von Damm had considerable leverage with the president and Reagan's California advisors. But Lyn Nofziger, Reagan's California political advisor, had also known Faith since her late husband's work on Richard Nixon's 1968 presidential campaign, and he may have recommended Whittlesey.

Faith also had earned the respect of establishment Republicans such as Drew Lewis, who worked with her in Pennsylvania Republican politics for years as she emerged as the highest-ranking woman politician of either party in that state. Lewis served as cochairman, with Whittlesey, of Reagan's 1980 presidential campaign in Pennsylvania and as secretary of transportation (a cabinet-level post) since 1981. During her time in Bern, Faith maintained close contact with Lewis, who consistently encouraged her to pursue a position in Washington. After the November 1982 midterm elections for Congress, Lewis had alerted Whittlesey to expect an offer.[7] According to syndicated columnist Sandy Grady, "A cynic could see the hand of the departing Drew Lewis in Mrs. Whittlesey's hiring, which gives the state another White House insider and provides Lewis with a Washington pipeline."[8]

Regardless of the source of Whittlesey's name, a consensus in favor of her appointment emerged. In Borcherdt's recollection, Chief of Staff Baker, who represented the Republican Party establishment, spoke up against Whittlesey.[9] Yet, von Damm does not mention any such disagreement in her memoir. She claimed that Baker opposed "Reaganite" candidates only when he believed that the individual in question would prove to be "an embarrassment to the administration." Baker's unfamiliarity with Reagan, von Damm claimed, led him to limit his objections.[10] Baker had gained experience in Washington as a member of the Nixon and Ford administrations (and as campaign manager for George H. W. Bush during his 1980

---

6   Ibid., p. 248.
7   Faith Whittlesey, interview by Ann Miller Morin, December 7, 1989.
8   Sandy Grady, "Heading 'Em Off at Gender Gap," *Miami Herald*, January 7, 1983, p. 19.
9   Wendy Borcherdt, interview by author, telephone, June 25, 2011
10 Von Damm, *At Reagan's Side*, p. 253.

bid for the Republican presidential nomination). If he did indeed oppose Whittlesey, Reagan's long-term supporters may have outweighed his opinion.

As the incoming head of outreach to organized interest groups, Faith would encounter major challenges. President Reagan's popularity had declined significantly since 1981. In the November elections, voters had sent 27 new Democrats to the House of Representatives, which had remained in the hands of a solid Democratic majority for nearly three decades.[11] Polling data indicated that less than 20 percent of the public believed the economy was improving.[12] By January 1983, President Reagan's approval rating had declined to 35 percent—lower than any other U.S. president beginning his third year in 40 years of recorded public opinion polling.[13]

THE OFFER: JANUARY 1983

Reagan's White House team unsurprisingly interpreted the negative midterm election results as requiring some staff adjustments. In the early days of January 1983, Chief of Staff Baker phoned Whittlesey in Bern. Elizabeth Hanford Dole, director of OPL since 1981, would be nominated to replace Lewis as transportation secretary, Baker informed her. Would Faith agree to replace Liz Dole? Baker's request came with a sense of urgency. Whittlesey wanted some time to think, but shortly after she hung up the phone, it rang again. This time, Deputy Chief of Staff Michael Deaver, Baker's assistant, was on the line asking her to accept right away. "They were just telling me over and over, 'Reagan needs you now!'" Whittlesey recalled.[14]

Faith took a political risk by departing her post as an ambassador who had led an effective embassy. In about 15 months, she had helped resolve a tense bilateral disagreement over Swiss banking privacy while also establishing effective public diplomacy initiatives. Her decision also meant leaving the luxury of a 21-room residence with two cooks, parlor maid, housekeeper, and a chauffeured car in charming and serene Bern. Why would she exchange this secure post for full immersion in the pressure cooker of the White House?

---

[11] Since 1958, Republicans had never held more than 44 percent of the seats in the House of Representatives. James E. Campbell, "Party Systems and Realignments in the United States, 1868–2004," *Social Science History* 30, no. 3 (Fall 2006): 363.

[12] Sean Wilentz, *The Age of Reagan: A History, 1974–2008* (New York: Harper Perennial, 2008), p. 150.

[13] Jules Tygiel, *Ronald Reagan and the Triumph of American Conservatism* (New York: Pearson Longman, 2006), p. 169.

[14] Faith Whittlesey, discussion with author, February 20, 2011.

On the other hand, the opportunity to serve the president directly in Washington appealed to Whittlesey's commitment to the success of the Reagan agenda. As a strong believer in Reagan's policies, Faith was inclined to respond favorably to a request by the president. She had volunteered countless hours since the mid-1970s in support of Reagan's long pursuit of the presidency. In 1976, when Reagan had come to personify an effective alternative to the Republican establishment, she endorsed him despite the Pennsylvania party leadership's steadfast alignment behind President Ford. Although her act of resistance contributed to a moment of great intraparty anxiety—one syndicated columnist characterized the party's national convention as a "bloodbath"[15]—Whittlesey explained her own position in an understated manner: "My views were more closely identified with Ronald Reagan than Gerald Ford."[16]

Many Wall Street Republicans much preferred the status quo to Reagan's more unsettling calls for change. But Whittlesey was a politician who had challenged and virtually taken over Pennsylvania's Delaware County Republican machine, and she thus perceived Reagan as a kindred political spirit. Reagan embodied the values of individual responsibility, decentralized and limited government, anticommunism, and military preparedness which she and many of her constituents—Main Street Americans—desired to see implemented. Reagan's election in 1980 was described by some political analysts as a revolution.[17] In the strong Democratic successes of 1982, however, Whittlesey perceived the potential problem that Reagan's political momentum might diminish without an active and vigorous defense. She agreed to be part of the solution.

MEDIA DEBATE ABOUT WHITTLESEY'S APPOINTMENT: JANUARY 1983

The press conference which jointly announced the appointments of Dole and Whittlesey inspired media speculation that the president was making a special appeal to women. A front-page *Washington Post* story reported that Chief of Staff Baker and other Republican officials eagerly sought to improve the president's standing with women.[18]

---

[15] Grady, "Heading 'Em Off," p. 19.
[16] Faith Whittlesey, discussion with author, February 20, 2011.
[17] E.g., Rowland Evans and Robert Novak, *The Reagan Revolution* (New York: Dutton, 1981).
[18] Lou Cannon, "Elizabeth Dole to Head Transportation Dept.," *Washington Post*, January 6, 1983, p. A1.

Syndicated columnist Sandy Grady further argued that Reagan's advisors were responding to "the gender gap." Survey data from the midterm elections revealed a large disparity between men—who generally approved of the president—and women—who largely viewed Reagan with suspicion. "The Reaganites are aware that they were ambushed at the Gender Gap in the midterm elections, when women voted Democratic by 6 percentage points more than men." Some political analysts attributed this difference in voter preference to a male focus on national security and economic issues. By contrast, the theory held, women opposed tax cuts, increased military spending, and limits on the growth of social programs and education. "The polling gurus say women are harder hit by Reaganomics, more dismayed by Reagan weapons spending and saber-rattling."[19] In this view, Reagan needed to soften his message or perhaps reverse his call for a strong defense and reexamination of the federal government's domestic spending.

An alternative view, in an op-ed by David Broder—one of Washington's most highly regarded journalists—highlighted Whittlesey's experience and skills rather than her gender. In the widely distributed Sunday edition of the *Washington Post*, Broder wrote a glowing appraisal of Whittlesey, whom he knew better than most political commentators in the nation's capital. During research for his 1980 book *Changing of the Guard*, Broder had discovered Whittlesey, whom he featured as one of the rising female politicians of her generation. Now in 1983, Broder recalled how impressed he had been upon meeting her in 1978. Having traveled to cover the Pennsylvania governor's race in that year, Broder had found himself drawn to Whittlesey as the most forceful of the six Republican nominees for lieutenant governor. "You do not have to hear her talk for more than 15 minutes to know what a tough, self-assured politician she is. She had to be that to survive." In his view, Whittlesey's experience confronting the Republican Party's establishment in Delaware County would serve her well in the Reagan administration. "She took on one of the last of the corrupt, old-line Republican patronage machines, the Delaware County 'War Board,' and became its new master."[20]

Reagan had not chosen Dole and Whittlesey as window dressing, Broder asserted. These women—as transportation secretary and OPL director, respectively—would occupy "two of the most important political jobs in government," he noted. More than merely a symbolic effort to diversify

---

[19]   Grady, "Heading 'Em Off," p. 19.
[20]   David S. Broder, "Two Good Choices," *Washington Post*, January 9, 1983, p. C7.

a predominantly male staff, Reagan's choices of Dole and Whittlesey enhanced his potential for reelection in 1984, according to Broder. In addition to helping himself, the president had also made the right choice for "his country," in Broder's words.[21]

DIVERSITY OF WOMEN'S VIEWS: THE ERA AND ABORTION

But Broder and Grady failed to recognize how Whittlesey's appointment offered the Reagan administration an opportunity to attract a constituency of women who did not endorse standard feminist policies. Many political commentators appeared to assume that all Americans, led by women, were gravitating in a kind of evolutionary movement toward endorsement of the feminist perspective on policy. Faith's political experience told her otherwise.

Sandy Grady suggested that Whittlesey might alienate women because she opposed the Equal Rights Amendment (ERA) and abortion rights. "Women who want a strong White House voice on feminist issues, abortion, and lower Pentagon spending may not be thrilled by Mrs. Whittlesey's views," Grady noted. "She's probably as far right as Reagan himself. She was among the Republicans who knocked the ERA out of the platform at the 1980 convention. She is anti-abortion. And she made an '80 convention speech for a stronger defense."[22] Faith's views did appear to clash with those of the Republican establishment. After all, Republican President Gerald Ford's wife Betty had spoken publicly in favor of the ERA and abortion in 1974.[23]

By 1983, however, organized opposition to the ERA and abortion had gained momentum as well as the support of many women who had previously avoided politics. Cadres of women embraced conservative policies during the 1960s and 1970s.[24] Whittlesey had recruited these types of volunteers in Delaware County. On a national level, Phyllis Schlafly had successfully campaigned to prevent the ERA from securing the 75 percent of the vote of states required for ratification. These women believed that congressional legislation previously enacted had already provided women with equal constitutional rights and were opposed to the ERA for a variety

---

[21] Ibid.

[22] Grady, "Heading 'Em Off," p. 19.

[23] Donald Critchlow, "Mobilizing Women: The 'Social' Issues," in *The Reagan Presidency: Pragmatic Conservatism and Its Legacies,* eds. W. Elliot Brownlee and Hugh Davis Graham (Lawrence: University Press of Kansas, 2003), p. 298.

[24] Lisa McGirr, *Suburban Warriors: The Origins of the New American Right* (Princeton, NJ: Princeton University Press, 2001).

of other reasons.[25] As Grady correctly noted, Reagan and the Republicans had gone clearly on record against the feminist perspective on the ERA and abortion in the party's 1980 platform.

Neither Grady nor Broder suggested that Whittlesey might mobilize women behind a conservative response to feminism, perhaps because she had built her prior political career in Pennsylvania on economic and fiscal issues. National opinion makers in the 1980s also may have assumed that all more highly educated professional women accepted feminism as the only means for achieving equal opportunity. Reagan's first OPL director, Elizabeth Dole, had originally supported the ERA. Since President Reagan opposed the ERA, however, Dole modulated her enthusiasm for the amendment, saying "There's more than one way to reach equal rights for women."[26] Few women offered conservative leadership to those who admired Reagan for defending traditional values and openly vowing to win the Cold War.

TWO TYPES OF FEMALE REPUBLICAN:
FAITH WHITTLESEY AND ELIZABETH DOLE

Similarities between these two women may have persuaded some members of the media and administration alike to expect that Whittlesey would perpetuate the tenor and direction which Dole had initiated at OPL. Both women had earned law degrees from Ivy League institutions during the mid-1960s, when men represented more than 95 percent of law school graduates. Like Whittlesey, Dole had initially been a Democrat. Both women chose careers in public service rather than the private sector. These basic qualifications had enabled them to be considered for the White House staff.

But Faith Whittlesey and Liz Dole also had come to Washington along very different paths. Dole hailed originally from North Carolina, where a wealthy Scottish-Irish family raised her in "a Southern belle type of genteel life."[27] She attended Duke and Oxford universities as well as Harvard

---

[25] Donald Critchlow, *The Conservative Ascendancy: How the GOP Right Made Political History* (Cambridge, MA: Harvard University Press, 2007), p. 139. In this view, Congress had previously secured equal rights for women through the 1963 Equal Pay Act, Title VII of the Civil Rights Act (1964), and the Equal Employment Opportunity Act (1972). Women's educational opportunity was achieved through Title IX of the Educational Amendments (1972), and women's credit protection had been assured through the Depository Institution Amendments of 1974. See also Donald Critchlow, *Phyllis Schlafly and Grassroots Conservatism: A Woman's Crusade* (Princeton, NJ: Princeton University Press, 2005).

[26] "President Names Elizabeth Dole His First Woman Cabinet Secretary," *Miami Herald,* January 6, 1983, p. 1.

[27] Molly Meijer Wertheimer and Nichola D. Gutgold, *Elizabeth Hanford Dole: Speaking From the Heart* (Westport, CT: Praeger, 2004), p. 6.

Law School.[28] Born Elizabeth Hanford, she had arrived in Washington in 1966, and in 1975 she married Robert Dole, the powerful U.S. senator from Kansas. A year later, her husband was selected as the vice presidential running mate for President Ford, whom Reagan had tried to unseat during the hotly contested 1976 campaign for the Republican Party nomination.

In contrast to Whittlesey, therefore, Dole at the time was a Washington insider who had spent her entire professional life in appointed federal offices within the nation's capital.[29] In 1980, the Doles originally backed George H. W. Bush for the presidency, but they campaigned for Reagan's victory after he won the Republican Party nomination. Dole was appointed as head of OPL, while Whittlesey was posted abroad to the U.S. embassy in Bern. Liz Dole's strong connections to the city's political establishment may explain why she demonstrated less enthusiasm than Faith did for Reagan's positions on social issues and active anticommunism.

Faith's small-town roots in upstate New York may have oriented her toward a more conservative view of public policy. She had relied on scholarships to secure travel to Europe, education at Wells College, and law school at the University of Pennsylvania. As a member of both the state legislature and the governing council of Delaware County she served a suburban, middle-class constituency. Whittlesey, of course, had also actively supported Reagan's unsuccessful 1976 bid to unseat President Ford.

In addition, Liz Dole and Faith Whittlesey may also have developed contrasting views toward feminism in response to their personal experiences. Polling data showed that married women tended to support Reagan more than single women.[30] While Liz Dole did not marry until her late-30s and had no children, Whittlesey married in her mid-20s and gave birth to three children in 11 years. She had also carried the entire responsibility of child care and financial support of her family following her husband's death in 1974.

Whittlesey's background may partially explain her willingness to challenge the Republican establishment. Without longtime status in the national party hierarchy, she was relatively free to exercise her own independent judgment. As OPL director, therefore, she actively promoted President Reagan's

---

[28] Dana Meachen Rau, *Elizabeth Dole: Public Servant and Senator* (Minneapolis, MN: Compass Point Books, 2008), p. 17; Wertheimer and Gutgold, *Elizabeth Hanford Dole,* pp. 6, 8.

[29] Wertheimer and Gutgold, *Elizabeth Hanford Dole,* pp. 8–9.

[30] Critchlow, "Mobilizing Women," p. 301.

conservative agenda—which would shift the direction of the Republican Party and "brand name" for the next generation.[31]

RESISTING "A DEMOTION": JANUARY–MARCH 1983

Whittlesey considered the impact on her family in making the transition to life in Washington. She realized that her children would be affected by the change in status from plenipotentiary envoy in sedate Bern to a staff position in the turbulent U.S. capital city. Having had real-world experience of the liabilities of public office, Faith understood that such a high-profile metropolis might be a difficult place for a widowed, single mother to raise teenagers.

For example, her children had endured listening, during the 1970s, to constant criticism of their politically ascendant mother by political adversaries and the liberal press in Pennsylvania, even during the heart-wrenching circumstances of her husband's passing. "My children noticed that after I became ambassador that there was a marked change in the way I was treated by these people."[32] Upon returning to the rough-and-tumble of U.S. politics, therefore, she decided to educate her two eldest children—17-year-old son Henry and 15-year-old daughter Amy—in New England boarding schools while keeping 10-year-old son William at home with her. The distance between parent and child proved difficult, but Faith maintained a close relationship with them through telephone calls, mail, and occasional visits. Her late husband's uncle, William M. Weaver, Jr., generously offered to pay the private school tuition of her three children so that she could afford to accept the White House position.

The difficulty of these arrangements contributed to her shock at hearing, from Deputy Chief of Staff Deaver, of how he conceived of her White House role. In early January, upon speaking with Baker and Deaver via telephone, she had asked several questions prior to accepting the position. After Deaver's initial briefing to her in the White House, however, she realized that they had not fully explained their view of her job description. Deaver now announced that her primary responsibility would be outreach to national women's organizations. Whittlesey was utterly shocked. Considering this restricted role demeaning, she essentially refused.

---

[31] On this theme, see Chapter 5.
[32] Faith Whittlesey, interview by Ann Miller Morin, December 7, 1989.

While arguably insubordinate, Faith viewed Deaver's proposal as belittling her ability to explain a variety of policy subjects to the public. "When it came to women's issues, none of these men wanted to deal with the women members of the establishment Republican Party like very moderate U.S. Representative Olympia Snowe from Maine, who wanted to have a big conference on women's issues. They wanted me to do that, which was, I believe, a completely sexist approach," she later recalled. "In my entire political career I had repeatedly declined to be pigeonholed as someone dealing with women's issues. I have made almost a *cause célèbre* of that view."[33] Whittlesey's enthusiasm for public life derived from her drive and ability to mobilize support for a policy agenda that included subjects as diverse as fiscal policy and national defense.

She had disrupted her family life for the opportunity to serve the Reagan administration by promoting the president's full range of administration policies, not to perform the role of token woman on the senior staff. After all, the unique profile of a female politician with aptitude in various policy areas helped explain her rapid ascent as a politician in Pennsylvania. As her brother Tom noted in a 1983 interview, "It's my impression that there's an enormous shortage of solid women at the upper levels of government, women who have a broad view and are not one-issue people. So someone with Faith's talent has been drawn along very quickly."[34] In Whittlesey's view, OPL needed a leader who would address the full range of policies which she had worked hard to articulate over several years. If she had known that administration officials planned to limit her role in this manner, she would not have left Switzerland.

"SAGA OF THE DRAGON LADY": APRIL 1983

This initial "dust up" with Deaver more than likely contributed to the beginning of a media campaign against Whittlesey. A series of news articles and editorials, which appeared in prominent national publications, portrayed Whittlesey's appointment as a mistake and a detriment to the president. Reporters quoted unnamed White House officials who claimed that Faith misrepresented Reagan's beliefs, particularly regarding "social issues." In the early 1980s, this phrase referred primarily to the divisive debate about abortion, school prayer, and tuition tax credits for nonpublic

---

[33] Faith Whittlesey, discussion with author, telephone, July 20, 2012.
[34] Beth Gillin, "Tough as Males," *The Philadelphia Inquirer Magazine*, October 2, 1983, p. 17.

schools. These administration sources—commonly known as "leaks" in the administration's otherwise trustworthy "plumbing system"—claimed that Whittlesey frustrated their efforts to make Reagan more acceptable to women. Ironically, these male staff members found themselves seeking to ostracize the senior staff's only female.

Special Counsel Edwin Meese later lamented the treatment of Whittlesey as part of a phenomenon he called "Government by Leak." In Meese's opinion, certain members of Reagan's staff mobilized the media against loyal advocates of the president's policies. According to Meese, these "pragmatists"—including Baker and assistants to the president Richard Darman and David Gergen—shared Reagan's basic ideology, but they constantly sought ways of "adjusting Reagan" in certain policy areas to gain more sympathy within the Washington press corps and government bureaucracies. Meese believed that Faith, himself, Clark, and other "Reaganauts" were more closely aligned with "the direction of Reagan's thinking."[35] Thus, Whittlesey's enemies in the White House attacked her mainly because of her straightforward efforts to advance the president's entire agenda to the maximum degree possible. "Faith, like many others loyal to the President," Meese concluded, became a target because of her insistence on "following [Reagan's] policies and doing what he wanted done."[36] Meese lamented that this anonymous, unauthorized release of staff comments at official meetings discouraged honest expressions of opinions which might be misquoted or misinterpreted in the media.[37]

Although Faith did not insist on any special treatment as a woman, negative gender stereotypes unfairly arose in many of the news reports about her arrival at the White House. Whittlesey emphasized her work ethic and persistence when asked how she had advanced in the "man's environment" of politics, saying she succeeded by "running harder and faster."[38] But many reporters chose not to emphasize Whittlesey's strength of character as a woman who had broken through a glass ceiling to reach high-ranking positions in the U.S. government. Some articles instead quoted critics who portrayed her as uncaring. One anonymous source called her

---

[35] Edwin Meese III, *With Reagan: The Inside Story* (Washington: Regnery Gateway, 1992), p. 102.
[36] Ibid., p. 107. Meese also mentioned Secretary of Defense Caspar Weinberger as a victim of anonymous media attacks for trying to pursue the president's reform agenda.
[37] Ibid., p. 116.
[38] Francis X. Clines, "White House: Public Liaison Aide Has 'Go-out-and-do-it' View," *New York Times*, April 13, 1983, p. 28; Joyce Gemperlein, "Reagan Aide Doesn't Like 'Tough' Label," *Miami Herald*, April 14, 1983, p. 18.

"steel straight through," "tough and intelligent," and "a dragon lady." This unnamed person—who was identified only as a "woman active in Delaware County [Pennsylvania] feminist issues"—appeared to harbor political and/or personal grudges against Whittlesey. But the writer failed to note the irony of a self-described advocate for women employing the term "dragon lady," which originated as a misogynistic slight to depict a woman as enigmatic, aggressive, and domineering.[39]

The image evoked by this supposed Pennsylvania feminist proved powerful, however, and subsequent media coverage of Whittlesey embraced this theme. In late April 1983, the *Washington Post* featured a story about Faith on the front page of the style section. The title, "Saga of the Dragon Lady," revealed the tone of the story, which quoted several anonymous sources who characterized Whittlesey as a difficult woman to manage. Of course, Faith had previously upset the Pennsylvania Republican Party establishment by supporting Reagan over Ford in 1976. But reporter Elisabeth Bumiller suggested that Whittlesey's gender contributed to the problem, writing that "[the White House] men aren't sure what to make of her."[40] She also cited anonymous sources which described Faith contradicting David Gergen when he suggested the administration needed to make policy changes to attract women's support.[41]

Perhaps this emphasis on Whittlesey's gender reflected the heightened political sensitivity to women's issues in 1983. To her credit, Bumiller expressed some healthy skepticism toward negative assessments of Whittlesey's performance. "It's hard to know how much of this criticism is inspired by sexism, by being the new assistant in the West Wing or by an honest assessment of her ability," she wrote.[42] But Bumiller also falsely characterized Faith as an inexperienced political outsider trying to survive amidst men from elite colleges. Calling her "a rare Reagan conservative among the Ivy League moderates who run the West Wing,"[43] Bumiller ignored her law degree from the University of Pennsylvania—an Ivy League institution. This assertion ignored the fact that several other conservatives shared leadership roles in the White House, especially Special Counsel Meese, a Yale University

---

[39] Joyce Gemperlein, "Reagan Aide Doesn't Like 'Tough' Label," *Miami Herald*, April 14, 1983, p. 18.
[40] Elisabeth Bumiller, "The Saga of the Dragon Lady; Faith Whittlesey, Reagan's New Public Liaison Officer, Tackles a Tough Job," *Washington Post*, April 24, 1983, p. G1.
[41] Ibid.
[42] Ibid.
[43] Ibid.

graduate. Being a woman in power appeared as such an anomaly that media coverage did not highlight her credentials and accomplishments as much as her reputed role in a battle of the sexes.

The backstabbing behavior of her leaking White House colleagues did not bode well for Faith's tenure at Public Liaison. Whittlesey's boss, James Baker, defended Whittlesey from the attacks, saying "Sure, it's difficult for someone coming in cold, but you give her a chance—and you watch."[44] Nonetheless, in only her second month on the job, Whittlesey might rightly have expected a more supportive work environment.

"AN UNLIKELY SCAPEGOAT": JUNE 1983

Whittlesey's critics repeatedly quoted Democratic Party and liberal voices which argued that women would vote as a bloc against President Reagan in 1984. When Faith denied that the gender gap would harm the president, Democrats disagreed, as might be expected. But Republicans within the administration increasingly appeared to concede the claim that Reagan was less popular with women than with men and wanted him to modify some policies and his rhetoric in response.

The White House's chief political advisor Edward Rollins publicly endorsed the gender gap theory in June 1983, and *Washington Post* columnist Judy Mann immediately exploited Rollins' words to discredit Whittlesey's position. Mann's column targeted Faith's argument that "the gender gap will vanish along with the recession." The economy was not the issue, Mann insisted, but women primarily opposed Reagan's goal of increased military expenditures.[45] Anyone at the White House who emphasized the gender gap provided Mann and other liberal voices with a wedge to widen the policy disagreements within Reagan's staff.

Mann correctly observed that Rollins' speech represented a deliberate maneuver "in the battle between rival factions in the White House for the president's mind." Baker, Deaver, Gergen, and Rollins wanted Reagan to downplay abortion, school prayer, tuition tax credits, outspoken anticommunism, and military spending. Similar to the unnamed White House critics of Whittlesey, Mann presented the OPL director as someone whose opinions seemed foreign to most women. Mann also linked Whittlesey with Dee Jepsen (one of the two special assistants whom Whittlesey retained

[44]   Ibid.
[45]   Judy Mann, "Gender Gap," *Washington Post*, June 8, 1983, p. C1.

after Elizabeth Dole's departure), whom she described as an "antiabortion crusader."[46] In this West Wing war, liberal Democrats clearly favored one camp—to which Mann effectively provided logistical support.

Other newspaper and magazine stories, uncritically quoting anonymous administration officials, perpetuated the idea that Whittlesey was misrepresenting Reagan as a heartless warmonger who frightened females. A *Newsweek* article titled "The Wrong Woman for the Job" asserted that Whittlesey's bosses had curbed her role after she characterized the gender gap as "overrated."[47] Subsequent reports in the *Washington Post* quoted unnamed White House officials calling her "a cold woman" who adopted a "more-conservative-than-thou style."[48] In the *Miami Herald*, a female White House official reportedly claimed that Whittlesey failed to appreciate the challenges of working-class women.[49]

Some fundamental contradictions went unnoticed in these media accounts which criticized Whittlesey. If Reagan and the Republicans in fact experienced difficulties recruiting women, the problem certainly predated Faith's arrival in early 1983. Moreover, this working mother spoke for many women who shared her challenges, and perhaps even her opinions, about how best to govern the country. But many administration officials failed to recognize Whittlesey's career as a tribute to Reagan's message of individual responsibility and self-reliance.

In one notable exception, *New York Times* writer Francis X. Clines addressed the inconsistencies within these uncritical stories filled with unnamed White House sources criticizing Whittlesey. He questioned why multiple White House officials blamed the new female staff member for Reagan's weakening popularity. In Clines' view, the "anonymous carping ... from the president's predominately male inner circle about the latest woman to join the Administration" amounted to an effort to blame Whittlesey for problems she did not create. Whittlesey seemed "an unlikely scapegoat for reelection anxiety about the 'gender gap' since she only recently joined the Administration and she reflects the President's own view that the gap is exaggerated and economic recovery will cover a multitude of dissatisfactions."[50]

---

[46]   Ibid. Mann misspelled her name as "Jepson."
[47]   Eric Gelman, "The Wrong Woman for the Job," *Newsweek*, June 6, 1983, p. 19.
[48]   Juan Williams, "Women's Liaison Duties Taken from Whittlesey," *Washington Post*, June 11, 1983, p. A2.
[49]   "GOP Takes New Tack to Woo Women; White House Replaces High-Ranking Female," *Miami Herald*, June 12, 1983, p. 11.
[50]   Francis X. Clines, "'Vengeance Vote' Worries White House," *New York Times*, June 12, 1983, p. 5.

Clines implied that the administration's leading men should examine their own failure during the president's first 2 years to rally the public behind Reagan's agenda. Neither did Whittlesey deserve contempt, Clines suggested, for clearly stating the president's long-standing views on the economy, national defense, and abortion.

"WAR BY RECEPTION": JULY 1983

Although Whittlesey's opponents appeared intent on orchestrating her removal from the White House staff, she mounted a strategic defense. Whittlesey was a key early advocate in Pennsylvania of Reagan's efforts to realize the goals of the conservative movement. She had contributed substantially to his 1980 election in that closely divided "battleground" state which ultimately contributed 27 electoral votes (the third-highest total of any state) to his victory. Many supporters of the president appreciated her contribution to the conservative movement which helped elect Reagan.

While some administration officials spread criticism about her in the media, Faith arranged to associate herself prominently with important Republican and conservative fund-raisers and organizers. Richard Viguerie, who began a direct mail company in 1964 to raise money for Republican candidates, admired Whittlesey's ability to articulate this agenda for change.[51] She had also become friendly with the Reverend Jerry Falwell, who had founded the Moral Majority organization in 1979 and mobilized previously apolitical Protestant evangelicals behind Republican Party candidates.[52]

These activists and many others rallied around Whittlesey to show their support. At a July 4th party sponsored by Viguerie in 1983, Whittlesey and Falwell participated in a mock contest that humorously referenced the anonymous sources which plagued Whittlesey. The game, called "Plug the Leak," had Whittlesey and the other participants trying to cork the holes in barrels to prevent water from escaping. According to the *Washington Post*, a "free-form water fight" ensued and Whittlesey found herself "cheerfully drenched." Apparently alluding to the anonymous "leaks" against her in the press, she told the reporter with more than a hint of irony, "Obviously,

---

[51] Critchlow, *Conservative Ascendancy*, p. 130.
[52] William Martin, *With God on Our Side: The Rise of the Religious Right in America* (New York: Broadway, 1996), pp. 224–225. See also Daniel Williams, *God's Only Party: The Making of America's Christian Right* (Oxford, UK: Oxford University Press, 2010), p. 198.

I don't know how to play this game."[53] The underlying message appeared to be that Whittlesey was unaffected by the anonymous media attacks because she enjoyed support from several important figures in Reagan's governing coalition and the conservative movement.

Faith did not merely seek to project an image of stoic valor. After years of experience in the art of political warfare, she understood how government officials could employ "character assassination" in the media to propagate or spread negative assessments about her. If she did not mobilize a defense, she might face a popular call for her resignation; so, she actively cultivated allies. "I realized I had to develop my own constituency. The conservatives rallied around me."[54]

Her assistant for communications, Mary Ann Meloy, whom Whittlesey had known for nearly 10 years, contributed to a strategy she called "war by reception." "Washington is a town of cocktail parties," noted Meloy, and social events provided individuals on the White House staff with opportunities to make or maintain personal connections and alliances. When powerful lawmakers and fund-raisers attended these gatherings, the reception became a coveted venue to meet and greet the people who might perpetuate one's status and power. In Pennsylvania politics during the 1970s, and as U.S. ambassador in Bern, Faith had developed great skill at entertaining with a purpose.

Therefore, with Faith's adversaries within the administration pillorying her incessantly by leaks in the media, Meloy helped coordinate cocktail-and-*hors d'oeuvres* gatherings with Whittlesey as the guest of honor. With each party hosted by a prominent Republican politician or organization, these events reminded Republican leaders of Whittlesey's importance to the GOP's governing coalition. "We would invite all of the high-level conservatives to show up and stand shoulder-to-shoulder with Faith. And then we would invite all of the people who were on the attack."[55] This strategy served to remind the Washington elite that Whittlesey deserved respect as a key member of the Republicans' conservative coalition.

In one apparent example of this "war by reception" technique, U.S. Senator Paul Laxalt, a Republican from Nevada, hosted a party for Whittlesey

---

[53] Paul Barrett, "Jerry Falwell, All Wet; Fun at Viguerie's Party," *Washington Post*, July 4, 1983, p. B1.

[54] Faith Whittlesey, interview by Ann Miller Morin, December 7, 1989.

[55] Mary Ann Meloy, interview by author, telephone, March 9, 2011.

in his Senate office on July 19, 1983. Laxalt enjoyed a reputation as a powerful Washington politician whom Ronald Reagan had considered (and perhaps even preferred) as his vice presidential nominee in 1980, and the *New York Times* called him the president's "First Friend" in 1982.[56] Laxalt's decision to honor Whittlesey in such a public fashion sent a signal which served to buttress her credibility in Washington. About 75 people attended this wine and cheese event, according to a *Washington Post* style section report. The news coverage also helped counter the months of anonymous reports about Whittlesey's alleged ineffectiveness. A *Post* photograph captured Chief of Staff Baker and Whittlesey laughing side by side in casual conversation with Senator Laxalt. This image clearly conveyed an atmosphere of harmony between the OPL director and her immediate boss.

Quotations in the text further buttressed the view that Whittlesey enjoyed Baker's complete confidence. A reporter asked them both to comment on the multiple reports that Michael Deaver had removed her from authority over the newly formed White House council on women. In separate conversations, Whittlesey and Baker offered the same interpretation. Faith denied that she had been demoted, and she suggested, "Giving Mike Deaver that responsibility was an elevation to a Big Four [i.e., Baker, Clark, Deaver, and Meese] concern. ... I never had [responsibility for] issues, policy or legislation. I am the outreach person." Baker agreed, saying, "The Deaver thing is not in any way meant to downgrade Faith but to bring more resources into the picture."[57] The chief of staff had appeared to signal his full support for Whittlesey.

These receptions were not confined to the Washington circuit. In one example, Australian-born entrepreneur Rupert Murdoch and his wife hosted a cocktail reception in Whittlesey's honor. While building a global media empire, Murdoch had entered the world of Republican Party politics. Several prominent public figures—including New York Archbishop John Cardinal O'Connor, New York City Mayor Ed Koch, philanthropist David Rockefeller, and neoconservative leader Irving Kristol—attended this party in the Murdochs' Manhattan apartment.[58]

---

[56] Sean Wilentz, *The Age of Reagan: A History, 1974–2008* (New York: Harper Perennial, 2008), p. 265; Daniel J. Galvin, *Presidential Party Building: Eisenhower to George W. Bush* (Princeton, NJ: Princeton University Press, 2010), p. 127.

[57] Jacqueline Trescott, "Filling in the Gaps," *Washington Post*, July 20, 1983, p. B10.

[58] David Rockefeller to Faith Whittlesey, December 8, 1992, letter in Faith Whittlesey's possession.

WHITTLESEY'S LIBERAL DEFENDERS: JULY–AUGUST 1983

As Faith continued to receive anonymous disparagement in the media, a couple of liberal women defended her. Kathy Wilson, a self-described feminist and chair of the National Women's Political Caucus, and the *Washington Post* Pulitzer Prize-winning editorial page editor Meg Greenfield viewed Whittlesey as a strong woman who deserved admiration rather than ridicule from her White House colleagues.

Wilson, as a supporter of the ERA and legalized abortion, certainly did not support Whittlesey's ideological viewpoint. She had attended the 1980 Republican National Convention pregnant with her first child and with an abortion rights pin on her lapel.[59] In May 1983, Wilson had criticized Whittlesey's view that Reagan could attract more female supporters through economic growth rather than an expansion of federal social services or a feminist agenda.[60]

By July, however, she suggested that the predominantly male White House officials were unfairly treating Whittlesey as "a fall guy" for their own mistakes. In Wilson's view, the White House men had unjustly punished Faith for merely restating Reagan's position that the gender gap would not defeat him. Referring to the media accounts that White House officials curtailed Faith's responsibilities for women's issues, Wilson charged Reagan's senior staff with acting "in some way sexist."[61] As a mother herself, Wilson perhaps sympathized with Whittlesey's special challenges of balancing professional and maternal duties.

Meg Greenfield, a savvy Washington insider, also frequently disagreed with Reagan's policies, such as his opposition to abortion, but she admired Whittlesey's achievements as a woman in politics. In an August 31 op-ed piece, she suggested that Reagan could benefit from the "pronounced, unmousy fortitude" she witnessed in several of Reagan's female appointees. The title of her piece, "Is There Hope for Reagan?," highlighted the president's political challenges as an election year approached. In Greenfield's view, Reagan needed candid and courageous supporters such as Whittlesey. Greenfield characterized Faith as a "forthright, resolute woman who seems not to mind making trouble and to rather enjoy taking the heat—she in fact

---

[59] Margalit Fox, "Kathy Wilson, 54, Women's Rights Advocate," *New York Times*, September 9, 2005, p. C15.

[60] Bumiller, "Saga of the Dragon Lady," p. G1.

[61] Donnie Radcliffe, "The White House's New Script on Women's Issues," *Washington Post*, July 24, 1983, p. G1.

invites it—that comes from pressing her extremely unfashionable views on certain issues."[62] Greenfield's recognition of Whittlesey, furthermore, was not merely a passing fancy. Much later, in a posthumously published book, Greenfield credited Whittlesey as one of a few women in Washington who "though publicly less well known ... held down heavy jobs."[63] Greenfield appeared to admire how Whittlesey forcefully and effectively promoted the president's principal policy goals, even those unfashionable in the nation's capital.

Several books on the Reagan presidency have overlooked this insight from one of Washington's preeminent media insiders and thus failed to recognize the contributions of Whittlesey and Public Liaison. Only a few authors have interviewed Whittlesey. Chroniclers of the Reagan administration rarely, if ever, sought the comments of any of the 38-member staff who worked at the OPL under her directorship. Why? Whittlesey believed that members of the Republican establishment preferred to downplay certain of Reagan's conservative positions—which she had tried to bring to the public's attention—by giving them and her the silent treatment.

REAGAN GETS INVOLVED

If Whittlesey had received so much criticism for merely defending Reagan's policies, one might expect the president to take action on her behalf. William Clark, one of the president's longtime friends and partners in government service, recalled that Reagan did address the anonymous media attacks against Faith after he brought them to the president's attention. In the process, Whittlesey temporarily appeared at the center of a bitter White House power struggle.

Reagan's staff divided into two distinct camps during the president's first few years. James Baker and Michael Deaver, on one side, tried to persuade the president to adopt a more moderate approach to many issues, while William Clark and Edwin Meese, on the other side, believed Reagan should actively promote the conservative agenda he campaigned on. In Baker's most recent book, he characterized these struggles as "barely civil" wars.[64] Although

---

[62] Meg Greenfield, "Is There Hope for Reagan? The women the president has appointed tend to be the kind who count for something," *Washington Post*, August 31, 1983, p. A25.

[63] Meg Greenfield, *Washington* (New York: PublicAffairs, 2002), p. 143.

[64] James A. Baker III with Steve Fiffer, *"Work Hard, Study, and Keep Out of Politics!": Adventures and Lessons from an Unexpected Public Life* (New York: G. P. Putnam's Sons, 2006), p. 193.

neither Baker nor Deaver[65] mentioned Whittlesey in their multiple memoirs, Clark and Meese have discussed the leaks against Faith in some detail.

Both Clark and Meese maintained that such egregious leaks as these never occurred when each served (at different times) as Reagan's chief of staff in California. In Clark's view, all White House leaks undermined Reagan's policy initiatives and potentially threatened the nation's defense. Unattributed quotations also fostered internal divisions and the impression of disorder in the White House. Clark blamed Baker's staff for the attacks. According to Clark's 2007 biographers, he attributed "the bad press Whittlesey received" to "a campaign of leaks carefully planted by the Baker people." Clark asked Baker to stop the leaks.[66]

But negative stories supported by unnamed White House officials continued to appear, and Clark decided to inform the president. Clark had much less experience in Washington than Baker, who had served President Gerald Ford as undersecretary of commerce. Having worked for Reagan since the 1960s, however, Clark sensed that his boss would share his indignation about the smearing of Whittlesey's name in the media. In a meeting with the president and Baker, Clark accosted the chief of staff: "Jim, someone on your staff is brutalizing Faith in the media, and she has done nothing to deserve this." According to Clark, "Reagan took notice, and sternly ordered Baker: 'I want this to stop.'"[67]

A long-standing disagreement between the two men had now emerged as an open argument. Baker exploded at Clark when they left the Oval Office. "It was the only time Baker lost his temper with me," recalled Clark.[68] Clark's intervention on Whittlesey's behalf suggested that Reagan was aware of the leaks. But the anonymous character of the anti-Whittlesey quotations limited the president's means of stopping them.

---

[65] E.g., Michael Deaver, *A Different Drummer: My Thirty Years with Ronald Reagan* (New York: Harper Collins, 2001); Michael Deaver, *Nancy: A Portrait of My Years with Nancy Reagan* (New York: Harper Collins, 2004).

[66] Paul Kengor and Patricia Clark Doerner, *The Judge: William P. Clark, Ronald Reagan's Top Hand* (San Francisco: Ignatius Press, 2007), p. 247.

[67] Ibid.

[68] Ibid. Baker never commented on this incident but admitted to often speaking "on background" or off the record with reporters. In September 1983, when Clark proposed lie detector tests to determine who might have leaked information related to national security, Baker protested strongly. Reagan eventually sided with Baker, and Clark left the national security advisor post in October. James A. Baker III with Steve Fiffer, *"Work Hard,"* pp. 193–195.

READY FOR THE 20TH CENTURY?: MARCH 1984

After Clark and Meese left their White House offices in late 1983 and early 1984, respectively, Whittlesey could no longer rely on these ideological allies for guidance and protection. The "Big Four" no longer competed as seriously for Reagan's ear after Clark's departure to become secretary of the interior in October 1983 and Meese's appointment as attorney general in January 1984. Baker and Deaver now had more exclusive access to Reagan's ear. The *Washington Post* speculated that Whittlesey might serve, in the absence of Meese and Clark, as the bearer of the torch for conservatives in the White House.[69]

Leaks against Whittlesey continued, and the general source now became an open secret. On the 10th anniversary of her husband's tragic self-inflicted death, a March 26, 1984, *Washington Post* story appeared on its front page under the headline "Whittlesey Pushed to Leave; Reagan Aide Called 'Disappointment.'" The article quoted an unnamed official who disparaged her as full of "crazy, right-wing ideas."[70] In response, syndicated columnist Sandy Grady stated publicly that most of Washington knew who surreptitiously disparaged Faith. "You don't need inside knowledge to guess that the anti-Whittlesey stories should carry the byline of Michael K. Deaver, longtime Reagan crony who is deputy chief of staff, or at least one of Deaver's minions," Grady wrote.[71]

As other reporters had noted, Deaver could not justly criticize Whittlesey for articulating the ideas upon which Reagan had built his political reputation. The prospect of dismissing Faith seemed ridiculous, in Grady's view. For the conservative President Reagan, Grady suggested, "Firing a woman because she's too right-wing is like [the 300-pound President] William Howard Taft firing somebody for being overweight." The constant attacks on Whittlesey said as much about the White House's chauvinist character as the administration's ideological differences, he argued. "The whole Whittlesey episode makes you wonder," Grady concluded, "if the Reagan team is quite ready for the 20th Century if it means giving equal status to an assertive female."[72]

---

[69] Lou Cannon and David Hoffman, "Clark Backed Meese for Attorney General," *Washington Post*, January 24, 1984, p. A4.
[70] Juan Williams, "Whittlesey Pushed to Leave; Reagan Aide Called 'Disappointment,'" *Washington Post*, March 26, 1984, p. A1.
[71] Sandy Grady, "White House's Inner Circle Undermines Lone Woman," *Miami Herald*, March 28, 1984, p. 29.
[72] Ibid.

On at least two occasions in 1984, reporters speculated about Whittlesey's possible departure from the White House, perhaps for a judgeship.[73] When a position on the Third Circuit Court of Appeals was offered to her, she seriously considered the opportunity. An old friend from Pennsylvania, U.S. Senator Arlen Specter, strongly urged her to accept, and he promised to support her fervently in the confirmation process.[74]

But Whittlesey wanted to complete the mission for which she had been called to Washington. She later admitted that a position in the judicial branch might have made her life more comfortable in subsequent years.[75] Ultimately, however, she got used to the unpredictable, contentious struggles in the West Wing. "Every day was a knock-down, drag-out struggle," she recalled.[76] After two decades in politics, she seemed accustomed to the challenges.

GERALDINE FERRARO AND THE GENDER GAP: JULY–NOVEMBER 1984

The Democratic Party's 1984 presidential nominee, Walter Mondale, appeared eager to prove the Michael Deaver–David Gergen–Edward Rollins theory that the so-called gender gap threatened Reagan's reelection. The prospect of a women's bloc of votes against Reagan remained at the center of public discussion. Contributing to this media attention, Mondale selected New York Congresswoman Geraldine Ferraro as his vice presidential running mate on July 13, 1984.

As the first woman ever nominated for a major-party presidential ticket, Ferraro embraced the opportunity to turn the election into a referendum on women's issues. Many Catholics had appeared to relish the opportunity to end the Protestant monopoly on the U.S. presidency in voting for the Catholic candidate John Kennedy in 1960, and Democrats hoped that women would similarly rally behind Ferraro in 1984. Ferraro specifically believed that "the gender-gap vote could make all the difference in the Presidential

[73] William E. Farrell and Warren Weaver, Jr., "Briefing: Two Sides of a Staff," *New York Times*, March 2, 1984, p. 16; David Hoffman, "The White House," *Washington Post*, August 8, 1984, p. A15.

[74] Faith Whittlesey, discussion with author, February 20, 2012.

[75] Ibid.

[76] Deal Hudson, *Onward Christian Soldiers: The Growing Political Power of Catholics and Evangelicals in the United States* (New York: Threshold Editions, 2008), p. 234.

election of 1984. And besides, we weren't a minority!"[77] Ferraro's high-profile leadership role threatened to realize the fears of Whittlesey's critics and to persuade women to desert President Reagan *en masse* at the polls.

In response to Ferraro's nomination, President Reagan repeated his belief—which Whittlesey had also advanced—that men and women shared the same basic policy priorities. "[The Democrats] have their ticket and I'm looking forward to campaigning against it on the issues," Reagan told the media.[78] The president did not address the gender gap theory, and he refused to concede the claim that Mondale's selection of Ferraro demonstrated a greater commitment to placing women in leadership positions than Reagan's. In response, the president listed the many women he had appointed to office. Ferraro's nomination was "historic," Reagan acknowledged, but "so was appointing Sandra Day O'Connor to the United States Supreme Court." After mentioning Ambassador to the United Nations Jeane Kirkpatrick and Transportation Secretary Elizabeth Dole, Reagan named 13 other women—including Whittlesey—whom he had appointed to the executive branch. "We Republicans think women should change America," Reagan asserted. He characterized the idea that only Democrats promoted women's rights as "foolishness."[79]

Whittlesey had spent months in the White House attempting to reframe national politics away from a strictly feminist focus. Faith had advocated for an agenda of strengthening national defense to win the Cold War, generating economic growth, and championing traditional social values. Reagan's statements similarly sought to neutralize any attempt to make the election a referendum on women's place in politics and society. Despite these efforts, however, Ferraro presented American females with the opportunity to prove or disprove Faith's assumptions about women voters. Ferraro clearly endorsed the policies which feminists believed—and which Deaver and some other Republicans feared—that most American women wanted to enact. "I truly hoped to increase the gender-gap throughout the campaign," she recalled.[80]

---

[77] Geraldine Ferraro with Linda Bird Francke, *Ferraro: My Story*, new ed. (Evanston, IL: Northwestern University Press, 2004), p. 49. On the 1960 election, see Thomas J. Carty, *A Catholic in the White House? Religion, Politics, and John Kennedy's Presidential Campaign* (New York: Palgrave, 2004).

[78] "Excerpts from Reagan's Remarks," *New York Times*, July 14, 1984, p. 7.

[79] Ibid.

[80] Ferraro, *My Story*, p. 97.

Ferraro's support for the ERA and abortion rights placed her at the opposite end of the ideological spectrum from Whittlesey and Reagan. In her 2004 memoir, she characterized Reagan's policies as "anti-women" because the president opposed Democratic Party initiatives such as federal funding of child care.[81] In campaign speeches, Ferraro frequently referred to the extraordinary nature of her candidacy, and Democratic Party polls estimated that her presence on the ticket might boost Mondale's vote several percentage points, perhaps enough to determine the election.[82] Democrats hoped that Whittlesey's opponents would prove prescient and a majority of women would rally behind Ferraro.

While Ferraro appeared to assume that American women would favor her feminist views, many voters challenged her on the abortion issue. Some of Ferraro's strongest criticism came from religious conservatives. New York's Cardinal O'Connor explicitly declared that Ferraro's support for legal abortion was contrary to the church's teachings. Such statements by O'Connor risked alienating some Catholics, such as New York Governor Mario Cuomo, who expressed the opinion that religious leaders should not offer opinions on candidates for office. President Reagan, by contrast, ultimately defended such participation by church authorities in public debate.[83] Thus, religion complicated the Democratic nominee's effort to attract women voters.

THE REAL GENDER GAP: REAGAN'S POPULARITY WITH MEN

The expected gender gap did not appear to have an impact in Reagan's overwhelming 1984 victory. A majority of American women—56 percent—voted for Reagan, while Mondale and Ferraro secured only 44 percent of female voters. Four years earlier, Reagan had won only 46 percent of females in the three-way 1980 election (with Democratic President Jimmy Carter garnering 45 percent and independent candidate John Anderson 7 percent).[84]

The president won 49 states, 525 votes in the electoral college, 59 percent of the popular vote, and political analysts perceived the gender gap as nonexistent or perhaps even favoring Reagan. The Rutgers University Center

---

[81] Ibid., p. 49.
[82] Ibid., pp. 298, 282.
[83] Carty, *Catholic in the White House*, pp. 167–169.
[84] Center for the American Woman and Politics, *The Gender Gap: Voting Choices in Presidential Elections,* Eagleton Institute of Politics, Rutgers, the State University of New Jersey, New Brunswick. Accessed on June 29, 2012, at *www.cawp.rutgers.edu.*

for the American Woman and Politics labeled Reagan's gender gap as 6 percent because he won 62 percent of men but only 56 percent of women.[85] While ABC News pollster Jeffrey Alderman also perceived a gender gap in the election results, he claimed that Mondale, not the president, suffered from the disparity. The Democratic nominee "had bigger problems with male voters than Reagan had with females."[86] Mondale won only 37 percent of male voters (vs. 44 percent of females—a "gap" of 7 percent).[87] Political scientist Everett Carll Ladd similarly noted this irony, writing: "Is the gender gap, such as it is, better understood in terms of relative Reagan weakness among women, or strength among men? Survey data suggest that this glass may be both half empty and half full."[88] Whittlesey had similarly noted that "the gender gap works two ways—if Reagan might have received less support from women, he made up the difference in gaining support from many more men than Mondale."[89] The election results provided vindication to Whittlesey, Reagan, and other Republicans who refused to alter long-standing principles and policy goals based on the gender gap theory.

Faith received no credit for her efforts to defend Reagan's principles against feminist critiques, nor did she pursue accolades. Whittlesey's goals at Public Liaison had not included higher status within the administration's bureaucracy. She had not intentionally laid groundwork for any personal advancement in the national Republican Party. Interestingly, more than a year after the election, a *Washington Post* reporter recognized Whittlesey's foresight in deemphasizing the gender gap's potential to undermine Reagan's popularity. But Whittlesey, rather than Reagan, suffered most from the gender gap flap, the writer implied. Feminists were angry with Faith for defending Reagan's opposition to the ERA and abortion. The gender gap debates may have contributed to Whittlesey's eventual departure from Washington, according to the *Post*: "The 1984 election eventually proved her to be right, but without a support system among women's groups or key presidential aides, it was not a victory for her."[90] By standing on her

---

[85] Ibid.
[86] Jeffrey D. Alderman, "ABC News Poll, Yearend Wrap-up 1984," cited in Lou Cannon, *President Reagan: The Role of a Lifetime* (New York: PublicAffairs, 1991), p. 871.
[87] Center for the American Woman and Politics, *The Gender Gap. www.cawp.rutgers.edu.*
[88] Quoted in Everett Carll Ladd, "On Mandates, Realignments, and the 1984 Presidential Election," *Political Science Quarterly* 100, no. 1 (1985): 17.
[89] Donnie Radcliffe, "Faith Whittlesey In Switzerland: Behind the Scenes as Ambassador," *Washington Post*, November 18, 1985, p. B1.
[90] Ibid.

principles, Whittlesey did not secure broad-based loyalty among women's groups and the more ascendant members of the White House staff.

Many analysts have talked about Reagan's achievement in redefining the political landscape, and Whittlesey and her office arguably contributed to this president's ability to alter popular perceptions of gender. As of 2012, no Democratic presidential nominee repeated Mondale's strategy of selecting a woman for the national ticket. Republicans no longer appeared vulnerable to the argument that women might abandon a candidate who opposed abortion on demand, supported limitations on the growth of federal spending, and pursued a more muscular foreign policy. Whittlesey appears as a pioneer in light of the 21st-century ascendance of more conservative women to leadership roles in the Republican Party.

But Whittlesey did not choose to make the personal sacrifices necessary for career advancement in Washington. Many political supporters had advised her to attend evening parties and social events "on the circuit." Female government officials told her to spend more time "promoting yourself." She decided that her own advancement in the power structure was "not my primary motivation." Instead, her "maternal responsibilities" weighed on her.[91] She believed that she simply could not, in good conscience, leave her 12-year-old son William home alone every night to attend receptions. She also missed her two older children who attended New England private schools.

Rather than concentrate on ascending the party's national hierarchy, therefore, she had decided to use her position as manager of a large White House office to cultivate constituencies which the Reagan White House and national Republican Party had previously virtually ignored. She recognized that Reagan had won the support of Americans from working-class, Catholic, evangelical Protestant, Jewish, Hispanic, and many other demographic groups whose individual members had before Reagan voted Democratic. The next chapter addresses how Whittlesey's work in the White House from 1983 to 1985 contributed to long-term expansion of the core constituency of the national Republican Party.

---

[91] Faith Whittlesey, interview by Ann Miller Morin, December 7, 1989.

CHAPTER 5

Holding on to Reagan Democrats
The White House Years (part 2)

Despite Ronald Reagan's 1984 landslide victory, many Americans viewed the president as an unintelligent cowboy whose political views ranged far out of the mainstream. Some analysts explained the election results as merely reflecting Americans' fascination with a simple-minded but charismatic former movie star. So strongly did this opinion persist that nearly three decades later, in 2009, historian Gil Troy included a chapter titled "Was Reagan a Dummy?" in a book on the former president.[1]

Apart from committed Reaganites (or Reaganauts), most Americans did not consider Reagan the leader of an intellectual movement in the early 1980s. After all, only 28 percent of the electorate identified themselves as conservative in 1980.[2] Democrats were the majority party. From 1952 to 1980, 54 percent of eligible voters identified themselves with the Democratic Party as compared with 39 percent who identified with the Republicans—a margin of 15 points.[3]

WHY DID THE DEMOCRATIC PARTY SO DOMINATE AMERICAN LIFE?

A generation of Americans who came of age during the Great Depression of the 1930s and World War II had come to revere Democratic President

---

[1] Gil Troy, *The Reagan Revolution: A Very Short Introduction* (Oxford, UK: Oxford University Press, 2009).
[2] Ibid., p. 32.
[3] James E. Campbell, "Party Systems and Realignments in the United States, 1868–2004," *Social Science History* 30, no. 3 (Fall 2006): 363.

Franklin D. Roosevelt (FDR). During these crises, FDR had created a lasting alliance, known as the New Deal coalition, of various demographic groups— such as religious and racial minorities, working-class trade unionists, and big-city residents. FDR's New Deal—the name given to the many laws he proposed to empower the federal government and executive branch—formed the foundation of modern liberalism for more than a generation.

Faith perceived Reagan's victories in 1980 and 1984 as signifying an important opportunity to revive the Republican Party. Reflecting on this trend in 1989, Whittlesey asserted that Reagan "broke up the old FDR coalition [by winning support in] the traditional Democratic strongholds of the ethnics, the Catholics, the Jews, the southern evangelical Protestants, and the big-city machines."[4]

Faith's experience as a politician in the 1970s and 1980s had led her to this conclusion. Whittlesey, like Reagan, had encountered many Americans who expressed dissatisfaction with liberalism and the Democrats. Both she and the president had been raised in small towns by an Irish Catholic father and Protestant mother. The Ryans and the Reagans viewed independence and self-reliance as fundamental virtues. Faith and Ronald Reagan had both held Democratic Party loyalties at a younger age, but later became Republicans.

This common experience may have made Whittlesey and Reagan especially aware of a potential shift in U.S. party politics. While campaigning for election in diverse communities—Reagan in California, and Whittlesey in Delaware County, Pennsylvania—they recognized conservative Democrats and independents who might potentially support Republican Party candidates. These conservatives made up an important portion of their electoral majorities, and they had helped Reagan win the White House in 1980.

As director of the Office of Public Liaison (OPL) from March 1983 to March 1985, Whittlesey worried that these "Reagan Democrats" might revert to being "Roosevelt Democrats." Faith identified two essential challenges that she would have to confront. First, how could she demonstrate to these "Reagan Democrats" that the president would continue to defend their interests? Second, how would Reagan's White House mediate between the often disparate views of business leaders and working-class Americans?

---

[4]   Faith Whittlesey, interview by Ann Miller Morin, June 21, 1989. Frontline Diplomacy, Manuscript Division, Library of Congress, Washington, DC.

WALL STREET AND MAIN STREET

While campaigning for Reagan in 1976 and 1980, Whittlesey had recognized his unique ability to secure the support of both Wall Street and Main Street. Historians have largely ascribed Reagan's popularity among independents and Democrats to these Americans' economic concerns. As "middle-class suburbanites … prospered and moved from the cities," according to this theory, they became Republicans.[5] But social and foreign policy issues also contributed to the "Reagan Democrat" phenomenon. Less-privileged whites had supported Reagan's vision of a strong national defense, traditional social values, limited government, and lower taxes. According to Gil Troy, "Reagan started weaving together the disparate strands of American conservatism [in the 1970s]."[6]

Would this tapestry remain strong? Although Reagan had run and won on a peace-through-strength, prolife, and limited-government agenda, many applicants for the administration's government positions came from the party's establishment wing. These experienced Republicans presented resumes which emphasized their prior service in Washington as members of the Richard Nixon and Gerald Ford presidential administrations. Few blue-collar Americans had any previous connections with Republicans, and thus they could not offer the same credentials in applying for administration jobs. "Reagan Democrats" in general, Whittlesey noted, "were very unaccustomed to having any relationship with a Republican White House."[7]

In the absence of conscious efforts to maintain bonds with Reagan Democrats who voted for the Republican president in 1980, Whittlesey feared that these Main Street Americans might easily slip back into their previous Democratic Party voting habits. In her view, "We had to show them that they counted and mattered."[8] Reagan's continued success as president depended on a strong alliance between these newer foot soldiers and the Republican Party establishment, she believed.

Even within the Reagan administration, Whittlesey discovered, some appointed staff resisted the president's social and foreign policy conservatism. As part of Reagan's effort to incorporate his prior adversaries within the party into his governing team, the president had appointed many individuals who had originally supported his Republican presidential primary opponent,

---

[5] Troy, *Reagan Revolution*, p. 23.
[6] Ibid., p. 25.
[7] Faith Whittlesey, interview by Ann Miller Morin, June 21, 1989.
[8] Ibid.

Vice President George H. W. Bush. These Washington-based officials had more political experience working with the country's Wall Street, business, and country club constituencies. But they often looked askance at his full embrace of the prolife movement, the National Rifle Association (NRA), and the uncompromising anticommunism characteristic of refugees from Cuba, Eastern Europe, Vietnam, and other communist-dominated regions. In Gil Troy's 2009 analysis, the "traditional conservative alliance of Main Street sensibilities and Chamber of Commerce business interests needed reinforcing."[9]

Whittlesey, as the OPL director, set about this task of actively recruiting Main Street Americans to become long-term Republican Party loyalists. In an office which catered to literally hundreds of groups with diverse policy goals, she attempted to establish common cause between the administration's agenda and each group's core values.

Whittlesey's management of Public Liaison specifically targeted constituencies which did not have strong connections to the Republican Party establishment—the NRA and gun owners in general; labor union members and other working-class Americans as well as veterans; and religious traditionalists within the Christian evangelical, Catholic, and Jewish communities. Whittlesey actively solicited the continued support of these individuals and groups through a marked increase in White House briefings for visiting interest groups designed to emphasize clear-cut themes. Whittlesey's goal—to paint Reagan's ideas in well-defined, bold strokes—also included inviting speakers and authorizing newsletters which would better explain the president's agenda.

While the administration's establishment-minded members sought to recast Reagan as a moderate or centrist, Faith endeavored to maintain close ties between the president and the particular interest groups which she credited for his 1980 victory. As an experienced elected official, Whittlesey believed that the success of Reagan's ideas required proof of his commitment to fulfilling the campaign promises which the president had made to these constituencies. In her view, such authentic demonstrations of integrity would prove important in securing their long-term loyalty.

---

[9] Troy, *Reagan Revolution*, p. 25.

THE OPL'S CORE CONSTITUENTS

When Faith arrived, the White House was undergoing a period of critical self-examination. President Reagan's popularity remained very low. The Democratic Party had made significant gains in the November 1982 midterm congressional elections.[10] In response, Whittlesey's new boss James Baker had initiated a full review of the White House offices.[11]

When Faith assumed responsibility for Public Liaison in March 1983, the office appeared to require changes. One Reagan administration official publicly—though anonymously—cited Public Liaison as having been ineffective prior to Whittlesey's arrival. This source claimed that the OPL seemed to lack the cohesion required to meet the diverse, and changing, needs of its constituents. "Public liaison has been a shop suffering from what I call the Andy Warhol syndrome. ... Everybody working there is famous for 15 minutes."[12] In this official's estimation, the multiple persons with the title "special assistant to the president for public liaison" competed for a brief, if only fleeting, moment in the media spotlight.

In addition to the challenge of managing these special assistants, Faith would direct a large staff that approached 40 members at one point during her tenure. Below the special assistants in the office hierarchy, associate directors worked on special projects. In addition, Whittlesey hired a number of consultants and interns to support their work.

The sizable OPL team found themselves constantly occupied by the immense challenge of responding to the hundreds of pressure groups which sought access to the White House. In the 1980s, such organizations appeared to have become a national tradition. "Just think of anything, and there is an interest group to represent them. And if zebras could talk, we would have one to represent them, too," recalled Mary Ann Meloy, Whittlesey's assistant for communications.[13] Public Liaison members were assigned to maintain communication with a broad array of at least 500 different organizations, ranging from farmers and longshoremen to nurses. Edward Lynch, whom Faith hired as a consultant, remembered the dauntingly comprehensive nature of Whittlesey's OPL: "I was asked about every issue

---

[10] Sean Wilentz, *The Age of Reagan: A History, 1974–2008* (New York: Harper Perennial, 2008), p. 150.

[11] Francis X. Clines, "White House; An Outsider (Soon to Be an Insider) Stirs Concern," *New York Times*, February 4, 1983, p.14.

[12] Francis X. Clines, "White House; Public Liaison Aide Has 'Go-out-and-do-it' View," *New York Times*, April 13, 1983, p. 28.

[13] Mary Ann Meloy, interview by author, telephone, March 9, 2011.

from the economy to abortion. The only issue I don't recall being asked about was snow removal in the District of Columbia."[14]

With the prospect of so many pressures emanating from various directions, any incoming OPL director might have simply decided to maintain bureaucratic continuity and manage the office in the more traditional low-key manner of her predecessors. But Faith did not merely want to perpetuate the status quo. She viewed Public Liaison as an important means of maintaining and strengthening Reagan's governing coalition, concentrating especially on the "Reagan Democrats." She adopted a more entrepreneurial approach to public service by pursuing creative, innovative strategies to maximize benefits for both the administration and the constituencies it served.

When an interest group raised an issue with her office, she listened. Then she asked the group to hear the administration's view on an important, perhaps related, policy goal. This new procedure encouraged a sundry range of individuals to consider a common mission.

WHITE HOUSE OUTREACH WORKING GROUP ON CENTRAL AMERICA

Although Whittlesey's boss, Chief of Staff James Baker, had not given her many specific tasks, he did instruct her to mobilize support for Reagan's active opposition to the spread of Soviet-style communism in Central America. This directive immediately expanded the role of Public Liaison beyond a focus on domestic issues, which had been its original mission. But Faith believed completely in this new objective. She understood that President Reagan had identified hemispheric stability as a high national security priority and Central America as a major front in the Cold War.

From 1975 (when the United States failed to stop communism's expansion in Southeast Asia) through Reagan's election in 1980, socialist leaders had seized power in 10 countries. President Reagan believed that these governments were potential or actual surrogates of the Soviet Union.[15] The president wanted to prevent the extension of this trend to Central America, so close to the U.S. southern border. This region thus emerged as an important theater of the late Cold War struggle.[16]

Furthermore, as the U.S. and Soviet negotiators met in Geneva to pursue armaments reductions, Reagan believed that military advances by Soviet

---

[14]   Edward A. Lynch, interview by author, telephone, May 9, 2011.
[15]   Andrew E. Busch, "Ronald Reagan and the Defeat of the Soviet Empire," *Presidential Studies Quarterly* 27, no. 3 (1997): 451.
[16]   Faith Whittlesey, discussion with author, telephone, March 12, 2012.

allies in Central America would weaken America's leverage at the arms talks table. Seeking a bargaining position of strength, the president wrote a June 26, 1983, diary entry, "If the Soviets win in Central Am. we lose in Geneva & every place else."[17] The administration therefore determined it would conduct a public information campaign to explain the security imperative in that region for the United States.

Although many characterized Reagan as the "Great Communicator," he recognized that he needed help to educate U.S. citizens about this region. After addressing a joint session of Congress and a national television audience to advocate for U.S. aid to anti-Soviet forces in Central America, Reagan lamented that polling data revealed widespread American ignorance about the region. In an April 27, 1983, diary note, the president wrote "It was astonishing how few people even know where El Salvador & Nicaragua are."[18] Complicating the message, the threat of Soviet expansion in Central America took different forms in the various nations. Reagan had to explain why the United States was on the side of the rebels in one country (Nicaragua) but supported the existing government in others (El Salvador, Honduras, and Costa Rica, for example).

Given these challenges, Whittlesey sought creative ways to amplify—and multiply the audience for—Reagan's message. Responding to Baker's request, Whittlesey created the White House Outreach Working Group on Central America, which institutionalized the goal of explaining the administration's plan to halt Marxist-Leninist expansion in that region. She utilized her role as OPL director to spread this message. For example, when Faith received inquiries and requests from businesses about administration policies toward various private-sector industries, she took the opportunity to advocate for Reagan's foreign policy mission: "Every businessman who asks me about natural gas or consumer product safety, I ask to help us on Central America," she told *Washington Post* reporter Lou Cannon, according to a front-page story on June 17, 1983.[19]

In Whittlesey's view, such conversations merely clarified the mutual benefit which could result from corporate cooperation with Reagan's anticommunism. Many U.S. companies had self-interested reasons to favor the administration's policies. As OPL director, Faith encouraged her staff to

---

[17]   Douglas Brinkley, ed., *The Reagan Diaries* (New York: Harper Collins, 2007), p. 163.
[18]   Ibid., p. 150.
[19]   Lou Cannon, "Public Relations Campaign; U.S. Promoting Latin Policy," *Washington Post*, June 17, 1983, p. A1.

explain the economic as well as political consequences of such realities as communist Cuba's denial of access to U.S. companies. To highlight the lost opportunity for U.S. exports to Soviet-dominated countries (which refused to receive American products), the OPL's liaison to the business community asked rhetorically, "How many Hershey bars do U.S. businessmen sell in Cuba?"[20] Public Liaison Associate Director Linas Kojelis recalled that OPL staff reworked Defense and State Department publications to create policy papers designed for business groups. Since corporate executives and managers faced financial market pressures to focus single-mindedly on bottom-line profits, the OPL attempted to demonstrate for these individuals how U.S. corporations benefited from specific U.S. government actions, such as guaranteeing the secure passage of consumer goods through the Panama Canal.[21]

Critics of Reagan believed that financial and military aid to Nicaragua's Contra rebels would eventually lead to U.S. military commitments in Central America. On July 4th weekend 1983, thousands rallied at the Vietnam Memorial to protest Reagan's support for the Contras. Paralyzed Vietnam veteran Ron Kovic (who later became famous when actor Tom Cruise portrayed him in the antiwar movie *Born on the Fourth of July*, based on his autobiography) made the connection explicit: "We will never let them do what they did to us in Vietnam."[22]

Given this powerful and compelling opposition to administration policy, Whittlesey labored to capture equal media coverage of Reagan's viewpoint. At the same location that day, therefore, Faith participated in a counterdemonstration to highlight the "captive nations" that suffered under Soviet domination. Immigrants who had fled Soviet-backed regimes in Vietnam, Cuba, Nicaragua, and Eastern Europe related their experiences of communist tyranny. Whittlesey herself delivered a message from President Reagan in which he recalled "the millions of people who have died as victims of communist oppression."[23] Perhaps motivated by her firsthand observations of pervasive police surveillance and economic underdevelopment when visiting communist Yugoslavia in the 1950s and China in 1979, Faith perceived those who sympathized with Soviet-style communism as ill

---

[20]   Ibid.
[21]   Linas Kojelis, interview by author, telephone, May 3, 2011.
[22]   Peter Perl and Caryle Murphy, "Opposing Groups Air Latin America Views at Vietnam Memorial," *Washington Post*, July 3, 1983, p. A1.
[23]   Ibid.

informed, and she believed she could persuade them with well-researched and cogent arguments. As it turned out, the *Washington Post* covered both rallies in a front-page story.[24]

In the coming months, Whittlesey continued to try to inject the administration's voice into media coverage of Central America. In another page-one article, the *Washington Post* quoted from an August 1983 press conference in which she criticized U.S. news agencies and several mainline churches for having wrongly depicted Nicaragua's Sandinista rulers as "Robin Hoods." Faith called the Sandinistas "bad guys" who "persecuted Jews, Protestants and Catholics."[25] Whittlesey's remarks echoed and amplified President Reagan's unequivocal message, stated earlier that year, that he considered the Soviet Union an "evil empire."[26]

Such statements mobilized Reagan's critics and supporters alike. Charles Bergstrom, executive director of the Office of Government Affairs for the Lutheran Council, charged her with turning Public Liaison "into campaign headquarters."[27] On the other hand, Faith's activism inspired strong praise from leaders who had rallied the conservative movement behind Reagan's agenda for change during the late 1970s. Paul Weyrich, who cofounded the Heritage Foundation in 1973, affirmed her message that popular opposition would evaporate when the American public understood the administration's Central American policies.[28]

ASSEMBLING AN OUTREACH TEAM

Whittlesey's capacity to make quick, tough choices helped her to assemble a creative and motivated support staff to advocate for Reagan's policies. As with many incoming officials, Faith sought individuals whom she knew and trusted on a professional and personal level. After consulting with several high-ranking members of the administration, therefore, she asked for the resignation of five of the seven incumbent special assistants. She decided that this approach would avoid any appearance of her dissatisfaction with

---

[24] Ibid.

[25] Lou Cannon, "News Media, Churches Blamed; 'Distortion' on Latin Policy Decried," *Washington Post*, August 10, 1983, p. A1.

[26] "Excerpts From President's Speech to National Association of Evangelicals," *New York Times*, March 9, 1983, p. A18.

[27] Lou Cannon, "Vacationing President's Aides Seek End to 'Unnecessary News'; Reagan & Co.," *Washington Post*, August 22, 1983, p. A3.

[28] Joanne Omang, "Reaction to Kissinger Panel; Right Plans Assault on Latin Policy," *Washington Post*, August 22, 1983, p. A1.

the staff based on her personal observations. Furthermore, she believed time was of the essence to find the most effective personnel.

This rapid and widespread overhaul of OPL caused quite a stir among certain media outlets, especially the *Washington Post*. Later, she regretted only one dismissal, Wayne Valis, who she now believes would have served the administration well and for whom she maintains high regard.[29] She assigned Morton Blackwell, one of the two special assistants whom she retained, as project office manager for the Working Group on Central America. Blackwell's credentials among Reagan loyalists dated back to 1964 when he was the youngest elected convention delegate favoring U.S. Senator Barry Goldwater's presidential nomination. Blackwell cheerfully accepted this responsibility in addition to his role—begun during the leadership of Whittlesey's predecessor, Elizabeth Dole—of coordinating outreach with Protestant evangelicals and conservative groups.[30]

Whittlesey then hired individuals who she believed would make Public Liaison responsive to, and supportive of, Reagan's diverse governing coalition. For example, one of Whittlesey's new hires, Linas Kojelis, appealed to Americans of Central and Eastern European descent. As a Lithuanian American, Kojelis could confidently predict that these individuals would share Reagan's strong opposition to communism. "They opposed President Jimmy Carter's 'mushy' approach to the Soviet Union, which had acted very aggressively in the 1970s." Kojelis' personal background helped him identify with many of these immigrants from communist governments in Poland, Hungary, Romania, Czechoslovakia, Lithuania—and other Central and Eastern Europeans from areas Reagan called captive nations. Kojelis' family had fled Lithuania upon finding evidence that the Soviet Union was prepared to kill or imprison financially successful farmers and educated persons.[31]

As she had done throughout her political career, Faith pursued dynamic new staff members whom she could trust. In June, she hired Assistant for Communications Mary Ann Meloy, who, as a longtime member of the Republican Women of Pennsylvania, had also directed Whittlesey's Southwestern Pennsylvania operation during Faith's unsuccessful run for lieutenant governor in 1978.[32] In October, Whittlesey appointed Robert

---

[29]   Faith Whittlesey, discussion with author, telephone, March 12, 2012.
[30]   Morton Blackwell, interview by author, telephone, March 4, 2011.
[31]   Linas Kojelis, interview by author, telephone, May 3, 2011.
[32]   Mary Ann Meloy, interview by author, telephone, March 9, 2011.

Reilly, who would soon receive a promotion to associate director and later to special assistant. Reilly directed outreach to the Catholic community and the prolife movement. After Morton Blackwell departed in 1984 to devote himself full-time to the nonprofit Leadership Institute he had created, Reilly would lead the Working Group on Central America.

Whittlesey also provided early opportunities to several young people beginning their careers. Both Edward Lynch, who was hired as a consultant, and Michael Waller, who worked as an intern, later became book authors after earning doctoral degrees and university faculty positions in political science. Another intern, Mark Klugmann, would become a speechwriter for Presidents Reagan and George H. W. Bush prior to an international consulting career that has included advising six Latin American presidents on policy reforms. Whittlesey also hired Mona Charen, who later earned national recognition as a syndicated columnist, one of the earliest female political commentators on cable television, and the author of several books. These young staff members brought enthusiasm, intellectual firepower, and creative perspectives to the OPL.

In order to avoid the "Andy Warhol syndrome," Whittlesey coordinated this talented staff's operations by adopting several methods of distributing the OPL's messages. First, she invited administration officials or representatives to address special-interest groups in Room 450, a large auditorium in the executive office wing of the White House complex. Second, Faith cultivated a network of speakers whom she might mobilize to articulate the administration's policies at interest-group gatherings in Washington. Third, she made it a point to hire staff members who could speak and write particularly well. Some of these individuals were assigned to produce a publication, known as the *White House Digest*, which was created to articulate and disseminate the administration's policy agenda. Fourth, Whittlesey's office discovered resourceful approaches to outreach, such as distributing the president's message directly to interest-group publications and local news outlets. These internal and external initiatives helped the office compound the impact of the administration's outreach efforts.

ROOM 450

Faith knew by experience how to create compellingly dramatic moments for an audience. Beginning at age 17, she had worked two summers as an intern in a live musical comedy theater-in-the-round near Niagara Falls,

New York. "I was a song-and-dance lady," she recalled. In Switzerland, she had excelled in using the embassy as an instrument of public diplomacy. Her elegant embassy events had helped endear her to Swiss society. But her small office on the crowded second floor of the West Wing did not even come close to approaching the size of the ambassador's residence in Bern.

In order to create a space where she could welcome large audiences, she utilized the greater White House complex, which included the adjacent Executive Office Building (EOB; later renamed the Eisenhower Executive Office Building) for her public outreach purposes.[33] Whittlesey frequently invited delegations from various interest groups to a Greek-style theater in Room 450 on the fourth floor of that structure. This routine enabled a steady stream of visitors. Such access to the epicenter of presidential power often inspired "a sense of marvel, and sometimes even awe," in the guests, recalled Whittlesey.[34]

Faith organized these EOB briefings to provide members of various voluntary organizations with regular direct access to administration policymakers. After discussing the issues of greatest interest to the visiting group, Faith or her surrogates would then ask the visitors to listen to a presentation about an administration priority, often relating to a pressing foreign policy or defense issue.

OPL personnel explained the significance of educating and mobilizing key constituencies to work in support of President Reagan's policies. Mark Klugmann, who worked as assistant director of the White House Outreach Working Group on Central America, later recounted that Whittlesey had initiated a significant strategic shift in Public Liaison's strategy. A tour of the White House, a photographic remembrance, a pair of cufflinks, or a jar of Reagan's favorite candy (jellybeans) all might help establish some rapport with the visitors. But Whittlesey, who brought years of experience in building political coalitions in Pennsylvania, had a "laser focus" on how to bring together very diverse organized constituencies around issues, such as Nicaragua, that had not before been at the center of their agendas.[35] Mona Charen echoed this assessment. "In most White Houses, the Liaison Office is, 'Come, let us pat your hand. You know we're very concerned about

---

[33] This structure had the same mailing address as the White House (1600 Pennsylvania Avenue), so visitors could legitimately claim that they had been to "The White House" even when they had only attended an event at the EOB.

[34] Faith Whittlesey, discussion with author, telephone, March 12, 2012.

[35] Mark M. Klugmann, interview by author, Skype, February 17, 2011.

this issue for Hispanics and that issue for blacks and this issue for women and this issue for business people,'" she explained. "Faith continued that tradition, but she also provided information about Reagan's foreign policy, especially in the American hemisphere. Every single group that came to the White House got a talk about what was important to the administration, and what were our priorities; and Central America was key to that."[36]

Prior to the proliferation of information technology through cable news stations and the Internet, many Americans lacked knowledge of the sophisticated global power networks operating outside U.S. borders. Whittlesey and the OPL staff sought to explain these connections by inviting expert speakers to Room 450. These policy specialists could give details about—to Christian and Jewish Americans, for example—communist insurgents' limits on religious freedom in Central America. Speaking to Jewish organizations, Faith would argue that Central American and Eastern European communists worked hand-in-hand with the same groups threatening Israeli security (such as Libya and the Palestinian Liberation Organization).[37]

Linas Kojelis highlighted these international connections when speaking with Americans of Central and Eastern European heritage. For example, after inviting the Polish American Congress to hear a speech about human rights violations in Eastern Europe's communist nations, he would then ask this group to listen to an address about communism's increasing strength in Nicaragua. Many Polish Americans had never considered the parallels between communist efforts in Eastern Europe and Central America, or the general threat of Soviet expansion worldwide, Kojelis recalled.[38] Since some of these U.S. citizens had suffered or fled communist rule in their respective countries, however, Faith believed they might come to an even greater appreciation of Reagan's steadfast and determined resistance to the expansion of Soviet power worldwide.[39]

Klugmann vividly recalled characterizing the corridor outside his first-floor office as "Main Street USA," because he saw "every face of the country" on the way to these meetings.[40] In the Executive Office Building, diverse segments of American life converged—Future Farmers of America, Orthodox Jews, Wall Street executives, movie stars and TV evangelists. "Whittlesey

[36] Mona Charen, interview by author, telephone, August 15, 2010.
[37] Cannon, "Public Relations Campaign," p. A1.
[38] Linas Kojelis, interview by author, telephone, May 3, 2011.
[39] Faith Whittlesey, discussion with author, telephone, March 12, 2012.
[40] Mark M. Klugmann, interview by author, Skype, February 17, 2011.

skillfully bundled together all these relationships to create a powerful tool for building support for the president's agenda," Klugmann concluded.[41]

Previous Reagan biographers have completely failed to note this public outreach initiative, in Whittlesey's view, because many other senior staff members were unaware of most of her activities. She rarely spoke up in senior staff meetings led by Chief of Staff Baker.[42] "I knew the White House moderates wouldn't understand," Faith reflected, "so I decided to say virtually nothing and just go about my business quietly."[43]

THE SPEAKERS NETWORK

Whittlesey recruited a wide variety of powerful and charismatic individuals to address these Room 450 gatherings, Monday staff meetings, interest-group seminars, or convocations in the nation's capital. In the first few weeks of the Central American Outreach Group's existence, she had arranged for EOB presentations by several specialists from the State or Defense Departments, Nicaraguan rebels, and church leaders. The speakers included administration heavyweights, such as Chief of Staff Baker, National Security Advisor William Clark, presidential counselor Edwin Meese, Vice President Bush, and the president himself.[44] Whittlesey carefully tailored the presenter to the particular audience in attendance, and she engaged with interest groups that might not otherwise have considered foreign policy as a priority.

For example, Faith used the EOB briefings to develop relationships with U.S. citizens of Latin American descent. In the period prior to the proliferation of Spanish television, radio, and Internet sources of information, such outreach might represent this constituency's only source of contact with Reagan's policy goals. Whittlesey often asked President Reagan to address groups whose roots were firmly in the Latin American community. At her invitation, State Department official Otto J. Reich, whose mother was Cuban, also frequently spoke with Hispanic organizations that came to the EOB.[45] As a means of reaching out to this community and looking for speakers who might address these audiences, Faith herself traveled to Cuban American rallies in south Florida. These groups sometimes supported the Democratic

[41] Mark Klugmann, email to author, July 6, 2012.
[42] Faith Whittlesey, discussion with author, telephone, March 12, 2012.
[43] Faith Whittlesey, email to author, June 20, 2012.
[44] Cannon, "Public Relations Campaign," p. A1. See also Faith Whittlesey, interview by Ann Miller Morin, June 21, 1989.
[45] Juan Williams, "White House Pitches Latin Policy to Public," *Washington Post*, September 24, 1983, p. A5.

Party's domestic policy, she recalled, but they typically applauded Republican vigilance against the spread of communism in the Western Hemisphere.[46]

Whittlesey then invited several of these Cuban American groups to Washington. Carlos Perez, a Cuban-born entrepreneur who challenged multinational food giants Del Monte, Dole, and United Fruit by creating the Turbana Banana Company in 1970, recalled as many as 10 visits to the White House by groups of U.S. citizens of various Latin American origins. "Faith reached all sectors of the population—medical doctors, engineers, famous singers and musicians. This was something never done before from the White House," said Perez. In his view, this kind of outreach allowed otherwise marginalized groups to develop a more positive perspective on the federal government. "She made special arrangements to show us rooms in the White House which had historical significance," he recalled. "During these visits, Faith created ways to allow Latin Americans to appreciate how the presidency and Congress operates." Whittlesey's ability to arrange for the president to address these visitors particularly made a strong impression, in Perez's view. But the mainstream media paid little or no attention to this demographic group in the 1980s.[47]

Room 450 speakers included eyewitnesses to the impact of Marxism-Leninism on Central America. One example, *Commandante Cero* ("Commander Zero") Eden Pastora, had joined with Sandinista rebels in overthrowing Nicaragua's dictatorship but became disillusioned when the new Sandinista government aligned with the Soviet Union.[48] Individuals who alleged having suffered persecution by the Sandinistas also addressed assembled interest groups. Robert Reilly, who assumed responsibility for the Working Group on Central America in January 1984, recalled bringing to the White House a Nicaraguan Protestant pastor who had had his ears cut off by the Sandinistas: "That was one night we made network news."[49] President Reagan made similar attempts to attract media attention to these causes. In Reagan's 1990 memoir, the president mentioned holding a press conference regarding two clergymen who had "their ears cut off with bayonets." As Reagan recalled, "I told their story in front of the television

---

[46]   Faith Whittlesey, discussion with author, telephone, June 23, 2011.
[47]   Carlos Perez, interview by author, telephone, September 30, 2011.
[48]   On *Commandante Cero*, see Jack Anderson, "Ex-Sandinista Led Capture of Nicaraguan Port," *Washington Post*, May 9, 1984, p. E19.
[49]   Robert Reilly, interview by author, Vienna, VA, September 15, 2010.

cameras, but it never received the attention I thought it deserved."[50] The president appeared to agree with Whittlesey that mainstream news coverage never appropriately compared the administration's views with Sandinista propaganda in a balanced manner. But she tried. When a *Washington Post* reporter challenged the accuracy of these accounts, Whittlesey wrote a letter to the editor to document the credibility of these witnesses.[51]

In her constant effort to spread the president's foreign policy message beyond American elites and to reach the average American, Faith arranged for members of the National Security Council (NSC) to visit conferences of interest groups which had primarily dealt with domestic issues. This initiative served two purposes. First, the administration could promote its agenda directly to the public without a media filter. Second, the speakers could gain popular support for their message, which might sometimes meet opposition from various actors within the White House, State Department bureaucracy, or Congress.

For this particular form of outreach, Whittlesey selected administration officials who had impeccable intellectual credentials and who shared her personal commitment to resist totalitarianism. For example, NSC members John Lenczowski and Constantine Menges frequently spoke at her request. Both men had earned doctorates—Lenczowski from The Johns Hopkins School of Advanced International Studies in Baltimore and Menges from Columbia University in New York—and both hailed from families who had fled European totalitarian regimes. Lenczowski's parents had left Poland and the Soviet Union. His father had served as a Polish army officer in North Africa and diplomat in Iran, and his Polish mother had been deported, imprisoned in the Soviet Union, and escaped to Iran. The two never returned to Poland, which had fallen under Soviet control. Instead, they sought freedom in America because "those Soviet-bloc countries persecuted people who had higher education, owned businesses, or were capable of defending Polish culture."[52] Menges' father had escaped from Nazi Germany to Turkey, where Menges was born. Menges

[50]   Reagan, *An American Life*, p. 481.
[51]   Faith Whittlesey, "Sandinistas: Unfortunately, the Truth Is Unpleasant," *Washington Post*, July 28, 1984, p. A11.
[52]   John Lenczowski, interview with author, telephone, June 15, 2011.

later praised Whittlesey's efforts to present Reagan's foreign policy vision in a comprehensible, coherent way.[53]

Lenczowski personally welcomed the chance to address varied interest groups. "She gave me the opportunity to build my own independent constituency, because many of these leadership groups came to appreciate the ideas I shared with them." For example, Whittlesey arranged for Lenczowski to give the first speech at the first conference held by the Concerned Women for America. "I originally thought I was going to have to speak to 200 people in Room 450 in the Old Executive Office Building when my secretary told me, 'Dr. Lenczowski, you've got to meet Ambassador Whittlesey in her car down in front.' Faith whisked me away to this ballroom with 3,000 women!"[54] Lenczowski's talk gained the support of a large audience and the group's founder Beverly LaHaye, who had become one of the nation's best-known Christian conservative leaders. Giving more than 65 speeches a year at Whittlesey's request, Lenczowski estimated that this exposure helped him gain wide public support for certain policies within the administration: "I had to be engaged in my own fights about Soviet policy within the White House."[55] Whittlesey adeptly used her position as the OPL director to help many such intellectuals in the Reagan White House promote their ideas to the public at large.

MYSTERIOUS NSC STAFF MEMBER

In her efforts to illustrate in a compelling manner the communist threat in Nicaragua, Whittlesey introduced a particular career military officer and NSC senior staff member. This individual conducted himself largely beneath a cloak of secrecy but presented compelling stories to her EOB visitors.

When he spoke in Room 450, he asked the audience not to take any photographs, record the meeting, or reveal his name. Since he traveled frequently and covertly to Latin America, the official claimed that his anonymity was necessary to protect his security. Under dimmed lights, he projected aerial maps and photographs as evidence for his claim that the Soviet Union provided 10 times more assistance to the region than the United States. The NSC official tugged at the audience's heartstrings by portraying the persecution of Nicaragua's native Miskito Indian population

---

[53] Constantine Menges, *Inside the National Security Council: The True Story of the Making and Unmaking of Reagan's Foreign Policy* (New York: Simon & Schuster, 1989), p. 172.
[54] John Lenczowski, interview with author, telephone, June 15, 2011.
[55] Ibid.

in a photograph of a small child who he said was "fleeing from internment camps in Nicaragua."[56] Several groups found this man's briefings so compelling that they requested to hear him on subsequent visits. He spoke before several labor groups, and Linas Kojelis recalled feeling as if he were this man's personal scheduler after coordinating so many of his visits to Room 450.[57]

The NSC staffer was a household name among the OPL personnel, but he would remain in obscurity until 1986. A U.S. Marine major, he learned of his promotion to lieutenant colonel at the Room 450 podium, Morton Blackwell recalled, just prior to delivering one of his briefings.[58] The popular briefer, Lt. Col. Oliver North, emerged from public anonymity years later when the media uncovered North's role as an emissary for the U.S. government's covert funding of Nicaragua's Contra rebels. To determine if North and other members of the administration had violated congressional statutes, the U.S. Senate called for televised hearings and issued him a subpoena which required him to testify in 1987.

Having seen North mesmerize audiences in the EOB many times, Faith would not be as surprised as the senators who discovered that North possessed a polished and supremely confident stage presence. In Whittlesey's view, "Many senators appeared to believe that their law degrees and research staff would prepare them to expose an inarticulate marine defending Reagan's policies."[59] But North would deliver passionate and eloquent defenses of the effort to stop Marxist-Leninist expansion in Central America. Whittlesey later noted the irony that the senators inadvertently provided an even larger audience than the White House's Room 450 for North's compelling case on behalf of Nicaragua's anticommunist rebels: "He won the media show the Democratic senators had staged."[60] In her view, "Had that Senate committee done its homework [by attending—or sending staff to—the Room 450 briefings], they would have realized what a star performer Ollie North was."[61]

Although North's actions threatened to undermine the administration by his disregard for constitutional restrictions on the executive branch, Whittlesey believed nonetheless that he "made a heroic defense of

[56] Williams, "White House Pitches," p. A5.
[57] Morton Blackwell, interview by author, telephone, March 4, 2011; Douglas Riggs, interview by author, telephone, June 20, 2011; Linas Kojelis, interview by author, telephone, May 3, 2011.
[58] Morton Blackwell, interview by author, telephone, March 4, 2011.
[59] Faith Whittlesey, discussion with author, telephone, February 20, 2011.
[60] Ibid.
[61] Faith Whittlesey, interview by Ann Miller Morin, June 21, 1989.

the anticommunist cause in this hemisphere in this encounter" with the senators.[62] Faith denied playing any role in North's illegal funding of the Contras through weapons sales to Iran, but she admitted to giving him a lot of public speaking practice in defending the president's policy toward Central America.[63]

THE *WHITE HOUSE DIGEST*

In addition to arranging these public presentations of administration goals, Whittlesey used the White House brand name as a means of spreading Reagan's foreign policy agenda through a variety of alternative media. In 1983, she initiated the creation and distribution of a newsletter called the *White House Digest*. Intended to attract readers through large print and brief, easily understandable, articles, the publication emulated the widely popular *Reader's Digest*.

Ed Lynch served as the primary researcher, writer, and editor for the new publication. His skills had come to Whittlesey's attention when he published an article for the Heritage Foundation (where he worked as an intern) about the October 1983 U.S. invasion of Grenada, an eastern Caribbean island just off the coast of Venezuela. Faith had known Lynch's prominent father, Frank Lynch, with whom she had served in the Pennsylvania legislature during the 1970s. She asked the scholarly young Lynch to leave the foundation and accept a consulting position at the White House.[64]

In Whittlesey's view, the U.S. government had failed at generating sufficient publicity for Reagan's Central America policy, and the *White House Digest* offered a means of spreading the word. In order to generate widespread support for the administration's Cold War agenda, Faith believed it was necessary "to explain specific foreign policy details to groups like the Turkey Farmers of America, the National Florists, or the National Cattlemen's Association."[65] While the departments of State and Defense provided information valuable to scholars and interest groups related to international relations issues, Faith sought to create materials specifically intended for ordinary Americans. The proliferation of ideologically driven news media outlets during the 1990s later demonstrated that a healthy appetite existed for such an alternative to the mainstream media.

---

[62] Faith Whittlesey, discussion with author, telephone, February 20, 2011.
[63] Ibid.
[64] Edward A. Lynch, interview by author, telephone, May 9, 2011.
[65] Faith Whittlesey, interview by Ann Miller Morin, June 21, 1989.

While Americans may have wanted such inside-the-beltway information, bureaucratic jealousies and restrictions made publication slow and difficult. Lynch recalled that the White House Office of Media Relations refused to approve the *White House Digest* until its contents had undergone a lengthy process of internal review by various offices in the executive branch. While a vetting process made some sense, especially since this publication carried the White House name and logo, the administration proceeded with exceptional—excessive, according to Lynch—caution.[66] Many moderate senior administration officials wanted to downplay the entire subject as "too controversial." Whittlesey and like-minded conservatives insisted that President Reagan needed to demonstrate commitment to an issue on which he had campaigned.[67]

White House officials also required that other executive branch entities inspect articles designed for the *Digest*. Personnel from the departments of Defense and State and the Central Intelligence Agency were asked to examine Lynch's assertions for factual accuracy and proper terminology. For example, Lynch explained, the State Department might disagree with his characterization of the Palestinian Liberation Organization as a terrorist group if the U.S. government had not officially placed that designation on the PLO.[68] In Whittlesey's view, members of these departments were also being protective of their bureaucratic turf since they distributed their own publications on these issues. "The *White House Digest*, after all, was something new," Whittlesey recalled. "The battles raged."[69]

The networks of voluntary associations with which Public Liaison had contact enabled Whittlesey to expand substantially the audience for President Reagan's agenda. Information from Room 450 briefings and the *White House Digest* gained wider distribution through numerous special-interest organizations such as the American Legion or the National Rifle Association. These groups occasionally reprinted facts and opinions originating from Whittlesey's office within their own membership publications. Since an

---

[66] Edward A. Lynch, interview by author, telephone, May 9, 2011. Blackwell and Whittlesey also described this experience. Morton Blackwell, interview by author, telephone, March 4, 2011. Faith Whittlesey, discussion with author, telephone, April 4, 2011.

[67] Faith Whittlesey, discussion with author, telephone, April 4, 2011.

[68] Edward A. Lynch, interview by author, telephone, May 9, 2011. In his 2011 book *The Cold War's Last Battlefield*, Lynch detailed his struggles with the State Department and those White House staff members who worried about the political consequences of statements in the *White House Digest*. Edward A. Lynch, *The Cold War's Last Battlefield: Reagan, the Soviets, and Central America* (Albany: State University of New York Press, 2011), pp. 199–201.

[69] Faith Whittlesey, discussion with author, telephone, April 4, 2011.

organization the size of the Southern Baptist Convention, for example, had about 15 million members and even more supporters, the message might get a very wide distribution, indeed.[70]

ALTERNATIVE MEDIA

Such coordination with interest groups proved especially important in the media environment of the mid-1980s. In an age prior to cable television, national talk radio, and the Internet, most people learned about issues relating to the federal government and foreign policy through television news broadcasts, which were largely limited to three major TV networks—ABC, CBS, and NBC.[71]

The Big Three monopolized the extremely popular dinnertime nightly newscast programming. Thus a small coterie of editors and producers had largely cornered the market on delivering national and international policy information to Americans. In one study of the typical TV news program's power, research psychologists found evidence to support the conclusion that a broadcaster's smile could determine voter preference in presidential elections.[72]

In order to bypass this heavily filtered medium, Faith cultivated "on the ground support" for the president's policies and initiatives.[73] Whittlesey and the OPL staff always searched for effective by-products of their communications initiatives. At a Room 450 briefing, for example, one audience member suggested that the administration should contact local talk-radio hosts to disseminate the same information which had just been shared. Back in 1984, Rush Limbaugh was just beginning a regional AM-radio broadcast program prior to rolling it out nationally via syndication during the 1990s. A few similar radio personalities enjoyed large local audiences during Whittlesey's tenure at Public Liaison. Lynch made himself or Whittlesey available for interviews on both conservative and liberal programs with regional audiences across the country.[74]

---

[70] Mary Ann Meloy, interview by author, telephone, March 9, 2011.
[71] CNN began in 1980, but only established a firm reputation during the 1991 Gulf War. Jane L. Chapman and Nick Nuttall, *Journalism Today: A Themed History* (West Sussex, UK: Wiley-Blackwell, 2011).
[72] Brian Mullen, David Futtrell, Debbie Stairs, Katherine E. Dawson, and Catherine A. Riodan, "Newscasters' Facial Expressions and Voting Behavior of Viewers: Can a Smile Elect a President?" *Journal of Personality and Social Psychology* 51 (1986): 291–295.
[73] Mark M. Klugmann, interview by author, Skype, February 17, 2011; Michael Waller, interview by author, Washington, DC, September 16, 2010.
[74] Edward A. Lynch, interview by author, telephone, May 9, 2011.

The OPL staff members also searched local newspapers for op-eds, editorials, and letters to the editor about administration priorities, especially Central America. Lynch recalled several such opinion pieces written by church leaders who had visited Nicaragua. The prelates praised the communist Sandinista government's land reform policies after having received tours by guides sympathetic to the government. In Lynch's view, they had been duped, and he requested equal space to submit an opposing viewpoint in an op-ed piece or letter to the editor. Lynch's response would typically detail multiple cases of the Nicaraguan government's human rights violations and restrictions of liberty which Public Liaison had researched. Lynch also argued that the proliferation of Soviet allies within the Caribbean and Central American region threatened U.S. economic and security interests.[75]

These strategies provided Public Liaison with several ways of delivering the administration's agenda, which the mainstream media might not otherwise have presented in the same manner. "Faith found ways to leap past media gatekeepers of that pre-cable/pre-Internet/pre-talk radio era and communicate directly with the grassroots," explained Mark Klugmann.[76] In Lynch's words, "A lot of what we decided to do is sort of de rigueur now, especially via the Internet, but no one was doing it at the time."[77] Whittlesey had turned Public Liaison into a productive public information office for President Reagan—way ahead of her time.[78]

Whittlesey measured the impact of her efforts by the administration's ability to create dialogue where anti-Reagan opinions had predominated. Rather than avoiding uncomfortable areas of disagreement, she sought instead to construct stronger arguments for the president's point of view. "As a politician, I like to turn political minuses into political pluses," she told a journalist in June 1983. Some moderate establishment Republicans believed that the mere discussion of the Soviet threat in Central America would inspire a general fear about possible U.S. military action too reminiscent of the Vietnam war. But Faith had confidence that honest factual discussions would engage rather than alienate Americans, saying: "I believe that, when people understand what the stakes for the United States are in

---

[75] Ibid.
[76] Mark Klugmann, email to author, July 6, 2012.
[77] Edward A. Lynch, interview by author, telephone, May 9, 2011.
[78] Despite the growth of communications technology in recent years, Linas Kojelis reported that many Washington colleagues later told him that subsequent administrations failed to duplicate the creativity and effectiveness of the outreach effort the OPL engaged in during the 1980s. Linas Kojelis, interview by author, telephone, May 3, 2011.

Central America, this issue has the potential of becoming a political plus for the administration."[79] By July 1984, the *Miami Herald* had acknowledged that the publicity generated by Whittlesey and the State Department's Otto Reich "widened the national debate on the issue."[80]

THE NRA AND "A TRIGGER-HAPPY NUCLEAR COWBOY": MARCH–OCTOBER 1984

Just as Faith did not shrink from addressing potentially divisive issues such as communism in Central America, she viewed the National Rifle Association as an important constituency for the Republican Party. Her own strong support of the Second Amendment right to bear arms further distanced her from national feminist organizations. But Whittlesey's personal policy views enabled her to appreciate better Reagan's unique appeal for gun owners. Reagan's longtime status as an NRA member clearly endeared him to the organization.

Three days prior to the 1980 presidential election, the NRA announced its support for Reagan. During its 130-year history prior to that date, the organization had never endorsed a presidential candidate. In Whittlesey's role as head of outreach to organized interest groups, she viewed the NRA, which boasted 2.6 million members in 1984, as an important group to maintain and cultivate as a loyal supporter of the administration.[81] On May 6, 1983, at the NRA's annual meetings in Arizona, Reagan became the only sitting U.S. president to address the organization. Three days later, the NRA made a strong sign of support by selecting Reagan as an Honorary Life Member—a title bestowed on only 19 individuals in the organization's 13 decades of existence. A smiling and waving President Reagan graced the cover of the NRA's monthly magazine *The American Rifleman* in July 1983, the caption below reading "President Reagan Voices His Support For NRA's Objectives."[82]

While Whittlesey constantly sought opportunities to promote the president's policies among the NRA's members, some other White House officials—especially Deputy Chief of Staff Michael Deaver—voiced the opinion that close associations between Reagan and the NRA might alienate

---

[79] Lou Cannon, "Public Relations Campaign," p. A1.
[80] Alfonso Chardy, "Outreach Group Tries to Sell Public on Reagan's Latin Policy," *Miami Herald*, July 26, 1984 p. 4.
[81] Accessed June 22, 2011, at *www.nra.org/article.aspx?id=224*.
[82] Accessed June 22, 2011, at *www.nra.org/article.aspx?id=224* and *www.nraila.org/Issues/Articles/Read.aspx?id=453&issue=011*.

those Americans, in particular women, who viewed gun owners with ambivalence, or hostility. Acting as a conduit for this organization, Faith presented the president with a large engraved handgun on a wooden plaque, and afterward relayed an NRA request to Deaver for a photograph of the president with the award. Not only did the image-conscious Deaver veto the idea, but also this internal matter hit the *Washington Post* front-page in a story quoting unnamed administration officials.[83]

Whittlesey had endured such tactics on several occasions throughout 1983 regarding her disagreement with Deaver and his allies about how best to maintain the support of American women. The leaks appeared designed to generate sufficient negative press about Faith to discourage other Washington officials and politicians from associating themselves with her.[84]

Although they did not feel confident enough to have their names associated with the story, the anonymous sources heaped contempt on Whittlesey's proposal. On March 26, 1984, the *Washington Post* reported on the NRA photo-op idea. In the piece, reporter Juan Williams wrote that a "top White House advisor" explained "with a smirk" how such a photograph could be easily exploited by Democratic presidential candidates. Democrats would hold up the image as proof, this source claimed, of Reagan's reputation for "being a trigger-happy nuclear cowboy holding a big gun." Two other unnamed White House staff members told the reporter that Deaver had twice rejected Whittlesey's proposal, as if to suggest that she was being unreasonably insistent.[85] But if Faith's opponents thought they could intimidate her into self-censorship, they definitely underestimated her tenacity.

Whittlesey and her associates refused to accept defeat. The OPL Assistant for Communications Mary Ann Meloy, in a last-ditch effort to rescue the proposal, asked Deaver's office to approve an alternative means of satisfying the organization's request for a photograph presenting Reagan in an appealing way to gun owners. Meloy's alternative scenario would have Reagan pose with the U.S. Olympic Rifle Team. Given that Los Angeles was hosting the 1984 Summer Olympic Games, Meloy thought that Deaver (who loved

---

[83] Juan Williams, "Whittlesey Pushed to Leave; Reagan Aide Called 'Disappointment,'" *Washington Post*, March 26, 1984, p. A1.

[84] See Chapter 4 for a detailed discussion of the campaign of leaks instigated against Whittlesey and reported in the *Washington Post*.

[85] Williams, "Whittlesey Pushed to Leave," p. A1.

pictures of Reagan with the American flag) surely could not characterize such a patriotic image as controversial.[86]

Having relayed this idea to Deaver on a Friday afternoon, Meloy decided to stay late in the office waiting for a reply. She typically spent weekends at home in Pennsylvania with her husband and daughters. On this occasion, however, Meloy wanted to be available for a final personal appeal if Deaver remained opposed to what she believed was a perfectly reasonable compromise—or, alternatively, to start acting on Deaver's response if the answer was "yes." At about 10 o'clock Friday night, Meloy received a phone call. The president would be available at 9:30 on Monday morning if the U.S. rifle team could come to the White House.

Since several Olympic Team members were on military bases, Meloy immediately called her friend, NRA Executive Vice President Harlon B. Carter, who used his contacts with U.S. military commanders to seek permission for the soldiers to leave their bases and arrive at the White House early on Monday morning. The photograph appeared on the October 1984 cover of *The American Hunter*—a month prior to election day. "To this day, I have the cover of that magazine … plain and simply because it was a personal victory," Meloy recalled.[87] Whittlesey and Meloy had run the extra mile because they believed political loyalty obliged the president to provide an eminently reasonable favor to a strongly pro-Reagan organization with nearly 3 million politically active members. Furthermore, they surely recognized that this image would further encourage the magazine's readers to support the president's policies.

This form of outreach reaffirmed trust between NRA leaders and the administration. Whittlesey and Meloy had asked Reagan's chief advisors to take a small risk of controversy as a sign of gratitude for the organization's unprecedented election endorsement. The NRA had only recently chosen to mobilize their millions of members behind a Republican president. By supporting Reagan so openly, the NRA gambled with the potential loss of Democratic voters and fund-raisers.

As it turns out, the NRA soon emerged as a core Republican constituency, and the organization's membership subsequently swelled to 4.3 million by June 2011. While the NRA certainly has been a target of criticism by Democratic Party leaders, feminist groups, and gun control activists,

---

[86]   Mary Ann Meloy, interview by author, telephone, March 9, 2011.
[87]   Ibid.

politicians of both parties have frequently pursued the group's endorse-ment.[88] By the 1990s, the NRA had become a formidable political force. In 1997, *Forbes* magazine rated the NRA sixth most important among pressure groups, behind such powerful organizations as the American Association of Retired Persons (AARP), the American Israeli Public Affairs Committee (AIPAC), and the American Federation of Labor–Congress of Industrial Organizations (AFL–CIO).[89]

LABOR UNIONS AND "HIGH HEELS"

At Whittlesey's arrival in 1983, Reagan did not have much contact with unions. The powerful AFL–CIO bureaucracy and membership had aligned themselves closely with Democrats for many decades. The Professional Air Traffic Controllers Organization (PATCO) had endorsed Ronald Reagan in 1980, but after PATCO voted to strike in disregard of federal law in 1981, Reagan fired half of the union's more than 20,000 members.[90]

Now, in 1983, some administration officials sought to distance the president deliberately from another union, the International Brotherhood of Teamsters truck drivers, who had also endorsed Reagan in 1980. While some Republicans appeared willing to write off labor unions, their members, and other working-class Americans, Faith considered it important to pursue their support, and she developed several creative strategies to cultivate this traditionally Democratic constituency.

In late 1980, President Reagan had asked Teamster President Jackie Presser to coordinate the administration's transition team handling labor issues. By 1983, however, administration counsel Fred Fielding discouraged further contact with this union leader. The Labor Department had begun to investigate several Teamster members, including Presser, for alleged embezzlement and ties to organized crime.[91] Faith publicly argued for continued cultivation of good relations with this organization, saying "I don't think you can turn your back on a union that has been so supportive and so large." Other administration officials, such as Director of the Office

---

[88] In a 2004 congressional election in South Dakota, for example, Democrat Stephanie Herseth's campaign ran television advertisements boasting proudly of her "A" rating by the NRA. Jon K. Lauck, *Daschle vs. Thune: Anatomy of a High-Plains Senate Race* (Norman: University of Oklahoma Press, 2007), p. 172.

[89] Accessed June 22, 2011, at *www.money.cnn.com/magazines/fortune/fortune_archive/1997/12/08/234927/index.htm.*

[90] Wilentz, *Age of Reagan*, p. 143.

[91] Lou Cannon, "Reagan Aides Advised to Keep Presser at Distance," *Washington Post*, August 17, 1983, p. A1.

of Political Affairs Edward Rollins, agreed with Whittlesey that the union deserved special treatment.[92] According to Douglas Riggs, whom Whittlesey appointed as associate director for outreach to labor unions in July 1983, "Elements in the White House were paranoid about being associated with the Teamsters," and there was "constantly a little dance that took place." In Riggs' recollection, Whittlesey deserved a lot of credit for reaching out to the Teamsters: "Whatever Faith did, she did it very well."[93]

Presser appeared to appreciate such loyalty, as the Teamsters invited Whittlesey to one of their large conventions. Whittlesey attended and spoke on behalf of the president. Facing that hard-boiled, overwhelmingly male audience of truck drivers, she assured them that a woman could demonstrate the resilience that they respected. After mentioning that many people had questioned her ability to keep pace as a widowed mother of three children and the sole woman on the president's senior White House staff, Faith uttered her most memorable quotation: "Remember that Ginger Rogers did everything Fred Astaire did—only backwards and in high heels." The crowd rewarded her with hearty and sustained applause.[94]

Whittlesey perceived several areas of mutual agreement between the administration and the Teamsters. Many of the union's members strongly agreed with Reagan's anticommunism, and she thus believed they could communicate the seriousness of the Soviet threat in Central America and the world at large to other Americans.[95] Furthermore, unlike most other union leaders, Presser publicly supported Reagan's economic policies, which he perceived as beneficial to U.S. workers. In September 1983, he indicated that the Teamsters would most likely endorse Reagan in a presidential contest because the administration had lowered interest rates and opposed those federal spending programs which "had wasted billions of dollars."[96] These positive links between the Reagan White House and the Teamsters surely contributed to the unanimous vote on August 30, 1984, of the union's 21-member board to endorse Reagan's reelection bid.[97]

---

[92] Francis X. Clines, "President Said to Keep Ties to Labor Leaders," *New York Times*, August 18, 1983, p. A21
[93] Douglas A. Riggs, interview by author, telephone, June 20, 2011.
[94] Faith Whittlesey, discussion with author, telephone, June 23, 2011.
[95] Ibid.
[96] William Serrin, "Teamster Says Union Prefers Reagan to Mondale," *New York Times*, September 26, 1983, p. B12.
[97] Gerald R. Boyd, "Teamsters Vote to Endorse Reagan," *New York Times*, August 31, 1984, p. A12.

Other unions, such as the AFL–CIO, predictably supported Reagan's Democratic opponent, Walter Mondale, in 1984, but Whittlesey's office developed a strategy for attracting rank-and-file union members. Labor liaison Doug Riggs gained Faith's confidence by devising a comprehensive plan to recruit Reagan Democrats. Having worked with the Teamsters and the AFL–CIO in Alaska while serving as special counsel to Alaska Governor Jay Haymond, Riggs had far more experience with labor unions than did most Republican politicians. In his first month at Public Liaison, Riggs prepared a strategic analysis ("white paper") on how the Reagan administration might approach working-class Americans. The White House was frustrated that the AFL–CIO, as the most recognizable union organization, and its President Lane Kirkland steadfastly opposed Reagan and the Republican Party. Riggs asserted that the administration could not hope to reach working-class Americans through such national labor unions, which shared long-established bonds with the national Democratic Party. In Riggs' estimation, the White House should focus its outreach on regional unions or nonunion organizations which working Americans frequently joined. For example, Riggs proposed opening channels of communication with veterans' societies, such as the American Legion and the Veterans of Foreign Wars, and voluntary entities, such as the Elks, which included blue-collar workers who might be rank-and-file union members as well.[98]

Whittlesey very much liked Riggs' proposal, which she supported with the full weight of her position as director of Public Liaison. By arranging a meeting with White House political advisor Ed Rollins and several other senior staff members, she allowed Riggs to present his ideas in a more formal setting. All of those in attendance approved of the plan. As Riggs' recalled, "They liked the approach of reaching working-class Americans without being tangled up in the barbed wire of the Kirkland AFL–CIO, which always supported Democratic Party candidates." Riggs received a promotion with the prestigious title Special Assistant to the President in October 1983. Whittlesey then authorized Riggs to implement his scheme. "If you were trustworthy, and you were executing, she was very supportive," Riggs noted. As a result, he cultivated alliances with the heads of veterans groups and with less prominent labor organizations, such as maritime laborers based primarily in New York City. In Riggs' recollection, he invited these

---

[98] Douglas A. Riggs, interview by author, telephone, June 20, 2011.

leaders to the White House "all the time," much to Whittlesey's delight.[99] Riggs impressed her as "a master strategist and thinker during my time at Public Liaison."[100]

Riggs also recognized the potential to establish common cause with labor union members by explaining Reagan's goals in Central America. Whereas corporate executives and union leaders in the United States traditionally clashed on economic policies, national security issues offered an area for discussion which more easily crossed class lines. The subject of Soviet power also represented a type of "wedge" issue which might potentially divide blue-collar workers and intellectuals—two typically Democratic Party constituencies. "Working-class Americans had a natural predilection to oppose communism, especially compared with the editorial staff of the *New York Times*," Riggs observed. The OPL hosted several meetings in Room 450 with groups of union members. Some of these workers had a strong predisposition to support Reagan's vigorous anticommunism. Eastern and Central Europeans, for example, tended to identify strongly with the anticommunist Solidarity movement of Poland's working class. In Riggs' view, these Americans came to admire Reagan's resolve in blocking the spread of communism to Caribbean and Central American nations such as Grenada, El Salvador, and Guatemala: "Under Reagan, it no longer looked like it was the 'new reality' that revolutionary forces would advance."[101] Reagan's muscular approach to international relations definitely appealed to this group.

Reagan's foreign policy stance thus helped Public Liaison address the challenge of finding common cause between the Republican White House and the AFL–CIO. Republicans had often engaged in tense disagreements with blue-collar workers on wages, profit sharing, and other economic issues. Therefore, Riggs and Whittlesey selected topics for conversation between the White House and labor union leaders with very careful advance planning. "I remember the discussions about bringing [AFL–CIO President Lane] Kirkland to the White House," Riggs said: " 'We cannot talk to Kirkland about any domestic policy,' [White House officials affirmed,] 'but on the communist issue we can talk to him.' " By emphasizing national security and foreign policy subjects in meetings with labor leaders as well as rank-and-file

---

[99] Ibid.; Faith Whittlesey, discussion with author, telephone, June 23, 2011.
[100] Faith Whittlesey, discussion with author, telephone, June 23, 2011.
[101] Douglas A. Riggs, interview by author, telephone, June 20, 2011.

union members, Riggs could build and maintain some alliances where negative relationships, or none at all, had previously existed. In Riggs' recollection, "I would go to see Lane [Kirkland] once a quarter and his top lieutenant once a month."[102] Whittlesey herself paid a visit to Kirkland in his Washington office as a gesture of respect.[103] In regard to organized labor, Whittlesey and Riggs had created the conditions to conceive of turning a political minus into a plus.

THE RELIGIOUS RIGHT

Whittlesey actively pursued the support of religious traditionalists, another group whose loyalty the Republicans had not yet decisively secured. In the 1980 presidential election, Reagan had demonstrated the ability to attract a majority of Protestant and Catholic Americans. Whittlesey's efforts in the Reagan White House to maintain the loyalty of these groups paid dividends both in the short and in the long run for Reagan and the Republican Party. "At that point in time, the early 1980s, most evangelicals were not registered to vote in the United States," recalled Mary Ann Meloy.[104]

Reagan's campaign benefited from this loose alliance of Protestant, Catholic, and some Jewish citizens who supported his campaign message. In 1980, Reagan's opposition to abortion on demand and the Equal Rights Amendment, and his endorsement of prayer in schools, helped persuade many evangelicals to eschew their earlier support for Governor, and later President, Jimmy Carter, a Baptist Sunday school teacher.

But Reagan's first 2 years in office had somewhat disappointed this constituency, which inevitably felt taken for granted as the administration chose to focus primarily on economic issues, especially a tax cut. Shortly before the assassination attempt on Reagan in March, 1981, little more than 2 months into his presidency, Chief of Staff James Baker and Republican Senate Majority Leader Howard Baker had jointly announced that the administration and its supporters in Congress would prioritize financial recovery at the expense of "collateral" and "emotional" social issues, and Reagan appeared to endorse this viewpoint in a *Washington Post* interview the following day.[105] Heritage Foundation cofounder Paul Weyrich recalled

---

[102] Ibid.
[103] Faith Whittlesey, discussion with author, telephone, June 23, 2011.
[104] Mary Ann Meloy, interview by author, telephone, March 9, 2011.
[105] See Bill Peterson and David Broder, "Split in the Senate: Senate Increasingly Divided on 'Social Issues' Timing," *Washington Post*, March 27, 1981, p. A1; and Cannon, *President Reagan*, p. 318.

expressing his outrage to other conservative Christian leaders, "Could you imagine if the Democrats had won and they issued a statement saying Civil Rights legislation has to go on the back burner?"[106] While many members of the religious right continued to view Reagan favorably, such incidents may have contributed to the president's low approval ratings by 1982.

Protestant evangelicals immediately found an ally in Whittlesey. In March 1983, Faith's first month as director of Public Liaison, the president prepared to meet with Reverend Jerry Falwell, who cofounded the powerful Moral Majority conservative movement. As with the working-class and NRA interest groups, she viewed Falwell's constituency as having been recruited by Reagan away from apolitical or pro-Democratic Party worldviews. In one of her first memos to the president, she advised that the president might utilize this opportunity to "recapture the enthusiasm in the fundamentalist and evangelical community. Clearly their political activism has declined between 1980 and 1982."[107] Faith demonstrated her keen awareness of this group's importance to the president's governing coalition. With the "invaluable" assistance and advice of Morton Blackwell, the OPL's liaison for evangelicals, she underscored Falwell's continued loyalty despite the disappointment in the president expressed by some disgruntled conservatives: "Unlike some other national conservative organization leaders, Dr. Falwell has never criticized you or Reagan administration policy."[108] Whittlesey encouraged the president to maintain a warm welcome for Falwell and other members of this emerging constituency of traditionalist religious believers. She viewed the minister as a potential linchpin in establishing evangelicals as full partners in a new Republican Party governing coalition.

Faith considerably improved the religious right's status in the West Wing. She became this group's "most aggressive ally in the White House," according to sociologist William Martin in his landmark book *With God on Our Side: The Rise of the Religious Right in America*. Martin noted that Whittlesey arranged for visits of "substantial numbers of major and minor evangelical leaders and pastors" who had their photograph taken with

---

[106] David John Marley, *Pat Robertson: An American Life* (Lanham, MD: Rowman and Littlefield, 2007), p. 71.

[107] Faith Whittlesey, memo to Ronald Reagan, March 14, 1983. Cited in David John Marley, "Ronald Reagan and the Splintering of the Christian Right," *Journal of Church and State* 48, no. 4 (Autumn 2006): 858; and Marley, *Pat Robertson*, p. 71.

[108] Marley, "Ronald Reagan," p. 858; Faith Whittlesey, discussion with author, telephone, April 4, 2011.

President Reagan in the White House.[109] Just as with the NRA, Whittlesey continued to emphasize that the loyalty of evangelical leaders could not be taken for granted.

Whittlesey's outreach to Catholics proved similarly robust. This constituency had voted 80 percent for the Democratic Party's Catholic presidential nominee John F. Kennedy in 1960, and a majority of Catholics supported Jimmy Carter in 1976.[110] Upon arriving in the White House, Whittlesey endeavored to expand contact with important ethnic constituencies, such as the predominantly Catholic Italian, Polish, and other Central and European American groups. Linas Kojelis coordinated outreach to the Polish American Congress, for example. He also recalled that the OPL invited 20–30 Catholic bishops for lunch at the White House.[111] Whittlesey included even those bishops who disagreed with Reagan's policies. Robert Reilly pursued common cause with a strongly Democratic priest, Father Bryan Hehir, who held several important positions at the National Conference of Catholic Bishops. Rather than treat Father Hehir as an enemy, Reilly arranged for a meeting between the priest and Whittlesey in her West Wing office for a substantive discussion of foreign and domestic policy issues.[112]

But these efforts did not win approval from several of Whittlesey's White House colleagues. To her great surprise, one of James Baker's staff members wanted to cancel Reagan's meeting with the Catholic bishops on the same day it was set to occur. This individual feared that the bishops would go out on the White House lawn afterward and criticize the president. Some did just that, she recalled, but the newspapers the next day were filled with prominent photos of Reagan smiling with all the Catholic bishops. On another occasion, Faith wanted the president to appear with the Sons of Italy or Knights of Columbus on Columbus Day, but Michael Deaver preferred to schedule Reagan to meet with Italian movie stars and fashion designers at the Italian embassy instead. In Whittlesey's view, this resistance revealed a blind spot among Republican establishment leaders, who "failed utterly"

---

[109] Cal Thomas, vice president of the Moral Majority (which represented many of these ministers), saw so many of these photos displayed in churches around the country that he recalled feeling that "Ronald Reagan became the surrogate messiah." William Martin, *With God on Our Side: The Rise of the Religious Right in America* (New York: Broadway Books, 1996), p. 225.

[110] See Thomas Carty, *A Catholic in the White House? Religion and Politics in John Kennedy's Presidential Campaign* (New York: Palgrave Macmillan, 2004).

[111] Linas Kojelis, interview by author, telephone, May 3, 2011.

[112] Deal Hudson, *Onward Christian Soldiers: The Growing Political Power of Catholics and Evangelicals in the United States* (New York: Threshold Editions, 2008), p. 238.

to recognize the importance of this religious institution and its members for Reagan's governing coalition.[113]

Faith also extended the White House's outreach to Jewish Americans. Although the Democratic Party typically won the overwhelming support of Jews, Whittlesey's Public Liaison actively recruited a specific Jewish constituency—war veterans—which the Republican establishment had overlooked. This particular constituency was new to Republicans. "Everybody wants to deal with all the big Jewish developers, the national Jewish groups, because they have lots of money to contribute to campaigns," but Whittlesey believed that Reagan needed to cultivate the common man's loyalty as well. "The Jewish veterans are the local butcher and tailor," she noted. "These were the people [to whom] we tried to give a sense of recognition and feeling that they had some relationship with Ronald Reagan's White House."[114] She hired highly regarded young conservative Jewish scholar Marshall Breger for this effort and other outreach to Jewish leaders.

THE POPE AND THE PROTESTANTS: JANUARY 1984

Faith had particularly encouraged the administration to cultivate relations with both evangelical Protestants and Catholics, but an historic administration policy decision in January 1984 threatened to revive divisions between these two constituencies dating back to the Reformation in the 16th century.

When President Reagan appointed an official ambassador to the Holy See, many Catholics perceived the decision as courageous. For more than 100 years, anti-Catholic prejudice had precluded previous presidents from formal recognition of the Vatican as a sovereign country. While some religious bigotry existed, many Protestants (especially within the evangelical community) had long argued that the appointment of an official envoy to any religious entity would violate the principle of separation of church and state.[115]

Evangelical leaders did not suppress their displeasure with President Reagan. Reverend Falwell—whom Whittlesey had praised in a memo

---

[113] Faith Whittlesey, discussion with author, telephone, June 23, 2011.

[114] Faith Whittlesey, interview by Ann Miller Morin, June 21, 1989.

[115] Evangelicals formed an important part of the coalition which opposed FDR's appointment of a personal representative to the Vatican in 1939, and they successfully lobbied President Harry S Truman to revoke his nomination of an ambassador to the Holy See in 1951. Michael H. Carter, "Diplomacy's Detractors: American Protestant Reaction to FDR's 'Personal Representative' at the Vatican," in *FDR, the Vatican, and the Roman Catholic Church in America, 1933–1945*, eds. David B. Woolner and Richard G. Kurial (New York: Palgrave, 2003), pp. 179–208.

to Reagan less than a year earlier for never criticizing the administration—decried the legal precedent which the president's choice appeared
to establish. In Falwell's perspective, all religious institutions could now
justly request an official ambassador from the U.S. government: "I wonder
when Mecca will want one. I told the White House if they give one to the
Pope, I may ask for one."[116]

Southern Baptists, who represented a large constituency within the
conservative Moral Majority, also rejected Reagan's move. James Dunn,
executive director of the Baptist Joint Committee for Religious Liberty,
labeled the action "a dumb, bumbling move by an Administration that
doesn't seem to understand the first lesson about church-state relations."[117]
U.S. Senator Jesse Helms, another close ally of Whittlesey, refused to vote in
favor of Reagan's nominee to serve as the first ambassador to the Vatican.
Ironically, Helms had cosponsored the congressional act which allowed the
president to recognize the Vatican. But he likely harbored second thoughts
after witnessing the strong reaction from many Baptists, especially within
his home state of North Carolina.[118]

In order to address these protests, Whittlesey immediately invited a large
group of evangelical Protestant leaders, including Falwell, to a meeting in the
White House. She carefully prepared talking points in an effort to persuade
the ministers, whom she had long cultivated as an essential part of Reagan's
governing coalition. Armed with a list of facts which explained the policy
change in its full legal context, she articulated the case for Reagan's decision.

U.S. recognition of the Vatican had precedents, which Faith explained.
The United States had formal relations with several "religious states such as
Israel, Saudi Arabia and [the United Kingdom]."[119] Whittlesey's notes drew
a comparison between the Vatican and the United Kingdom, where "it is
worth noting that the Queen of England is also the head of the Anglican
Church and head of State." Furthermore, more than 100 nations had already
granted this status to the Vatican. The memos also detailed how official
relations with the Vatican benefited the administration's agenda. The pope's
statesmanship and the Vatican's diplomatic efforts closely aligned with

---

[116] Kenneth A. Briggs, "Church Groups Denounce Reagan Move," *New York Times*, January 11, 1984, p. A4.
[117] Andrew M. Essig and Jennifer L. Moore, "U.S.-Holy See Diplomacy: The Establishment of Formal Relations, 1984," *Catholic Historical Review* 95, no. 4 (October, 2009): 760.
[118] Ibid., p. 758.
[119] "U.S.-Vatican Diplomatic Relations Talking Points," Faith Whittlesey Papers, Box 10F, Ronald Reagan Presidential Library.

U.S. foreign policies regarding refugee assistance, family planning, and geopolitics, such as the resolution of a territorial dispute between Argentina and Chile.[120]

Looking back on the experience of facing the Protestant ministers, Whittlesey found this event one of the most daunting moments of her political career. Faith's Methodist mother Amy had been ostracized by some of her brothers for marrying a Catholic. Faith seriously worried that lingering anti-Catholic attitudes might overwhelm her own best efforts to persuade these Protestant leaders to understand and accept Reagan's policy shift. In the end, Whittlesey believed that the ministers listened to her, especially when she reminded them about the suffering of Catholic martyrs within the Soviet empire. Christians should unite in opposition to both atheistic communism and abortion, she suggested.[121]

Fortunately for Whittlesey, she had established a substantial reservoir of trust and goodwill with Falwell and other conservative Protestant leaders. Although a couple of organizations—such as Americans United for Separation of Church and State and American Baptist Churches in the U.S.A.—filed lawsuits intended to reverse the president's decision, no widespread public opposition gained traction. Scholars have noted other reasons for the lack of a sustained resistance to U.S. diplomatic recognition of the Vatican. Overwhelming public respect for Pope John Paul II and the gradual assimilation of Catholics into mainstream American society certainly proved to be important.[122] But Faith explained this contentious policy shift in a way that satisfied a disgruntled, yet vital, constituency within the conservative coalition.

No one has credited Whittlesey for this important avoidance of a rift within the religious right at a time when President Reagan was preparing for his reelection campaign. Whittlesey's consistent willingness to advocate the school prayer and prolife agendas helped sustain the evangelical Protestant commitment to cooperate with conservative Catholics. This interfaith alliance was impossible without Protestant tolerance of Catholicism. Whittlesey and Reagan both seemed to understand this reality, perhaps because their mothers had both shown this freedom from prejudice in selecting Catholics as their husbands.

---

[120] Ibid.
[121] Faith Whittlesey, discussion with author, telephone, April 26, 2011.
[122] Essig and Moore, "U.S.-Holy See Diplomacy," pp. 760–764.

1984 PRESIDENTIAL ELECTION

Whittlesey's outreach efforts at Public Liaison certainly contributed to Reagan's 49-state landslide victory, although the president's inner core of advisors never publicly acknowledged the important role she played. James Baker managed Reagan's "Rose Garden" approach to the campaign by generally keeping the president from venturing outside of the White House grounds, purportedly to prevent the media from engaging Reagan in detailed policy discussions.[123]

In the end, however, most Americans expressed basic agreement with the Reagan agenda which Faith had creatively promoted as the OPL director. A November 1983 *Los Angeles Times* poll recorded that 59 percent of Americans claimed to like "most of [Reagan's] policies."[124] And a month before the election, sociologist Amitai Etzioni told the *New York Times* that "No matter how great an actor he is, the script is still what matters most to most Americans."[125] During her 2 years at Public Liaison, Whittlesey had worked hard—"virtually under the radar," in her view—to present and explain Reagan's story line to the American public at large.[126]

In addition, Whittlesey had tried to attract certain key audiences to whom she believed the president's policies would appeal. While some of her critics charged that she often pitched her appeals to groups who were already sympathetic to Reagan's point of view, Faith assumed that these dedicated supporters could help her amplify Reagan's message. In Ed Lynch's words, "We may have been preaching to the choir, but we wanted to make sure they knew the words."[127] Or as Whittlesey similarly phrased the idea, "The choir had to have music!"[128]

Having arrived in Washington in January 1983 to work for a president with 35 percent public approval ratings, Faith privately interpreted Reagan's popular triumph 22 months later in part as an implicit endorsement of the OPL's broad range of innovative initiatives. In addition to Reagan's winning nearly every state, Republicans gained 16 House seats (while losing only one Senate seat). Reflecting on the victory, Whittlesey said in April 1985: "My goal here was to help strengthen and expand the President's governing

---

[123] Cannon, *Role of a Lifetime*, p. 496.
[124] Quoted in Everett Carll Ladd, "On Mandates, Realignments, and the 1984 Presidential Election," *Political Science Quarterly* 100, no. 1 (1985): 4.
[125] Cannon, *Role of a Lifetime*, p. 496.
[126] Faith Whittlesey, discussion with author, telephone, April 26, 2011.
[127] Edward A. Lynch, interview by author, telephone, May 9, 2011.
[128] Faith Whittlesey, discussion with author, telephone, December 13, 2011.

coalition, to assure the success of his Administration. I think one could say the results were measured in the 1984 election."[129] While political analysts could debate about the various factors explaining the election results, one could not deny that she had served creatively and actively, if unsung, within Reagan's White House.

The 1984 election certainly shook the foundations of the political consensus which President Franklin Roosevelt had fashioned during the 1930s. A preliminary analysis in the *New York Times* suggested that "the old New Deal coalition … remains very much alive," despite the overwhelming Republican victory. But several political scientists soon challenged this assertion. Writing in *The Election of 1984: Reports and Interpretations*, Wilson Carey McWilliams asserted that Mondale's lopsided defeat revealed a serious reduction in the core Democratic constituencies, to include only racial minorities, Jews, trade unionists, big-city residents, and the unemployed: "The New Deal *coalition*—the majorities that four times elected FDR—began with the Democratic party that Roosevelt inherited, a party built around southern whites and northern Catholics."[130] Reagan had pealed many of these white southern Protestant and northern Catholic Americans away from a long-standing fidelity to the Democrats.

Based on this research, one can argue that Whittlesey's vastly expanded outreach to evangelical Christians and the Catholic prolife movement, for example, played a key role in helping Reagan break the historically strong bond that connected many Protestants (especially southern ones) and Catholics to the Democratic Party. Faith had emphasized issues which appealed to these religious traditionalists. By publicizing the president's support for prolife policies, school prayer, and tuition tax credits, Whittlesey's office encouraged these groups to rethink their commitment to Democrats, whose appeal became reduced to wealth disparity. In the words of one Democratic leader in 1984, "If we don't have an economic issue for ["born-again" Christians], we don't seem to have any issues."[131] As McWilliams noted, this perspective left Democrats "reduced to waiting for a recession." Reagan's campaign clearly benefited from economic good news in 1984, but Whittlesey had also ensured that these groups recognized profound

---

[129] "Q and A: Faith Whittlesey On White House," *New York Times*, April 8, 1985, p. A14.

[130] Wilson Carey McWilliams, "The Meaning of the Election," in Gerald Pomper et al., *The Election of 1984: Reports and Interpretations* (Chatham, NJ: Chatham House, 1985), p. 167 (emphasis in original).

[131] Ibid., pp. 167–168.

intangible reasons for supporting the president. As McWilliams observed, "Political allegiance involves our deepest feelings and our highest aspirations as much as our prosaic needs; in the last analysis, political loyalties are a matter for the soul."[132] Even as some members of his administration wanted Reagan to keep a respectable distance from traditional religious believers, Whittlesey actively lobbied him for just the opposite.

Most Republicans had written off working-class Americans, especially members of labor unions, as unapproachable for Reagan in 1983 and 1984, but Whittlesey had cultivated their support. After the election, political scientist Everett Carll Ladd reported data which affirmed Whittlesey's instincts in this regard. Blue-collar voters—one of the "mainstays of the New Deal coalition"—voted for Reagan in 1984. Even though labor union leaders "went all out for Mondale," the Democratic nominee only marginally defeated the president among voters from households where at least one adult belonged to a union.[133]

All of this evidence suggested to scholars the theory that Faith had advanced—Reagan had proven his ability to secure several key Democratic constituencies and to orchestrate a political realignment. The National Opinion Research Center produced surveys in 1983 and 1984 which revealed that Republicans received more popular support in the 1980s than in any previous period dating back to the 1930s.[134] Historians soon began to chronicle this remarkable phenomenon in such books as *The Rise and Fall of the New Deal Order* and *The Conservative Ascendancy*.[135]

SCREENING *THE SILENT SCREAM* IN THE WHITE HOUSE
Although Faith had requested and received a reassignment to an ambassadorial post after the election, she continued to recruit ordinary Americans to view Reagan's agenda favorably. By Christmas 1984, she knew that Reagan would appoint her again to head the U.S. mission in Bern, but she needed to wait several months for Senate confirmation. In the meantime, Whittlesey determined to maintain strong connections with the interest groups that Reagan had promised to support during the campaign.

---

[132] Ibid., p. 168.
[133] Everett Ladd, "1984 Presidential Election," p. 13.
[134] Cited in ibid., p. 18.
[135] Steve Fraser and Gary Gerstle, eds., *The Rise and Fall of the New Deal Order* (Princeton, NJ: Princeton University Press, 1989); Donald Critchlow, *The Conservative Ascendancy: How the GOP Right Made Political History* (Cambridge, MA: Harvard University Press, 2007).

In February 1985, she organized a significant gesture of support for the prolife movement. Reagan had addressed prolife rallies each year via video recordings. Robert Reilly now arranged for the screening in Room 450 of a recently produced documentary film called *The Silent Scream*, which featured ultrasound images of a mother's womb during an abortion at 3 months. Narrated by Dr. Bernard Nathanson—who had cofounded the National Abortion Rights Action League and who reported having performed some 60,000 abortions over the course of his medical career prior to disavowing the practice—the 28-minute video footage confronted viewers with heart-wrenching visual displays of a very human-looking fetus appearing to resist and scream while a doctor performed the procedure. Chief of Staff Donald Regan, who had replaced James Baker after the election, tried to cancel the screening on the morning of the same day it was scheduled to occur. Regan's justification, which he stated to Whittlesey, was that the film was "too controversial." Whittlesey answered Regan directly with a degree of puzzlement, "It's not controversial, Don—it's the president's *policy!*"[136]

In Whittlesey's view, this decision fully supported the president's principles. "Ronald Reagan was convinced of the sanctity of human life of both mother and child," she asserted.[137] Whittlesey had defended Reagan's policies for more than 8 years in three presidential campaigns. Her own direct experience with the president convinced her that he believed strongly that abortion is the taking of the life of an unborn child—a grave moral offense. On one particular occasion, she recalled sitting with the president and Chief of Staff Baker in the back of a limousine. In Whittlesey's recollection, Baker was "telling the president about poll numbers on his prolife position with the implication that [Reagan's] views were hurting him." Reagan's response made a strong impression on Whittlesey. "It was one of the few times I saw Reagan express a twinge of irritation. He said to Baker, 'Jim, I do not care what the polls say. This is the right thing to do. Do it.'"[138] According to the *Washington Post*, Reagan had even endorsed the message of *The Silent Scream*. In Reagan's words, "If every member of Congress could see this film ... Congress would move quickly to end the tragedy of abortion."[139] Despite his administration's strong focus on economic growth

---

[136] Faith Whittlesey, email to author, February 25, 2011.
[137] Ibid.
[138] Deal Hudson, *Onward, Christian Soldiers*, p. 236.
[139] William McPherson, "Abortion and Other Images of Horror," *Washington Post*, February 19, 1985, p. A19.

and undermining communist governments, Reagan also "defined himself as an advocate for the sanctity of human life."[140]

Robert Reilly asked several White House staff members if they could secure the president or another high-level administration official to introduce the film, but only Whittlesey would agree to do it. In Faith's view, she wanted to offer her status as a senior staff member as a testimony to Reagan's support for human life. "Ronald Reagan would not have been elected and reelected in such landslides had it not been for his prolife supporters," she later asserted. "These 'values voters' expected moral leadership from the president."[141] For them, "sanctity of each human life" equaled, if not surpassed, the significance of the administration's economic policies.

As she had done several times during her more than 2 years at Public Liaison, Whittlesey staged a dramatic event in Room 450. "Faith with her uncanny sense for what gets the press's attention had us build several pyramids out of these hundreds of cassettes on each side of the speakers on stage," Reilly recalled. "And, sure enough, I saw cameramen on their knees—as if they were adoring these pyramids—filming them." These images would make the cut for the highly valued few minutes of nightly televised news coverage on the major networks. To generate the greatest political impact possible, Reilly arranged for the film's producer to donate 535 cassettes for White House distribution to each member of Congress.[142]

Reilly and Whittlesey had courted this attention to create political momentum for those Americans who believed in the rights of unborn children. As Reilly recalled, "We were well aware that this event would cause a sensation, if not an uproar. That is why we were doing it—to bring maximum attention to *The Silent Scream*."[143] Rather than viewing Reagan's opposition to abortion as a stance which might alienate Americans, Faith believed that opponents of this procedure expected such dramatic demonstrations of the president's commitment to their cause. She had also grown even more personally committed to the prolife position after witnessing both *The Silent Scream* and the sincere dedication of those Americans who sought to defend human life.[144]

---

[140] Faith Whittlesey, email to author, February 25, 2011.
[141] Ibid.
[142] Robert Reilly, interview by author, Vienna, VA, September 15, 2010.
[143] Robert R. Reilly, "A Safe Place," accessed on February 22, 2011, at *www.Insidecatholic.com*.
[144] Faith Whittlesey, discussion with author, telephone, June 22, 2011.

Nathanson's "gentle ... dignified, thoughtful" presentation impressed Whittlesey but also made an impact on some Americans who did not share her commitment to the prolife cause. Perhaps because Nathanson was "not in any way bombastic or confrontational," Whittlesey suggested, his presentation mesmerized the audience. Furthermore, the images spoke volumes. "The audience of approximately 225 in Room 450 sat in stunned silence," Faith recalled. "I remember having to avert my eyes ... as the baby struggled to escape the dismemberment of the suction machine."[145] William McPherson, a member of the *Washington Post* editorial page staff, noted that Whittlesey had introduced the film accurately as "a powerful testament for the prolife position." He also acknowledged that "it is no longer possible to claim ignorance of the pain of abortion." McPherson's column went on to criticize the Reagan administration for not supporting population-control measures aimed at alleviating comparable suffering, such as the effects of extreme poverty in Ethiopia and elsewhere. But, he conceded, "Whether one agrees or disagrees with the president, any person of normal sensibilities would have to find the film disturbing." This honest recognition of "horror" at the sight of an actual abortion, from a liberal news source, testified to the powerful impact of the film and—by extension—the temerity of Whittlesey and her staff.[146]

Whittlesey and Reilly viewed such actions as important as the administration crafted its policy messages at the outset of Reagan's second term. In his first 4 years, the president had achieved only limited progress toward his goal of changing the government's abortion policies. Reagan appointed many federal judges who restricted the nearly unfettered access to abortion provided for in the 1973 Supreme Court decision *Roe v. Wade*, and yet Congress had failed to agree on legislation about this widely debated Supreme Court decision.[147] The prolife movement was becoming dispirited, but Whittlesey's efforts to publicize the moral principles underlying the cause provided a glimmer of hope for future action in this policy sphere.[148]

---

[145] Faith Whittlesey, email to author, February 25, 2011.
[146] William McPherson, "Abortion and Other Images of Horror," *Washington Post*, February 19, 1985, p. A19.
[147] David M. O'Brien, "Federal Judges in Retrospect," in *The Reagan Presidency: Pragmatic Conservatism and Its Legacies*, eds. W. Elliot Brownlee and Hugh Davis Graham (Lawrence: University Press of Kansas, 2003), pp. 297–300.
[148] Faith Whittlesey, discussion with author, telephone, March 12, 2012.

"LAST OF THE CONSERVATIVES"

Many conservatives lamented the reports of Whittlesey's impending departure from the White House. Unsurprisingly, given previous evidence, the news leaked to the press in early January. Faith had defended conservative causes with strong commitment and some success. In Reagan's second term, the president's most conservative staff members would leave the White House for the private sector or other public-sector positions. In coming years, Baker and Secretary of State George Shultz came to imprint their agenda on the Reagan legacy. Whittlesey believes that Bill Clark, Ed Meese, and CIA Director William Casey—if they had retained leadership roles in the White House—might otherwise have more noticeably defined the brand of Reagan conservatism to which she subscribed for the next generation.[149]

An ad hoc organization honored her on January 8, 1985, with the first McDonald Memorial ("Grace Under Fire") Award. This prize was named after U.S. Navy veteran and conservative Democratic Congressman Lawrence Patton McDonald from Georgia—who died in the Korean Air Lines Flight 007 passenger jet which Soviet fighter pilots shot out of the sky on September 1, 1983—and it testified to the high regard and esteem with which this group of anticommunist and social conservatives regarded her. Although few high-profile establishment Republicans attended, the newly elected U.S. Senator Mitch McConnell of Kentucky explained his attendance as a sign of appreciation for the conservative activists who had organized the event: "I'm here because a lot of these people helped me when no one else would. Most of the business PACs [political action committees] were so busy trying to pick a winner they paid no attention to a challenger, especially a little-known challenger." Longtime Republican fund-raiser and activist Richard Viguerie lamented Whittlesey's departure from Washington as a further blow to the administration officials, such as Clark and Meese, whom he admired.[150]

Whittlesey's name again surfaced in newspapers when Jeane Kirkpatrick, Reagan's ambassador to the United Nations, announced her resignation from the administration. Disappointed administration conservatives bemoaned Kirkpatrick's decision along with those by Faith, Clark, and Meese to leave the White House. As one unnamed source viewed the situation, "We're losing

---

[149] Ibid.
[150] Elizabeth Kastor, "The Right Angles; Talking Politics at the McDonald Dinner Conservatives," *Washington Post*, January 9, 1985, p. D1.

one member after another of the real Reaganaut team."[151] The conservative *Washington Times* portrayed Whittlesey in a headline as the "Last of the Conservatives" in the Reagan White House. At a farewell roast for her on March 27, 1985, Senators Jesse Helms and Arlen Specter attended as well as Whittlesey's firm friend and ally, CIA Director Casey.[152] Social and foreign policy conservatives generally trusted very few of Reagan's remaining staff members to help promote their agenda, and Whittlesey had earned deep and widespread respect among this group for having done so.

"IT WAS THE CONTENT"

Perhaps Whittlesey did not make greater claims to have affected the 1984 election results because she pursued a more significant long-term impact on American opinion. She also gave President Reagan all the credit. But in an understated manner, she did imply that Public Liaison perhaps contributed to the results by making the case for Reagan's policies among the working class. "It's quite unique for a conservative Republican President to have the support of blue-collar Americans," she noted. "And I knew that in order for that success to grow and translate into a successful governance, that emerging new [Reagan Republican] coalition had to be attended to."[153] Faith Whittlesey had certainly endeavored to preserve and expand this constituency during her more than 2 years at the helm of the OPL.

Under Whittlesey's leadership, the White House Office of Public Liaison engaged in a spirited public information mission, but the OPL personnel did not view her as having engaged in the pursuit of political gain at the expense of ideas. As White House consultant Ed Lynch recalled, "You never doubted the reasons for her actions. When she said she wanted to stop communism in Central America, she always said it was because she wanted to stop communism, not to gain the Cuban vote in Florida."[154] Neither did Whittlesey appear to have an overriding personal ambition which might have otherwise tainted her policy views. In her assistant Mona Charen's recollection, "It was never about her. That was one big distinction between Faith and the other public figures I've known. There was such tremendous lack of vanity in her." Whittlesey's commitment to ideals defined her

---

[151] John M. Goshko and Lou Cannon, "Kirkpatrick to Quit Government," *Washington Post*, January 31, 1985, p. A1.

[152] Donnie Radcliffe, "No Charity for Faith," *Washington Post*, March 28, 1985, p. B2.

[153] "Q and A," p. 14.

[154] Edward A. Lynch, interview by author, telephone, May 9, 2011.

tenure in the White House, Charen believed.[155] This absence of ambition to climb the party power ladder further kept her rooted in beliefs rather than political expediency.

Whittlesey also seemed less motivated by short-term crisis management (or "spin control," which became part of America's political lexicon in the wake of the 24-hour cable TV news explosion during the 1990s) than by changing people's minds about big ideas. "She wasn't thinking in terms of a news cycle or an election cycle. She was thinking next generation," recalled Michael Waller.[156] Whittlesey herself had viewed her work in this manner. She expressed a "profound sense of obligation to the grassroots voters who had elected Reagan believing him to be a man of deep principle and traditional faith."[157] From 1983 to 1985, Whittlesey employed the White House brand name, talented speakers and writers, and existing alternatives to the mainstream media to disseminate the administration's messages in increasingly effective ways.

President Reagan valued Faith's contributions. On October 29, 1984, the president called Whittlesey "one of my most important aides in the White House," during a Reagan-Bush rally in Media, Pennsylvania.[158] In a November 1, 1984, letter to Whittlesey mere days prior to the election, Reagan wrote "to offer you my personal thanks for the invaluable assistance you've given me."[159] Whittlesey greatly appreciated Reagan's gratitude since she had given many hours, and great effort, to fight for the man and the values and ideals he represented to her.

Whittlesey had clearly contributed to Reagan's reputation as a principled politician who implemented significant changes in U.S. foreign and domestic policies. In his January 11, 1989, farewell address, he conceded that his message held more importance than the medium by which he connected with the public. "I won a nickname: 'The Great Communicator.' But I never thought it was my style or the words I used that made a difference—it was the content."[160] As OPL director and a member of the White House senior staff, Whittlesey helped explain this "content" to the public. She would bring this wealth of new experience and enhanced skills in public information

---

[155] Mona Charen, interview by author, telephone, August 15, 2010.
[156] Michael Waller, interview by author, Washington, DC, September 16, 2010.
[157] Deal Hudson, *Onward, Christian Soldiers*, p. 235.
[158] Accessed on June 27, 2012, at *www.reagan.utexas.edu/archives/speeches/1984/102984b.htm.*
[159] Ronald Reagan to Faith Whittlesey, November 1, 1984, letter in Faith Whittlesey's possession.
[160] Quoted in Fred Greenstein, *Presidential Difference: Leadership Style from FDR to Barack Obama*, 3rd ed. (Princeton, NJ: Princeton University Press), p. 259.

management back to Switzerland when she returned to her duties as U.S. ambassador in April 1985.

CHAPTER 6

Geneva Summitry and Technology Transfers
The Second Bern Tour (part 1)

State Department officer Douglas Sears graphically recalled riding 100 miles per hour on a Swiss highway sometime between 1986 and 1988. The large, heavy, four-door Oldsmobile sedan, specially retrofitted and armored for U.S. government use, did not handle very well, and the passengers could feel each bump in the road. U.S. Ambassador to Switzerland Faith Whittlesey sat next to Sears in the backseat while the ambassador's chauffeur barreled the limousine down the highway. Attempting to insert contact lenses into her eyes all the while, Faith kept inquiring, "*Where* is my speech?" In Sears' retelling more than 20 years later, he pauses frequently while trying to contain his laughter at an event which *still* seems surreal to him: "I'm watching this, and I've got my seatbelt on—because I don't want to die young—and she has no seatbelt on!"[1]

Fortunately, Sears was immediately able to provide Whittlesey one of several copies of her speech which he had drafted. At Sears' request, Whittlesey's residence manager had dutifully placed a copy in the ambassador's purse. Sears had kept another in his hand, stuck a third copy in his back pocket, and gave Whittlesey a fourth prior to leaving the ambassador's residence.[2] In her second tour as U.S. ambassador in Bern from 1985 to

---

[1] Douglas Sears, interview by author, Boston, July 9, 2009.
[2] Ibid.

1988, Faith seemed to be motivated to push her limits. "It was the height of the Cold War. The stakes were high," she recalled.[3]

Whittlesey's commitment to her duties as U.S. ambassador led her to travel frequently for social occasions and speaking engagements all over Switzerland. Several embassy staff people who worked with Faith recalled her as a dynamic, energetic, and engaged ambassador. "She was always interested in getting the message out as effectively as possible," related Intelligence Officer Joseph Hayes.[4] DeLynn Henry, Whittlesey's secretary and a career federal government employee, remembered the ambassador "constantly thinking of things she had to do," even to the point of "giving me notes on a ski lift" during an embassy outing.[5] According to Richard Devine, an economics officer in the embassy and an acting deputy chief of mission for several months during her second tour, "She was very accessible—she was a very active ambassador."[6]

Faith viewed her mission—to increase the number of America's friends and diminish the number of its enemies—as an important component in Ronald Reagan's overall foreign policy vision. In addition to preserving and strengthening bilateral commercial, cultural, financial, and scientific ties, Whittlesey pursued four major areas of mutual interest between the two countries. First, in 1985, she used the media attention accorded President Reagan's meeting with Soviet Premier Mikhail Gorbachev in Geneva to demonstrate how Reagan's foreign policy principles were compatible with Swiss views of the world. Second, Whittlesey worked with Swiss businesses, the financial community, and the government to maintain vigorous trade without allowing excessive transfer of U.S. military-related technology to America's adversaries through Swiss borders. Third, Whittlesey urged stronger commercial and military ties between the two countries by promoting the sale of U.S. aircraft to both Swissair and the government of Switzerland. Fourth, she facilitated contacts between U.S. intelligence agents and Swiss political and financial elites. In Whittlesey's view, these four areas of potential agreement would help preserve her nation's position in the eyes of the Swiss as the world's primary military and economic power while at the same time maintaining moral legitimacy.

---

[3]   Faith Whittlesey, discussion with author, telephone, December 13, 2011.
[4]   Joseph Hayes, interview by author, McLean, VA, May 29, 2009.
[5]   DeLynn Henry, interview by author, Washington, DC, May 29, 2009.
[6]   Richard Devine, interview by author, Annapolis, MD, May 28, 2009.

GENEVA: AN ARMED, NEUTRAL HOST

In one of Faith's first assignments after returning to Switzerland in 1985, she met her counterpart—Ivan Ippolitov, the Soviet ambassador to Switzerland— at the Swiss Foreign Ministry in Bern.[7] The United States and the Soviet Union had engaged in a global competition since the close of World War II in 1945, and accordingly the two governments armed themselves with tens of thousands of nuclear warheads attached to various kinds of missiles—known in military terms as "delivery vehicles." Although President Reagan had characterized the Soviets as criminals in his first press conference in 1981 and as an "evil empire" in a 1983 speech, the U.S. president had also written Soviet General Secretary Konstantin Chernenko to request a direct dialogue with him. Upon Chernenko's death in 1985, Vice President George H. W. Bush attended the funeral and delivered a letter to his successor, Mikhail Gorbachev. The note included an invitation for the Soviet head of state to meet with Reagan in the United States.[8] As Reagan later recalled, "I wanted to convince Gorbachev that we wanted peace and they had nothing to fear from us."[9] After some negotiations, Gorbachev agreed to a bilateral summit, but the two heads of state had decided to meet in a neutral location—Geneva.

The choice of Switzerland was an important component in ensuring that the summit would occur at all. Some Reagan advisors had believed the president should insist on Washington as the location for any summit since the last two meetings between these two nations' leaders had been held in the Soviet Union. Moreover, U.S anticommunists had wanted Gorbachev to appear more anxious for an agreement by having to travel to American "turf." Perhaps for similar reasons, the Soviet premier suggested that Reagan come to the Soviet Union. U.S. Secretary of State George Shultz weighed in, suggesting that a U.S. *or* Soviet location would unrealistically raise public expectations for a major bilateral agreement. A neutral site alternatively promised to create a comfortable environment where the two leaders might initiate a path toward later agreements.[10]

---

[7]   Donnie Radcliffe, "Faith Whittlesey in Switzerland: Behind the Scenes as Ambassador," *Washington Post*, November 18, 1985, p. B4.

[8]   Jack F. Matlock, Jr., *Reagan and Gorbachev: How the Cold War Ended* (New York: Random House, 2004), p. 108.

[9]   Ronald Reagan, *An American Life: The Autobiography* (New York: Simon & Schuster, 1990), p. 12.

[10] Matlock, *Reagan and Gorbachev*, pp. 124–126.

Switzerland had established a centuries-old tradition of providing expert diplomatic "good offices" to belligerent parties and an equally long practice of strict political neutrality. These characteristics gave confidence to both the United States and the Soviet Union that they would receive even-handed treatment from their Swiss hosts. Switzerland's long-standing and internationally recognized commitment to disavowing military alliances had proved important to this nation's survival as a small independent member of the community of nations. During the 20th century, neutrality had helped the Swiss avoid invasion and the widespread destruction wrought by two world wars that raged in Europe. Geneva, in particular, had a venerable reputation as the international headquarters for many humanitarian and political organizations, such as the League of Nations, International Red Cross, the World Health Organization, and several United Nations missions. In 1985, U.S. and Soviet negotiators had already been working on arms control talks in that city for several years.

As a well-armed nation, furthermore, Switzerland offered excellent security. A high-profile meeting between heads of the world's two most powerful governments might well attract assassins or terrorists. But Switzerland's thoroughgoing military preparations to resist invasion served the needs of the superpowers. Whittlesey explained Switzerland's quiet, serious dedication to protecting citizens' safety to a *Washington Post* reporter in 1985: "Many Americans don't realize that Switzerland is one of the best defended nations in Europe. They think of the Swiss as neutral and of neutralism as pacifism." The Swiss military, Faith also noted, could mobilize one of the largest militia armies in Europe within 48 hours: "There are no conscientious objectors and every man keeps his rifle at home with him."[11] These factors heightened Switzerland's value as a secure venue.

THE SWISS, HUMAN RIGHTS, AND GOD

Despite Switzerland's nonaligned status, Whittlesey believed Reagan enjoyed a subtle strategic advantage by meeting with Gorbachev in that particular nation. Switzerland and the United States shared basic values, and Geneva offered fertile ground for advancing Reagan's foreign policy agenda. For example, despite Switzerland's political neutrality as a precept underlying its foreign policy, the Swiss were, by no means, morally neutral. Both Swiss and American citizens valued Judeo-Christian traditions and the

---

[11]   Radcliffe, "Faith Whittlesey in Switzerland," p. B4.

concept of morally ordered liberty under the rule of law. In Whittlesey's view, therefore, the United States should be able to persuade the Swiss that Americans understood and defended their commitment to political, economic, and religious freedom.

Since Soviet communism presumed to ensure equality of condition by limiting the individual's religious, economic, and political liberties, U.S. leaders could expect Swiss sympathy for Reagan's claim to defend basic freedoms, Faith believed. "It's a battle of ideas," Whittlesey averred.[12] The Swiss and Americans thus had a strong affinity for close cooperation even though Switzerland's historic neutrality prevented any formal alliance.

At the same time, Faith feared that the Soviets were gaining ground in the ideological struggle by portraying the United States as a nation of robber barons and President Reagan as a hyper-individualistic, selfish man ambitious for profit and power. Most Europeans recognized Soviet tactics as deceptive propaganda, but Reagan's image as a reckless cowboy capitalist persisted in Europe, including Switzerland. This widespread impression of Reagan alienated many Swiss and other Western Europeans, who feared that his policies might lead to a third world war in Europe. Whittlesey recognized the sophistication of Soviet messaging: "They're trying to convince Western Europe that its future stability lies with the Soviets rather than continued friendship with the United States."[13] In her view, therefore, the U.S. government needed to articulate a clear, sustained, credible American message, or else, more and more, the Swiss and other Europeans might choose to distance themselves from the United States. For this reason, upon returning to Switzerland in early 1985, Whittlesey endeavored to re-create the public information initiatives to promote Reagan's policies which she had begun during her first tour.

Leading up to the Geneva summit, however, the White House did not appear to be conveying the U.S. perspective on human rights effectively to the Swiss and other media sources covering the events. A presummit *Washington Post* article stated that Whittlesey "won't get into what she thinks about the administration's failure to dispatch an advance team of Americans to Geneva to counter the Soviets."[14] The reporter's observation of Whittlesey's reluctance signaled to the administration—without stating it

---

[12] Ibid.
[13] Ibid.
[14] Ibid.

directly—that they were failing to lay the public information groundwork for President Ronald Reagan's first meeting with his chief worldwide adversary, Soviet Premier Mikhail Gorbachev.

U.S. representatives had largely prepared for the meeting in administrative rather than issue-oriented ways. According to Jack Matlock, Reagan's chief advance man William Henkel focused on "every detail of imagery: where the press pool would be located so as to present Reagan in the most favorable light, what would be in the background of photographs, how to position Reagan to be seen as the dominant partner in the dialogue."[15] This presummit stage management certainly made a very positive impression for Reagan. Henkel's concept of starting a lighted fireplace to create a soothing backdrop for the two leaders became a defining photographic icon of what Reagan called the "fireside summit."[16] Some of Reagan's advisors suggested that the mere imagery of the two smiling leaders would reassure people that the president had no intention of starting another war in Europe. This picture, however, might also engender in some the impression that the president was too friendly and did not take seriously enough the Soviets' routine violations of human rights.

Worried about substance more than style, Whittlesey believed a capable advance team was needed to prepare the location intellectually as well as physically, and in particular she wanted to emphasize the differing conceptions of human dignity in these systems. In her view, there would be a contentious struggle to influence global public opinion at the summit. Soviet Premier Gorbachev had already fully committed himself to engage in this battle. In a presummit visit to Paris, Gorbachev granted several long interviews on French television and attempted to persuade the U.S. and Western publics that the Soviet Union, not the Reagan administration, truly promoted social justice and peace.[17] Whittlesey wondered whether Reagan's staff properly advised the president about how he might counter Gorbachev's public relations offensive, which clearly showed the Soviet leader's ambition to shape the summit's public diplomacy agenda in important ways.

Rather than publicly critiquing the Reagan administration, however, Faith tried to fill the void by speaking out on behalf of human rights herself.

---

[15]   Matlock, *Reagan and Gorbachev*, p. 147.
[16]   Ibid.
[17]   Ibid. Gorbachev also presented himself in a *Time* magazine interview as a charismatic, youthful leader. He could make persuasive arguments in unscripted encounters with Western media analysts and commentators.

Having spent two decades in politics, Whittlesey understood the importance of surrogates promoting the leader's ideas. As the date of the summit approached, she accepted every invitation to speak that she could. She also represented the administration's viewpoint by attending key events sponsored by groups dedicated to protesting Soviet restrictions on freedom. "To emphasize Reagan's position on human rights," the *Washington Post* reported, "she attended a benefit [on November 15] for the Russian Orthodox Church [in Geneva] with about 400 members of the Russian exiled community."[18]

On November 16, President Reagan finally landed on Swiss soil, and Faith was the first in the receiving line as he deplaned. Her mother, Amy Ryan, wrote her a letter expressing her excitement: "What a thrill [to] see you on TV last night as we watched Reagan's arrival in Geneva."[19] Mrs. Ryan also noted the news coverage, which clearly showed that vocal and aggressive anti-American protests continued to erupt in Switzerland: "The antinuclear parades and the burning of the U.S. flag [were] frightening and horrible to watch."[20]

Despite these signs of resistance to American power, Faith continued to subscribe to the concept that Switzerland and the United States were, in essence, "sister republics." In October 1981, upon submitting her credentials to Swiss President Kurt Furgler at the start of her first tour, Whittlesey had noted that the two nations shared a commitment to constitutional democratic government as well as economic and religious liberty.[21] Over the years, Furgler and Whittlesey developed a mutual respect for each other. She arranged for him to speak at Boston University's World Leaders' Summit in October 1985.[22]

When President Reagan met with Swiss President Furgler in Geneva, Faith was present. Her notes recorded that the two leaders expressed to each other across the table a common, profound commitment to their core belief in inalienable human rights deriving not from the state, but from God. Publicly rejecting the atheistic principles underlying Soviet communist philosophy,

---

[18] Radcliffe, "Faith Whittlesey in Switzerland," p. B4.
[19] Amy Ryan to Faith Whittlesey, November 17, 1985. Box 2, Folder 10. From the Faith Whittlesey Collection, Howard Gotlieb Archival Research Center at Boston University (hereafter referred to as FW).
[20] Ibid.
[21] "Remarks on presentation of credentials to Swiss President Furgler," October 23, 1981. See Box 23, Folder 11, FW.
[22] Furgler's remarks are available in Box 2, Folder 1, FW.

the two men solemnly affirmed their common dedication to the principle that human rights derive from spiritual rather than material roots.[23]

"STAR WARS," THE SOVIETS, AND THE SUMMIT

Whittlesey also worked discreetly to support Reagan's missile defense system, which emerged as the centerpiece subject in public debates about the summit. In March 1983, Reagan had announced that the U.S. government would begin research and development of a space-based system of lasers to target and destroy incoming enemy missiles. In the White House, Whittlesey had actively assisted the efforts of those who viewed this Strategic Defense Initiative (SDI) as, potentially at least, the key to victory in the Cold War.

In Geneva, SDI advocates defended Reagan from charges of warmongering by asserting that he sought military modernization chiefly to create "peace through strength." William Clark and other conservative supporters of the president had argued that SDI would ultimately force Soviet leaders into making concessions in disarmament discussions because the Soviets lacked sufficient technology to compete with such an ambitious program.[24] In November 1985, the Geneva summit offered a choice opportunity to test Clark's theory.

But, for this to happen, Reagan would have to resist pressures to abandon SDI not only from the Soviet leadership but also from liberal Democratic opponents in the United States. Liberals had long rejected Reagan's plan as fantasy, most famously when U.S. Senator Edward Kennedy mocked the president's "reckless Star Wars schemes" (in a reference to the popular *Star Wars* movie trilogy of the 1970s and 1980s).[25] The phrase captured the popular imagination, and many reporters (and soon the general public) came to use the term "star wars" instead of SDI when referring to the program. Opponents also portrayed SDI as dangerous. By granting the United States a "first-strike capability," claimed Soviet leader Gorbachev in 1985, "star wars" would generate insecurity and increase the likelihood of nuclear

---

[23] Whittlesey's handwritten notes are in Box 2, Folder 10, FW. Political scientist Paul Kengor has documented many similar examples of the U.S. president's consistently opposing communism's human rights violations on religious grounds, not merely as a strategic calculation. See both Paul Kengor, *God and Ronald Reagan: A Spiritual Life* (New York: Regan Books, 2004), and Paul Kengor, *The Crusader: Ronald Reagan and the Fall of Communism* (New York: Harper Perennial, 2006).

[24] Paul Kengor and Patricia Clark Doerner, *The Judge: William P. Clark, Ronald Reagan's Top Hand* (San Francisco: Ignatius Press, 2007), p. 201.

[25] Lou Cannon, "President Seeks Futuristic Defense Against Missiles," *Washington Post*, March 24, 1983, p. A1.

war.[26] The Soviets focused some 80 percent of their propaganda on SDI, according to a study conducted by Reagan's director of the Arms Control and Disarmament Agency.[27] While Reagan hoped SDI would provide him leverage in conversations with the Soviets, critics encouraged him to give it up. A few weeks prior to Reagan's departure for Geneva, longtime UPI White House correspondent Helen Thomas pointedly asked the president, "Will you negotiate Star Wars at all?"[28]

Whittlesey was determined to work against such an outcome. Upon greeting the president in Geneva, she had handed him a 54-page document containing arguments with supporting facts to counter the Soviet talking points on SDI, disarmament, and security issues.[29] It is unlikely that Reagan would have received this book without her intervention, she was certain. Faith did not seek prior approval of the State Department: "After all, I reported directly to the president as ambassador."[30] Produced by the nonprofit conservative Heritage Foundation, this unofficial "briefing book" provided the president with "ready ammunition" to rebut Soviet claims relating to their vaunted positions on peace, individual freedoms, and human rights.[31] Such well-researched factual data and analysis could prove important in the high-level one-on-one debate characteristic of bilateral summits. Whittlesey understood that Reagan's private deliberations with Gorbachev would have public consequences, and she was determined to help the U.S. president advance a clear and powerful message in whatever way she could.

In one measure of the impact of Whittlesey's intervention, Gorbachev reportedly complained to President Reagan about this Heritage book. Richard Allen, who had served as Reagan's national security advisor from 1981 to 1982, told the media that the Soviet leader raised the subject of the publication during the first 10 minutes of the initial United States–Soviet group meeting on November 19. According to Allen's account (which he claimed

---

[26] Matlock, *Reagan and Gorbachev*, p. 122.
[27] Ken Adelman, quoted in Stephen K. Knott and Jeffrey L. Chidester, *At Reagan's Side: Insiders' Recollections from Sacramento to the White House* (Lanham, MD: Rowman and Littlefield, 2009), p. 105.
[28] Paul Kengor, *Dupes: How America's Adversaries Have Manipulated Progressives for a Century* (Wilmington, DE: Intercollegiate Studies Institute, 2010), p. 416.
[29] Philip M. Boffey, "Heritage Foundation: Success in Obscurity," *New York Times*, November 17, 1985, p. 62.
[30] Faith Whittlesey, discussion with author, telephone, December 13, 2011.
[31] Ibid.

to have received from someone present at the meeting), Gorbachev cited the manuscript as proof of "right-wing pressure" on the summit proceedings.[32]

Although the Soviet leader disparaged such interest-group activism, Faith considered public advocacy as the foundation of a healthy democracy. In her political career, she had consistently recruited Americans to participate more actively in the political process. True to form, Whittlesey distributed 100 copies of Heritage's briefing book in Geneva.[33] This action boosted the spirits of conservatives, many of whom believed that moderates had nearly exclusive access to the president's ear in 1985, especially after the departure of Clark, Edwin Meese, Jeane Kirkpatrick, and Whittlesey from the White House. Several leaders of the interest groups which had helped elect Reagan began to question the administration's continued commitment to a strong anticommunist foreign policy.[34] But Whittlesey worked to reassure many of the president's advisors and supporters who worried that Reagan might, under the weight of negotiations, back off on his previously stated goals.

Certain administration officials insisted that Reagan could secure a reputation as a peacemaker by making concessions to reduce the stress and strain on Gorbachev. But the Heritage briefing book buttressed the president's goal of maintaining consistent pressure on the Soviet Union to abandon its totalitarian system. Faith had also helped Heritage attract some good publicity, such as a November 17 feature in the *New York Times* which touted Heritage's "Success in Obscurity."[35]

Despite condemning "right-wing" meddling in the summit, the Soviet leader appeared more than willing to egg on American left-wing interest groups in their calls for the U.S. president to remove SDI from the negotiating table. Between sessions during the summit's first day of formal talks (November 19), Gorbachev spoke publicly with American activist Jesse Jackson at the Soviet mission in Geneva.[36] Given Jackson's outspoken critique of Reagan and SDI during his 1984 bid for the Democratic Party presidential nomination, Gorbachev saw an opportunity to weaken Reagan's bargaining position by highlighting internal U.S. divisions about "star wars." To

---

[32] James F. Clarity, "Briefing: Summit Excitement," *New York Times*, November 27, 1985, p. 6.
[33] Ibid.
[34] See John M. Goshko and Lou Cannon, "Kirkpatrick to Quit Government," *Washington Post*, January 31, 1985, p. A1; and Elizabeth Kastor, "The Right Angles; Talking Politics at the McDonald Dinner Conservatives," *Washington Post*, January 9, 1985, p. D1.
[35] Boffey, "Heritage Foundation," p. 62.
[36] Joseph Lelyveld, "Jackson, in Impromptu Session, Presses Gorbachev on Soviet Jews," *New York Times*, November 20, 1985, p. A1.

Gorbachev's delight, Jackson brought 45 U.S. peace activists, who decried Reagan's military modernization as destabilizing to global security.[37]

It soon became clear that Gorbachev wanted actual, or implicit, support from Jackson in the Soviets' efforts to disparage SDI.[38] Despite Jackson's best efforts to make him account for Soviet violations of Jewish human rights, Gorbachev proceeded "to hammer home his positions against the U.S. Strategic Defense Initiative."[39] When the Soviet leader finally acknowledged Jackson's questions about individual liberties, he merely dodged them by saying that "the so-called problem of Jews in the Soviet Union does not exist."[40]

Who would the world trust—Gorbachev or Reagan? Switzerland's small city of a few hundred thousand inhabitants had temporarily become a global public relations battleground.

THE GENDER WARS IN GENEVA

Owing to Whittlesey's continued close connections with U.S. interest groups, she learned that Phyllis Schlafly, president of Eagle Forum, had organized a delegation of SDI supporters to demonstrate in Geneva on behalf of the president's policy. Schlafly had written five books and spoken extensively on the subject of U.S.-Soviet relations since the 1960s.

Schlafly came to Geneva to counteract the Committee for a SANE Nuclear Policy, one of the groups which accompanied Jackson to the Soviet mission on November 19. SANE leaders had created a coalition of more than 30 feminists (including such well-known individuals as former U.S. Congresswoman Bella Abzug and Oscar-nominated actress Jane Alexander) who traveled to Geneva under the title Women for a Meaningful Summit to demonstrate for an immediate halt, or freeze, to the manufacture of nuclear weapons.[41] In Schlafly's view, SANE threatened the president's plan to demonstrate U.S. resolve through military preparedness, including provision for increased missile security in Europe. Schlafly believed that

---

[37] Robert W. Merry and Frederick Kempe, "U.S., Soviet Officials Are Upbeat As the Summit Gets Under Way—But Gorbachev Creates Stir by Meeting With Jackson, Peace Activists," *Wall Street Journal*, November 20, 1985, p. 1.

[38] Steven Erlanger, "Jackson Meets Gorbachev, Says Disarmament the Issue," *Boston Globe*, November 20, 1985, p. 25.

[39] Merry and Kempe, "U.S., Soviet Officials Are Upbeat as the Summit Gets Under Way," p. 1.

[40] Ibid.

[41] Donald T. Critchlow, *Phyllis Schlafly and Grassroots Conservatism: A Woman's Crusade* (Princeton, NJ: Princeton University Press, 2005), p. 291.

these left-wing protestors would "basically back up Gorbachev."[42] Anti-SDI protests strengthened the Soviet leader's arguments that Reagan's policy threatened global peace and stability, she believed.[43]

About 40 women traveled with Schlafly to form a group they called Women for a Real Defense.[44] "Specifically designed, presented, and advertised" to the media as an alternative women's voice, they pursued equal time in the summit's media spotlight to argue in support of Reagan.[45] Schlafly's colleagues included Florida conservative activist Alyse O'Neill and Elaine Donnelly, a member of the Defense Department Advisory Committee on Women in the Services.

Schlafly recalled that Jesse Jackson had refused to allow Women for a Real Defense to attend his press conference in Geneva. Nonetheless, they held their own meetings with reporters, made themselves available for interviews, and demonstrated in the park with pro-SDI signs and balloons.[46] These "elegantly dressed articulate ladies," Whittlesey recalled, ensured that opponents of Reagan's policy did not totally dominate discussion of the summit among opinion makers and the general public.[47]

Faith actively offered her support to the Schlafly effort. Donnelly especially recalled the warmth of Whittlesey's reception at the airport in the cold, snow-capped Swiss city. Schlafly found Whittlesey "extremely helpful in guiding us around Geneva."[48] These personal connections helped the group contend with their busy schedule. On November 16, Faith attended a luncheon with the Schlafly group. After they held an official press conference at Geneva's Noga Hilton Hotel on the 17th, Whittlesey hosted a party (at Senator John Tower's Geneva residence, where her own staff was staying during the summit) to recognize in a formal way the contributions of Women for a Real Defense to achieving the administration's foreign policy goals in Geneva.[49]

Donnelly considered it important that Whittlesey invited the delegation to receptions where she and the other women could interact with media figures such as the influential network broadcasters Tom Brokaw and Peter

---

[42] Phyllis Schlafly, interview by author, telephone, November 23, 2010.
[43] Ibid.
[44] Critchlow, *Phyllis Schlafly*, p. 291.
[45] Phyllis Schlafly, interview by author, telephone, November 23, 2010.
[46] Ibid. See also Critchlow, *Phyllis Schlafly*, p. 291.
[47] Faith Whittlesey, discussion with author, telephone, December 13, 2011.
[48] Phyllis Schlafly, interview by author, telephone, November 23, 2010.
[49] Phyllis Schlafly, email to author, November 26, 2010; Faith Whittlesey, discussion with author, telephone, December 13, 2011.

Jennings, to whom they could communicate their message.[50] Faith further facilitated Women for a Real Defense's publicity efforts by inviting these women to her Bern residence, where they could engage directly with many prominent Swiss government and business leaders.

At a time when reporters continued to scrutinize the administration's popularity with women, Faith's introductions of Schlafly's group to prominent U.S. news commentators and media spokesmen proved especially significant. Following a 1984 election campaign in which many feminist groups had predicted incorrectly that women would vote as a bloc against Reagan, allegations of female displeasure with the administration naturally attracted special attention from the press. Two months prior to the summit, the *Wall Street Journal* quoted several of Reagan's senior female officials—including Whittlesey—who expressed the belief that some of the president's staff did not accept women as equals.[51]

In this information context, the president's new chief of staff, Donald Regan, all but confirmed the perception of White House insensitivity to female opinions. When asked about the meeting between Ronald Reagan's wife Nancy and Raisa Gorbachev, the wife of the Soviet premier, the chief of staff downplayed the role of women, saying, "They're not going to understand [missile] throw weights, or what is happening in Afghanistan or what is happening in human rights." Regan's subsequent statement that "most women … would rather read the human interest stuff" definitely contributed to the widespread impression that the White House was marginalizing females' opinions. By appearing to belittle women's interest in foreign policy, Regan unintentionally reignited the lingering embers of the gender gap issue. More importantly, these comments distracted the media from the president's summit agenda.[52]

Fortunately for the president, Faith and Women for a Real Defense counteracted the perception that the administration was an all-male preserve by earnestly defending SDI and Reagan. Moreover, the attention-grabbing nature of the story encouraged reporters to interview the engaging and

---

[50] Elaine Donnelly, interview by author, telephone, July 26, 2010. As noted in Chapter 4, these powerful spokesmen for the mainstream U.S. TV media had a near-monopoly on setting the information agenda for the American public through their selection of content for the dinnertime nightly newscasts.

[51] Amy E. Schwartz, "'She Is No Executive': They said it about Frances Perkins and they've been saying it about women in high office ever since," *Washington Post*, October 15, 1985, p. A23.

[52] Elizabeth Kastor, "Regan Gets Summit Glare," *Washington Post*, November 21, 1985, p. A29. See also Ellen Goodman, "Woman's Place at the Summit," *Washington Post*, November 30, 1985, p. A27.

knowledgeable women who came to Geneva *in support of* Reagan's policies.[53] The ready availability of Schlafly's group also enabled reporters to
redirect discussion to the president's message—and away from whether or
not women were being treated fairly by his senior staff.

Most importantly, Whittlesey's access to Reagan allowed her to inform
him about Schlafly's activities. The president called Schlafly to thank her
personally for traveling to Geneva in support of his policies: "[Reagan] was
very grateful that we were backing him up because he always did believe
that SDI was absolutely essential."[54] Whittlesey's success in keeping the
president aware of Women for a Real Defense and giving him the Heritage
Foundation materials may well have strengthened his resolve not to compromise on SDI. By working to demonstrate that SANE did not speak for
a majority of American women, Schlafly and Whittlesey also contributed
to building public confidence about Reagan's peaceful intentions, helping
to counterbalance European perceptions of American foreign policy as
militaristic and bellicose.

Reagan remained committed to resisting the USSR without compromise,
and his refusal to bargain away the SDI program thoroughly frustrated
Gorbachev, who recognized Reagan's superior leverage and thus desper-
ately sought to rebalance the argument. In 1997, political scientist Andrew
Busch asserted that SDI was one of the primary causes for the fall of the
Soviet Union.[55]

The Soviets' abject failure to develop even *the pretense* of a comparable
high-technology counterprogram enabled Reagan to negotiate from a position of relative strength. During Faith's second tour in Switzerland, she played
a role in maintaining this wide gap between U.S. and Soviet know-how.

CURBING TECHNOLOGY TRANSFERS

As the Soviets faced the prospect of falling further behind relative to the
United States in military modernization, they sought to obtain and import
America's high-tech products through third-party countries. But President
Reagan, from the beginning of his first term, had acted to suppress any

---

[53] For example, Schlafly was quoted in Kastor, "Regan Gets Summit Glare," p. A29.
[54] Phyllis Schlafly, interview by author, telephone, November 23, 2010. See also Critchlow, *Phyllis Schlafly*, p. 291.
[55] Andrew E. Busch, "Ronald Reagan and the Defeat of the Soviet Empire," *Presidential Studies Quarterly* 27, no. 3 (1997): 451–461.

"Remember,
Ginger Rogers did
everything
Fred Astaire did,
but she did it
backwards
and in high heels."

FAITH WHITTLESEY

First campaign for the
Pennsylvania legislature, 1972.

"New Look" Council Members Charles Keeler and Faith Whittlesey enter
Delaware County courthouse in Media, Pennsylvania, to take charge of the
Delaware County Council, 1976.

Faith, noticeably pregnant with her third child William, on the campaign trail for the Pennsylvania House in 1972.

Faith and husband Roger with children Henry and Amy and Swiss mother's helper Edith Conrad McCartney, Avalon, New Jersey.

Faith's parents Amy Covell Ryan and Martin Roy Ryan, circa 1977.

Faith's husband Roger Weaver Whittlesey, circa 1972.

Bulletin Photo by Salvatore C. DiMarco Jr.

Delaware County Councilwoman Faith Ryan Whittlesey introduces President Ford at the Valley Forge Music Fair.

Faith supported Governor Ronald Reagan's challenge to President Gerald Ford for the Republican Party presidential nomination in 1976. But after the convention delegates nominated the president, she campaigned for Ford's election.

Faith introducing presidential candidate Ronald Reagan with Nancy at the Folcroft Firehouse in Delaware County, Pennsylvania, Reagan's first campaign stop after declaring his candidacy in New York City in late November 1979. Upper Darby Mayor Sonny Kane is in background on the right. *Photo by Bill Wilson © 2011.*

Polling the Pennsylvania delegation at the 1980 Republican National Convention in Detroit.

U.S. Chief of Protocol Lee Annenberg at left directs Faith's installation as U.S. ambassador to Switzerland at swearing-in ceremony in the State Department in Washington, DC, as children Henry, Amy, and Will look on, September 1981.

William Scranton III, Faith's rival for lieutenant governor of Pennsylvania in 1978, attended her installation and offered words of congratulations.

Fellow Pennsylvanians U.S. Secretary of Transportation Drew Lewis (far left) and U.S. Senator Arlen Specter at the swearing-in ceremony.

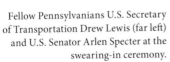

Whittlesey family portrait. Faith, Henry (15), Amy (13), William (8), 1980.

U.S. Embassy Residence, Bern, Switzerland, about 1981.

Former Iranian Ambassador to the U.S. Ardeshir Zahedi at right, at embassy reception; in the background at far right, E. Luk Keller, chairman of the Swiss daily newspaper *Neue Zürcher Zeitung (NZZ)*.

Faith participated in Art in Embassies program with the Pennsylvania Academy of the Fine Arts.

Embassy receiving line. Faith greets Swiss diplomat Raymond Loretan. At right U.S. Defense Attaché Colonel William Serchak.

In Commemoration of the 209th Anniversary
of the Independence of the United States of America

Ambassador Faith Ryan Whittlesey

requests the pleasure of your company
at a Fourth of July Celebration

on Thursday, July 4, 1985 from 12:30 p.m. to 2:30 p.m.

R.S.V.P.   Rainmattstrasse 21
031-43 73 21 / 43 72 74   3005 Berne, Switzerland

Please present this card at the entrance

July 4th celebration, U.S. Embassy Bern, 1985. Faith broke with tradition and served hot dogs, hamburgers, and fudge sundaes to 400 guests. *(Top)* Invitation. *(Middle)* Marines appeared in dress uniform for occasion. *(Bottom)* Kitchen and volunteer wait staff numbered more than 20.

U.S. Securities and Exchange Commission (SEC) Chairman John Shad representing the United States and Ambassador Jean Zwahlen representing Switzerland shake hands at signing of Memorandum of Understanding in Washington, DC, 1982. Faith was a key player in negotiations that led to the first agreement between the two nations on banking secrecy laws. At rear, SEC Director of Enforcement John Fedders. In front, SEC Counsel Edward Greene.

Mixing with the Swiss. *(Left)* In the piano room of the embassy residence, Faith plays as Swiss friends Margot and Annina Bodmer and Egon Zehnder and his two sons sing along. *(Right)* E. Luk Keller, chairman of Switzerland's most influential daily newspaper known as "the *NZZ*," enjoys conversation and skiing with Faith and son Will in Arosa in the Swiss Alps.

Leaning over the president's desk, "Mr. President, can you read my handwriting?" Oval Office, 1983.

Oval Office, 1984.

Whittlesey family. Faith with Henry, Amy, and William on White House steps.

Some of the White House Office of Public Liaison staff of 39 in Faith's West Wing office. Left to right, Douglas A. Riggs, Marguerite Fry, Mary Ann Meloy, Trudy Morrison, Mary Jo Jacobi-Jephson, Linas Kojelis, Susan Graf.

Faith Ryan Whittlesey
Assistant to the President
for Public Liaison

The White House
Washington, D.C. 20500   (202) 456-2270

White House Cabinet Room meeting with President Reagan. Seated left to right, Reverend Jerry Falwell, Secretary of State George Shultz, President Reagan, Chief of Staff James Baker, and Faith. Special Assistant to the President Robert Reilly is in the background.

Peppi Wister of Philadelphia, showing off a gift jar of President Reagan's favorite candy, jelly beans, honored Faith at a luncheon in her home. Foreground: Julie Nixon Eisenhower.

National Journal

THE WEEKLY ON POLITICS AND GOVERNMENT   APRIL 30, 1983/NO. 18

Contracting Out
Budget Bloodletting

Wooing
the Working
Class
FAITH RYAN WHITTLESEY

Faith struggled to recruit and maintain support of Main Street "Reagan Democrats" and other working-class Americans who espoused Reagan's conservative values and foreign policy positions.

Reception in honor of Faith at the home of media magnate Rupert Murdoch in Manhattan. *(Above)* Rupert Murdoch at left with New York City Mayor Ed Koch, a Democrat. *(Right)* New York Archbishop John Cardinal O'Connor. *(Below)* Cardinal O'Connor in conversation with Faith and neoconservative intellectual Irving Kristol.

(Left) Faith with National Security Advisor William Clark at left and U.S. Senator Orin Hatch of Utah. *(Middle)* U.S. Congressman Bud Shuster of Pennsylvania. *(Bottom)* Morton Blackwell, who worked with Faith in the White House Office of Public Liaison as a special assistant to the president.

President Reagan meeting with senior aides in the Executive Office Building: Faith is on the right in the front row; Chief of Staff Don Regan is seated in the middle.

Faith, circa 1988, as she returned from Bern and began to work full-time in the private sector.

(Above) Faith with National Football League star Roosevelt Grier at left and U.S. Congressman Phil Crane (R-IL) at dinner honoring U.S. Senator Jesse Helms (R-NC). (Right) Senator Helms and Faith applaud Charlton Heston who spoke at the dinner.

Faith led a delegation of Reagan women to the lift-off of the first woman astronaut Sally Ride at Cape Canaveral on June 18, 1983. Judith A. Buckalew is on the left next to a NASA official. Susan Graf and Mary Jo Jacobi-Jephson are to the right.

Faith was the first to welcome President Reagan as he deplaned from Air Force One in Geneva for the summit with Soviet leader Mikhail Gorbachev in November 1985.

To Faith Whittlesey
With admiration and best wishes,
Ken Dam

National Security Advisor Robert McFarlane, former Secretary of State Henry Kissinger, and Faith listen to Deputy Secretary of State Kenneth Dam at White House briefing. U.S. Ambassador to Brazil Tony Motley is on the far right.

Q & A in Basel, Switzerland. Faith traveled throughout the country to address audiences and also made herself available for interviews as part of her public diplomacy mission to spread the administration's foreign policy message to audiences beyond the Swiss government.

(Left) Faith at 1985 summit in Geneva with U.S. Arms Control and Disarmament Director Kenneth Adelman at the center and USIA Director Charles Wick.

(Below) Faith at the summit with Foreign Service officer James Fees at left and White House staffer Barbara Hayward, Republicans Abroad President John McCarthy of Geneva, and President of Eagle Forum Phyllis Schlafly.

Skiing in St. Moritz with Vice
Chairman of the Republican
Jewish Coalition George Klein.

At New York party with U.S. Ambassador to Austria
Ron Lauder and his mother Estée Lauder.

Faith with Cuban Americans in Miami, at event organized by Carlos Perez (fourth from left).

Assistant Susan Graf and Faith on the South Portico
of the White House.

Sing-along at the end of the evening at the home of Erna and Paul Jolles in Bern. Left to right, Erna Jolles, Jean Pierre Cuoni (currently the president of EFG International), Dr. Paul Jolles, and Dr. Francis Pribula of Geneva. Dr. Jolles was chairman of Nestlé and a former high-ranking Swiss diplomat and state secretary of Switzerland.

(Left) Dancing with Swiss president, Federal Councilor Kurt Furgler.

(Below) Learning Swiss songs from a Swiss president, Federal Councilor Jean-Pascal Delamuraz.

Dining with Credit Suisse CEO Rainer Gut at left and Swiss businessman Jean-Pierre Bruderer in Zürich.

Chairman and President of the Swiss-American Chamber of Commerce Quincy Hunsicker in Zürich.

Faith's favorite pastime in Switzerland—skiing in the glorious Swiss Alps.

Daughter Amy weds in New York City. Reception at the Union Club, September 29, 1989.

Faith with former U.S. Attorney General Ed Meese at right, who had been one of her conservative allies during her White House days, and then son-in-law George D. O'Neill, Jr., circa 1991.

Family gathering at the funeral of Faith's mother Amy Covell Ryan in Lake Wales, Florida, October 1996. Left to right, son William, nephews Sam Ryan and Lt. Ben Ryan (U.S. Navy Seals), son Henry, and brother Tom Ryan.

Testimonial dinner in Washington, DC, 2003, brought almost 200 friends and colleagues together to honor Faith. Left to right, Chris Manion, Louise Oliver, Dolf Droge, Patricia Schramm, James Price, Faith, Kelly Waering, Gene Waering, Cathi Cremaldi, Pauline Price, Cosmo Cremaldi, Peppi Wister, and Nancy Price.

The 2001 Young Leaders Conference was sponsored by Holcim at Bad Ragaz, Switzerland. Faith joins Holcim Chairman Thomas Schmidheiny at right and Young Leaders including James Hauslein at left, founder and former CEO of Sunglass Hut, for breakfast.

Faith in conversation with Holcim Vice Chairman Anton Schrafl at right and Young Leader Michael Sullivan, who had served two terms as mayor of Cambridge, Massachusetts.

American Swiss Foundation Young Leaders Conference, 2005, visit to Swiss Parliament. Left to right, Nancy Price of Pennsylvania, Stefan Altner of Bank Julius Bär, Hon. Scott Nishimoto of Hawaii, Mario Armstrong of Baltimore, Faith, Gabriela Lippe-Holst of Swiss Re, Hon. Adam Hasner of Florida, and Hon. Frank Lasee of Wisconsin.

Nestlé Chairman and CEO Peter Brabeck-Lemathe, the Union League Club, New York, 2006.

Ambassador Jean Zwahlen, who later became a member of the governing board of the Swiss National Bank, was the Swiss negotiator of the historic 1982 Memorandum of Understanding on insider trading and banking secrecy.

This group photo of 2007 American Swiss Foundation Young Leaders Conference in Thun, Switzerland, was typical of the conferences moderated by Faith annually since the program's inauguration in 1990, a year after she became chairman and president of the American Swiss Foundation. Fifty participants—roughly half American and half Swiss—aged late 20s to 40, attend the bipartisan conference held in Switzerland for one week.

The American Swiss Foundation annual dinner in 2001 featured U.S. Secretary of Health and Human Services Tommy Thompson of Wisconsin at left. Dr. David Wolf of Cornell Medical College and UBS Executive Vice Chairman Alberto Togni of Zürich also attended.

Faith with former Young Leader Chris Ruddy, CEO of Newsmax Media, in Mr. Ruddy's office with Alaska Governor Sarah Palin in West Palm Beach, 2010.

Ambassador (and U.S. Brigadier General) Patrick Jay Hurley (second from left) flanked by Chinese leaders Chou En-lai at left and Mao Tse-tung, standing in front of Whittlesey Hall in Yan'an, August 1945. To the present day, Captain Whittlesey is a hero in China for his role in the U.S. government's Dixie Mission, discussed in Chapter 9. He was shot by Japanese soldiers in 1944, the only member of the U.S. mission killed in action.

The American Council of Young Political Leaders delegation to China in 1979 included Faith and also later-to-be U.S. Senators Kit Bond of Missouri to her left and Charles Robb of Virginia at rear center. Zhang Zhijun, standing between Bond and Robb, was the group's driver and translator. By 2012 Zhang Zhijun had become Vice Foreign Minister of China. "The Chinese always assigned their brightest young people to escort dignitaries, even sometimes serving in lower positions, for their training and to make contacts. This is an aspect of Chinese education we might want to note and perhaps even emulate," Faith later commented.

Faith teaching the popular American "Hokey Pokey" song and dance routine to the Chinese, 1979. U.S. Congresswoman Barbara Rose Collins of Michigan is third from the right; in foreground is Peter McPherson, director of USAID under Reagan. Later-U.S. Senator Kit Bond of Missouri is next to Congresswoman Collins.

Faith led the first all-Republican delegation to China in 1994, which included former U.S. Senator Roger Jepson at left. Zhang Zhijun on the far right was designated by the Chinese as the group's translator. By 2012, as Vice Foreign Minister of China, he was the #2 man in the Foreign Ministry.

President Hu Jintao of China greets Faith in Beijing at the 60th anniversary dinner marking China's victory over Japan in World War II in 2005. At right is Colonel John Easterbrook, grandson of General Joseph Stilwell, who commanded U.S. troops in the China-Burma-India theater during World War II.

Former American Swiss Foundation Young Leader and President of the Brooklyn Botanic Garden Scot D. Medbury presents Faith with new tea rose named for her at dinner at Union League Club in New York, 2006. *(Right)* Cover of September–October 2012 *American Rose* magazine featured a drawing of the 'Faith Whittlesey'™ rose by artist Maria Cecilia Freeman.

Nicole and William Whittlesey with children Charles (12), Jack (10), Will, Jr. (9), and Mary Aza (6), Sherborn, Massachusetts, 2012.

Ellen and Henry Whittlesey, Cambridge, Massachusetts, 2012.

Faith with her youngest of 10 grandchildren, Joseph Ryan Whittlesey (6), Boynton Beach, Florida, 2012.

indirect transfer of strategic equipment to the Soviet bloc. During the mid-1980s, the administration tightened export controls with even greater rigor.

Owing to her previous experience in the White House, Whittlesey maintained contacts with the administration's highest-level officials, and she thus understood Reagan's strong views on this issue. Recognizing that neutral Switzerland had no treaty obligations to help the U.S. government investigate and prevent illicit third-party transactions, Whittlesey nonetheless appreciated the Swiss desire to maintain friendly relations as well as the free flow of economic exchange with the United States. Her efforts to find a mutually amicable solution to this bilateral disagreement proved important for both nations.

Since 1981, the Reagan administration had taken several steps to confront head-on those countries and groups which threatened U.S. security by transferring high-level technology to America's sworn enemies. In early 1981, Assistant Secretary of Defense Richard Perle received a CIA report that the Soviet Union had created more than 5,000 weapons systems which depended upon technology obtained from Western countries.[56] Working with North Atlantic Treaty Organization member governments, the United States attempted to strengthen the power of CoCom (the Coordinating Committee for Multilateral Export Controls) to regulate technology transfer in NATO countries. During the hot summer of 1984, CoCom had expanded the embargo lists it had created. Law enforcement officials could clearly identify the threat to national security whenever a U.S. adversary bought nuclear materials or a machine tool specifically designed to create state-of-the-art submarine propellers.[57]

The United States also led worldwide in the research and production of "dual-use" innovations—such as computer microchips—which had both consumer and military applications. Hand-held computer games contained semiconductor chips which could also be used to improve accuracy in weapons' targeting capabilities, even for nuclear missiles.[58] CoCom now sought to limit exports of "computer software, telecommunications equipment, and small military-relevant computers" to the Soviet bloc nations.[59]

---

[56] Richard Perle, "Foreword," in Seth Cropsey, *A New Balance in the New Economy* (Washington: AEI Press, 2001), p. viii.
[57] Peter Schweizer, *Victory: The Reagan Administration's Secret Strategy That Hastened the Collapse of the Soviet Union* (New York: Atlantic Monthly Press, 1994), p. 200.
[58] Daniel Harris, interview by author, Paris, August 24, 2009.
[59] Schweizer, *Victory*, p. 200.

The United States needed to protect such dual-use technology—along with standard military equipment—from passing into Soviet hands, in Perle's view. This initiative supported President Reagan's widespread efforts to find nonmilitary means of undermining Soviet power.[60]

When CoCom member nations agreed to prevent the transfer of Western technology to the Soviet Union and its allies through third-party nations, this decision threatened to reduce U.S. trade with Switzerland. In the mid-1980s, several *Time* magazine stories suggested that the Swiss could not prevent the proliferation of technology transfer to America's enemies without U.S. law enforcement assistance. In April 1983, *Time* had reported that the commercial attaché in Bern prevented the purchase by the Soviets of two particularly sophisticated U.S.-produced machines for making microcircuits. The Reagan administration believed this technology could have enhanced Soviet weapons systems.[61] Switzerland had been the inadvertent conduit for nuclear proliferation materials, according to another *Time* story which claimed that U.S. officials worked to try to prevent Libyan dictator Muammar Gaddafi from obtaining nuclear-related technology via the Swiss nation.[62] In June 1985, on the heels of Whittlesey's Senate confirmation for a second tour as ambassador, *Time* claimed that U.S. marshals apprehended a suspect who allegedly transported a state-of-the-art VAX II/780 mainframe computer to Czechoslovakia via Switzerland.[63]

As one of Whittlesey's mandates in Bern, therefore, she leveraged the full weight of the embassy's personnel to implement a reduction of technology transfers effectuated through Switzerland. Complicating the issue somewhat, the Swiss were themselves world leaders in the development of highly advanced technologies. Nonetheless, administration officials were determined to put an immediate end to sensitive high-tech transfers. It was rumored that if the Swiss could not prevent the release of high-value and dual-use technology to U.S. adversaries, the American government might decide to limit (or regulate heavily) U.S. exports to, and commercial cooperation with, Switzerland.[64]

Swiss neutrality prevented the United States from creating a system of formal export controls through Switzerland. But the Swiss had conceded to

---

[60]   Busch, "Ronald Reagan," 451–455.
[61]   "Switzerland: Short Circuit," *Time,* April 25, 1983, p. 41.
[62]   "Switzerland: Sheik Down," *Time,* March 21, 1983, p. 60.
[63]   Evan Thomas, "Moles Who Burrow for Microchips," *Time,* June 17, 1985, p. 25.
[64]   Faith Whittlesey, discussion with author, telephone, December 13, 2011.

U.S. pressure and signed on to abide by several CoCom regulations relating to "strategic" exports in the secret Hotz-Linder Agreement (whose provisions were not revealed publicly until after the Cold War ended) of July 1951.[65]

The Swiss government, however, never explicitly recognized any political or legal obligations to prevent sensitive U.S. technologies from passing to the Soviet Union or other nations which had unfriendly relations with the United States. According to Intelligence Officer Hayes, "This was not a major security concern for them or for their country, but it was a major security concern for us." In the absence of any Swiss law preventing the sale of these technologies, U.S. officials remained convinced that financial incentives would inevitably tempt Swiss companies to ignore U.S. pleas for stricter limits on the transfer of weapons-based and dual-use technology to America's adversaries. According to James Shinn, DCM in the Bern embassy from 1982 to 1986, "The Swiss are a very export-oriented country, and they produce high-technology machinery and equipment which they'd like to sell, and frequently their business community would like to sell it wherever they can find a buyer."[66] These divergent American and Swiss interests created considerable tension because U.S. efforts to regulate Switzerland's imports and exports appeared to the Swiss as an obvious infringement of sovereignty.

Whittlesey's return to Bern in 1985 led to a noticeable shift in the embassy's approach to technology transfer. Aware that pressure exerted by U.S. law enforcement agents on the Swiss might damage the bilateral relationship and the substantial commercial exchanges between the two nations, Faith decided to mobilize sufficient staff time and resources to find a mutually agreeable solution. Commerce Officer Daniel Harris viewed Whittlesey's arrival as "a very positive change."[67]

As she had done frequently during her political career, Faith evaluated the personnel resources. The embassy's ECON officer appeared to her unable or unwilling to implement a more activist approach to technology transfer negotiations.[68] Whittlesey identified Harris as an individual who would

---

[65] Jürg Martin Gabriel, "The Price of Political Uniqueness: Swiss Foreign Policy in a Changing World," in *Swiss Foreign Policy, 1945–2002*, eds. Jürg Martin Gabriel and Thomas Fischer (New York: Palgrave Macmillan, 2003), p. 12.

[66] James Shinn, interview by author, Kensington, CA, March 16, 2010.

[67] Daniel Harris, interview by author, Paris, August 24, 2009.

[68] Faith Whittlesey, discussion with author, telephone, December 13, 2011. See also Faith Whittlesey, interview by Ann Miller Morin, December 7, 1989. Frontline Diplomacy, Manuscript Division, Library of Congress, Washington, DC. Dan Harris also "noticed that technology transfer was a very important issue which the ECON section was not handling in a very dynamic fashion." Daniel Harris, interview by author, Paris, August 24, 2009.

find a solution if given greater responsibility for technology transfer. Since Harris' superiors in the Commercial section also recognized the geostrategic and financial importance of this issue, they allowed him the time to pay more attention to this challenging matter.

Despite Harris' demonstrated ability, he recognized that Whittlesey took a significant risk in granting him extensive authority for this complex and important issue. Harris had come to the Commerce Department with a wide-ranging skill set. In addition to his being fluent in French, German, and Spanish, he had worked for such large corporations as Bell Telephone and the British chemical giant Imperial Chemical Industries. But his valuable "real-world experience" did not negate the fact that—in government bureaucratic parlance—he still remained strictly a "first-tour officer."[69]

Nonetheless Faith assigned near-total control of the technology transfer area to Harris. In Harris' view, this demonstration of trust in him was "rather astonishing, and it's probably not something that a career ambassador would have done."[70] This would be neither the first nor the last time that Faith would elevate a capable young person to sudden leadership status.

To explain the full significance of Whittlesey's decision, Harris detailed the wide-ranging responsibilities which she granted him. The ambassador had asked him to manage "all three threads of the technology transfer portfolio—the commercial aspect, enforcement, and policy." In the first area, commerce, Harris was assigned the duty of articulating the delicate balance that the U.S. government sought in terms of trade in dual-use items to the Swiss people, and to ask their cooperation in the export licensing process. In Harris' recollection, he had to explain why the United States sought to "protect our technology from a communist threat which represented 'a life-and-death struggle' to the Reagan administration." Second, regarding enforcement, Harris accepted responsibility to keep alert for, and evaluate reports on, possible violations of U.S.-Swiss agreements relating to technology transfers. "I got the walk-ins. That is, if somebody wanted to dime out on their competition [i.e., divulge confidential information] and walked into the embassy, they were referred to me." Working closely with the FBI and intelligence officers in the embassy, Harris would then make "a judgment call as to what to do with that information." Finally, undertaking to perform his third function, Harris would soon initiate discussions with

---

[69]   Daniel Harris, interview by author, Paris, August 24, 2009.
[70]   Ibid.

Swiss officials about the specific policy disagreements between the two nations on this issue.[71]

This final component, policy negotiations, in the end proved quite problematic. Richard Perle and other Defense Department officials evidenced precious little tolerance for Switzerland's long-standing tradition of political neutrality. The Swiss appeared to be pursuing their own economic gains through maximum trade with the Soviet Union while at the same time denying any obligation on their part to temper such trade—owing solely, they would claim, to the nation's historically neutral status in geopolitical terms. Harris and his Swiss counterpart, Willi Jaggi, engaged in thoughtful detailed discussions about how a suitable agreement between the two nations might conceivably look. Both negotiators were obliged to convincingly present their respective government's views in a candid and honest manner while still pursuing common ground and maintaining credibility with each other. Ultimately, the two men built a strong, trusting relationship, and they remain friends to this day.[72]

In the hope that the U.S. side would not resort to bullying tactics in pressing the smaller nation to submit, Harris constantly sought to instill in his American colleagues a greater appreciation of Swiss traditions. "I put together several discussion groups with Swiss and Americans in which the Swiss were explaining Swiss neutrality to us—why it was not just convenient, but why it was deeply embedded in the Swiss national identity."[73] The Swiss also pointedly observed on several occasions that certain NATO-member nations regularly violated U.S. technology transfer rules without suddenly precipitating American pressures to conform or face penalties for obvious infractions.[74]

Harris particularly appreciated Ambassador Whittlesey's willingness to vest in him sufficient authority to handle all aspects of this technology transfer negotiation on his own. Another, more traditional, ambassador might have divided responsibility for the three aspects of the technology transfer issue among three different officers. "The typical thing to do is to parcel it out—you give me responsibility for commercial relations, and you give ECON responsibility for policy, and somebody else for enforcement." Such a command structure, however, often could lead to inefficiency and

---

[71] Ibid.
[72] Ibid.
[73] Ibid.
[74] Faith Whittlesey, discussion with author, telephone, December 13, 2011.

impotence, Harris maintained. "And then you have interagency meetings and not a lot happens, or it's difficult sometimes to make anything happen. You spend a lot of time communicating with each other."[75]

Delegating substantial authority to a first-tour officer required courage and resolve, Harris asserted. If he had failed to manage this multifaceted task, Faith's State Department opponents "would have been all over me and would have sort of used it to try to embarrass her." Fortunately, Whittlesey's decision to entrust this important subject to Harris alone ended up paying dividends several times over. He was ultimately able to secure an acceptable bilateral trade arrangement that both parties could live with (while preserving U.S.-Swiss goodwill) during a period of intense Cold War competition between the United States and the Soviet Union.

Whittlesey's relationships with CEOs of major Swiss firms also allowed her to advance the U.S. case on a separate—diplomatic—track. Faith sometimes addressed her acquaintances in a direct and personal manner to advance U.S. interests. At other times, she mobilized her contacts with administration officials to improve communication with the Swiss public. For example, she asked Richard Perle, who was personally responsible for the stricter U.S. export controls, to visit Switzerland and address Swiss audiences on the subject in January 1986, just 2 months after the Geneva summit. She and Perle were on the same page on this subject and were very friendly.[76]

In order to maintain protocol during this delicate negotiation, Faith sometimes asked Joseph Hayes, the embassy's intelligence officer, to act as her surrogate. In Hayes' view, she demonstrated a keen understanding of the nuances of diplomacy by allowing him to represent her on occasion. "If Faith had a conversation with a senior Swiss person—it was, by definition, a formal expression on the part of the U.S. government," Hayes explained. "That's who she was—and their response would necessarily incorporate a kind of formal response embodying the Swiss view." In an effort to establish a more expansive and free-flowing dialogue with the Swiss on this issue, Whittlesey would schedule Hayes to meet with Swiss business and political leaders to discuss subjects under the most favorable circumstances that she could possibly devise. Representing the United States at a lower level—in diplomatic terms—Hayes could speak in a less restrained but yet more thorough manner. "I could have a conversation in which I was not a formal

[75]   Daniel Harris, interview by author, Paris, August 24, 2009.
[76]   Faith Whittlesey, discussion with author, telephone, December 13, 2011.

representative—I was there to exchange information, to understand points of view—and it was a qualitatively different experience." The Swiss very much appreciated U.S. willingness to explain the policy ramifications in a discreet but comprehensive manner. Hayes came to respect this "straightforward and honest" approach to diplomacy: "Too often the United States makes a *demand*; we don't make a request with an explanation."[77] As she had done many times previously in Switzerland, Whittlesey consistently insisted on cooperation rather than coercion. This method significantly improved communication and understanding between the two governments.

From the U.S. perspective, these efforts appear to have proved successful. Harris recalled that he and Swiss trade representative Jaggi successfully negotiated a mutually agreeable working relationship between the two governments on this complex and troublesome trade issue.[78] Political scientist Jürg Martin Gabriel has speculated that U.S. Assistant Secretary of Defense Perle and Swiss diplomat David de Pury likely concluded a confidential accord similar to the Hotz-Linder Agreement of 1951, but there was never any official announcement regarding the issue's resolution.[79] Government documents on this matter are not publicly available in either country.

In a 1988 address to the Swiss-American Chamber of Commerce, Whittlesey noted the outcome's benefits to both the United States and Switzerland: "In the area of the transfer of sensitive dual-use technology originating in the [United States], U.S. confidence in the integrity of Swiss re-export licensing controls has facilitated the import into Switzerland of advanced technologies from the United States." She counted this achievement as among the most significant of her second tour in Bern.[80]

Harris and Hayes believed that Ambassador Whittlesey's leadership in resolving U.S.-Swiss differences over technology transfers likely impeded the Soviet Union's efforts to keep pace with the United States in the Cold War. In Hayes' view, "My sense is that the work she did contributed substantially to our ability to mitigate some of the progress the Soviets would have made."[81] Harris concurred, concluding that the embassy's coordinated actions helped

---

[77] Joseph Hayes, interview by author, McLean, VA, May 29, 2009.
[78] Daniel Harris, interview by author, Paris, August 24, 2009. Harris also credited the assistance in Washington of Jean-Daniel Gerber, who had been posted to the Swiss embassy in Washington. Ibid.
[79] Gabriel, "The Price of Political Uniqueness," p. 13.
[80] Luncheon remarks for Swiss-American Chamber of Commerce General Meeting, June 28, 1988, Box 4, Folder 4, FW.
[81] Joseph Hayes, interview with author, McLean, VA, May 29, 2009.

in "driving the Soviet Union to the edge of its ability to compete." Despite disagreeing with certain Reagan initiatives, he nonetheless praised the president unreservedly "for forcing the Soviet Union into an arms race that they could never win ... because arms were increasingly moving up a steep technology curve."[82] Harris believed that U.S. vigilance drove up the costs for the Soviets to acquire the latest technological innovations. "They had to pay a premium and probably did not get the quantities that they wanted."[83]

As ambassador to Switzerland in her second tour, Whittlesey succeeded in curbing technology transfers effectuated through Switzerland while simultaneously maintaining cordial relations with that important nation. This delicate balancing act proved crucial in both advancing U.S. security interests and continuing strong trade and commerce between the two republics.

SELLING MILITARY AIRCRAFT TO THE SWISS

Faith also placed a high priority on facilitating the efforts of U.S. companies to sell military equipment to the Swiss. In her first tour, she had undertaken an ambitious initiative to help persuade Switzerland to purchase the Abrams M1 tank. Although this particular effort failed, Whittlesey resolved upon returning to Bern to have greater success whenever a new sales opportunity presented itself. As it happened, the Swiss had just recently invited bids for a major purchase of interceptor aircraft.

Two U.S. corporations indicated their intention to compete for the contract with several other nations whose products were also in the competitive mix. In Whittlesey's view, both McDonnell Douglas' F-18 Hornet and General Dynamics' F-16 Fighting Falcon stood a good chance of winning the contract with the Swiss military. The Hornet boasted state-of-the-art aeronautic technology, while the Fighting Falcon provided a more cost-effective alternative choice.[84]

Faith well understood that the process of actually completing such a sale might take years. During a preevaluation phase, Switzerland's Federal Military Department would review planes made in France, Israel, the Soviet Union, Sweden, and the United States. After this comprehensive process, two finalists would be chosen for a more intensive testing regime prior to

---

[82] Daniel Harris, interview with author, Paris, August 24, 2009.
[83] Ibid.
[84] Faith Whittlesey, discussion with author, telephone, December 13, 2011.

the Swiss government's final decision. In Whittlesey's view, the time and effort expended promised to pay worthwhile dividends since Switzerland would likely spend billions of Swiss francs on one of these fighter aircraft systems.[85]

Weapons sales to U.S. allies and friends made sense for a number of reasons. All exports strengthened the American economy by creating new (and maintaining existing) domestic jobs as well as contributing to the U.S. government's tax base. Furthermore, more sales reduced unit costs because larger production runs permitted greater efficiencies of scale. Increased profits from these sales, in turn, could be reinvested in further research and development, which likewise would enhance the probability of continuing technological innovations. As a result, America's military would maintain continuing superiority vis-à-vis its adversaries.[86]

Even more direct political and economic gains accrued from the export of American-made products to the armed forces of friendly foreign nations. Of course, for obvious national security reasons, U.S. leaders would not likely countenance the sale of its most technologically advanced armaments and weapons systems to non-NATO countries or—especially—to its adversaries. Nonetheless, in military-strategic terms, any country that purchased U.S. armaments effectively initiates attendant professional connections with the armed forces of the United States. While not a formal alliance, such exchange of military merchandise builds bilateral lines of communications because U.S. technicians typically provide for the training, maintenance, and modernization features implicit in recent weapons systems.[87] The U.S. government also establishes greater financial interdependence—and secures some leverage—with the purchasing nation by accumulating that country's currency. In the case of Switzerland, moreover, Swiss francs maintained a strong value over time relative to other nations' legal tender.[88]

Faith's appreciation of the many potential benefits deriving from such sales encouraged her to present this goal to her staff in very clear and direct terms. President Reagan, in stark contrast to his predecessor Jimmy Carter, wanted embassies to be active in marketing U.S. armaments to

---

[85] Ibid.
[86] Ibid. See also Michael G. Roskin and Nicholas O. Berry, *The New World of International Relations*, 7th ed. (New York: Prentice Hall, 2007), p. 303.
[87] William Serchak, interview by author, Rockville, MD, August 12, 2009.
[88] Faith Whittlesey, discussion with author, telephone, December 13, 2011.

foreign nations.[89] Whittlesey brought an entrepreneurial spirit to the sale of American planes to the Swiss. Intelligence Officer Hayes recalled that, even during the first staff meeting upon her return to Switzerland in 1985, Ambassador Whittlesey made a distinct and immediate impression on him. She minced no words in explaining that her chief mission was to promote President Reagan's policies—which, she emphasized, voters had overwhelmingly endorsed by electing him to a second term in a landslide. In particular, Faith announced that she would ask all embassy officials to support her objective of persuading the government of Switzerland to purchase one of the two American-made fighter jets—the F-16 or the F-18—being actively promoted to the Swiss. Nearly 25 years later, Hayes retained a vivid recollection of how Whittlesey dramatically concluded this thought: "And then she said, memorably, 'Does anyone here have a problem with that?' "[90] Whittlesey had instantly established herself as a results-oriented leader who routinely expected high performance from the entire embassy team.

Faith well understood that the two U.S. aircraft manufacturers faced stiff competition from many nations (the French, in particular) for this aircraft sale to Switzerland. In the preevaluation phase, McDonnell Douglas and General Dynamics would vie with Sweden's Saab Corporation, which marketed the JAS-39 Gripen,[91] and the Soviet Union's MiG-29.[92] France's Avions Marcel Dassault-Breguet Aviation appeared in a favorable position as the producers of an updated version of the 30 Mirage planes which the Swiss Air Force had employed since the Swiss government's last major aircraft purchase during the 1960s.[93]

Such a large expenditure of public funds—especially for a squadron of fighter jets—immediately grabbed the Swiss public's imagination and attention. Whittlesey arranged to have the U.S. aircraft available for viewing at a prominent air show in the southern part of Switzerland. The U.S. Air Force attaché also attended to answer questions about how the U.S. plane compared favorably to the Mirage, which French officials energetically marketed to the Swiss.[94] As Defense Attaché William Serchak recalled: "Sale negotiations were going on at that time—that made it a very popular

---

[89]   Ibid.
[90]   Joseph Hayes, interview by author, McLean, VA, May 29, 2009.
[91]   Eric Beech, "Defending Neutrality," *Flight International,* November 14, 1987, p. 23.
[92]   "Swiss Declined Soviet Offer, Narrowing Fighter Competition," *Aerospace Daily,* March 1, 1991, p. 362
[93]   Beech, "Defending Neutrality," p. 25.
[94]   Faith Whittlesey, discussion with author, telephone, December 13, 2011.

thing for a lot of people. If I want to see this airplane we're spending all this money on, I want to go down there and check it out."[95] These air shows were always well attended, and thus local politicians and the general public often had substantially more knowledge of these weapons systems than would be the case, say, in the United States. Unlike the United States and most nations, Switzerland required universal male military service, which made the armed forces a more common topic of daily conversation and thus a great force for social cohesion in Switzerland.[96]

Throughout this period, Whittlesey actively publicized the U.S. aircraft in speeches to various Swiss organizations and in personal contacts with her numerous government and business acquaintances within Switzerland. Always seeking to develop an edge on the competition, Whittlesey decided that she could talk about these aircraft in a more authoritative and convincing fashion if she were able to sit in the cockpit and even fly in one of the jets. Just as an auto executive might encourage his salesmen to sit behind the wheel of the cars they sold, General Dynamics was more than pleased to have Ambassador Whittlesey take an F-16 for a "test drive." Defense Attaché Serchak explained how this gesture might enable her to make the case even more persuasively in her various presentations: "This isn't somebody just trying to sell me a piece of hardware—she's actually been in the thing and knows something about it, where they haven't been."[97]

Despite Faith's commitment to the sale, she did have moments of doubt upon arriving at the U.S. military base in West Germany where a U.S. pilot escorted the ambassador in the fighter jet. Embassy officer Sears recalled with a chuckle that she "regretted" this particular mission. Sears knew well firsthand that Whittlesey could endure fast driving on Swiss highways. But after the jet landed, he recognized that Faith had not enjoyed the steep angle of ascent, nor the heavy "g" (gravitational) forces which distinguished the experience of jet flight from that aboard a commercial airliner. Nonetheless, Whittlesey's pilot and flight crew in due course received pleasant personal notes from the ambassador thanking them for their graciousness and patience.[98] "I had gained a new, keener appreciation of their professionalism,"

---

[95]　William Serchak, interview by author, Rockville, MD, August 12, 2009.
[96]　Faith Whittlesey, discussion with author, telephone, December 13, 2011.
[97]　William Serchak, interview by author, Rockville, MD, August 12, 2009.
[98]　Douglas Sears, interview by author, Boston, July 9, 2009.

she recalled.[99] She also generated a considerable amount of publicity for herself and the American aircraft in Switzerland, as she had fully intended.

After all this effort, Faith received several pieces of good news regarding U.S. exports to Switzerland in the final months of her second tour. First, the Swiss had chosen the F-16 and F-18 as the two finalists.[100] Second, this announcement added to her sense of accomplishment because Swissair had also recently decided to purchase 6 long-haul MD-11 passenger aircraft from McDonnell Douglas Corporation. Whittlesey had helped advocate for this U.S. company's efforts in both the F-18 and the MD-11. This $780 million order "dealt a blow to Europe's Airbus consortium," according to the *New York Times*, because the two companies had engaged in cutthroat contests which had "grown into a major trade issue between the United States and European governments."[101] While the relative quality of the products most certainly proved crucial in the Swiss decision, U.S. marketing and Whittlesey's efforts to maintain the bilateral friendship likely helped, as well. "We were sophisticated, I think, in the way we went about persuading the Swiss to buy American products," Faith later concluded.[102] America's European competitors had initially enjoyed the advantage of being Switzerland's neighbors, after all.

Whittlesey would consider these aircraft sales among the most significant accomplishments of her second tour. The Swiss Federal Military Department announced the awarding of a $1.8 billion contract for 34 F/A-18 Hornets in early October 1988.[103] Between the two contracts, Faith could rightly claim to have contributed to the export of some $2.58 billion of U.S. products.

HUMAN INTELLIGENCE

Whittlesey also mobilized her political power behind the embassy's efforts to obtain covert information vital to U.S. national security. Faith's assistance to Intelligence Officer Hayes made him more effective in gathering human intelligence. Whittlesey arranged personal introductions which proved especially valuable to Hayes' work in, among other things, countering terrorism and nuclear proliferation.

---

[99]   Faith Whittlesey, discussion with author, telephone, December 13, 2011.
[100] John H. Cushman, Jr., "Justice Dept. Is Pressed to Inform Pentagon of Inquiry," June 26, 1988, p. 22.
[101] "Swissair Orders 6 MD-11's," *New York Times*, March 20, 1987, p. D3.
[102] Faith Whittlesey, interview by Ann Miller Morin, December 7, 1989.
[103] Andrea Adelson, "McDonnell Douglas Wins Swiss Contract," *New York Times*, October 4, 1988, p. D5.

Global terror campaigns waged by small rogue nations and extremist groups increasingly began to occupy Whittlesey's attention during her second tour. Palestinian gunmen hijacked the Italian cruise ship *Achille Lauro* and killed a handicapped Jewish American passenger in October 1985.[104] On April 5, 1986, a bomb that was detonated in a West Berlin discothèque killed two U.S. servicemen and injured more than 150 patrons.[105]

Even in typically tranquil Switzerland, the dangers were considered serious enough to warrant precautions. Whittlesey's secretary DeLynn Henry recalled briefings in which she was warned to change her route to work on occasion. In July 1986, Faith received "soft body armor" from an embassy security officer who grimly advised her to "make use of it whenever you are scheduled to appear/speak at a large function or during periods of terrorist threats."[106] Faith, however, continued her unaccompanied walks along the river Aare, into the town of Bern and in the Bernese Oberland. And she did not wear the bullet-proof vest.[107]

Whittlesey nonetheless accepted her responsibility to assist U.S. intelligence and law enforcement organizations with great seriousness. Intelligence Officer Hayes later characterized counterterrorism and counterproliferation of nuclear weapons in this period as issues "of enormous consequence to U.S. national security."[108] The seeds of terrorism's emergence as America's foremost national security issue were being sown as the decade progressed.

As an active ambassador who frequently met with key figures from both the public and private sectors, Whittlesey had a sophisticated understanding of how her extensive political and social contacts could prove valuable for CIA initiatives. As Hayes recalled, "She was extremely good and very generous in making introductions and connections."[109] Whittlesey often invited Hayes and a senior Swiss businessman to lunch or dinner at her residence. These arrangements leveraged Whittlesey's status, since the contact person was typically "someone who would be honored to receive an invitation from the U.S. ambassador but who would have probably been a bit more guarded about receiving a U.S. official with a security portfolio." After some polite

---

[104] Michael K. Bohn, *The Achille Lauro Hijacking: Lessons in the Politics and Prejudice of Terrorism* (Washington, DC: Potomac Books, 2004), p. 2.
[105] John Tagliabue, "2 Killed, 155 Hurt in Bomb Explosion at Club in Berlin," *New York Times*, April 6, 1986, p. 2.
[106] Wolfgang G. Fuchs to Faith Whittlesey, June 25, 1986. Box 2, Folder 11, FW.
[107] Faith Whittlesey, discussion with author, telephone, December 13, 2011.
[108] Joseph Hayes, interview by author, McLean, VA, May 29, 2009.
[109] Ibid.

conversation, Whittlesey would generally "rise and excuse herself, leaving me free to engage with the guest."[110]

During the 1980s, the agency particularly sought to establish human intelligence related to international terrorism, and Whittlesey shared her sources in that area. On one particular occasion—Hayes recalled in 2009—Whittlesey's arrangements enabled Hayes to meet a "very, very senior, well-placed and still very influential political leader from the Middle East who had left his home country—for political reasons—and had settled in Geneva."[111] This person provided Hayes access to an international network which the CIA's upper echelon had long sought to penetrate.

Whittlesey noted with pride that Hayes, one of her most critically important Bern allies, subsequently rose to the highest ranks of the CIA. Hayes had been the founding director of the Center for the Study of Intelligence and, toward the end of his government career, was appointed by the director of Central Intelligence to the first Richard Helms chair for espionage. In this role, Hayes contributed to the formulation of the current code of ethics and training curriculum for the clandestine service. Hayes himself acknowledged the importance of his work in Bern during Whittlesey's tenure, saying, "Many of the awards and distinctions I was honored to receive derived in part from my service in Switzerland, although I cannot be more specific."[112]

PERSON-TO-PERSON DIPLOMACY AT THE HEIGHT OF THE COLD WAR

As ambassador, Whittlesey seized opportunities to demonstrate her personal sympathy for individuals who lived under communist rule in Eastern Europe, the Soviet Union, and elsewhere. On one particular occasion, Hayes recalled that a very senior East European intelligence official came to the U.S. embassy in Bern to ask for asylum. This kind of "walk-in" defection occurred occasionally, and such cases were referred to Hayes' office as a matter of process. Typically, the intelligence agencies might handle the logistics as an internal matter, but *this* man had asked for protection for his wife and child, who had also been spirited out of his home country.

Hayes decided to inform the ambassador that he might need her political contacts in Washington to help ensure that this more complicated

---

[110] Ibid.
[111] Ibid.
[112] Joseph Hayes, email to author, November 19, 2011.

request might receive an expedited response from the agencies and officials charged with handling these cases. Whittlesey's reply surprised Hayes with its warmth of spirit: "Her instant reaction was 'I would like to meet with them.'"[113] Hayes discouraged her intervention prior to his following some standard operating procedures such as identifying the man's objectives and background. Whittlesey understood Hayes' cause for caution and immediately withdrew her request for a meeting.[114]

But Faith did not feel comfortable delegating complete responsibility for the family's well-being to the intelligence officer. To Hayes' surprise, she "literally got up from her desk" and went to her residence. She soon returned with a container in which she had prepared some cosmetics and other personal-care items for the wife, a baseball glove and cap for the young boy, and a handwritten letter of welcome for the East European intelligence officer. Whittlesey had asked Hayes to translate the letter for their unexpected guest, and he was shocked to witness the man's emotional response: "As I read this to him, his eyes welled up and it was clear that he was so deeply moved and touched by this personally generous offer."[115]

Practical benefits accrued from Whittlesey's uncommon sensitivity to the family's apprehension in the face of their uncertain future. By sending the family this personal note signifying her special interest in their welfare, Whittlesey had helped build trust between the U.S. embassy and the Eastern European family as they fulfilled the usual procedural safeguards associated with the asylum-granting process. Faith had created "a context in which the man and his family became instantly less guarded, less defensive—more fully cooperative," in Hayes' view. This smooth and rapid relationship building helped the CIA remove the family posthaste from Switzerland "where they were vulnerable to the search activities" that might be employed by the government they had fled—and they were successfully transported immediately to a neighboring country prior to going on to the United States, where they subsequently sought out and gained U.S. citizenship.[116]

Whittlesey believed that effective resistance to communist expansion required such personal forms of outreach. She invited two former Czech political prisoners to her residence in Bern during her second tour as ambassador. Hoping they would speak more freely there than in her embassy

---

[113] Joseph Hayes, interview with author, McLean, VA, May 29, 2009.
[114] Ibid.
[115] Ibid.
[116] Ibid.

office, she was pleased when they showed her "words of Reagan's speeches they had written out in English on well-worn scraps of paper they carried with them." She was inspired that the president's rhetoric had made such an impact—but not surprised, because she believed that Reagan's oratory "moved men and nations" and was a source of great inspiration and encouragement to the oppressed peoples of Eastern Europe. She also received from them a large scroll listing the names of many former Czech political prisoners who admired Reagan.[117]

On another occasion, while she was visiting Brussels for a U.S.-European ambassadors' meeting, Whittlesey requested a meeting with the members of Polish Solidarity (the labor organization which had valiantly resisted one-party communist rule in Poland during the early 1980s). "The office, in a remote location, was small and staffed by only one man, who to my great surprise told me that I was the *only* U.S. ambassador who ever had visited," she recalled. "I wished him well and gave him the good wishes of the president for whom I worked."[118]

These accounts epitomize Whittlesey's philosophy that the United States would win the Cold War one person at a time. In her view, *each* individual counted in the global struggle to defeat "the evil empire." Whittlesey believed victory required more than merely focusing on the macro-level goals of changing military and economic structures. In other words, Faith did not lose sight of the primary purpose of her opposition to communism—liberating the human spirit.

PUBLIC DIPLOMACY

Confident that individuals would always select the Western over the Soviet system if given the freedom to decide, Whittlesey resolved to make the Bern embassy an information center for the administration's agenda. This dedication to presenting Reagan's policies as widely as possible made some people uncomfortable in neutral Switzerland, including some career U.S. government officers who did not personally agree with Reagan's outspoken defense of the Nicaraguan Contras and SDI (the U.S. plan to develop a space-based missile defense system).

Commerce Officer Harris recalled some Swiss discomfort with Whittlesey's advocacy of assistance to anticommunist rebels in Nicaragua.

---

[117] Faith Whittlesey, email to author, January 11, 2010.
[118] Ibid.

Some Europeans worried that the U.S.-Soviet proxy struggle in Central America might ultimately prompt a military, perhaps nuclear, confrontation. In a country where people did not like to "rock the boat," Harris believed that the Swiss winced at her "being so forthright on an issue that was guaranteed to irritate the Russians badly."[119] Although neutral, Switzerland's government provided some humanitarian aid for agrarian reform in Nicaragua. This Swiss policy frustrated the Reagan administration's objective of stopping Nicaragua's pro-Soviet regime from promoting communist revolutions throughout Central America. Given the nature of totalitarian rule, Whittlesey assumed the Sandinista government would distribute the money solely to those farmers who supported it.[120]

When Secretary of State George Shultz visited Bern, Whittlesey recalled, she mentioned this Swiss agricultural assistance as the two conversed en route to their meeting with Switzerland's secretary of state. This item was not on the list of talking points the Bern Foreign Service officers had proposed for him. Shultz's anger was instantly aroused that he had not been informed, and he raised protests with the Swiss officials he met. Since the U.S. career diplomats responsible for his briefings had not provided these facts to the secretary of state, they were not pleased that she had informed Shultz, Faith recalled. She had been out of the country just prior to the Shultz meeting, and so did not participate in the drafting of his briefing materials.[121]

Many Swiss also responded very tepidly to Whittlesey's advocacy of SDI. Not only did Faith instruct all embassy officers to promote SDI with their Swiss government and military contacts, but also she personally used social events, such as the annual Fourth of July party at the ambassador's residence, to raise the subject of SDI with any high-ranking Swiss military officer she encountered. U.S. Defense Attaché William Serchak, who was sure the neutral Swiss would never openly support SDI (which he did not himself), recalled one such social occasion at which he was having a discussion with the chief of staff of the Swiss army when the ambassador joined them: "Five minutes into the conversation, she's saying, '... and then about "star wars," General, I'd like to know your opinion.' And he just sort of rolled his eyes and very politely said, 'How was your holiday, Madam Ambassador?'"[122]

---

[119] Daniel Harris, interview with author, Paris, August 24, 2009.
[120] Faith Whittlesey, discussion with author, telephone, December 13, 2011.
[121] Ibid.
[122] William Serchak, interview by author, Rockville, MD, August 12, 2009.

Since SDI represented a highly significant component of Reagan's "peace through strength" approach to the Soviet threat, Whittlesey believed in raising the issue for discussion whenever possible. Faith understood the administration's strategy regarding SDI because of her work in the White House. She also had known Dr. Robert Jastrow—one of America's top physicists and SDI proponents—for 25 years. Jastrow had explained to her that the SDI *concept* alone was exerting significant pressures on the Soviet Union in a variety of ways.[123] Assessing SDI's full impact remains speculative, but political scientist Paul Kengor accumulated a list of sources—including high-ranking Soviet officials, Democrats, and Reagan biographers—who credited the president's SDI strategy for accelerating both U.S.-Soviet missile reductions and the demise of the Soviet Union.[124]

Despite their clearly evident discomfort with some of her views, the Swiss consistently continued to seek out her point of view. Whittlesey's political savvy and personal charisma contributed to Swiss tolerance for her policy positions. DCM James Shinn recalled that Reagan appeared excessively militaristic and imperialistic to many Swiss, but he also noted that Whittlesey enjoyed a reputation as a person with access to the seat of power, especially after having worked in the White House in close proximity to the American president. Furthermore, she approached the Swiss with uncommon charm and gentility. In Shinn's view, "She was a player in Washington, and she could keep them in touch with people that were important to them. I think also that they just personally liked her."[125] Given Whittlesey's strong commitment to Reagan's policies ("she's got a backbone of titanium steel,"[126] noted Hayes), combined with her temperate disposition and unquestioned decorum, the Swiss could not ignore the administration's voice despite some bilateral disagreements from time to time.

Whittlesey's grace and sensitivities to her audience softened her strongly held belief in Reagan's wisdom. Commerce Officer Harris, prior to knowing Whittlesey, recalled hearing about her reputation as a member of "the hardest of the hard core of the Reagan revolution" in the White House. Would she abide frank and open discussions about administration policies? Harris recalled a conversation with Whittlesey nearly a quarter of a century earlier in which he expressed an opinion which did not conform

---

[123] Faith Whittlesey, discussion with author, telephone, December 13, 2011.
[124] Kengor, *Dupes*, p. 417. See also Kengor, *The Crusader*, pp. 300–302.
[125] James Shinn, interview with author, Kensington, CA, March 16, 2010.
[126] Joseph Hayes, interview with author, McLean, VA, May 29, 2009.

at all to the Reagan party line. Aware that some ambassadors might scorn or punish dissent, Harris nonetheless spoke up (albeit gingerly), "kind of expecting I was going to get my ears pinned back." To Harris' surprise, the ambassador responded, "With respect ... ," and then she offered her own perspective "in a very sort of professional way." Whittlesey's willingness to discuss the issue seriously and intelligently impressed Harris. "She could have said, 'Dan, that is not my view. Here is my view. Write it down.' She was too classy a person to do it quite that way, but that could have been the message." Despite Whittlesey's reputation for passionately defending conservative causes, she consistently wanted to persuade rather than to intimidate those with whom she interacted.[127]

This openness to alternative viewpoints also may have helped Whittlesey retain the goodwill of the Swiss. Joseph Hayes remembered that Faith occasionally inquired whether she was advancing Reagan's policies with too much vigor: "And she would ask, 'Joe, do you think I'm pushing too hard? What do you hear from the people that you talk to?'"[128] In Hayes' recollection, Whittlesey welcomed his frank suggestions in a "really serious, straightforward, nondefensive" manner.[129] Whittlesey's forbearance of criticism even permitted Hayes to pepper his recommendations with some irony, saying, for example, "Madam Ambassador, that speech you gave in Zürich last week ... dynamite speech—if you'd given it in Cleveland, but it's not going to work in Zürich."[130] Not all Foreign Service officers may have had the courage to question or contradict the ambassador, and Whittlesey always projected a commanding presence. But these officers did not characterize her as domineering.

The Swiss also respected Whittlesey's persistence in seeking Switzerland's understanding, if not support, on these controversial issues. Rather than ignore Switzerland as an inconsequential player in world politics, having deliberately chosen to remain outside the NATO alliance and even the UN (except as an "observer" until 2002 when the Swiss voted by referendum to join as a full member nation), she made a consistent effort to explain Reagan's policies, demonstrating a significant respect for the Swiss perspective from the United States government. Regarding Nicaragua, SDI, and other issues, Whittlesey remained confident that official declarations of political neutrality

---

[127] Daniel Harris, interview by author, Paris, August 24, 2009.
[128] Joseph Hayes, interview by author, McLean, VA, May 29, 2009.
[129] Ibid.
[130] Ibid.

did not prevent the Swiss from sharing U.S. views on human rights and the need for a strong defense. As Intelligence Officer Hayes recalled: "One of the senior Swiss officials once said to me, 'We may be neutral, but we're not stupid—we understand where the threats really come from. They come from the East—we do not consider NATO or the United States to be a threat to Swiss interests and Swiss sovereignty—certainly not on a scale like the Soviet Union and Warsaw Pact are.' "[131] Commerce Officer Harris agreed: "The Swiss, clearly, were not neutral as to the outcome of the Cold War."[132]

Whittlesey appreciated the deeply held Swiss understanding of their own sovereignty. Switzerland wanted to avoid alliances but understood that close friendship with the United States would be in its national interest.[133] By engaging the Swiss in political exchanges on contentious (although relevant) issues of international relations, Faith signaled that the United States desired a long-term friendly relationship with Switzerland based on mutual understanding and deep respect.

Counselor for Public Affairs Robert Reilly, who had worked closely with Whittlesey for more than a year in the White House, believed that mutual admiration best explained the Swiss tolerance for Whittlesey's persistent expression of sometimes unpopular beliefs. "The friendship she exhibited and developed for the Swiss was not manufactured. And that was contagious to them—that they saw an American ambassador so enthusiastically embrace their country."[134] As the highest-level representative of the United States in Switzerland, Whittlesey worked hard to ensure that the Swiss viewed her country in the most honest, and hopefully favorable, light. She obviously very much enjoyed their mountains, culture, music, and people. Almost every weekend, she visited museums or hiked or skied with her children and Swiss friends, and she entertained them on her grand piano by playing well-known Swiss folk songs as well as teaching them "Oh! Susannah" and "Home on the Range."[135]

Ultimately, the Swiss appeared to recognize Whittlesey's genuine esteem for the country's core values and rich history. She respected Switzerland's delegation of power to local governments, military readiness, innovativeness,

---

[131] Ibid.
[132] Daniel Harris, interview with author, Paris, August 24, 2009.
[133] Faith Whittlesey, discussion with author, telephone, December 13, 2012.
[134] Robert Reilly, interview with author, Vienna, VA, August 15, 2009.
[135] Faith Whittlesey, discussion with author, telephone, December 13, 2011.

frugality, discipline, high levels of education, scientific achievements, and humanitarian tradition.

While Whittlesey engaged in fighting the Cold War in Europe, however, a coterie of political opponents deliberately targeted her. Within the Bern embassy, a few State Department officials sought to undermine her authority. While their plan appeared feeble at first, all Reagan loyalists came under intense suspicion in Washington during the unfolding Iran-Contra scandal which at one point briefly threatened to end with President Reagan's possible impeachment.

The next chapter recounts Faith's relationship with the embassy staff and determination not to allow political adversaries to succeed in undermining her second tour achievements.

CHAPTER 7

Madam Ambassador Under Fire— Much Ado About Nothing?
The Second Bern Tour (part 2)

U.S. Attorney General Edwin Meese came to Switzerland in late 1985 in order to request that the Swiss Parliament make money laundering a federal crime in Switzerland. The absence of such a law complicated the work of U.S. law enforcement officials.

In this visit, Meese explained why he sought to expand the range of crimes for which America could request judicial assistance from the Swiss. A 1977 treaty signed between the United States and Switzerland pledged that the two countries would cooperate in cases where illegal activity was suspected. But when individuals allegedly violated American law by attempting to conceal illegally obtained assets ("dirty money") in Swiss financial institutions, Switzerland's legislation provided protections for bank account holders' privacy. Swiss banks were required by law to keep account holders' names secret. Therefore, when U.S. officials tried to fight drug cartels which allegedly laundered money in Swiss banks, Swiss courts had little, if any, legal means of redress to support American prosecutors.

During her first tour as U.S. ambassador in Bern, Faith Whittlesey had facilitated agreement in a similar case. Following her diplomatic intervention, Swiss banks and the government of Switzerland had agreed to assist U.S. agencies which attempted to prosecute "insider trading." The Swiss pledged to cooperate with U.S. requests for information about individuals who allegedly violated U.S. law by trading U.S. securities while in possession of privileged, or "insider," information.[1]

Upon Meese's arrival in 1985, Whittlesey discussed with him and his staff the importance she thought should be attached to clearly demonstrating U.S. respect for the Swiss government, its laws, and its people. Faith urged the naturally diplomatic Meese to *persuade* rather than appear to pressure the Swiss to align their national laws more closely with U.S. policy. She understood how strongly the Swiss prized their status as an independent, sovereign nation that upheld the rule of law *established by their own democratic system.*

Whittlesey fully supported Meese's initiative, which she viewed as an extension of the bilateral cooperation between the "sister republics" that she had consistently encouraged during her first tour as ambassador. Now in her second tour, she arranged for Meese to meet and discuss this latest contentious issue with key decision makers in the Swiss financial community and governmental leadership circles.

Meese understood Whittlesey's counsel, and he acted accordingly. Rather than portray himself as attempting to threaten this small nation, the attorney general presented the U.S. case in a thoughtful, deferential manner. Through the Swiss-American Chamber of Commerce in Zürich and similar venues, Meese outlined to members of the Swiss financial center the specific U.S. goal of targeting four discrete types of criminal activity: drug trafficking, organized crime, terrorism, and economic crime.

Faith wanted to convey her appreciation to Meese for coming to Switzerland himself rather than sending deputies. She therefore hosted a large dinner in his honor at the ambassador's residence.

Less than a year later, this embassy dinner for Attorney General Meese would be made the focal point of a small, yet significant, campaign to reprimand and perhaps even remove Whittlesey from her Bern post. She had received reimbursement for this event in part from a special State Department fund. Private individuals, whom Faith had solicited, had donated money to this account, which State Department officials controlled and managed. Contribution checks went directly to the State Department. But a handful of Bern embassy staff members judged this fund's very existence to be inappropriate.

Whittlesey could not understand this complaint, since she had submitted a formal application to the State Department in order to set up the

---

[1]   See Chapter 2.

fund, which the department's representatives had approved. Therefore, Faith believed she was entitled to reimbursement from the fund for diplomatic events such as hosting the attorney general. Furthermore, a State Department administrative officer in Bern had approved her requests for reimbursement for this event.

The way in which her accusers presented their complaint also upset her. These embassy officials brought their criticism directly to Democratic staff members of the U.S. Congress. They did not approach her directly as their immediate superior to discuss their concerns. Nor did they use the State Department grievance policy. Instead, after the fact and anonymously, they took their case to her political adversaries in Washington. To this day, she does not know precisely who brought the specific charges into the political hotbed of the Beltway environment.[2]

As had occurred during her White House years, Whittlesey's critics used the media—especially the *Washington Post*—as a megaphone for advancing their case. As a result, a sustained critique of Faith's leadership persisted even after extensive investigation by the State and Justice departments exonerated her of any wrongdoing. Congressional Democrats and sympathetic media expanded the scrutiny to include her personnel procedures, her official objectives as ambassador, and her judgment. Skeptical sources even linked her to the Iran-Contra scandal, which threatened to bring down President Reagan himself.

In sharp contrast to these very few critics, many embassy employees expressed deep admiration for Whittlesey. For example, Faith helped Drug Enforcement Agency (DEA) officers deal more effectively with a large caseload, she cultivated an intellectually stimulating environment in the Bern embassy, and she earned the lasting respect and affection of her residence staff.

FIGHTING DRUG MONEY

Greg Passic, who came to Switzerland as the Bern embassy's first DEA officer in 1984, viewed Whittlesey's role as critical to the success of his work. Passic recognized how her diplomatic bearing with Meese (counseling him and his staff to avoid lecturing the Swiss) had ensured that his mission succeeded in improving understanding between the two nations.[3]

---

[2]   Faith Whittlesey, discussion with author, telephone, April 12, 2012.
[3]   Greg Passic, interview by author, telephone, January 20, 2012.

In Passic's recollection, some U.S. State Department officers had opposed her recommendation that Meese meet with Switzerland's top-level banking executives. These in-house skeptics were convinced that the Swiss had no interest at all in listening to Meese's arguments for tougher money-laundering statutes or closer banking regulation of suspect activities. Meese did, in fact, encounter some strong contrary Swiss opinions during the question-and-answer period following his Zürich appearance: "He was almost lectured to by the bankers about what the U.S. government should not be able to do," Passic said.[4]

Passic nonetheless believed that Meese's visit proved beneficial because the Swiss people as a whole agreed that Switzerland should provide judicial assistance to help Americans prosecute money laundering. "Switzerland's law enforcement community and the Swiss people supported the case that drug cartels like the *Cali* and *Medellín* should not have access to Swiss banks," in Passic's view.[5]

Whittlesey's handling of the Meese visit demonstrated strong support for the DEA, and Passic considered her treatment of law enforcement officers exceptional. Not all high-level politicians showed police officers such respect, in Passic's view. "When she held social events at her residence," he recalled, "she always let us cops in—and all my counterparts from the Swiss side."[6] For Passic, Faith's invitations symbolized her appreciation for the bilateral cooperation between the law enforcement institutions of the United States and Switzerland.

The DEA's presence in Bern grew from one to three officers during Whittlesey's tenure. Passic credited Faith's support for facilitating these new hires.[7] Upon her arrival in 1985, she recognized that he was shouldering an excessive workload as the only DEA officer in Switzerland. In Passic's pursuit of international drug dealers, he needed assistance, Whittlesey believed. "I was motivated to help Passic in part because of my previous experience as an assistant U.S. attorney in Pennsylvania," she recalled.[8] Having worked in law enforcement herself, she understood his challenges. In spite of President Reagan's often stated vision of reducing the size of government, Whittlesey

---

[4] Ibid.
[5] Ibid.
[6] Ibid.
[7] Ibid.
[8] Faith Whittlesey, discussion with author, telephone, April 12, 2012.

expanded the U.S. commitment to drug law enforcement. Faith sincerely regarded U.S.-Swiss cooperation in this area as a top national priority.

Whittlesey's skills and judgment consistently helped strengthen the bilateral relationship, Passic believed. "She was always thinking about the big picture, while the rest of us were just focused on our specific missions. That was her role as ambassador."[9]

THE EMBASSY FAMILY

Whittlesey also understood the pressures of working overseas for the U.S. government, and she attempted to alleviate the inconveniences of living abroad for the embassy staff members. During her second tour, from April 1985 to July 1988, Faith made concerted efforts to sustain excellent morale in the embassy.

Intelligence Officer Joseph Hayes recalled her as "an incredibly gracious hostess" when she served as ambassador. Whittlesey's wide contacts at the highest levels of the U.S. government and politics allowed her to attract several very prominent Americans ("the kinds of people embassy staff members would love to meet and talk to," in Hayes' words) to the embassy.[10] When these individuals visited, Whittlesey did not restrict access to high-level officers, but she invited the entire embassy staff to meet these visitors at afternoon receptions featuring coffee and cake.[11]

Faith conducted herself with a definite seriousness of purpose, but staff members appreciated that she did not jealously guard her privacy or erect rigid boundaries between her family life and professional life. The ambassador arranged for her secretary DeLynn Henry (née Rushing), a career federal government employee, to take classes in German so she could better communicate with the Swiss in such Swiss-German areas as Bern and Zürich. When in 1988 she learned of DeLynn's upcoming nuptials, Whittlesey offered the use of her embassy residence for the wedding reception and dinner. DeLynn gratefully accepted Faith's offer—and remained appreciative a generation later.[12]

The ambassador did not limit such generosity to a select few. Intelligence Officer Hayes recalled many invitations for all embassy employees to attend

---

[9]   Greg Passic, interview by author, telephone, January 20, 2012.
[10] Joseph Hayes, interview by author, McLean, VA, May 29, 2009. For some of the individuals who visited U.S. embassy Bern during her tours, see Chapter 3, pp. 78–79.
[11] Joseph Hayes, interview by author, McLean, VA, May 29, 2009.
[12] DeLynn Henry, interview by author, Washington, DC, May 29, 2009.

social events in the ambassador's residence. "I don't know how many times she opened her home to the embassy staff—just invited people to come over and have dinner and dance in the residence."[13] In Hayes' recollection, these gestures helped unify the roughly 125 people who worked under her authority in the U.S. mission. "It was family. And she worked very hard to create that sense of community. It was very touching."[14] Hayes served under 10 ambassadors during his 30-year career as an intelligence officer in U.S. embassies, and he rated Whittlesey "among the most conscientious and most caring."[15] Whittlesey's style certainly leveled some of the common societal barriers which separated an ambassador from the average embassy staff member.

Faith's guests at embassy receptions and parties also appreciated the sophisticated, balanced level of intellectual exchange available there. Mona Charen, who had worked with Whittlesey in the White House Office of Public Liaison, visited her in Bern several times. In Charen's view, Faith had successfully re-created at the embassy the modern equivalent of the 18th-century French salons where educated elites often gathered to discuss ideas and culture. "There was this constant flow of really interesting and exciting people," she recalled, "including those with whom Faith didn't necessarily see eye to eye politically." Whittlesey certainly wanted to advance Reagan's foreign policy agenda, but she much preferred a free exchange of opinions rather than a heavy-handed or one-sided effort to indoctrinate people.[16]

Charen received invitations to address Swiss audiences from Whittlesey, and she constantly marveled at how Faith managed to construct conditions for a comfortable, meaningful dialogue. For example, Whittlesey invited leaders of Switzerland's Jewish community to one of Charen's lectures. As a Jewish American, Charen could easily establish instant camaraderie with this group. Faith's gesture had set a favorable tone for the night's proceedings. "It was a great evening," she recalled. "I gave a talk, I told a lot of jokes, and everyone had a good time—good public diplomacy, too!"[17]

On another occasion, Charen remembered that two ex-U.S. Army officers led Whittlesey's guests in singing Soviet Red Army songs. Having met and interacted with Soviet officers during World War II, these Americans had

---

[13] Joseph Hayes, interview by author, McLean, VA, May 29, 2009.
[14] Ibid.
[15] Ibid.
[16] Mona Charen, interview by author, telephone, August 15, 2010.
[17] Ibid.

learned to impersonate Russian officers. Since it was commonly understood that the Soviets specialized in placing surveillance equipment in U.S. embassies abroad, the group joked that Russian intelligence agents were likely listening and "scratching their heads and asking each other, 'What is going on at the American embassy?'"[18]

In Charen's view, Whittlesey prioritized mutual understanding between Americans and Swiss. "You can't just go to people and say 'support us,'" Charen suggested. "People need reasons, and you have to try and persuade— and Faith was very, very committed to that."[19]

ASSISTANCE TO RESIDENCE STAFF

The experiences of several Filipino immigrants in the ambassador's residence provide some revealing examples of Whittlesey's compassionate treatment of local embassy employees. The household staff at one point included two chefs, a residence manager and assistant, a butler, a laundress, a gardener, and a parlor maid.

Faith expected a lot from her staff, but she also demonstrated a genuine concern for their well-being. More than 20 years later, the assistant residence manager (housekeeper) and parlor maid—who lived in the residence with Whittlesey—remembered her with abiding affection. These migrant workers held very demanding positions—performing diverse duties from early morning hours to late in the evening—while living far from their childhood homes. For example, the housekeeper and parlor maid served meals, washed dishes, dusted furniture, cleaned silverware, answered the door and telephone, made beds, and ironed clothes. They worked hard to keep these jobs, which allowed them to maintain a work visa and pursue opportunities in Switzerland unavailable in the Philippines. Their accounts of Whittlesey's leadership are unequivocally favorable.

For example, Nenalyn Alicarte, who served as the parlor maid at the ambassador's residence during Whittlesey's second tour, developed a profound respect and appreciation for her boss. As might be expected for a young woman living in a country totally foreign to her, Nenalyn struggled. Both maintaining employment and managing her personal life proved very challenging. Having previously left her job at the Lebanese embassy in Bern because she believed her bosses were not respecting her basic rights,

---

[18] Ibid.
[19] Ibid.

Alicarte had certainly experienced the uncertainties of having to fend for oneself while living abroad on a work visa.[20]

Soon after starting at the U.S. ambassador's residence, Alicarte encountered another formidable, though very different, challenge. After trying to hide her swelling midsection for several weeks, she soon could no longer conceal the fact that she was pregnant. Nenalyn raised the subject with the embassy residence manager Nicola Champeaux, who proceeded to inform the ambassador. In many cases, this story would end with an abortion or the firing of a maid who could not balance work and maternal duties. Having originally come to Switzerland with a work permit issued in 1979, Alicarte worried that leaving the job would mean not just the loss of income but also her forced return to the Philippines, where she would find even greater difficulty in securing work to support herself and her child.[21]

Rather than quietly releasing Alicarte, however, Whittlesey made determined efforts to help the pregnant woman. Committed to the prolife position, Whittlesey suddenly encountered an opportunity to put her principles into practice. When Alicarte could not find an opening for her newborn child in a daycare facility or nursery, the ambassador allowed her to keep the baby upstairs in the residence. Nenalyn recalled that certain State Department officials openly opposed this decision, claiming that Whittlesey did not have the authority to allow Alicarte's baby to live with her in U.S. housing. But Faith asserted her right to decide who stayed as a guest in her place of residence.[22] On several occasions, such as dinner parties during which Alicarte needed to work late-evening hours, Whittlesey's teenage children—Amy and Henry, who spent their school vacations in Switzerland—volunteered to help care for the infant.[23]

Nenalyn frequently broke down with emotion when relating this story in 2009. In Alicarte's view, Whittlesey had treated her as a family member rather than a dispensable staff person. Faith made a profound impression on her by demonstrating such uncommon understanding during her unexpected pregnancy and her child's earliest years.[24]

Whittlesey maintained contact with Alicarte for several years after resigning as ambassador, and she came to Nenalyn's aid on other occasions.

[20] Nenalyn Alicarte, interview by author, Geneva, August 16, 2009.
[21] Ibid.
[22] Faith Whittlesey, discussion with author, telephone, April 12, 2012.
[23] Nenalyn Alicarte, interview by author, Geneva, August 16, 2009.
[24] Ibid.

Alicarte credited Whittlesey's example and words with helping her to develop a greater appreciation for religion and morality, as well.[25] "For me she is a hero," Alicarte recalled. "She's really like, for me, Mother Teresa—because she saved my life."[26]

Annabelle Latu-Ab, a fellow Filipino friend of Alicarte who had recommended that she apply for this position at the residence, also spoke glowingly of Whittlesey. After working for Whittlesey as parlor maid for a while, Annabelle had received a promotion to housekeeper. Whittlesey was an exacting but fair boss, she recalled. Latu-Ab particularly remembered how the ambassador stressed that she should answer all telephone calls "even in the middle of the night."[27] Owing to the 5- and sometimes 6-hour time differential with the United States, family or professional contacts might be trying to reach Faith at odd hours in Switzerland. Alicarte and Latu-Ab also remembered Whittlesey's meticulous attention to every detail associated with entertainment functions or formal dinners, all of which they were expected to implement with rigorous care.

Despite the ambassador's high expectations, both women remembered Faith as exceptionally appreciative of their work, considering her among the most caring and understanding of all the people they had served. After any social event, Whittlesey made a special point of personally thanking each staff member.[28] In Latu-Ab's recollection, the ambassador made a conscious effort to downplay differences among the U.S., European, Filipino, and other staff members. She and her children were even comfortable enough to confide in her while engaged in conversations about their private lives.[29]

This personal contact meant a lot to Latu-Ab, who had thought a barrier existed between herself and non-Filipinos based on her ethnic facial features, social class, and limited knowledge of English. Annabelle initially felt extremely nervous about socializing with the ambassador and her U.S. staff because she had little confidence in her ability to speak fluent English with Americans. Although Latu-Ab also doubted that she would be able to share common experiences with the non-Filipinos on the embassy staff, Whittlesey invited her to lunches and other social events with U.S. and European staff members, which helped her to relax. The ambassador's

[25] Ibid.
[26] Ibid.
[27] Annabelle Latu-Ab, interview by author, Geneva, August 16, 2009.
[28] Ibid. Nenalyn Alicarte, interview by author, Geneva, August 16, 2009.
[29] Annabelle Latu-Ab, interview by author, Geneva, August 16, 2009.

evenhanded treatment of all personnel reduced Annabelle's shyness and self-described "inferiority complex." When Whittlesey promoted her from housekeeper to residence manager, she recalled, the ambassador entrusted her with the combination to the residence safe, which presumably contained some of Faith's most valuable personal possessions.

Whittlesey's willingness to ignore racial and class differences astonished Annabelle, who also spoke about the ambassador with high praise in 2009. "She taught me how to be a human being and to respect others, rich or poor. There were no boundaries in terms of helping one another. I guarantee you she has a golden heart."[30]

ACCUSATIONS FROM EMBASSY STAFF MEMBERS

Despite this praise from embassy and residence employees, a small minority within the Bern mission exerted fierce resistance to Whittlesey's leadership during her second tour as ambassador. Their criticisms of her initially focused on the entertainment fund through which she had received reimbursement for the Meese dinner. As Faith answered these charges, investigators and political adversaries broadened the attack by questioning morale at the embassy, and ultimately by attempting to connect her with the emerging Iran-Contra scandal.

Prior to leaving Washington in the spring of 1985, Whittlesey arranged with, and gained the approval of, the State Department for the creation of the account which would later lead to such controversy. Known as the Unconditional Gift Fund, this account was modeled on another such fund created by U.S. Ambassador to Austria Helene von Damm (formerly personnel director in the White House). Faith had asked individuals to donate money "unconditionally"—that is, without placing any conditions or restrictions on the grant—to the U.S. State Department directly. Donors might, however, request that the contributions support a particular U.S. embassy. At a time of budget consciousness in Washington, Whittlesey viewed this fund as a valuable private-sector solution to shortages of public-sector resources.[31]

Independently wealthy ambassadors often made a practice of covering the expenses associated with entertainment purposes (and the improvement of embassy furnishings) from their own personal fortunes. As Faith did not

---

[30]   Ibid.
[31]   Faith Whittlesey, discussion with author, telephone, April 12, 2012.

have abundant private resources herself, she solicited donors to supply this State Department account from which she could request reimbursement for such extraordinary expenses. "Wealthy ambassadorial appointees could easily afford these expenses. I could not," Whittlesey recalled. "Switzerland was very expensive."[32]

Faith returned to Switzerland with an ambitious public diplomacy agenda. She viewed the Unconditional Gift Fund as a means of representing the United States to the Swiss in a dynamic and creative manner. After meeting with Mary Ryan, assistant to Ronald Spiers, the State Department's undersecretary for management, Whittlesey learned the agency protocols necessary to establish and utilize such a fund in total compliance with the law. Having worked in the executive, legislative, and judicial branches of state and national government, she fully understood the importance of operating within established government guidelines. "I had been a U.S. government prosecutor myself," she recalled, "so I knew how to follow proper legal procedures—and I did."[33] This scrupulous advance preparation made her especially surprised that some officials would later question her actions.

Soon after her arrival, the State Department assigned a new administrative officer, Donald Lynch, to the Bern embassy. Lynch's responsibilities included reviewing and approving expenditures and reimbursement claims. After less than a year in Bern, Lynch accused Whittlesey of requesting and receiving reimbursement from the Unconditional Gift Fund for personal expenditures, such as a blouse for her daughter.

Whittlesey denied any "blouse expenditure or request" and maintained that she used the funds for the specific purpose of advancing the administration's foreign policy goals and improving embassy staff morale. "I was incredulous," she recalled.[34] She could not understand how Lynch, who had personally certified every expenditure and reimbursement, could later claim improprieties. "I said, 'Don, you know, this is slanderous.' I insisted that he apologize in front of his whole section and retract what he had said, which he did."[35] The acting DCM, career officer Louis Segesvary, also conducted an investigation which exonerated her.[36] Lynch even wrote a memo (dated

---

32 Ibid.
33 Ibid.
34 Ibid.
35 Ibid.
36 Typed notes, Box 4, Folder 1. From the Faith Whittlesey Collection, Howard Gotlieb Archival Research Center at Boston University (hereafter referred to as FW).

July 30, 1986) stating that "I am satisfied that there have been no intentional improprieties committed."[37]

DEMOCRATIC CONGRESSIONAL STAFFERS RECEIVE A VISIT

But the allegations surfaced again about a month later when unnamed career Foreign Service officers from Bern approached two employees of Democratic members of the House of Representatives in Washington. Reviving Lynch's charges of misusing the Unconditional Gift Fund, these State Department officials also accused Whittlesey of having arranged a post in Bern for Robert Reilly (as a USIA[38] officer), in exchange for his father's $5,000 donation intended for the U.S. Embassy Bern.

The officers demonstrated a keen understanding of the power structure in Washington by presenting their case not to her but to the staff of Democratic House members. Through that branch's traditional "oversight" function, congressmen could claim constitutional authority to review the activities and operations in U.S. embassies. Within the 435-member House of Representatives, moreover, the accusers had specifically targeted the handful of legislators serving on the Subcommittee on International Operations of the Committee of Foreign Affairs. They did not make their differences known through normal departmental channels or through internal State Department means of redress—such as the agency's grievance process. If these officers surmised that Democrats would have the strongest motivation to investigate a member of the Republican Reagan administration, they guessed correctly.

Whittlesey now found herself in the middle of an interparty power struggle. She faced the prospect of an investigation by House Democrats, who had held majority rule in that chamber since the 1950s. The Republicans had gained slightly more than a dozen House seats during Reagan's 1984 landslide victory, however, and the Democratic congressmen certainly relished the possibility of reversing their fortunes in the November 1986 congressional elections.[39]

The Democratic committee members and their own respective staff members (Republicans having their own separate staff) decided to share the charges not with the ambassador herself but with H. Byron Hollingsworth,

---

[37] Donald J. Lynch to Louis S. Segesvary, July 30, 1986, Box 9, Folder 3, FW.

[38] United States Information Agency.

[39] Steven V. Roberts, "G.O.P. Adds to Total in House, but Democrats Retain Control," *New York Times*, November 8, 1984, p. A29.

who headed the Office of the Inspector General at the State Department. Hollingsworth's office had existed for only 6 days prior to learning of these allegations. If the charges were true, Inspector General Hollingsworth believed a federal criminal statute might have been violated, and he requested that Congress delay official action until his office had an opportunity to research the matter fully. After coordinating with the public integrity section of the U.S. Department of Justice, Hollingsworth initiated an investigation into Robert Reilly's appointment and the other allegation that Whittlesey had misused the State Department fund.[40] Although some congressmen had wanted to hold immediate public hearings, the committee members agreed to await a report from the two departments (State and Justice) that would study the charges.

Whittlesey could not understand the inspector general's willingness to take these allegations seriously. "None of these officials apparently was deterred by the fact that the fund was set up by the State Department," she noted. "State Department officials approved every request for reimbursement I made and received, and they accepted every contribution to the fund."[41]

Complicating the issue of who should lead the investigation, Congress had recently given the Justice Department the authority to appoint an independent counsel in certain circumstances. If the appearance of a conflict of interest existed within the executive branch in investigating its own members, the law created the possibility of hiring an attorney from outside of the administration to research the charges.

ANTI-WHITTLESEY LEAKS TO THE *WASHINGTON POST*, AGAIN!

In these pitched political battles, news reporters may conscientiously strive to maintain objectivity but sometimes end up serving as an informal spokesperson for one side or the other. During Whittlesey's time as director of Public Liaison in the White House, media sources—especially the *Washington Post*—had repeatedly reported anonymous leaks damaging to her reputation.[42] As the investigation process began to take form in 1986, this newspaper again appeared to provide uncritical publicity for

---

[40] *Investigation of the U.S. Ambassador to Switzerland, Hearing and Staff Report Before the Subcommittee on International Operations of the Committee on Foreign Affairs, House of Representatives,* One Hundredth Congress, First Session, March 10, 1987 (Washington, DC: U.S. Government Printing Office: Washington, 1988), p. 10.

[41] Faith Whittlesey, discussion with author, telephone, April 12, 2012.

[42] See Chapter 4, pp. 99–104.

anonymous accusers who seemed intent on damaging her effectiveness as a representative of the Reagan administration.

On September 26, 1986, the *Post* presented the case against Faith in a page-one article headlined "2 Departments Are Probing Whittlesey's Embassy."[43] Reporter Howard Kurtz chronicled the charges. Whittlesey had allegedly used "nearly all the money" from the $80,000 Unconditional Gift Fund "to entertain leading American conservatives, businessmen and administration officials."[44]

But the article failed to mention that "the State Department approved every contribution and expenditure," Whittlesey observed.[45] She considered her actions entirely justified since administrative officer Lynch had signed off on all her purchase orders and vouchers cleared through the Unconditional Gift Fund.

When critics questioned her invitations of conservative intellectuals to Switzerland, she countered that, as a member of the U.S. government's executive branch, she had the task of explaining and advancing the Reagan agenda which voters had endorsed first in the 1980 presidential election and even more decisively in his 1984 reelection. Inviting like-minded officials and intellectuals to Bern best served her public diplomacy goals of publicizing and explaining the administration's policies to both the Swiss and the wider world.[46]

In addition, Kurtz's story detailed the accusation that Faith had arranged for the embassy's hiring of USIA officer Robert Reilly as a *quid pro quo* for his father's $5,000 donation to the fund. Reilly's father had contributed the money 6 days prior to his son's swearing in on November 18, 1985, Kurtz noted.[47] But Whittlesey's selection of Reilly had received official State Department endorsement months prior to his father's gift. The idea that Whittlesey needed a financial incentive to select Reilly, moreover, strained common sense, since Faith had consistently praised Reilly's work when he served under her authority in the White House Office of Public Liaison.

Although Whittlesey believed that this unauthorized release of information pertaining to the investigation inevitably produced a tainted public

[43] Howard Kurtz, "2 Departments Are Probing Whittlesey's Embassy Fund," *Washington Post*, September 26, 1986, p. A1.
[44] Ibid.
[45] Faith Whittlesey, discussion with author, telephone, April 12, 2012.
[46] Ibid.
[47] Kurtz, "2 Departments," p. A1.

account of the events to her detriment, she chose not to defend herself in the media. Investigators had begun their research and interviews, and therefore Faith's lawyers discouraged her from engaging in a media public relations battle. "I now believe that this was a mistake," Whittlesey concluded from the perspective of 2012. "The 'take-no-prisoners' attitude underlying most politics in Washington required mounting a media campaign in my own defense."[48]

By the mid-1980s, the *Washington Post* had emerged as a formidable actor in the nation's capital. Slightly more than a decade earlier, this newspaper had established itself as a kind of government watchdog by launching the earliest probing reports into Republican President Richard Nixon and the Watergate break-ins. After Nixon's resignation in 1974, the *Post* enjoyed a reputation for having valiantly exposed corruption in the executive branch.[49] Apparently viewing the accusations against Whittlesey as promising another high-profile "scoop," the *Post* willingly (and uncritically) published the details in several front-page stories. These accounts relied on Democratic congressional staff members and anonymous State Department employees as sources to develop the public case against Whittlesey.

Daily life in the Bern embassy was affected negatively by these reports. DEA Officer Passic recalled that Eric Kunsman, who had recently arrived as the new DCM, straight away called a staff meeting which "was very nonsupportive of the ambassador." In Passic's recollection, Kunsman "delivered a pompous, self-serving speech which assumed she was gone, and about how badly U.S.-Swiss relations would be affected."[50] The news threatened to undermine morale among the embassy's 125 personnel. According to Commerce Officer Daniel Harris, "What I mostly recall is that you just had to be terribly careful, even talking to friends inside the embassy because you could have very different perceptions of what was going on." Rival camps formed around the issue. "People felt strongly about it, and you could wind up having an argument with a colleague or a friend. It was a very fraught time."[51]

---

[48] Faith Whittlesey, discussion with author, telephone, April 12, 2012.
[49] The two *Washington Post* reporters, Bob Woodward and Carl Bernstein who led the investigation of Nixon, won widespread fame and published a best-selling book, *All the President's Men* (New York: Simon & Schuster, 1974), which subsequently was made into a major motion picture released in 1976.
[50] Greg Passic, interview by author, telephone, January 20, 2012.
[51] Daniel Harris, interview by author, Paris, August 24, 2009.

In another consequence of the *Washington Post* news articles based on anonymous leaks, one political columnist seized the opportunity to express contempt and outrage over the still unproven charges against Whittlesey. *New York Daily News* Washington correspondent and syndicated columnist Lars-Erik Nelson, perhaps hoping to attract readership and create a reputation for hard-hitting stories, wrote a syndicated column titled "Swiss Accounts Show Lady's Not for Bern." Zealously portraying the allegations as a significant embarrassment to the conservative wing of the Republican Party, Nelson characterized Whittlesey as an uninformed ideologue and socialite.[52]

As it happens, Nelson's account contained several illogical statements. He portrayed Faith as having run afoul of many "Reaganites" who "complained to anyone who would listen that she was 'a crazy right-winger.'" In the same article, however, Nelson also called Whittlesey "just another Reaganite" who allegedly exploited "government service and public property to live well and show her pals a good time."[53] Nelson's two somewhat contradictory depictions of Whittlesey—first as a conservative pariah within the Reagan administration and then later as a typical representative of Reagan's White House—made little sense. Certainly it is fair to say that there had, indeed, been hard-fought battles among the White House inner circle over Whittlesey's designated functions as a member of the senior staff. But Nelson's dismissal of Whittlesey as a mere socialite totally ignored her impressive academic, governmental, and political background as well as her successful promotion of the administration's policies through an effective public diplomacy program in Switzerland.

After spending more than 600 words besmirching Whittlesey's character and reputation, oddly enough Nelson in effect exonerated her of any wrongdoing. In the column's final paragraph, he wrote that "it is likely that she did nothing against the law."[54] While Nelson's conclusion all but totally deflated the preceding fanfare of accusations, it also raised a question which he never explored, namely: Were Whittlesey's adversaries merely exploiting (for their own purposes) blatantly false accusations?

Newspaper writers rely on specific sources to provide the outline and details of any story. Faith's adversaries inside the U.S. embassy—protected

---

[52] Lars-Erik Nelson, "Swiss Accounts Show Lady's Not for Bern," *Miami Herald*, October 7, 1986, p. 11.
[53] Ibid.
[54] Nelson, "Swiss Accounts," p. 11.

by anonymity—had more than likely provided the case against her to the media. Alternatively, Democratic members of the House and their staff members might also have leaked anti-Whittlesey stories in the hope of discrediting her and, by extension, President Reagan. Such news might make Democrats appear to be noble watchdogs guarding against Republican mismanagement or even misdeeds. If the investigation did indeed reveal mistakes or even corruption, Democrats might re-create the climate of suspicion about Republican ethics in general which had brought down the Nixon presidency.

Alternatively, a few State Department careerists might have thought themselves likely to benefit from discrediting a noncareer ambassador. Some Foreign Service officers viewed political appointees such as Whittlesey and Reilly as threats to their professional advancement (or at least to their conception of the superiority of career diplomats). Individuals specifically trained as career diplomats might well consider themselves to be, by and large, more effective ambassadors than a president's selection of a political ally or personal friend, no matter how well-qualified the individual on his or her own terms. Imputing mistakes or infractions to Whittlesey could well strengthen the case, in the public's mind, for appointing ambassadors more frequently from the ranks of the career diplomats, or Foreign Service officers.

DEFENDERS OF WHITTLESEY

Although few administration officials spoke out on Whittlesey's behalf, several conservatives immediately rallied to her defense. When the *Washington Post* stories appeared, White House acquaintances (including Lt. Col. Oliver North) called her to inquire about her well-being and whether she needed legal advice.[55] More importantly for her public image, conservative writers began articulating her case in the media.

In the October 3 *Wall Street Journal*, for example, Suzanne Garment portrayed the media campaign as emblematic of a frightening trend of "gotcha" journalism. Whittlesey had violated neither the spirit nor the letter of State Department rules, she asserted. The government had provided no specific regulations or guidelines regarding expenditures from the Unconditional Gift Fund. Since the State Department had approved

---

[55] Faith Whittlesey, discussion with author, telephone, April 12, 2012.

Whittlesey's expenditures to date, Garment argued that efforts to charge her with misuse of funds *after the fact* were inherently unjust.[56]

Regarding the charges against Whittlesey, Garment articulated a theory—which she would later develop into a full-length best-selling book[57]—suggesting that partisan government officials increasingly manipulated scandal-seeking reporters to prosecute political adversaries in the court of public opinion. Garment characterized the media reports about Faith and the proposed congressional committee hearings to investigate her conduct as a "snake pit" in which "some people's resentment [of Whittlesey] has turned into venom."[58] In Garment's view, "No one operated with the slightest presumption that she might have been acting in good faith."[59] Invoking a theme which would prove illustrative of the 1990s (given President Clinton's subsequent bouts of controversy as his Lewinsky affair quickly enough morphed into impeachment proceedings), Garment warned that the "impulse to turn every clash or problem into a crime is poisonous, [and] if people do not stop rewarding its excesses, it will choke our public life."[60]

Jeane Kirkpatrick, who served as Reagan's first ambassador to the United Nations until 1985, also characterized Faith as an innocent victim of a broader attack on noncareer ambassadors. The *Washington Post* printed Kirkpatrick's case in its October 12 Sunday edition. Kirkpatrick explicitly described this newspaper as an unwitting accomplice to a concerted political campaign against Whittlesey and, by extension, Reagan. High-profile *Post* articles, Kirkpatrick charged, were actively aiding and abetting the drive to embarrass Faith. In Kirkpatrick's view, "When a front-page story conveyed the questions of a 'knowledgeable' but anonymous 'source' about Ambassador Whittlesey's use of a special fund for embassy entertainment, the story itself became part of an attack on Whittlesey."[61]

Through use of the *Post* as their uncritical conduit, Whittlesey's detractors in the State Department were actually waging a much wider struggle for power. "Bureaucrats" in the Foreign Service, Kirkpatrick asserted, wanted to create the impression that noncareer ambassadors could not demonstrate

---

[56]   Suzanne Garment, "Scandal Hits the Journal's Editorial Page," *Wall Street Journal*, October 3, 1986, p. 28.

[57]   Suzanne Garment, *Scandal: The Culture of Mistrust in American Politics* (New York: Times Books, 1991).

[58]   Garment, "Scandal Hits," p. 28.

[59]   Ibid.

[60]   Ibid.

[61]   Jeane Kirkpatrick, "Use Fewer 'Anonymous' Sources," *Washington Post*, October 12, 1986, p. D8.

sufficient professionalism and objectivity. Career diplomats considered themselves immune to charges of conflict of interest, Kirkpatrick believed. Those who argued against the appointment of political ambassadors assumed that Faith must have extended favors in exchange for monetary donations—however unfounded those beliefs might be. Whittlesey's unnamed critics had "ballooned an ambiguity [about the Unconditional Gift Fund's rules] into a scandal." In this context, the *Washington Post* emerged as "an unwitting accomplice in an ongoing bureaucratic war against political ambassadors."[62]

In concluding her article, Kirkpatrick urged the newspaper to lessen its reliance on such unauthorized leaks and "make sources more accountable for the reliability of their information." Absent such minimal standards, reporters would "remain vulnerable to willing and unwilling entrapment in personal vendettas and political and bureaucratic wars."[63]

Although Kirkpatrick did not make any reference to Whittlesey's time in the White House, she certainly knew that Whittlesey had borne the brunt of many such media battles throughout her political career, especially in the pages of the *Washington Post*.

ENTER IRAN-CONTRA

In another time and place, these two thoughtful opinion pieces by Garment and Kirkpatrick might have yielded some fruitful discussion and perhaps even soul searching within the media. But unexpected developments set in motion a series of events which cast a broad net of suspicion over the Reagan administration.

Beginning in October 1986 and continuing into 1987, the "Iran-Contra scandal" came to dominate news headlines and public conversations throughout the country. Revelations relating to covert weapons sales and the diversion of funds threatened to derail Reagan's presidency. The administration's enemies aggressively pursued evidence against Reagan allies, including Faith, throughout the executive branch.

In rapid-fire succession, the media launched accounts of White House officials who sold weapons to Iran in exchange for the release of U.S. citizens held hostage in the Middle East. A portion of the profits from these sales had eventually been funneled to anticommunist Contra rebels in Nicaragua. Some Democrats compared the emerging scandal to White House efforts

---

[62] Ibid.
[63] Ibid.

to cover up the Watergate burglaries slightly more than a decade earlier. The media soon started experimenting with names, such as "Reagangate" and "Contragate," for the cloak-and-dagger stories they related.[64] Some of Reagan's opponents even began calling for his impeachment.[65]

Faith's time spent as a high-ranking former White House official now automatically brought her under suspicion. Veteran Washington reporters summoned to mind Whittlesey's consistent efforts as Office of Public Liaison director between 1983 and 1985 to publicize the administration's Central America policy. In the Sunday *Washington Post* on October 19, 1986, a long and detailed article recounted how Whittlesey had organized briefings for interest groups visiting the White House. Two of the covert operation's key players, Lt. Col. Oliver North and National Security Advisor Robert McFarlane, had spoken frequently at her request. This story clearly linked her by association—though without evidence—to the secret scheme suddenly being exposed.[66]

ANOTHER CHARGE: OBSTRUCTION OF JUSTICE

On October 27, 1986, State and Justice Department officials were preparing to conclude their investigation of Whittlesey when Bern embassy DCM Eric Kunsman suddenly accused her of attempting to obstruct justice. Faith had pressured him, he alleged, not to cooperate with investigators seeking to obtain her telephone records. The Justice and State Departments, as well as the congressional subcommittee, immediately opened another line of inquiry. At that point, "It became a vendetta," Whittlesey concluded.[67]

The new charge derived from events unfolding earlier in the same month. From Bern, Whittlesey's secretary had phoned the ambassador in Washington (where she had returned to prepare her defense during the investigations). She reported to Faith that a U.S. embassy receptionist (who was a Swiss national) had begun photocopying the ambassador's confidential telephone logs from her residence and office phones. The request for copies had come from Administrative Officer Lynch, who had originally initiated the improper-funding accusations and who was also in Washington at the time.

---

[64] Tom Wicker, "Two Different Gates," *New York Times*, December 12, 1986, p. A35; Dorothy Gilliam, "Different Era, Same Arrogance," *Washington Post*, December 4, 1986, p. B3.

[65] "Students at Brown to Vote on Proposal to Oust Reagan," *New York Times*, November 9, 1986, p. 58.

[66] Richard Harwood, "Contras' Private Pipeline Pumps at U.S. Behest; That Reagan Backs Shipments Is No Secret," *Washington Post*, October 19, 1986, p. A1.

[67] Faith Whittlesey, discussion with author, telephone, February 18, 2012.

Whittlesey and her lawyers believed that such a request for embassy records should be made in writing and signed by an appropriate authority in the State Department. Thus, Whittlesey immediately contacted DCM Kunsman, who (in the ambassador's temporary absence) was then serving as *chargé d'affaires*, or acting head of the Bern mission. Kunsman specifically denied any knowledge of either the photocopying or any request for the ambassador's personal telephone records.[68]

Acting on the advice of her attorneys, Faith asked Kunsman to intervene. She believed that he had an obligation to prevent any unauthorized release of these records. "The fact that such copying and transmission was taking place in the Embassy without the knowledge of the Chief of Mission or the [*Chargé d'Affaires*] was contrary to the traditions of the Foreign Service, the protection of privacy, and basic management practices," she later wrote to the congressional subcommittee investigating her actions.[69] Kunsman's response did not inspire her confidence. In her recollection of events, Whittlesey characterized Kunsman as reluctant to implement these instructions, which he "preferred to delegate ... to the Regional Security Officer."[70] Whittlesey insisted, as she recalled, that he "take charge—in view of the seriousness with which I regarded the potential invasion of my privacy if these records were disclosed to unauthorized persons."[71]

Days later, Kunsman complied with a written order to send these records to the State Department. On October 23, officials in the inspector general's office had requested that the ambassador's telephone records be sent to them via diplomatic pouch.[72] Whittlesey again spoke with Kunsman by phone and "criticized his reluctance to take charge of this matter in my absence." In all of these conversations with Kunsman, two of Whittlesey's lawyers were in the room and could hear her side of the conversation, "and both flatly denied [Kunsman's] allegations, as do I, of any attempt to obstruct justice, or intimidate a witness."[73] This testimony persuaded investigators from the Justice Department and the State Department's Office of the Inspector General, Whittlesey noted, of the accuracy of her recollection.[74]

---

[68] *Investigation of the U.S. Ambassador to Switzerland*, p. 178.
[69] Ibid.
[70] Ibid.
[71] Ibid., p. 179.
[72] Fuller to Eric Kunsman, telegram, October 23, 1986; Kunsman to Fuller, telegram, October 24, 1986, both in Box 4, Folder 12, FW.
[73] *Investigation of the U.S. Ambassador to Switzerland*, p. 179.
[74] Ibid.

Kunsman's allegation, however, delayed the reports from the Justice and State Department examinations of Whittlesey until December.

EXONERATION, AND A SUBPOENA

In early December 1986, the report of the investigation by the State and Justice Departments exonerated Whittlesey of any illegal activities on her part. With the swirl of Iran-Contra and spy-novel intrigue still in the air, however, some critics of the Reagan administration refused to accept this conclusion. While Whittlesey's supporters praised her for defending herself against politically motivated attacks, the Democratic-controlled Subcommittee on Internal Operations of the House Foreign Service Committee decided to hold a hearing on the subject.

The vaunted "bipartisanship" of the subcommittee's leadership could be somewhat deceiving. Subcommittee Chairman Daniel Mica of Florida, a Democrat, and the ranking Republican member, Olympia Snowe of Maine, both appeared especially skeptical of Whittlesey's innocence. Mica and Snowe issued a joint letter to Attorney General Meese in which they criticized his failure to appoint a special prosecutor for the Whittlesey case. As a moderate Republican, Representative Snowe strongly differed with Whittlesey, Meese, and Reagan on the issues of abortion and the Equal Rights Amendment.[75]

Thus, both Democrat Mica and Republican Snowe perceived Whittlesey as a political adversary, and they showed no trust in the State and Justice Departments' report which had cleared Faith of wrongdoing. Instead, they criticized Meese's unwillingness to apply the Independent Counsel Act of 1978 in her case. Enacted to prevent members of the executive branch from shielding their colleagues in the White House (and elsewhere in the federal government) from prosecution, this legislation authorized the U.S. attorney general to appoint a special prosecutor. Whittlesey's White House service from 1983 to 1985 had made her fully subject to this law. Mica and Snowe further asserted that Meese could not evaluate Faith's case impartially because he had benefited personally from the Unconditional Gift Fund

---

[75] For example, Representative Snowe joined a group of liberal Republican women who unsuccessfully attempted to persuade Republican delegates to endorse the ERA in the party's platform in 1984. Bill Peterson, "GOP Women's Pitch for ERA Heard Coldly," *Washington Post*, August 14, 1984, p. A4.

(from which Whittlesey had received reimbursement for the $385 dinner she hosted at the Bern embassy in his honor).[76]

In the absence of an independent counsel, Mica and Snowe decided to make Faith answer the charges in person. "We feel the subcommittee now has no choice but to conduct formal hearings into the matter," the letter announcing the hearing read. Whittlesey would be subpoenaed to testify before them.[77]

Sympathetic media reports in the *Washington Post* supported the sub-committee's decision to hold the hearing. In yet another front-page headline ("Meese Rejects Special Counsel for Whittlesey"),[78] the *Post* highlighted what Attorney General Meese had decided *against* doing (i.e., invoking use of the independent counsel statute) rather than what Ambassador Whittlesey *had or had not done*—that is, the facts underlying her exoneration. After reviewing the report, Meese concluded that there was "no direct evidence that a donation was made to Ambassador Whittlesey's gift fund in return for the performance of an official act."[79]

But reporter Howard Kurtz, again citing unnamed sources, claimed that the case's principal investigator had recommended naming a special counsel. The story further questioned Meese's refusal to recuse himself from the case despite having been Whittlesey's guest at the Bern embassy dinner party which had been billed in part to the gift fund.[80] The story carried the implication that a more objective perspective might uncover wrongdoing, but the reporter failed to mention that State Department career officers had fully approved and reimbursed these expenses to the ambassador without at any time interjecting or evidencing any reservations.

"TRUE GRIT"

In sharp contrast, conservative outlets trumpeted Faith's exoneration as providing closure to the Whittlesey saga. A *Wall Street Journal* editorial titled "True Grit" praised Whittlesey for having passed a difficult test in which investigators closely examined huge volumes of information, including interview transcripts, correspondence, and telephone records. In particular,

---

[76] Michael Kranish, "Swiss Envoy Faces Questions," *Boston Globe*, December 12, 1986, p. 1.

[77] Howard Kurtz, "2 Lawmakers Criticize Meese for Role in Whittlesey Case," *Washington Post*, December 11, 1986, p. A7.

[78] Howard Kurtz, "Meese Rejects Special Counsel for Whittlesey," *Washington Post*, December 6, 1986, p. A1.

[79] Ibid.

[80] Ibid.

the editors highlighted the Justice Department report's footnote number 17, which asserted that investigators had employed a rigorously skeptical view of her actions and still found no evidence of wrongdoing. In other words, rather than presuming her innocence from the start, they claimed to have examined "the disputed facts in the light least favorable to Ambassador Whittlesey."[81]

Echoing the interpretations offered by Suzanne Garment and Ambassador Jeane Kirkpatrick, the newspaper's editors attributed the charges against Whittlesey to the "jealousies" of career Foreign Service officers. Career ambassadors resented political ambassadors, the editors argued, because these bureaucrats "usually have a harder time raising the representational funds politically powerful figures attract." Throughout the long and tortuous investigative process, the *Journal*'s editors concluded, Whittlesey had shown "True Grit"—the "combination of character, intelligence, humor and commitment" which Americans should cherish in any ambassador.[82]

One of America's best-known conservative writers, William F. Buckley, Jr., also came to Whittlesey's aid and defense, characterizing the charges against her as potentially damaging to U.S. diplomacy. In happier days, Whittlesey had enjoyed traveling to Buckley's chateau near Gstaad, where they had skied together in the Swiss Alps.[83] Now, in his nationally syndicated column in January 1987, Buckley specifically challenged critics of the Unconditional Gift Fund to develop a better alternative means of financing public diplomacy.[84]

Ambassadors such as Whittlesey lacked sufficient allocations from Congress, he argued. Unless they were independently wealthy, U.S. envoys needed to think creatively if they wanted to provide for a reasonable entertainment budget. Whittlesey's innovative resourcefulness in this instance may have appeared sinister to a Washington establishment which viewed conservatives with suspicion. In Buckley's view, however, the "State Department bureaucracy" and an anti-Reagan Beltway culture had promoted "a lazy public disposition to believe that Mrs. Whittlesey was caught up doing something improper, never mind that she was cleared on all counts."

---

[81] "True Grit" (editorial), *Wall Street Journal*, December 12, 1986.
[82] Ibid.
[83] James Shinn, interview by author, Kensington, CA, March 16, 2012.
[84] William F. Buckley, Jr., "Embassies Need Those Private Contributions," *Houston Chronicle*, January 13, 1987, p. 16.

On the contrary, Buckley argued, she was trying "to bring about important changes in public sentiment and understanding."[85]

In other words, Faith was engaged (even through her entertainment activities) in active public diplomacy, as she had consistently undertaken in Switzerland since day 1 of her first tour.

IRAN-CONTRA: A SWISS CONNECTION?

Notwithstanding such praise, the rapidly unfolding story of Iran-Contra's connections to Switzerland kept Whittlesey under the media microscope. By late November 1986, Oliver North had been fired for his alleged role in the secret Iran-Contra transfer of weapons and money.[86] News accounts emerged that he had used Swiss bank accounts in these covert deals.[87]

Observers of Washington politics attempted to muster up conclusions about events which seemed too coincidental to have happened by mere chance. From 1983 to 1985, Whittlesey's Public Liaison staff in the White House had arranged for multiple briefings by North in the old Executive Office Building (in Room 450). North's mysterious and charismatic manner of presenting his anticommunist message had made him the most popular speaker during Faith's tenure at Public Liaison.[88]

Faith offered her own theory, in which she suggested that North may have acted to help the Contras out of frustration. Following her departure from Public Liaison in April 1985, Whittlesey noticed that the White House had terminated the Central American outreach briefings. The administration appeared to have abandoned efforts to secure congressional funding of the Contras. "Ollie very much regretted this, and he may have felt that it was up to him to keep contra aid going," Whittlesey told the *Washington Post*.[89]

But several reporters dug through the facts looking for a more complicated explanation, perhaps a conspiracy which linked North, Whittlesey, and even Robert Reilly. A few questions revealed that Reilly had headed Public Liaison's Central American outreach group under Whittlesey's guidance, and, soon after she left the White House for Switzerland, he had

---

[85] Ibid.

[86] David Hoffman, "Iran Arms Profits Were Diverted to Contras; Poindexter Resigns, NSC Aide North Is Fired," *Washington Post*, November 26, 1986, p. A1.

[87] John Tagliabue, "Swiss Account Linked to Arms Deal Is Frozen," *New York Times*, December 8, 1986, p. A17.

[88] See Chapter 5, pp. 133–135.

[89] David Hoffman and Lou Cannon, "The Key Relationship Remains a Mystery," *Washington Post*, December 7, 1986, p. A26.

joined her in Bern. Then, Faith had assigned him to help her explain to the Swiss why Reagan perceived the Nicaraguan government as engaged in a form of indirect aggression against the United States with covert Soviet, East German, and Cuban assistance. As the U.S. Justice Department was asking Switzerland to assist investigations into North's alleged use of a Swiss bank account in his covert plot,[90] Whittlesey and Reilly appeared to be curiously situated at one of the focal points of the Iran-Contra operation.

Speculation suddenly abounded that Whittlesey's embassy might have participated in the funneling of secret aid to Nicaragua's anticommunist rebels. The widely read Zürich newspaper *Tages-Anzeiger* reported that the ambassador had in fact helped North gain access to the Swiss banks. Although Faith denied the claims in the story,[91] this left-of-center Swiss paper featured the accusation in a front-page article.[92] No proof of this charge ever emerged despite hours of questioning of Whittlesey in Washington and her driver in Switzerland.[93]

But international cross-fertilization of news proliferated suspicions about Whittlesey's alleged role in Iran-Contra. The *Washington Post* and *New York Times* had further distributed the Swiss newspaper's reports, which had been based on anonymous U.S. "congressional sources."[94] Failing to heed Jeane Kirkpatrick's admonition that reporters should scrupulously avoid printing purely anonymously sourced information, these media outlets now resorted to repeating allegations from unnamed individuals quoted in foreign newspapers. Anyone who might have intended to foster public doubts about Whittlesey's actions could find willing accomplices in these powerful U.S. publications.

The search continued for months to find hard evidence to demonstrate that Whittlesey had mismanaged the Bern embassy and had been involved in "Contragate." Immense American news interest in Iran-Contra encouraged the Swiss media, in turn, to focus attention on the U.S. mission in Bern.

According to a December 24 telegram from the U.S. embassy in Geneva, the Swiss weekly newsmagazine *L'Hendo* had reported all manner of connections between Whittlesey, the anticommunist Contra resistance, and

---

[90] Loren Jenkins, "U.S. Asks Swiss Aid in Criminal Investigation of Secord, North," *Washington Post*, December 9, 1986, p. A1.
[91] "Envoy Denies a Swiss Report," *New York Times,* December 18, 1986, p. A20.
[92] Reported in ibid.
[93] Faith Whittlesey, discussion with author, telephone, April 12, 2012.
[94] Ibid.; Loren Jenkins, "Swiss Expand Order Freezing Secret Accounts," *Washington Post*, December 18, 1986, p A29.; "Envoy Denies," p. A20.

Switzerland. For example, during Whittlesey's tenure as ambassador, a career diplomat and the U.S. consul general in Zürich, Louis Segesvary, had traveled to Nicaragua and secretly visited Swiss development aid projects. This paper also noted that political officer Frank Tumminia, who had served in the Bern embassy during both Whittlesey's first and second tours, had left Switzerland in 1985 for the U.S. embassy in Suriname (formerly Dutch Guiana). The reporter might have recognized Tumminia's transfer to the Caribbean area as the routine rotation of a career diplomat. Instead, the story implied that Faith had established a clandestine global operation in Bern to resist Cuba and other communist governments within the U.S. sphere of influence.[95]

L'Hendo and the left-wing U.S. publication *The Nation* even entered into a collaboration to investigate. Eric Burnand, staff writer for *L'Hendo,* contributed to a January 1987 *Nation* article in which he and his coauthor Mark Shapiro detailed their theory that North had worked through a Whittlesey-Reilly-Segesvary "*contra* support system" in Switzerland. The piece characterized North as "one of her closest advisors" in the White House. Shapiro and Burnand called on the House Foreign Affairs subcommittee to press Whittlesey on how much time she spent advocating for the Contras, whether she spoke with North in person or by telephone during his travels to Switzerland, and whether she knew of the secret Swiss fund created by North.[96]

Amid the daily drumbeat of charges and media reports, Whittlesey and Robert Reilly even came under suspicion from journalists representing conservative news outlets. Having read these elaborate accounts of the Bern embassy's alleged connection with Iran-Contra, some of Whittlesey's like-minded allies concluded that she and Reilly had indeed participated in covert operations against the Sandinistas. As Reilly recalled, "Faith and I had been so visible on the Central America issue that many people thought, 'Well, the administration just couldn't send them to Switzerland for no reason.'"[97] Reporters who knew Reilly personally even prodded him for exclusive rights to his story because they sought the publicity and prestige of giving the public the authoritative proof that Whittlesey and Reilly had indeed aided Oliver North. As Reilly related these events a quarter of

---

[95]   U.S. mission Geneva to USIA, Washington, DC, telegram, December 24, 1986, Box 2, Folder 14, FW.
[96]   Mark Shapiro and Eric Burnand, "Keeping Faith," *The Nation*, January 17, 1987, p. 42.
[97]   Robert Reilly, interview with author, Vienna, VA, August 15, 2009.

a century later, he chuckled at the widespread presumption of his guilt, saying, "Even friendly journalists from the *Washington Times* would say, 'Bob, could you let me know *first?*' "[98]

Leading conservative voices nonetheless denounced the subcommittee's treatment of Whittlesey as an "inquisition." In Whittlesey's case, the *Wall Street Journal* argued, the continued vilification that had been instigated by unnamed accusers served merely to "lay down a large, muddy public record of implied wrongdoing." In the editors' view, the politics of personal destruction had come to dominate life in DC: "It is becoming increasingly difficult to square the well-defined rights of the accused in a criminal proceeding with the interminable, anonymous, vague insinuations of guilt typified by the Faith Whittlesey affair."[99]

APPEARING IN CONGRESS

As the March 1987 congressional hearing approached, Whittlesey systematically prepared to defend herself in an increasingly bitter political climate. Further allegations surfaced about President Reagan and several senior administration officials. Whittlesey endeavored to demonstrate to anyone who inquired that she did not belong under the cloud of suspicion surrounding these policymakers or policy moves.

High drama and intrigue touched Faith personally upon learning about a suicide attempt by Oliver North's former boss and partner in the arms-for-hostages deals. On February 9, 1987, Robert McFarlane, Reagan's national security advisor from 1983 to 1985, had ingested a nearly fatal dose of (perhaps 20 or 30) Valium capsules.[100] As the event had occurred only days prior to his scheduled testimony before the U.S. Senate, some Americans might have speculated that conspirators seeking to suppress the truth about Iran-Contra had attempted to assassinate him. Faith had known McFarlane (who had supported her appointment as ambassador in 1981) for years.

Whittlesey could not help but imagine that some of the players or agencies which participated in this undercover operation might now want to silence anyone with any real or apparent connection to the events. As Faith prepared in Washington to face the subcommittee, she called Annabelle

---

[98] Ibid.

[99] "The Inquisition" (editorial), *Wall Street Journal,* December 22, 1986.

[100] Susan Okie and Chris Spolar, "McFarlane Takes Drug Overdose; Iran Probe Figure Hospitalized Shortly Before Testimony Due," *Washington Post,* February 10, 1987, p. 1.

Latu-Ab, the ambassador's residence manager in Bern. During the conversation, Whittlesey gave Annabelle the combination to the residence safe, saying, "Whatever happens to me, you just take out all the papers and everything I have there, look after it, and later give it to my daughter."[101] Approximately a month following McFarlane's near-death encounter, Whittlesey entered the House of Representatives to answer questions from the subcommittee.

The congressional hearing, which began on March 10, 1987, immediately descended into accusations of improper political maneuvering. On the heels of the November 1986 elections, in which Democrats regained a majority in the Senate and maintained control of the House of Representatives,[102] partisan political divisions frequently rose quickly to the surface.

As the public period of the hearing began, Representative Jack Kemp of New York (with whom Whittlesey had worked in writing the foreign policy portion of the 1980 Republican Party platform) requested time to speak, and he testified to Whittlesey's long and distinguished service to the country. Kemp's comments also specifically referenced Swiss praise of Faith's performance as ambassador by the Mayor of Zürich, the Swiss-American Chamber of Commerce, and the Jewish community of Switzerland.[103]

Kemp framed the investigation in broader terms by highlighting the national security implications of Whittlesey's public diplomacy mission. "The Soviet Union is engaged in a full-scale effort to separate and divide the West, and they devote enormous resources to influencing public opinion," Kemp told the subcommittee.[104] In his view, Faith "prepared [Americans] to meet that propaganda with our greatest weapon, the truth." Kemp also questioned the subcommittee's authority to pass judgment on Whittlesey, noting that ambassadors "serve strictly at the pleasure of the President of the United States."[105]

Kemp's testimony strongly endorsing the ambassador prompted Representative Peter Kostmayer, a Democrat from Bucks County, Pennsylvania, to reproach Whittlesey. "This hearing room reeks with politics," Kostmayer abruptly began his remarks when given a chance to speak. "I think bringing a Republican candidate [Kemp] for the presidency

[101] Annabelle Latu-Ab, interview by author, Geneva, August 16, 2009.
[102] Paul Taylor, "Democrats Wrest Control of Senate from GOP," *Washington Post*, November 5, 1986, p. A1.
[103] *Investigation of the U.S. Ambassador to Switzerland*, p. 7.
[104] Ibid., p. 8
[105] Ibid.

of the United States ... lends a kind of partisanship to the hearing."[106] Although the 1988 presidential election remained a year and a half in the future, Kostmayer's comments revealed his clear appreciation of the potential electoral implications of this hearing.

Other committee members also showed great sensitivity to how the public would perceive their actions. Chairman Mica and the ranking Republican Snowe spent several minutes justifying the hearing as part of Congress' oversight role vis-à-vis U.S. diplomatic missions. In Snowe's view, Congress might need to examine "if the Department of State has sufficient safeguards to ensure that any practices at our posts abroad do not run contrary to the policies of the Department."[107]

Mica's opening statement expressed outrage at those who had protested the subcommittee's investigation of Faith. In his first question to Whittlesey, he clearly suggested that she had sought to influence the hearing through various political pressures applied in advance. Several of Mica's Florida constituents had called his office to complain about the committee's preliminary treatment of Whittlesey. "I personally take offense and resent the fact that people would call my district office and have friends call me and say such things as my entire district is upset over the fact that this hearing is being held," Mica fumed.[108] Mica certainly well understood the wisdom of keeping one's constituents happy. "I was so upset that I was considering subpoenaing each of the people who has called a member of Congress to find out who asked them to call," Mica warned sternly.[109]

Why had so many of his constituents telephoned his office to protest the hearings? Having traveled frequently to Florida as a White House senior staff member, Faith certainly had friends in that state. But Whittlesey's carefully worded reply to Mica portrayed the circumstances as democracy in action: "I suppose they believed that there was something awry and they wanted to express their opinion." She also expressly denied having asked anyone to contact Mica's office.[110]

After some further discussion about the telephone calls to his office, Mica proceeded immediately to inquire about Whittlesey's contact with Oliver

---

[106] Ibid., p. 30.
[107] Ibid., pp. 4–5.
[108] Ibid., p. 1
[109] Ibid., p. 27.
[110] Ibid.

North and "the so-called Iran-Contra situation."[111] Whittlesey testified at length that she had not participated in the transfer of money or arms in any way. Even when the questions returned to the original improper-funding accusations that Lynch had brought, several congressmen insisted upon revisiting the diversion of weapons sale proceeds to the Contras. Some of the committee members' questions even scrutinized Whittlesey's public diplomacy efforts aimed at persuading the Swiss against providing agricultural aid to the communist-affiliated Sandinistas.[112]

Although the committee relatively quickly dispensed with discussion of the Unconditional Gift Fund, focusing instead on other accusations, the lawmakers cast a wide net in examining Whittlesey's activities. Hours of back-and-forth discussion and detailed accounts of events followed. The official transcript of the hearing's first session ran nearly 100 pages (and excluded material from the lengthy nonpublic session that covered matters touching on national security or employees' privacy and professional reputations).[113]

Representative Kostmayer (the Bucks County, Pennsylvania, Democrat) most aggressively accused Whittlesey of having pressured State Department officials to act in accordance with her wishes. Faith defended herself as an advocate of the policies of a president who had won the public's endorsement in overwhelming fashion in his November 1984 reelection. She believed that Kostmayer hoped to discredit her as a potential political opponent in a future Pennsylvania state election for U.S. House, U.S. Senate, or the governor's office: "Representative Kostmayer's actions were designed to drive up my negatives in Pennsylvania polling data."[114]

Not to be deterred, Kostmayer pursued the same line of questioning with State Department Undersecretary Ronald Spiers and George Vest, director general and director of personnel of the Foreign Service. These two senior officers had also been summoned to testify by the subcommittee. Questioning Vest, Kostmayer asked him to confirm a specific allegation from the subcommittee's report. Congressional staff members had written that Whittlesey had issued a "threat" of retribution from her White House friends if Vest would not approve an extension for James Shinn, the DCM who had carried over from her first tour. Upon Faith's return to Switzerland

---

[111] Ibid.
[112] E.g., ibid., pp. 39–40, 61, and 68.
[113] Ibid.
[114] Faith Whittlesey, email to author, May 29, 2012.

for her second tour, she had asked Vest not to rotate Shinn to another assignment, but he had denied her request.[115] Despite Vest's admission that he felt "pressure" from Whittlesey, he refused to agree with Kostmayer's charge that she had threatened him. In fact, Vest challenged the reliability of the congressional report where Kostmayer had unearthed this accusation. "I do not remember saying a number of things that are in that record," Vest stated to the committee.[116]

Despite Kostmayer's prosecutorial tactics, neither of these high-level State Department representatives supported the congressman's argument that Whittlesey violated the department's policies or procedures. In apparent frustration, Kostmayer accused Vest and Spiers of being "intimidated" by Whittlesey, a charge which both men denied earnestly and repeatedly.[117]

Vest and Spiers appeared to view the committee's investigation of Faith as completely out of bounds. Spiers later remembered the event as a totally unjustified attack. In a 1991 oral history interview (less than 5 years after the hearing), he told an interviewer: "The Committee was obviously intent on damaging her reputation. Although I was not a devotee of Whittlesey, neither George [n]or I testified as the Committee wished. I think they were greatly disappointed by what we had to say."[118] Spiers' refusal to take sides in this battle, he believed, damaged his working relationship with Representative Snowe, who would refuse to speak with him "either personally or on the phone" in the years following this hearing.[119]

Having failed to uncover evidence of wrongdoing, the subcommittee's leaders nonetheless charged her with mismanagement and bad judgment. At the end of the hearing, Mica and Snowe concluded that Whittlesey had committed no crimes, but they faulted her for permitting the appearance of impropriety which they claimed had resulted from the State Department's acceptance of donations from a man whose son (Robert Reilly) she had employed. The potential for conflict of interest was unacceptable, even if they could not establish that a *quid pro quo* had actually taken place. Notably, the ranking subcommittee members focused their critique on Whittlesey

---

[115] *Investigation of the U.S. Ambassador to Switzerland*, pp. 1, 69–70.

[116] Ibid., p. 70.

[117] Ibid., p. 71.

[118] Ronald I. Spiers, interview by Thomas Stern, November 11, 1991. Frontline Diplomacy, Manuscript Division, Library of Congress, Washington, DC.

[119] In the interview, Spiers detailed other disagreements with Snowe in addition to his differences with her over his testimony at the hearing. Ibid.

rather than commenting on the State Department's own failings, if any, in its monitoring function.

DIPLOMACY ON A "SHOESTRING" BUDGET

In light of the investigation of Whittlesey, the State Department had decided to ban such private funding of U.S. representation abroad. In Whittlesey's view, this change in policy would have negative consequences. She continued to defend the concept of the Unconditional Grant Fund as a tool for active public diplomacy.

Faith articulated her opposition to the State Department's decision by asking Americans to consider the true value of the nation's embassies. In an August 1987 opinion piece in the *Wall Street Journal,* Faith advocated for her signature theme, public diplomacy. As she had done since her first tour, Faith criticized the almost automatic assumption that U.S. embassies should serve solely to communicate government-to-government decisions on policy. Expressing a broader interpretation of official American missions, Whittlesey asserted that ambassadors should "engage a wide range of local opinion leaders."[120]

The declining legitimacy of authoritarian regimes and the global communications revolution had made foreign publics more politically active and thus significant to the United States, she noted. U.S. legations needed to seize the emerging opportunities to persuade the people of their host countries about the value of American ideals, she suggested. An imperative for heightened public diplomacy, Whittlesey argued, also derived from the potential *negative* consequences of these expanding international networks of exchange. In her view, a creeping "skepticism, if not outright hostility," toward U.S. policies required Americans to explain their country's intentions and values on a person-to-person basis.[121]

Faith suggested that private-sector funding of such public diplomacy seemed perfectly logical, and perhaps critical, at this historic juncture. In recent years, she noted, Congress had begun to limit the funding of U.S. missions abroad. Without private donations, Whittlesey warned, U.S. embassies would need to conduct diplomacy on a "shoestring" budget.[122]

---

[120] Faith Whittlesey, "Diplomacy on a Shoestring Has Its Price," *Wall Street Journal,* August 14, 1987.
[121] Ibid.
[122] Ibid.

Later reflections by Joseph B. Gildenhorn, who served as U.S. ambassador in Bern from 1989 to 1993, provided support for her argument that ambassadors (at least those posted to certain key countries) frequently required independent wealth to supplement congressional allocations. In Gildenhorn's reflections immediately following his 4-year tour, he asserted that the ambassador's residence in Bern had required money for improvements upon his arrival. As a wealthy businessman, he was able to finance the redecoration of the residence via a personal contribution which he made through the State Department. Gildenhorn also exceeded the embassy's budgeted expenditures for entertainment at times, but he covered the deficit through his own private resources. "If we were short at the end of the year, I would pay it myself and not expect the staff to contribute."[123]

The State Department's decision to accept personal donations from ambassadors but not from a pool of donors appeared to stack the deck in favor of the megarich. Presidents who wanted their ambassadors to pursue active public diplomacy would presumably need to exclusively select heads of mission with deep pockets (at least for high-profile or especially prominent postings).

During Whittlesey's congressional hearing, Democratic subcommittee chairman Dan Mica had acknowledged as valid the point that ambassadors of less substantial means might have to operate at a disadvantage. The Unconditional Gift Fund made sense, Mica conceded, "if the funds are there for a purpose that can be defined and guided."[124] Without such supplementation, he noted, "it leaves poor people like me out of the loop for ever becoming an ambassador."[125]

In a case of extreme incongruity, the State Department had itself accepted outside private donations for renovations to its Washington headquarters. On September 26, 1986, the *Post* ran its first front-page account detailing unsubstantiated charges about Whittlesey's solicitations for the Unconditional Gift Fund, which amounted to $80,000 in supplemental resources (beyond the standard congressional allocations) earmarked for U.S. embassy Bern.[126] When that same newspaper reported on October 1 that the State Department had raised more than $30 million from private

---

[123] Joseph B. Gildenhorn, interview by Charles Stuart Kennedy, May 13, 1993. Frontline Diplomacy, Manuscript Division, Library of Congress, Washington, DC.
[124] *Investigation of the U.S. Ambassador to Switzerland*, p. 42.
[125] Ibid.
[126] Kurtz, "2 Departments," p. A1.

tax-deductible donations to renovate the seventh and eighth floors of its main building, the story was tucked away on page D7.[127]

Similarly, as the State and Justice Departments vigorously investigated whether Faith had engaged in a conflict of interest by allowing the State Department to accept a $5,000 donation from the father of one of the embassy's new hires, the *Post* reporter was nonchalantly describing how a committee comprising seven tobacco companies had pledged $1.2 million to adorn the State Department's Treaty Room with 18th-century Delft tobacco jars, peace pipes, and "whorls of carved tobacco leaves, seeds and flowers."[128] No editorials or anonymous sources called for investigations to determine whether those donors received special favors, nor was any undertaken. When presented with these starkly contrasting stories in 2012, Whittlesey dryly and succinctly commented, "Selective indignation."[129] Moreover, these private donations for State Department projects seemed to vindicate Whittlesey's advocacy for the Unconditional Gift Fund concept.

Ironies abounded in the *Washington Post's* handling of the Whittlesey investigation. On December 4, the *Post* reported that Secretary of State George Shultz hosted a State Department fund-raiser in which $1,500 purchased an individual ticket to meet with Vice President George H. W. Bush, the guest of honor.[130] While this event received page C1 placement, Whittlesey's investigation again graced *page A1* just days later. This story quoted Reagan administration critics who suggested that Attorney General Meese could not show objectivity in the Whittlesey case because he had attended a $350 dinner partially financed through the Unconditional Gift Fund.[131]

The page C1 story actually focused more on the emerging Iran-Contra scandal and the alleged role of Swiss financial institutions than on the State Department renovations. Swiss ambassador Klaus Jacobi attended, and he responded to questions about whether Switzerland would help U.S. officials investigate whether Oliver North had diverted funds from Iran to Central America through Swiss banks. Jacobi's polite reply affirmed that the Swiss government would fulfill its treaty obligations and cooperate with U.S. law

---

[127] Sarah Booth Conroy, "Unveiling Stately New Décor: Spotlight," *Washington Post*, October 1, 1986, p. D7.
[128] Ibid.
[129] Faith Whittlesey, discussion with author, telephone, July 5, 2012.
[130] Sarah Booth Conroy, "Shultz's Big Show: Bush Is Guest of Honor at State Fundraiser," *Washington Post*, December 4, 1986, p. C1.
[131] Kurtz, "Meese Rejects Special Counsel," p. A1.

enforcement agencies insofar as possible within the terms of existing agreements between the two nations. "We know our banks were used to launder money. Our banks will reveal the owner, if they are authorized, or if it is done through judicial assistance."[132] Of course, the reporter failed to take note of this final irony: Whittlesey had done more to guarantee U.S.-Swiss cooperation in a variety of such sensitive legal matters than anyone else.

The excessive media coverage and expressions of outrage against Whittlesey lent credibility to her theory that a (or multiple) political vendetta(s) motivated these investigations. During these investigations, many career embassy officials wrote memoranda which described Donald Lynch and Eric Kunsman as consciously seeking to undermine Faith's leadership.[133] State Department officer Doug Sears recorded that Lynch unprofessionally sought to undermine the ambassador's authority during an introductory briefing in December 1986.[134] The multiple memos also suggest that Faith had many more supporters than enemies among the State Department rank and file.

Most significantly, partisan suspicions fueled the burning desire of Reagan's critics to find evidence of wrongdoing by Faith. In 1988, President Reagan nominated Stephen Trott, who had served as associate attorney general under Meese from 1986 to 1988, for Ninth Circuit judge on the U.S. Court of Appeals. U.S. Senators Edward Kennedy and Howard Metzenbaum refused to allow a Senate vote on Trott's nomination unless the Justice Department provided the senators with documents related to the Whittlesey case. Anonymous sources had claimed that Justice's public integrity section had recommended that Meese appoint a special counsel to investigate Faith, and the senators were clearly hunting for evidence that might uncover wrongdoing by Trott, Meese, Whittlesey, and perhaps the president. Although Reagan's Justice Department initially refused, claiming the confidentiality of "internal deliberative memoranda," the administration ultimately turned over the documents in March.[135] After this intense standoff between the executive and legislative branches, no further charges were advanced against Whittlesey.

---

[132] Conroy, "Shultz's Big Show," p. C1.
[133] E.g., Monica Scopelliti, memo to file, February 25, 1987, Box 4, Folder 10, FW; Richard Devine, memo for the record, May 19, 1987, Box 4, Folder 12, FW.
[134] Douglas Sears, memo to file, February 26, 1987, Box 4, Folder 10, FW.
[135] Louis Fisher, *The Politics of Executive Privilege* (Durham, NC: Carolina Academic Press, 2004), p. 79.

While no *Washington Post* headlines announced Faith's total and complete exoneration, Mona Charen had summarized the sordid tale in a *National Review* column titled "The Petty Inquisitors." According to Charen, "Faith Whittlesey's experience gives a clear picture of the symbiotic relationship between the bureaucracy, Congress, and the media. The press had a field day, the bureaucrats won their internal dispute, and the congressional Democrats carried the headlines, if not the day."[136]

"THE SWISS WILL MISS YOU"

While Faith had survived a battle for her professional life, the 6-month-long political and legal odyssey had exacted a personal toll. In late 1987, Whittlesey decided to leave public life, although she would remain at her post until July 1988.

The investigations had caused her great pain and emotional suffering, recalled John McCarthy, who ran the Geneva office for the executive search firm Russell Reynolds Associates in the late 1980s. Faith had recruited McCarthy to serve as chairman of Republicans Abroad (Switzerland), and he had come to regard her as his "personal mentor in conservatism."[137] In McCarthy's description of the lessons he learned from Whittlesey, he used martial metaphors. "Faith supported the Republican Party because parties are the armies that raise the money, sponsor the candidates, and fight the elections."[138] McCarthy called Faith "a heroic figure who carried the banner, but also a human figure who felt pain and who had difficulties."[139] In her most difficult days, Whittlesey would travel to see John and his wife Mary at their cozy Villars chalet in the Swiss Alps. "Faith used to say, 'That's the only place I can enjoy a restful night's sleep.' "[140]

Whittlesey appeared unhappy with the administration's lukewarm defense of her during that period, as well. By this time, moreover, it was increasingly evident that the Republican Party was verging in the direction of the more moderate George H. W. Bush as Ronald Reagan's likely successor, a prospect not likely to warm the hearts of such well-certified conservatives as Whittlesey.

---

[136] Mona Charen, "The Petty Inquisitors," *National Review*, December 18, 1987, p. 60.
[137] John McCarthy notes for "Tribute to Faith Whittlesey" testimonial dinner, Republicans Abroad (Switzerland), April 19, 2008. In John McCarthy's possession.
[138] Ibid.
[139] John McCarthy, interview by author, New York, August 11, 2009.
[140] Ibid.

Without expressing regrets but eager to return to private life, she composed her resignation letter to President Reagan. As she explained to the president, all three of her children now lived in America. But Faith assured the president that she would, upon returning to the private sector, continue to advocate "those principles which attracted me to you" when she first committed herself to Reagan as he challenged President Ford for the 1976 Republican Party presidential nomination.[141]

Whittlesey also provided the president with an assessment of Swiss-American relations as her tour came to a close. She cited four major recent accomplishments as signs that her mission had proved successful. "This year alone we have concluded four major agreements in the areas of judicial assistance, law enforcement cooperation, civil aviation, and export control."[142] In Whittlesey's view, Switzerland held "a deep reservoir of goodwill for the United States."[143]

As she had done for years, Faith described several important Swiss characteristics which spoke directly to the potential for continued good relations with the United States. In particular, she singled out for praise "[Swiss] devotion to the sanctity of the individual, decentralized government, democratic capitalism, and military preparedness as the best guarantee of peace with freedom." Whittlesey clearly perceived the Swiss as sympathetic to Reagan's core conservative ideas. In her estimation, the Swiss were truly "natural friends of liberty."[144]

President Reagan's reply "reluctantly" accepted her resignation, and acknowledged her desire to return to her three children. The president called Faith "one of my most steadfast and effective supporters" both in the White House and in Switzerland. "I have missed you since your return to Switzerland in 1985," Reagan wrote, and predicted "I am sure the Swiss will miss you, too."[145]

"IT KEEPS YOU CLEAN"

Prior to her departure in July, she delivered many farewell speeches to the Swiss individuals and groups with whom she had become so familiar and

---

[141] Faith Ryan Whittlesey to The Honorable Ronald W. Reagan, December 9, 1989. Letter in Faith Whittlesey's possession.
[142] Ibid.
[143] Ibid.
[144] Ibid.
[145] Ronald Reagan to Faith Whittlesey, December 17, 1987. Accessed July 12, 2012 at *www.reagan.utexas.edu/archives/speeches/1987/121687d.htm.*

close. In a handwritten note she prepared for one such address, she wrote, "As you know, I have been associated with some controversial issues both here and in Washington. While I do not seek controversy for itself, I have never shied away from it. In fact, I have always subscribed to G. K. Chesterton's remark, 'I believe in getting into hot water. I think it keeps you clean.' "[146]

This rhetorical nod to Chesterton, a conservative Catholic Englishman, demonstrated how ideas remained at the center of Whittlesey's public service. Faith was never one to avoid contentious disagreements about policy, and she seemed to believe that confronting these difficult questions head-on was the most important contribution she could make as a public servant.

In the summer of 1988, Ambassador Whittlesey left the small city of Bern, with slightly more than 100,000 residents, to join the 8 million people living in the "Big Apple." She would not be leaving Switzerland for the last time, however—far from it.

---

[146] Handwritten notes, Box 4, Folder 4, FW.

CHAPTER 8

New York and the American Swiss Foundation
Private Diplomacy (part 1)

Faith Whittlesey arrived in Manhattan during the summer of 1988 to circumstances that appeared promising. Lewis Rudin, a Reagan supporter known as "Mr. New York" for his extensive real estate holdings and political connections in that city, helped her find an apartment.[1] Situated in the city's Upper East Side, her residence placed her in a vibrant neighborhood of luxurious boutiques, the beautiful East River walkway, numerous famous restaurants, Fifth Avenue, Central Park, the Metropolitan Museum of Art, and, just across the park, Lincoln Center. Her 20-year-old daughter Amy lived with her. This new home also located her much closer to her two other children, especially the youngest, William, who was attending a boys' boarding school only a short distance from the city.[2]

As a New York City resident, Faith also was well positioned to continue the interests she had pursued as U.S. ambassador in Bern in a different forum. For more than two decades, Whittlesey had participated directly and indirectly in U.S. politics. During her nearly 5 years as head of the U.S. mission in Switzerland, she had actively engaged with that nation's people, especially key governmental and economic decision makers. Now, in a

---

[1]   On Rudin, see Bill Baily, "Lew Rudin, 'Mr. New York,' Dies," *New York Daily News,* September 21, 2001. Accessed July 27, 2012 at *http://articles.nydailynews.com/2001-09-21/ news/18353875_1_samuel-rudin-rudin-management-lewis-rudin.*
[2]   Faith Whittlesey, discussion with author, telephone, July 11, 2011.

private-sector role, Whittlesey would soon be asked to continue her work with U.S.-Swiss organizations and leaders of U.S. and Swiss multinational corporations to strengthen ties between the United States and Switzerland.

THE BIG APPLE

"From Bern, I had no time to search out the job market extensively in 1988," Whittlesey recalled.[3] Yet, her training as an attorney and her professional network attracted Harvey Myerson, a well connected New York lawyer known to many by his nickname "Heavy Hitter Harvey," according to the *New York Times*. Faith was impressed by Myerson's personally coming to Bern to recruit her to the firm.

Whittlesey would initially practice corporate law at Myerson's firm, which was a joint venture with Bowie Kuhn, the former commissioner of Major League Baseball. In the wake of the bankruptcy of the nation's fourth-largest law firm (of which Myerson was a partner), the two men had then launched their own firm with 135 lawyers in 1988.[4] Opening in November 1987, the new Manhattan office of Myerson and Kuhn soon had high-profile clients such as real estate developer Donald Trump and the Shearson Lehman Hutton Investment firm—the name (at the time) for mainstay (at the time) Lehman Brothers.[5] Myerson, whom *Fortune* magazine had dubbed the "master of disaster" for his ability to assist companies with serious legal troubles, boasted the ability to "knock the socks off" the world's most powerful financiers.[6]

Michael Horowitz, her trusted friend, had joined the firm and encouraged her to accept Myerson's offer. Horowitz, a former White House colleague, had represented her *pro bono* during the combined State/Justice Department followed by congressional investigations of her second tour as ambassador. She decided to join Myerson and Kuhn as a partner, a decision she would soon have occasion to regret.

Faith's family circumstances made New York City particularly suitable for her at this period in her life. Philadelphia carried melancholic memories

---

[3]   Ibid.
[4]   David Margolick, "Can a Tarnished Star Regain Luster?," *New York Times*, February 25, 1990, p. F1. Amy Dockser, "Former Envoy to Switzerland Joins Law Firm," *Wall Street Journal*, July 19, 1988.
[5]   Paul Richter, "Myerson & Kuhn Law Firm Files for Chapter 11: Attorneys," *Los Angeles Times*, December 29, 1989. Accessed on July 31, 2012 at *http://articles.latimes.com/1989-12-29/ business/fi-1235_1_baseball-commissioner-bowie-kuhn*.
[6]   Margolick, "Tarnished Star," p. F1.

of her deceased husband. Washington and its lobbying industry also held no appeal to her. But Manhattan offered Whittlesey closer access to her three children, Henry, Amy, and William, who were approaching the age when they would be making pivotal choices about applying to college, starting careers, and forming lifetime relationships.

In New York, she lived within hours of each child. Her eldest son Henry was an undergraduate student at Harvard. William attended Trinity-Pawling School, slightly more than an hour's drive away in Pawling, New York.[7] Amy was just about to start her sophomore year at Fordham College in the Bronx and only a year later, in September 1989, she would marry George D. O'Neill, Jr., a great grandson of John D. Rockefeller, Jr.[8]

The transition to life outside of government work appeared to benefit Whittlesey in a personal way: "I like being a private citizen," she said in a 1989 interview.[9] Public service had its drawbacks, such as limiting Faith's ability to assure financial security for her children and her own future. Political battles had invigorated her at times, but attacks by political opponents and hostile media had also exacted a toll.

Amidst all these changes, one phenomenon remained constant: Whittlesey continued to assign herself an active professional agenda. She embraced her role as breadwinner for her three children by working as a law partner, corporate board member for various companies, and later head of her own consulting firm. Throughout this period, she remained committed to several causes in which she believed most strongly. In addition, she continued to promote the bilateral friendship between the United States and Switzerland.

The Big Apple also proved convenient for Whittlesey's service on several corporate boards. For example, she accepted offers to serve as a director of Munich Reinsurance, the U.S. subsidiary of a large German insurance company, Allianz; the media and marketing company Valassis Corporation; and several Swiss companies, such as Schindler Enterprises Inc. (which had just purchased Westinghouse Elevator Company and Nestlé (for whom she served on the U.S. advisory board). At the point that she had joined six corporate boards, she began declining similar offers. Living in New York

7   Faith Whittlesey, discussion with author, telephone, January 19, 2012.
8   "Amy Whittlesey, a Student, Weds," *New York Times*, September 24, 1989, p. 70.
9   Faith Whittlesey, interview by Ann Miller Morrin, June 21, 1989. Frontline Diplomacy, Manuscript Division, Library of Congress, Washington, DC.

enabled her to participate actively in board meetings, which were frequently held in the city.[10]

In 1989, disaster struck the nascent Myerson and Kuhn law firm as it was suddenly charged with overbilling clients and soon filed for court bankruptcy protection. Whittlesey had not been the target of any of these charges, but as one of the firm's partners she had to contribute money to the legal settlement. Harvey Myerson went to jail, and Faith, as a partner, was assessed by the bankruptcy court a significant part of her small savings.[11] Although she soon found work at another legal firm, this first postambassadorial work experience left a bitter taste.

Whittlesey's next legal stint proved to be almost equally abbreviated. She joined a well-known Philadelphia law firm, Pepper, Hamilton & Scheetz, founded in 1890, but which was only then opening a New York office. She did not like the dynamics of a large law firm and did not stay long.[12]

"A BRAIN THE SIZE OF MANHATTAN"

In contrast, Whittlesey enjoyed her work as a member of several corporate boards. Beginning in 1992, for example, she served on the board of Valassis Corporation, a Livonia (Michigan)-based provider of media and marketing services. Founded in 1970, Valassis, then chiefly a supplier of newspaper advertising coupons, went public and began trading shares on the New York Stock Exchange in 1992, the same year Whittlesey joined their board.

Two longtime Valassis executives have credited Whittlesey with playing a significant role in that company's meteoric rise to prominence. Alan Schultz, the company's chairman of the board in 2012 (and a 28-year veteran of the company as of that year), explained that Valassis product offerings and revenues had expanded exponentially during Whittlesey's long association with the firm, rising from one product and $350 million in revenues in 1992 to some 30 products and services yielding $2.3 billion in prospective revenues in 2012.[13] Past General Counsel and Executive Vice President Barry Hoffman (who retired in 2012 as a 25-year veteran of the company) noted that the number of employees grew from 110 in 1982 to some 7,500 in 2007.[14]

---

[10]   Faith Whittlesey, discussion with author, telephone, January 19, 2012.
[11]   Ibid.
[12]   Ibid.
[13]   Alan Schultz, interview by author, telephone, May 21, 2012.
[14]   Barry Hoffman, interview by author, telephone, May 21, 2012.

Whittlesey demonstrated a consistently strong commitment to her role on the board, according to both Schultz and Hoffman. Neither man could recall her missing a board meeting. In fact, they both remembered being impressed that Faith accomplished such a feat despite her frequent overseas travel. On numerous occasions, she attended via conference call from Europe or Asia. "In many cases, she had to wake up at three in the morning because we scheduled meetings based on Eastern Standard Time, but she showed no signs of being tired," Schultz recalled.[15] Whenever they needed to contact board members quickly for their approval or consent on specific issues, recalled Hoffman, Whittlesey's responses were always exceedingly prompt, "just amazing!"[16] They both appreciated her diligence as a sign of sincere dedication to the welfare of the company.

More than merely being present, Whittlesey was consistently an active participant in the meetings. Hoffman and his fellow executives prepared a lot of research materials for board meetings because Faith—particularly in her role as chairperson of the compensation committee—would ask for data comparing the company with other organizations of similar size and scope. "She makes you a better manager because of her high expectations," Hoffman allowed. "You want board members to challenge you to ensure that everybody does their job."[17] Schultz also admired Whittlesey's commitment to preserving the company's continued financial health, saying, "She is passionate about her long-term fiduciary responsibility to shareholders, and she is always looking to avoid any 'short-term optics' which make the bottom line appear better than it is."[18] Both men appreciated her seriousness of purpose.

Over a period of two decades of service, Whittlesey established herself as a leader on the Valassis board. Board members looked to her to chair executive sessions during those times when only the outside directors—excluding senior management—would meet. As chairperson of the compensation committee, she reviewed and approved pay scales, hourly employee rates, bonus plans, and executive compensation. "This committee is key in terms of the shareholders' perspective," Hoffman noted. Whittlesey's experience on several other corporate boards also provided Valassis with a lot of value,

---

[15] Alan Schultz, interview by author, telephone, May 21, 2012.
[16] Barry Hoffman, interview by author, telephone, May 21, 2012.
[17] Ibid.
[18] Alan Schultz, interview by author, telephone, May 21, 2012.

in Hoffman's view. "She brought a lot of knowledge about how a diverse array of corporations worked."[19]

Schultz remembered that Whittlesey's long-term outlook particularly helped steer Valassis to diversify. Years prior to the decline in newspaper-based products, she encouraged the company's executives to look beyond advertising inserts (the company's chief product) within print media. "Faith Whittlesey recognizes future problems long before they become evident to most people," Schultz acknowledged.[20]

Schultz and Hoffman seemed to enjoy Whittlesey as an individual, as well. "She has a brain the size of Manhattan," Hoffman quipped, "and she's a great raconteur. I used to try to sit next to her at board meetings just to hear her stories about politics and world affairs."[21] Schultz admired her patriotism as well. "She's a great American, always serving her country, and looking for ways to improve relations with other countries around the world. She's taken Valassis employees on trips to Switzerland and China designed to help them understand the perspectives of others around the world and to help others understand the United States."[22]

LEADING THE AMERICAN-SWISS ASSOCIATION

Living in New York City provided Whittlesey with many opportunities to continue to cultivate relationships with the Swiss. Most of the large Swiss multinational companies had offices in Manhattan. In the fall of 1988, only months following her return to the United States, a delegation of three leaders of the American-Swiss Association approached Whittlesey with a proposal which would lead to one of the signature achievements of her private diplomacy initiatives.

These three men asked her to assume leadership of the American-Swiss Association. One of her visitors, the highly esteemed former U.S. Ambassador to Switzerland Shelby Cullom Davis, had been this organization's chairman for many years, but he would turn 80 years old in 1989. Whittlesey had served with distinction in Bern, they noted, almost as long as Davis's 6-year tenure as U.S. ambassador to Switzerland.[23] Faith promptly accepted their offer and the newfound responsibility attending it with characteristic

---

[19] Barry Hoffman, interview by author, telephone, May 21, 2012.
[20] Alan Schultz, interview by author, telephone, May 21, 2012.
[21] Barry Hoffman, interview by author, telephone, May 21, 2012.
[22] Alan Schultz, interview by author, telephone, May 21, 2012.
[23] Davis served Presidents Richard Nixon and Gerald Ford as U.S. ambassador in Bern from 1969 to 1975.

seriousness of purpose. "I was quite flattered, and yet not really knowing what I was getting into," she recalled more than two decades later.[24]

In the wake of the conclusion of World War II, the American-Swiss Association was created to explain Switzerland's unique foreign policy heritage. Some Americans strongly resented neutral Switzerland's refusal throughout the war to sign on to the U.S.-led military alliance—the "Allies"—against Nazi Germany. Thus, the American-Swiss Association's founders had long endeavored to host speakers who could educate Americans about Switzerland's traditions—in particular, the Swiss government's centuries-old tradition of maintaining political neutrality in foreign wars. Over the years, Americans with Swiss connections and Swiss temporarily based in the United States had periodically attended American-Swiss Association events (dinners and luncheons primarily) to exchange ideas about how relations between the two countries might best be improved.

As World War II faded in the public's collective memory, the American-Swiss Association's board of directors viewed Whittlesey as a person who might revitalize the organization and give it new purpose. Geoffrey C. Bible, chief executive officer of the Philip Morris Corporation, and other organization directors believed that more potential existed for the American-Swiss Association to strengthen bilateral relationships. At that time, Philip Morris was the largest U.S. corporate employer in Switzerland.[25] Several board members were convinced that Whittlesey could breathe new life into the largely quiescent voluntary organization.

Whittlesey perceived value in an organization which could advance, through the private sector, the goals of stronger bilateral relations and a deeper mutual understanding which she had pursued as ambassador. After accepting the board's offer to assume leadership, Faith relied heavily on the insights and advice of her New York–based Swiss-American lawyer friend, Hans Kaeser, who agreed to join the board.

Most Americans failed to recognize the importance of Switzerland's friendship to the United States, especially in the areas of job creation, capital flows, humanitarian commitments, and diplomatic "good offices," such as representing U.S. interests in Iran and Cuba. Approximately one-third of all offshore worldwide liquid assets were managed through the Swiss financial center. More and more, U.S. companies chose to locate their

---

[24] Faith Whittlesey, email to author, July 11, 2011.
[25] Ibid.

European offices in Switzerland. Faith frequently reminded U.S. citizens that this small nation "punched above its weight economically" and was one of the largest direct investors in the United States. In addition, the United States was one of the largest donors to the International Committee of the Red Cross, a Swiss-run institution headquartered in Geneva. In sum, the bilateral U.S.-Swiss relationship, Whittlesey believed, "needed to be nurtured."[26]

With this perspective in mind, Whittlesey proposed an idea which she believed would have a positive long-term impact on U.S.-Swiss relations. This new initiative would actively supplement the work of both nations' diplomatic corps.

ENVISIONING THE YOUNG LEADERS PROGRAM

Her principal scheme, the Young Leaders Conference, immediately gained support from the board of the American-Swiss Association. As she had demonstrated as U.S. ambassador in Bern, Faith believed in the potential impact of person-to-person diplomacy. Whittlesey now leveraged the experience and skill she developed in her government work to create a model of bilateral cooperation through the private sector.

Faith proposed a travel program which would bring together both American and Swiss professionals who had shown promise in the early stages of their careers. Models of foreign exchange programs existed, and Whittlesey traveled with Steven Hoch, a dual U.S.-Swiss citizen who had become active in the American-Swiss Association, to speak with the chairman and president of the American Council on Germany. This organization sponsored an American-German Young Leaders Conference.[27] Prior to Whittlesey's acceptance of the presidency and chairmanship, Hoch had proposed a similar idea to the American-Swiss Association board. "They listened politely, but they didn't really get it," he recalled.[28]

The strength of Whittlesey's personality surely contributed to the board's favorable response. One member, the board's secretary, George Gyssler, recalled that she made a very convincing case. Whittlesey's leadership qualities definitely impressed Gyssler, a Swiss national who served as CEO of certain Asea Brown Boveri (ABB) U.S. affiliates. Gyssler's recollection of

---

[26]   Faith Whittlesey, email to author, July 11, 2011.
[27]   Steven Hoch, interview by author, telephone, November 23, 2010.
[28]   Ibid.

Whittlesey, 20 years following their initial meeting, produced a bubbling stream of superlatives to describe Whittlesey's personality. "She develops an immediate affinity and this is an extraordinary characteristic of hers," Gyssler related. "Extremely intelligent, fast, demanding—but friendly, very friendly."[29] The rest of the board shared this view, according to Gyssler and Hoch.[30]

Faith envisioned a week-long series of events which would provide a platform for Americans to appreciate the Swiss on their own terms, and vice versa. Without careful, deliberative planning, however, she understood that the typically gregarious U.S. participants might not interact in a meaningful way with the generally more reserved Swiss. Thus, Whittlesey decided against creating a foreign exchange program which fêted participants with a vacation-style "Club Med" atmosphere. To the contrary, Faith insisted on full days of panel discussions, speakers, and educational tours that might include historical sites, factories, local government offices, museums, or an excursion into the Alps. While recognizing the attraction of Switzerland's "beautiful surroundings and abundance of good food and wine," Whittlesey wanted to foster more than superficial small talk and casual contact. Careful seating arrangement at meals would serve to encourage extension of the issue-oriented conversations which the day's events had stimulated. From dawn until long past dusk, the busy program prodded participants to "mix and mingle," just as Whittlesey had encouraged her embassy staff to imitate.[31]

Whittlesey's political experience in both the United States and Switzerland proved vital to the Young Leaders Conference. Very few Americans had a more intimate understanding of both nations. In 2 years as the White House director of Public Liaison, she had interacted with a broad spectrum of American interest groups representing professional associations, business, labor, religious, and ethnic organizations, and all 50 states. As U.S. ambassador in Switzerland for nearly 5 years, Whittlesey had similarly engaged with all regions and social sectors of that nation through her active public diplomacy agenda. This unique degree of contact with a wide spectrum of two countries helped her design a conference based on a truly consequential exchange. Whittlesey's knowledge of both the United States

---

[29] George Gyssler, interview by author, Zürich, August 19, 2009.
[30] Ibid. Steven Hoch, interview by author, telephone, November 23, 2010.
[31] Faith Whittlesey to author, July 11, 2011.

and Switzerland informed her preparation of all program details—such as setting, recruitment of participants, and curriculum.

In another critical divergence from predecessors, such as the German program, Whittlesey suggested that Switzerland host the Young Leaders Conference each year. A Swiss city or location would serve as the conference's home base rather than having a rotating schedule between Swiss and U.S. venues. There were multiple reasons behind Whittlesey's proposal. For one, U.S. citizens knew much less about Switzerland than the reverse. Second, many more Swiss citizens had traveled to the United States than Americans to Switzerland. Third, Whittlesey believed that the most talented corps of potential U.S. participants would respond more positively to an invitation to visit Switzerland than an opportunity to travel to another U.S. city. "I knew fewer high-level Americans would be willing to take a week from their busy lives for a program in Boston, for example, as opposed to one in Geneva," she explained in 2012.[32] Finally, Switzerland's comparatively small size enabled U.S. participants to immerse themselves in more than one of that country's diverse regional cultures. In the vast United States, a conference could expose the Swiss to only a small slice of multiple regions of the United States.

These decisions, Whittlesey believed, would help ensure that Americans came to know a country which they might have otherwise overlooked, and that the Swiss would reexamine their assumptions about a nation that they thought they understood. Aware that some U.S. citizens confused Switzerland with Sweden, Faith also believed the Swiss unintentionally contributed to this limited appreciation for their country. Switzerland was not "a splashy, self-promoting country," Whittlesey noted. "Understatement was their preferred style." People in the financial centers of New York and London, or perhaps the world of science and technology at MIT and Caltech, likely knew about Switzerland. But, outside of these specific professions, "the Swiss profile in the U.S. was so low, they were nearly off the radar screen entirely."[33]

Thus, few American opinion makers in the media, think tanks, and liberal arts colleges and universities appreciated Switzerland's impact on the U.S. economy, she believed. Many Americans enjoyed—and excelled in—the art of public relations, multimedia, and communications. Yet, the Swiss did

---

[32]   Faith Whittlesey, discussion with author, telephone, January 19, 2012.
[33]   Faith Whittlesey, discussion with author, telephone, July 11, 2011.

not typically have the same tendency toward (and skill in) promotion and self-presentation as did Americans, especially in a language not their own.

Whittlesey believed that an annual Young Leaders Conference in Switzerland would open American eyes to the Swiss and generate a fuller and more meaningful understanding of the United States among future leaders of Switzerland. The American-Swiss Association's board of directors agreed. In short order, she began to implement her idea.

CHOOSING THE YOUNG LEADERS AND PROGRAM SPONSORS

Two preliminary challenges confronted Whittlesey. First, she needed to recruit participants who would represent the United States in a respectful and positive manner.[34] Second, since the conference took place in Switzerland annually, Whittlesey also had to recruit new yearly sponsors from the Swiss business community to serve as hosts.

Neither task proved easy. The latter goal meant asking leaders of Switzerland's multinational corporations to underwrite the conference's expenses. "Providing room, board, and transportation for 50 people for a week is no small sum in Switzerland—so, my pleas for sponsorship had to be thought out very carefully and made in person-to-person meetings with the CEO or board chairman."[35] Whittlesey suggested that each of the major Swiss multinationals could host the conference once every 10 years so that "the burden would be spread out and not fall on one group disproportionately."[36] Fortunately, she had cultivated positive relationships with Swiss CEOs, who greeted her proposal more favorably because they knew well that Faith understood Switzerland and held their country in high regard. Credit Suisse, UBS, Schindler, and Nestlé sponsored the conference during the earliest years. The privilege of helping to select the Swiss conference participants strengthened the incentive for Swiss CEOs to justify sponsorship of this program to their boards of directors and investors.

In a related point, the quality of the U.S. delegation thus added to the perceived benefit of the conference for Swiss multinationals. If the program sent well-connected future decision makers from the many regions and political perspectives of the United States, Whittlesey believed, leaders of these companies could justify the conference's cost to their board members.

---

[34] A board composed primarily of representatives of Swiss multinational corporations chose the members of the Swiss delegation.

[35] Ibid.

[36] Faith Whittlesey, discussion with author, telephone, January 19, 2012.

The potential to establish positive relationships with the next generation of U.S. political and business leaders might satisfy Swiss sponsors that this new venture would benefit their country in the long term. Most of these companies had made large investments in the United States, in factories and in direct capital flows into American financial markets.

Whittlesey developed rigorous criteria for selecting American delegates. First, she focused on U.S. opinion leaders. Americans in state and local government, think tanks and colleges, business, and the media, she believed, had cultivated sufficient rhetorical skills to articulate the complex and multifaceted character of U.S. politics, culture, and economics in a conference setting. She described these candidates as coming from the American "chattering class," the very important group of U.S. citizens who influenced public policy in the United States. Future leaders in these particular fields would best contribute to the educational goals of the Young Leaders Conference because they would spread the lessons they learned about Switzerland through their personal interactions, public speaking, and writing.[37]

Second, Whittlesey sought U.S. candidates who had little previous knowledge of Switzerland. Since the conference's purpose was to create strong bilateral connections where they did not previously exist, she did not perceive value in inviting Americans who were employed by a Swiss company, had Swiss family or business ties, or had been educated in Switzerland.

Political and ideological diversity was a third characteristic of the selection process. Despite critics who might portray her as a knee-jerk conservative, Whittlesey maintained productive professional relationships with many Democrats and liberals. Proving herself more than a mere ideologue, she persuaded Republicans and Democrats to accept invitations. "In the early days," Hoch related, "she had the brilliant idea of going to senators from both parties—she was very balanced—and have them choose a young leader from their state."[38]

Fourth, to keep education at the forefront of the conference's activities, Whittlesey insisted on selecting people who would not primarily use the opportunities presented by the week-long conference to solicit clients. This requirement typically discouraged nomination of lawyers in private practice only, public relations specialists, lobbyists, and money managers. Neither

---

[37] Faith Whittlesey, discussion with author, telephone, July 11, 2011.
[38] Steven Hoch, interview by author, telephone, November 23, 2010.

did it seem appropriate to invite "conference tourists" who might view the Young Leaders Conference as merely an all-expenses-paid European vacation (a vacation—all would soon enough learn—it most definitely was not!).

To create a coterie of American candidates from diverse regions and professions, Whittlesey utilized her professional connections and broad knowledge of the United States. John Barrasso, who later was elected to the U.S. Senate from Wyoming, participated in the first conference, and Charlie Crist, who later was elected governor of Florida, attended in 1991. Whittlesey's extensive contacts with leading national Democrats—such as Vice President Al Gore, U.S. Senator Bill Bradley of New Jersey, U.S. Senator Charles Robb of Virginia, and Pennsylvania Governor Ed Rendell—allowed her to attract participants from both ends of the political spectrum. Former Democratic Congresswoman Gabrielle Giffords of Arizona attended in 2004, and another Democrat, Albert "Ben" Chandler, participated in 1998 and was later elected to the U.S. Congress.

LAUNCHING THE YOUNG LEADERS CONFERENCE

When it came to the conference agenda, "she was relentless," recalled Swiss entrepreneur and Young Leader Philibert Frick. "She would walk over the mountains, and—there was one guy from Credit Suisse—I think he had mapped out a 4-hour hike. She was there, and she would do everything—all these activities—from morning at 7 until midnight."[39]

Whittlesey approached conference events with the same degree of commitment she demonstrated in selecting participants and soliciting sponsors. Just as she had organized an excursion in the Bernese Alps for U.S. government officials prior to their negotiations with Swiss bankers and politicians in 1982 during her first months as U.S. ambassador, she made sure that the conference itinerary would include the Swiss mountains. "I wanted to share my love of Alpine scenery with the Young Leaders," Whittlesey recalled.[40] As an avid hiker and skier herself who had never missed the opportunity to enjoy the mountains in all seasons while ambassador, she led by example.

If organized correctly, Whittlesey believed, the conference schedule should offer an opportunity to create long-lasting positive personal relationships between delegations of Americans and Swiss. In her view, the American-Swiss Association could bring young Americans from all regions

---

[39] Philibert Frick, interview by author, Geneva, August 14, 2009.
[40] Faith Whittlesey, discussion with author, telephone, January 19, 2012.

of the United States into contact with the diverse people of Switzerland and the richness of Swiss culture and history. The Young Leaders Conference would also expose the Swiss to the varieties and depth of America in a far more significant way than Hollywood and other media purveyors had ever attempted. Given this potential formula for success, carefully chosen U.S. participants represented Whittlesey's number-one priority.

The Young Leaders Conference energized many of Switzerland's leading decision makers, who personally volunteered their time and knowledge to the program. When the Young Leaders visited government buildings, factories, and corporate offices throughout Switzerland, Faith had arranged for lectures or discussions to be led by leading Swiss politicians, entrepreneurs, and corporate managers. "From the beginning," Hoch recalled, "top executives in the Swiss companies really liked this idea. So, instead of sending some mid-level VP to talk to the Young Leaders, often you'd have a CEO of some of these top multinational companies in Switzerland like ABB, Holcim, Nestlé, Novartis, Schindler, and UBS."[41] This kind of commitment raised the conference's level of conversation, quality of information, and ultimately its prestige in both the United States and Switzerland as a coveted invitation.

Whittlesey joined the group in almost every activity. Faith's vision proved infectious as speakers imitated her example. "Chief executive officers from major Swiss multinational companies would come and spend an hour or more with the Young Leaders," recalled Hoch, who attended the first conference. "And sometimes they would get so excited, they'd stay for beers and talk all evening with the Americans." Whittlesey had created an outlet for a very healthy dialogue, Hoch believed. "There weren't too many venues where corporate executives could just freely talk to a bunch of smart people like that, expressing all kinds of different opinions."[42] Such high-level personal participation by senior Swiss executives and government officials ensured that the program provided Americans with a deep appreciation for Swiss foreign and economic policy, financial power, and tourist opportunities. For instance, Alberto Togni, executive vice chairman of UBS and for many years president of the American Swiss Foundation's Swiss Advisory Council, would often join the program for casual discussion following a formal talk.

And of course, Young Leaders soon enough would secure some of these prized executive posts in government and the private sector. Steven Bernard,

---

[41] Steven Hoch, interview by author, telephone, November 23, 2010.
[42] Ibid.

director of the Geneva Financial Center (which serves as the trade association for that city's financial community), characterized Whittlesey as "one of the favorite conduits that Switzerland can and should use to maintain positive relationships with the United States."[43] The Young Leaders Conference, which Bernard attended as a Swiss participant in 1997, helped Whittlesey create "a dedicated pool of dynamic and influential people" who believe in fostering mutual understanding between the two countries.[44]

According to Raymond Baer, a Young Leader in 1993 and chairman of the board of Julius Baer Holding AG since 2003, a leading private bank in Switzerland, the Young Leaders Conference demonstrated unique and positive characteristics which had no competitor. "I do not know any other effort where two countries are assuring a continuous pipeline of young and promising leaders across all sectors and political arenas who come together for a week of intense discussions."[45]

LOOKING BEYOND NATIONAL STEREOTYPES

The quality of participants contributed to the degree of trust with which participants conducted themselves in conversations. By maintaining the agreement that remarks would be considered "not-for-attribution" or "off the record," formal speakers and discussants could venture beyond official "talking points" which their business concern or government agency had authorized.

Conference members thus spoke frankly without fearing that their comments would appear in print for scrutiny by adversaries. This understanding raised the content of conversations from uncompromising, nonnegotiable talking points to more genuine give-and-take. Christoph Schaer, a Swiss national,[46] attended the conference in 1998 during a time of severe tensions between the two countries. To Schaer's surprise, he did not find his colleagues attempting to make "headline-grabbing" statements or seeking to score propaganda points. Instead, individuals honestly expressed deeply felt opinions which helped generate greater awareness and appreciation for another perspective.[47]

Many American participants also appreciated the quality of the discussions. David Holt, vice president of operations and business development

---

[43] Steven Bernard, interview by author, telephone, August 17, 2009.
[44] Ibid.
[45] Raymond J. Baer, email to author, August 12, 2010.
[46] Schaer had frequently asked Ambassador Whittlesey to provide U.S. speakers for events he organized during his university years. See Chapter 3, pp. 77–78.
[47] Christoph Schaer, interview by author, Zürich, August 24, 2009.

at Conexus Corporation in Indiana, agreed that the conference created conditions for open yet respectful debate. "Most political and religious debates end with animosity. In this forum, [however,] it was productive and enlightening to have the discussion without creating hard feelings between parties. This is hard to do in America."[48] University of Scranton history professor Kathryn Meier offered a theory to explain the openness of Young Leaders Conference exchanges. Switzerland's multiparty democracy had proved highly conducive to compromise, she believed, whereas in America's two-party system every issue "becomes politicized" by a tendency to maintain either Republican or Democratic doctrinal purity.[49]

From the Swiss perspective, participants appreciated the opportunity to present their country as more than the stereotypical images projected in U.S. popular culture. Philibert Frick, who attended the second conference in 1991, appreciated that Americans could recognize that "Switzerland is actually better than the cliché of a country with only cheese and secret bank accounts."[50] Luciano Gabriel—chief executive officer of PSP Properties, one of Switzerland's largest real estate companies, and a Young Leader in 1992—recalled that the usually reserved Swiss participants developed greater comfort speaking in English and engaging in vigorous dialogue with their American counterparts over the course of the week.[51]

Both Americans and Swiss recognized the Young Leaders Conference as a unique opportunity to surpass the boundaries of nationality. Raymond Baer believed that the conference reminded participants of the importance of understanding the other's cultural and political systems "since there are many wrong impressions on both sides." Such recognition of differences would also lead to an appreciation of common goals. In David Holt's words, "We might not agree on some key issues, but in the end we all want a better world."[52] Many other participants expressed an admiration for the Young Leaders Conference's method of giving them the opportunity to engage in honest and open exchange with people possessing a different global understanding.

---

[48] David W. Holt, email to author, August 12, 2010.
[49] Kathryn Meier, interview by author, telephone, February 2, 2012.
[50] Philibert Frick, interview by author, Geneva, August 14, 2009.
[51] Luciano Gabriel, interview with author, Zürich, August 21, 2009.
[52] David Holt, email to author, August 12, 2010.

BEHIND THE SCENES

Faith's long-standing support of various conservative interest groups during her political career had won her the admiration of many politically engaged Americans. When a tall, somewhat portly young man approached her at a 1988 election night party (hosted by George D. O'Neill, Jr., later her daughter's husband) in New York City, Whittlesey recalled having no recollection of his face. "You don't know me, but I know you," the man announced. "I just moved here from California to start a radio show." Whittlesey, and the rest of America, would soon become well acquainted with this person, Rush Limbaugh, as one of the nation's iconic media personalities for the next several decades.[53]

Many young Republicans admired her political experience as well as her generous mentoring of their careers. Faith continued to meet with Reagan administration veterans, such as speechwriter Josh Gilder (who participated in the 1991 Young Leaders Conference). In Gilder's view, Whittlesey enjoyed great respect among Reaganites as "one of the staunchest and most effective advocates of Reagan's freedom agenda."[54] Meanwhile, she cultivated new friendships in New York, such as reporter Christopher Ruddy, who would later found the highly successful and influential Newsmax Media, one of the leading conservative news outlets in 2012. "When I was teaching high school in the South Bronx and starting to write for a monthly conservative newspaper, the *New York Guardian*, she took an interest in my work, and that meant a lot to me," recalled Ruddy (a 2001 Young Leader).[55]

Faith believed that active and successful public diplomacy was one of Ronald Reagan's most valuable legacies, and she thus resolved to invest substantial time and energy in an academic institution which would train students in the strategy and techniques of statecraft and diplomacy. Soon after Reagan left office, John Lenczowski envisioned a graduate school for international affairs and national security in Washington, DC. As a National Security Council staff member in the 1980s, Lenczowski had worked with Whittlesey in the Reagan White House. Faith agreed to serve as a founding member of the board of trustees for Lenczowski's new institution, founded in 1990 and known as the Institute of World Politics (IWP).[56]

---

[53] Faith Whittlesey, interview by author, Sherborn, MA, March 25, 2010.
[54] Joshua Gilder, interview by author, telephone, August 26, 2010.
[55] Christopher Ruddy, interview by author, telephone, December 27, 2010.
[56] John Lenczowski, interview by author, telephone, June 15, 2011; Owen Smith, interview by author, telephone, May 15, 2012.

IWP benefited greatly from the strategic assistance of Whittlesey's numerous contacts, who proved important to the program's development in several ways. "Of all the people I worked with in Washington, she was my strongest supporter and mentor," Lenczowski recalled.[57] Prior to receiving accreditation from the association of peer institutions, for example, Whittlesey connected Lenczowski with her friend John Silber, president of Boston University. Because a new academic institution cannot even apply for accreditation until it has a full degree program in place and a student body willing to graduate from an accredited school, and because it would take time to complete the building of a degree program, Lenczowski requested that Boston University give credit for IWP courses during its initial years until it received independent accreditation—credit it ultimately received.

Whittlesey also helped IWP raise thousands of dollars. Lenczowski admired how Whittlesey could articulate the institute's qualitative long-term policy vision in language which impressed corporate decision makers who focused on bottom-line results, "She appreciated the nuances of policy decisions with acute discernment," recalled Lenczowski. Whittlesey's constant, unwavering support for the school's mission meant much more than mere financial donations, he stressed, noting, "The root of the word 'fiduciary' comes from the Latin *fides*, which means 'faith.' Faith keeps faith."[58] Faith would serve as chairman of the IWP board for 6 years, and in 2012 she received an honorary doctorate from that institution.

Whittlesey's contribution to IWP also impressed Michael Waller, who held the institution's Walter and Leonore Annenberg chair of international communication in 2012. "She was always planning future initiatives," recalled Waller, who served as an intern in the White House when Whittlesey was director of Public Liaison. "Faith never rested on her laurels."[59] For example, Whittlesey encouraged the theme of public diplomacy, which became a defining mission of the institute. IWP's faculty produced many articles and books which argued on behalf of extending U.S. foreign policy goals to engage foreign *publics*, not merely the government officials, in other countries— just as Whittlesey had done in Switzerland, through the American-Swiss Association and later in China through her private initiatives.[60]

---

[57] John Lenczowski, interview by author, telephone, June 15, 2011.
[58] Ibid.
[59] Michael Waller, interview by author, Washington, September 16, 2010.
[60] On China, see Chapter 9.

Based on this careful nurturing, IWP developed and expanded. After beginning by offering summer courses in 1992, the institute introduced a year-round program in 1994. By 1998, IWP granted certificates of graduate study, and the institute's first Master's degree candidates received diplomas in 2002. After working in affiliation with BU for 14 years, IWP became totally independent in 2005.

Despite Whittlesey's limited political engagement, she encouraged many young scholars and academics behind the scenes. As she had done in the White House and in the U.S. embassy in Bern, when emerging young intellectuals caught her attention, Whittlesey tried to connect them with leaders of think tanks, prospective donors, and influential politicians.

MANAGING HEALTH CHALLENGES

Each year since 1899, on the second Saturday of December, a nonprofit organization known as the Pennsylvania Society has hosted a festive holiday dinner in the grand ballroom of the Waldorf Astoria Hotel in midtown Manhattan. In 1994 Whittlesey attended, as she had done for many years.

This time, however, she could not enjoy the socializing because of blurred vision in her right eye. No matter what remedies she tried, the haziness persisted. "I kept removing my contact lens to clean it. Finally, when I held my hand up to my right eye, I realized I couldn't see out of that eye."[61] Mary Ann Meloy, her longtime friend and professional colleague from Pennsylvania and the White House Office of Public Liaison, recalled leaving the party with Whittlesey. Meloy's typically stoic friend seemed distracted. "As we were walking together until we had to split off," Meloy recalled, "Faith said, 'You know, that's my eye doctor's office. If it weren't so late at night, I'd go right in and see him. My eye is killing me.'"[62] When Whittlesey did visit him the following evening, he informed her that she had a detached retina, and he recommended complete bed rest for the remainder of the weekend. Whittlesey recalled sensing discomfort in the doctor's demeanor.[63]

On Monday morning, she returned to the doctor and learned that a strawberry-sized cancerous tumor was inside her eye. She had ocular melanoma, a rare and lethal illness, which had progressed to the most advanced

[61] Faith Whittlesey, discussion with author, telephone, January 19, 2012
[62] Mary Ann Meloy, interview by author, telephone, March 9, 2011.
[63] Faith Whittlesey, discussion with author, telephone, January 19, 2012.

stage—level 4. This diagnosis typically indicated a 9–15 percent chance for a victim's survival. Whittlesey underwent tests which showed positive news—the tumor had not spread to her brain. But the cancer prompted a series of harrowing procedures and treatments. First, doctors counseled removal of her eye so that no cancer cells would be transferred into the brain. Second, she was fitted with a plastic eye. Finally, she immediately began immunotherapy, which required daily self-injections.

The physical and psychological toll, while hard to quantify, proved severe. In the words of her longtime friend Meloy, "For most women, that would have been the end of them."[64] Whittlesey conceded having experienced life-changing personal challenges in the process. "I felt deformed and disfigured with an artificial eye," Whittlesey recalled, "and this fact made it even harder for me to have a normal social life."[65] She felt more awkward at the many public events which she attended, and struggled to overcome the limited vision she now experienced. "At that age, the brain doesn't compensate as much as it does in young people," she noted later.[66]

Despite suffering severe self-consciousness and losing half of her vision, Whittlesey rarely if ever complained to acquaintances. The rapidity of her recovery shocked Michael Waller, with whom she had worked in the White House and the Institute of World Politics. In Waller's recollection more than 15 years later, "We were afraid for her life, and she just bounced back. And now she acts like it's nothing. She's a courageous, gutsy, charitable, really tough, loving, aggressive, nasty-for-all-the-right-reasons person—the kind you want on your side. She's your wingman; she's watching your back."[67] Radio talk-show host Michael Smerconish agreed, saying, "She doesn't discuss adversity, and she is a strong-willed individual. These qualities help explain why she is such a loyal friend." As longtime friend Mary Ann Meloy noted with laughter in a 2010 interview, "You can't wear her out. She believes what she believes, and she will act on it until the day she dies."[68]

Whittlesey deflected much of the credit for her ability to defeat the negative prognosis. "I am grateful to the Swiss pharmaceutical corporations

---

[64] Mary Ann Meloy, interview by author, telephone, March 9, 2011.
[65] Faith Whittlesey, discussion with author, telephone, January 19, 2012.
[66] Ibid.
[67] Michael Waller, interview by author, Washington, September 16, 2010.
[68] Mary Ann Meloy, interview by author, telephone, March 9, 2011.

and the American doctors who saved my life."[69] And she never missed attending the entire Young Leaders Conference each year.

THE AMERICAN SWISS FOUNDATION AND PRIVATE-SECTOR DIPLOMACY

Despite Whittlesey's serious health challenge, she continued to dedicate energy and ideas to the bilateral relationship between the United States and Switzerland. Rather than decrease her commitment to organizations such as the American-Swiss Association, Faith came to imprint her signature on this organization, as well as her reputation for fostering the continued friendship between the sister republics, during this period.

Soon into Whittlesey's tenure as chairman, she had suggested changing the American-Swiss Association's name to the American Swiss Foundation. "Association" sounded too much like an organization which sponsored trade expositions. In Faith's view, "Foundation" better communicated the organization's educational mission. Similar to The Heritage Foundation—a conservative think tank in Washington with which she had worked—the American Swiss Foundation served to generate and promote an exchange of ideas more than merely act as a resource for connecting businesses with markets. Whittlesey conceived of the American Swiss Foundation's mission as private-sector diplomacy to maintain understanding and cooperation between the two countries at the highest levels.

Whittlesey also came to see even more clearly the value of both the American Swiss Foundation and the Young Leaders Conference during the 1990s. After President Clinton appointed hotel owner and millionaire Larry Lawrence as ambassador to Switzerland in 1994, Faith was concerned about the diplomatic message this gesture conveyed to the Swiss. Lawrence's qualifications appeared primarily to have been his nearly $200,000 in donations to Clinton's 1992 presidential campaign.[70] During Lawrence's confirmation hearings, he even admitted to possessing little knowledge of foreign policy (although Senator John Kerry of Massachusetts defended him, somewhat lamely, by citing the many kings, presidents, and prime ministers whom he had hosted in his luxury Hotel del Coronado in California).[71]

---

[69] Faith Whittlesey, discussion with author, telephone, January 19, 2012.

[70] David Binder, "M. L. Lawrence, Entrepreneur and Ambassador, Is Dead at 69," *New York Times,* January 11, 1996, p. D21. Lawrence had given some $10 million to Democratic candidates since 1952, and he paid more than $7,000 in fines to the Federal Election Commission for violating the $25,000 limit on contributions to candidates in 1988. Ibid.

[71] Steven Greenhouse, "Clinton Is Faulted on Political Choices for Envoy Posts," *New York Times,* April 13, 1994, p. A15.

As she well knew, the Bern embassy offered comfort and style, which made it a prize for high-end donors. But Whittlesey did not believe that electoral and fund-raising strategy should take precedence over U.S. foreign policy goals. Moreover, she realized that the Swiss viewed such appointments as a slight to their national dignity. The "Swiss desk" in the State Department amounted to only half time of a junior officer.[72] Absent an active ambassador, who would cultivate positive relationships between the sister republics?

Hoping to make a strong impression on the 1996 presidential candidates, Faith wrote an op-ed article, "No More Embassies for Sale, Please"—which the *International Herald Tribune* published.[73] Noting the trend of increasingly large sums of monetary donations to candidates of both parties, Whittlesey called on the presidential aspirants to disavow the tradition of offering an embassy appointment as a reward for the campaign's most effective fund-raisers.

In Whittlesey's opinion, U.S. foreign policy benefited significantly from ambassadors chosen primarily for their ability to convey an administration's goals and objectives in a clear and cogent manner. In the complex post–Cold War world, she argued, individuals who could articulate a president's philosophy abroad and engage socially and intellectually with foreign publics were more important than ever. How might presidents show gratitude for the fund-raising proficiency and generosity of wealthy contributors in a more appropriate manner? Invitations to the Kennedy Center, White House dinners, or Rose Garden events should suffice, she suggested.[74]

Faith was certainly not lobbying for another position as an ambassador, but she believed that someone should make the case for the skill set which she had brought to the Bern embassy. She was proud of her accomplishments as a political ambassador who had mobilized individuals and institutions in active, innovative ways behind the president's ideas and initiatives. As a private citizen now, Whittlesey called for presidents and their advisors to consider ambassadorial appointments—even to smaller nations such as

[72] Faith Whittlesey, discussion with author, telephone, January 19, 2012.
[73] Faith Whittlesey, "No More Embassies for Sale, Please," *International Herald Tribune*, May 4, 1995. Accessed on March 7, 2012, at *www.nytimes.com/1995/05/04/news/04iht-edwhit. html?pagewanted=print.*
[74] Ibid.

Switzerland—as critical tools of diplomacy rather than prizes primarily for those individuals who oiled the financial hinges of the two parties.[75]

THE UNITED STATES CONFRONTS SWITZERLAND ABOUT "NAZI GOLD"
Whittlesey's concern about the importance of nurturing U.S.-Swiss relations would prove prescient. During the mid-1990s, a crisis in U.S.-Swiss relations revived tensions dating back to World War II.

Steven Hoch recalled some soul searching during the early years of that decade among the board members of the American Swiss Foundation. The organization's importance seemed limited in the absence of serious controversy between the United States and Switzerland. In Hoch's recollection, "We [board members] were starting to ask some questions about the mission and to say, 'You know, relations are so friendly between the two countries, do we really need this organization?' "[76]

Fifty years after World War II's end, most Americans appeared to have forgotten the suspicions which some had harbored about Swiss neutrality. During the Cold War, both the United States and Switzerland shared a concern about expanding Soviet power. In the coming years, however, events would precipitate a serious strain in U.S.-Swiss relations.

The bilateral friendship soon seemed at risk when individuals at the highest levels of the U.S. government made damaging public accusations against Swiss actions during World War II. In 1995, the World Jewish Congress (WJC), an organization founded 60 years earlier in Geneva, asserted that Switzerland's government and several Swiss banks had inadvertently and at times purposely refused to return to their rightful heirs prewar bank deposits made by the victims of Nazi Germany's death camps.[77] Accusers also charged the Swiss with purchasing gold which Germany had allegedly stolen from the persecuted Jewish populations of Europe.

In a short period of time, Switzerland had a serious global public relations problem on its hands. WJC President Edgar Bronfman entered a class-action lawsuit against the Swiss banks in 1995 in New York City. Months later, in April 1996, U.S. Senator Alfonse D'Amato (R-NY), chairman of the Senate Banking Committee, convened Senate hearings to investigate. Democratic

---

[75] Ibid.

[76] Steven Hoch, interview by author, telephone, November 23, 2010.

[77] This mass extermination of millions of European Jews (as well as others), known as the Holocaust, evoked strong emotions because of the premeditated, gruesome nature of the killings as well as the wrenching stories told about these events in subsequent books and movies.

President Bill Clinton asked Undersecretary of Commerce Stuart Eizenstat to testify at D'Amato's hearings and to produce a report on the subject.[78] Eizenstat's written account directly challenged Swiss claims of political neutrality. A bipartisan consensus highly skeptical of Swiss motives had formed in the United States. Leading members of both parties wanted Switzerland to answer these claims, but the Swiss government did not issue a full explanation of its actions and/or rebut the charges.[79]

A widespread presumption of guilt appeared to take hold in the media. Reporters and opinion pieces depicted Switzerland as a thinly veiled ally of Nazi Germany. *Die Spiegel* of Hamburg claimed that the Swiss National Bank "financed the Nazi wars of aggression," and the *Frankfurter Allgemeine Zeitung* called Switzerland "The Thieves' Den."[80] In the United States, Switzerland's silence was interpreted as an admission of culpability. The *New York Times* wrote of the "Swiss neutrality lie," and the London *Evening Standard* characterized Swiss neutrality as "just an excuse to get rich."[81]

Whittlesey later explained that much of this initial analysis failed to recognize that Switzerland did not have banking account escheat laws as they existed in the United States. In U.S. states, escheat allowed the government to take funds in dormant bank accounts when the owner has not made contact with the bank for a specified period of time (typically 2 to 7 years, dependent on state law). The state will normally publish a list of these dormant accounts in local newspaper advertisements, but no further effort is required to find the account holder. Since the Swiss Parliament rejected several attempts to pass escheat legislation, there occurred a proliferation of small accounts in Swiss banks over time. In the United States, these monies would have been transferred years before to state treasuries "by means of escheat," Whittlesey noted.[82]

Such legal details rarely received their day in the court of public opinion. Jacques Rossier, managing partner for the Geneva bank Darier Hentsch & Cie in the 1990s, recalled a taxi driver in Washington during this period telling him, upon hearing that he was from Switzerland, "Oh, you took

[78] "U.S. Expanding a Search for Nazi Asset Records," *New York Times*, November 5, 1996, p. A5.

[79] See Angelo M. Codevilla, *Between the Alps and a Hard Place: Switzerland in World War II and the Rewriting of History* (Washington, DC: Regnery, 2000).

[80] Jean Ziegler, *The Swiss, the Gold, and the Dead: How Swiss Bankers Helped Finance the Nazi War Machine* (New York: Harcourt, Brace and Company), p. 5.

[81] Ibid., p. 6.

[82] Faith Whittlesey, email to author, May 16, 2012. "The Swiss just don't trust the growth of centralized power over private resources in banking or anything else." Ibid.

all the money of the Jewish families that perished in the Holocaust." In Rossier's view, there were "lots of emotions and lots of misconceptions."[83] American Swiss Foundation board member George Gyssler recalled that a U.S. campaign to boycott Swiss companies began to appear imminent in the late 1990s. In Gyssler's view, an anti-Swiss public relations movement had completely tainted Americans' opinion of his native land. "I got the impression that there were no friends of Switzerland whatsoever in the United States. Nothing!"[84]

Many Swiss responded with similar expressions of shock. The United States had always appeared as a kindred spirit (even an older sibling) for a small country like Switzerland, according to Jean Pierre Cuoni, chairman of the EFG International bank following a long career as a Citibank chief executive in Switzerland. U.S. politicians and courts now appeared to demand, in an aggressive and uncompromising manner, large and immediate financial payments from Swiss banks. In Cuoni's view, "The Swiss certainly felt like the little kid brother would feel if the big brother—who was always nice to the kid—all of a sudden gives the kid a hit in the stomach. You look up to the big brother, and you don't believe it!"[85]

As members of a nation of roughly 7 million in 1996, most Swiss perceived themselves as facing strong-arm tactics by a nation of more than 250 million. According to Peter Weibel, former member of the board of Credit Suisse Group, "It's like David and Goliath. But what we wish is to be treated and respected as a long-standing partner." In Weibel's view, Switzerland had contributed significantly to the U.S.-Swiss relationship. "We tried in the past, and still nowadays in several ways, to be helpful when it comes to protecting the interests of the United States. So, we will expect the United States also, at the very least, to understand our motivation."[86]

Several Swiss echoed Weibel's hope that Americans would try to appreciate the Swiss perspective during such disagreements. Herbert Oberhaensli, assistant vice president at Nestlé, could not understand why U.S. officials did not consult the Swiss before writing reports which made terrible accusations against Switzerland. "We expect conflict, but we want to have it within rules. And that has left some bad memories. It has damaged the

[83]   Jacques Rossier, interview by author, Geneva, August 17, 2009.
[84]   George Gyssler, interview by author, Zürich, August 19, 2009.
[85]   Jean Pierre Cuoni, interview by author, telephone, November 21, 2009.
[86]   Peter F. Weibel, interview by author, Zürich, August 19, 2009.

U.S. quite a lot."[87] The incident "was badly perceived here," agreed Gabriela Lippe-Holst, a Swiss lawyer who served as deputy head of the strategic and emerging claims management department of the Swiss Re reinsurance company. Lippe-Holst reported that many Swiss saw the event "as a show of a few people who wanted to get richer." Referring to U.S. class-action lawsuits, she noted that Switzerland does not really know such lawsuits and they are "widely perceived as a money making tool rather than a tool for the pursuit of equity."[88]

At the height of the crisis, Faith tried to interject some balance into the overwhelmingly negative discussion about Switzerland's role in World War II by writing a December 1996 opinion piece for the *Wall Street Journal*. She explained the long established Swiss principle of armed neutrality. While Americans might have preferred Switzerland to join the Allies, Whittlesey noted several benefits to the United States deriving from Swiss neutrality. Their neutral stance, for example, permitted the International Committee of the Red Cross, a Swiss institution, to assist Allied prisoners of war and refugees. U.S. intelligence operative Allen Dulles was allowed to operate and gather information under Germany's nose in Bern, where he spent the war. Approximately 1,700 American airmen shot down while flying over Nazi Germany made their way into neutral Switzerland and were safely interned there. More than 20,000 Swiss citizens of Jewish heritage were spared Nazi persecution in addition to the nearly 27,000 Jewish refugees who were admitted at the Swiss borders. More recently, she noted, the world benefited from Swiss neutrality. Geneva offered the world a secure site for international negotiations, and the Swiss financial center "has been the mainstay of a stable world banking system."[89] While none of these facts was offered as an excuse for unethical activity during World War II, she maintained that "as we search for the truth, we should be careful not to unduly antagonize or defame a country whose commitment to civilized diplomatic discourse continues to be important to our national interests."[90]

The Swiss appreciated her refusal to receive the groundswell of anti-Swiss opinions in silence. Cuoni later recalled believing for several months that "Faith Whittlesey represented this country's only friend in the United

[87] Herbert Oberhaensli, interview by author, Vevey, Switzerland, August 17, 2009.
[88] Gabriela Lippe-Holst, interview by author, Zürich, August 20, 2009.
[89] Faith Whittlesey, "Nazi gold: The Swiss side of the story," *Wall Street Journal*, December 11, 1996, p. 22.
[90] Ibid.

States."[91] According to Geneva banker Rossier, "She was about the only American writing in a significant paper trying to calm things down and speaking up for the Swiss."[92]

Faith's call for understanding the Swiss viewpoint ruffled some feathers in the United States. Switzerland's widespread unpopularity during this period made her support for that country controversial. After she wrote a piece titled "Switzerland on Trial" in *The Ambassador's Review*, another former U.S. ambassador to Switzerland asked her, disapprovingly, why she would take Switzerland's side in this case. In Whittlesey's view, she was merely acting to preserve a long-standing and valuable friendship with Switzerland and stating many facts which had heretofore been omitted from the narrative.[93]

SUPPORTING ACADEMIC STUDY OF SWITZERLAND IN ENGLISH

While the Young Leaders Conference had served to educate Americans about Switzerland, Whittlesey and the American Swiss Foundation now sought another means of increasing U.S. understanding of the Swiss. The "Nazi Gold" crisis had highlighted the need for a thoughtful, serious response—in English—to charges against the Swiss.

Aware that fuller accounts of Swiss wartime decisions existed, Whittlesey also knew that the vast majority of Americans could not access these works because they did not read German or French. Thus, she endeavored to support the publication and distribution of English-language scholarly works about Switzerland as well as the translation of existing works into English.

Years prior to the U.S.-Swiss imbroglio over World War II bank accounts, Faith had begun to assist scholars seeking to provide a more complete context to Switzerland's response to the events of the 1930s and 1940s. For example, through their mutual friendship with Wayne LaPierre, longtime executive vice president and CEO of the NRA, Whittlesey had met Steven Halbrook, who held Ph.D. and J.D. degrees and who had begun to research the circumstances of Switzerland's political neutrality, its militia, and its national defense system during World War II. Appreciating Halbrook's unique position as an English-speaking writer who knew Switzerland well, Whittlesey invited him to address conference participants in the

91   Jean Pierre Cuoni, interview by author, telephone, November 21, 2009.
92   Jacques Rossier, interview by author, Geneva, August 17, 2009.
93   Faith Whittlesey, discussion with author, telephone, January 19, 2012.

early 1990s. If future American and Swiss decision makers could better comprehend all the facts, she believed, this knowledge would improve the bilateral relationship.

As Halbrook prepared a book manuscript on this subject, Whittlesey offered assistance. Her extensive contacts within Switzerland helped him arrange interviews with people relevant to his work. In Halbrook's recollection, these conversations proved valuable because Whittlesey had facilitated a meeting between him and high-ranking members of the Swiss army general staff "who had either written books or had personal experience" in World War II.[94] Whittlesey's support for Halbrook helped counter a torrent of unbalanced negative books—more than a dozen in all—which portrayed Switzerland entirely in an uncomplimentary light.[95] Halbrook's 1998 book *Target Switzerland: Swiss Armed Neutrality in World War II* was translated into five languages and sold widely in the United States and throughout the world.[96]

In a more general way, Whittlesey also supported the creation of an American Swiss Foundation committee to encourage the translation of Swiss works of history. Research by board member Don Hilty, the former chief economist of the Chrysler Corporation and of Swiss heritage, had shown that U.S. libraries carried nearly no published books in English about Switzerland. According to board member George Gyssler, "Hilty came up with a horrible picture" of material available in U.S. libraries in English. In Gyssler's recollection, the negative publicity surrounding Swiss banks in World War II generated a series of "highly derogatory books on Switzerland" in the late 1990s.[97] Swiss entrepreneur Andreas W. Keller, chairman of the Diethelm Keller Group and a member of the Swiss Advisory Council of the American Swiss Foundation, recalled that Whittlesey "proved to us that if you go into an average American library and look for Swiss books in English, they would always be negative." By contrast, Keller noted, "We have a lot of positive books in German about Switzerland."[98] Whittlesey encouraged

94   Stephen P. Halbrook, interview by author, telephone, December 2, 2010.
95   E.g., Isabel Vincent, *Hitler's Silent Partners: Swiss Banks, Nazi Gold, and the Pursuit of Justice* (New York: William Morrow, 1997); Tom Bower, *Nazi Gold: The Full Story of the Swiss-Nazi Conspiracy to Steal Billions from Europe's Jews and Holocaust Survivors* (New York: Harper Perennial, 1998); Mark Aarons and John Loftus, *Unholy Trinity: The Vatican, the Nazis, and the Swiss Banks* (New York: St. Martin's Griffin, 1991, 1998).
96   Stephen P. Halbrook, *Target Switzerland: Swiss Armed Neutrality in World War II* (Rockville Center, NY: Sarpedon, 1998).
97   George Gyssler, interview by author, Zürich, August 19, 2009.
98   Andreas Keller, interview by author, Zürich, August 22, 2009.

the foundation to translate these books for distribution to American public and university libraries.

Jürg Stüssi-Lauterburg, a Swiss historian and head of the federal military library in Bern, took inspiration from the American Swiss Foundation's support for these publications. Having written books in German about Switzerland's actions during World War II, he believed that someone needed to defend his country's past decisions. Motivated by a sense of obligation to speak out against the perceived injustice against Switzerland, Stüssi-Lauterburg traveled—at his own personal expense—to a Columbia University conference on the subject of the World War II Swiss bank accounts. Although Stüssi-Lauterburg had not written in English, he determined to present the facts—as he understood them—to a U.S. audience. George Gyssler met the Swiss historian at the conference and provided him with a prepublication copy of Halbrook's *Target Switzerland*. This English-language account of Switzerland's World War II experience reassured Stüssi-Lauterburg that at least some U.S. citizens might judge the Swiss in a balanced and academic—rather than a superficial and sensationalist—manner.

In Stüssi-Lauterburg's recollection, his experience with the American Swiss Foundation now permitted him to believe that some Americans might "want to save the traditional friendship between the United States and Switzerland."[99] When Whittlesey learned of Stüssi-Lauterburg's commitment to explaining Switzerland's history to Americans, she asked him to speak at a Young Leaders Conference so that he might continue to help counter the overwhelmingly anti-Swiss message which predominated in the mainstream media.

SWITZERLAND'S "FOUL WEATHER" FRIEND

Despite efforts of Whittlesey and others to present the Swiss case to the American public, Switzerland's political and financial leaders were fearful. In August 1998, Swiss banks agreed to pay $1.25 billion in a global settlement of the class-action suit that had been instituted in New York City.[100] One American scholar portrayed the Swiss banks' reaction to the class action as succumbing to implied threats by New York's state treasurer to sanction Switzerland through withholding licenses and pension fund divestment

---

[99] Jürg Stüssi-Lauterberg, interview with author, Zürich, August 19, 2009. Stüssi wrote an endorsement for *Target Switzerland*—"The most comprehensive documentation to date of the Nazi threat and the Swiss will to resist it"—which the publisher cited on the book's back cover.
[100] Codevilla, *Between the Alps*, p. x.

of Swiss equities.[101] The Swiss continued mostly to avoid public comment on the subject except through formal diplomatic channels and activities.

Many Swiss citizens later recounted their admiration for Whittlesey's support for their country during this difficult period. Jacques Rossier lamented that the Swiss had "totally neglected public relations" such as "building up networks" with think tanks, politicians, and the media in the United States.[102]

In the late 1990s, the negative publicity about Switzerland's actions in World War II had provoked Rossier to investigate independently the details of the subject. Having served in the Swiss army's mountain infantry during the 1950s, Rossier took great pride in Switzerland's devotion to defending the country through a strong army. In Rossier's view, the United States had always represented a force for freedom, while Switzerland warily regarded the Soviet Union as a clear and present danger during the Cold War. Such confidence in the admirable intentions of both Switzerland and the United States inspired Rossier to research the allegations against the Swiss banks. After uncovering facts which contradicted some of the accusations U.S. politicians and media had reported, he began to write letters to the editors of Swiss newspapers and to speak on television programs, discussing his findings. At a meeting of Swiss bankers in Geneva during this time, Rossier met Whittlesey, who invited him to speak in May 1999 on the subject at an American Swiss Foundation-sponsored event at the Harvard Faculty Club in Cambridge, Massachusetts.[103]

In that speech, Rossier—who holds an MBA degree from Harvard— did not adopt the position of counsel for the defense, but rather he asked Americans to consider the positive as well as negative actions by Switzerland during World War II. Rossier's words did not seek absolution of Switzerland or Swiss banks. The August 1998 settlement had ended the class-action suit.[104] With no pending legal matter affecting the dialogue, Rossier retrospectively presented the good, the bad, and the ugly truth, as he understood it, of the standoff between the United States and Switzerland during this crisis. For example, he asked the audience to recognize Switzerland's maintenance of a free press and deterrence against Nazi aggression during World War II. Rather than collaborate with the Nazis, Rossier suggested, the Swiss

---

[101] Ibid., p. 187.
[102] Jacques Rossier, interview by author, Geneva, August 17, 2009.
[103] Ibid.
[104] Codevilla, *Between the Alps*, p. x.

government had struggled to maintain sufficient food supplies and gold to support its threatened currency—the Swiss franc—during a period when the U.S. government froze Switzerland's gold reserves held within the United States.[105]

Switzerland made terrible mistakes, Rossier conceded. In Rossier's estimation, the Swiss did fail in refusing to accept 30,000 additional Jewish refugees (27,000 had already been admitted to Switzerland) since the beginning of the war in Europe. He also faulted the Swiss Bankers Association for neglecting to seek out heirs of Holocaust victims in a more proactive and systematic manner. In brief, Rossier counseled greater sensitivity to "the moral aspects of the crisis." These missteps "lent credibility to the vilification of Switzerland [by] private class-action plaintiffs." U.S. leaders at the national and state levels, and the media, contributed to creating a perception that the Swiss intentionally exploited the plight of European Jews.

Rossier offered several lessons from the crisis. First, he quoted one of "Murphy's laws," saying "Friends come and go but enemies accumulate!" In Rossier's view, "In order to be heard in this U.S. court of public opinion, one needs strong allies among interest groups as well as opinion makers and opinion disseminators."[106] By cultivating his contact with Whittlesey, Rossier practiced what he had preached. Faith had substantial experience working with U.S. interest groups, and she arranged for a high-profile venue for Rossier's message. Through the foundation's network, Whittlesey also published and distributed his speech.

Several Swiss business leaders viewed the American Swiss Foundation as an important means of making the bilateral U.S.-Swiss relationship a positive one. In the view of former Credit Suisse board member Peter Weibel, who served on the Swiss Advisory Council of the American Swiss Foundation, typically negative stereotypes about Swiss bankers perpetuated the image that the "gnomes of Zürich" unfairly accumulate and jealously guard hordes of gold. Weibel argued that Switzerland needed to counter these "fairy tales" with facts, saying "It is important that we put [forth] something against these fantasies."[107] The Swiss had a factual, objectively based story to tell. The American Swiss Foundation's board and many

---

[105] Jacques Rossier, "Switzerland, Gold and the Banks: Analysis of a Crisis," American Swiss Foundation Occasional Papers. Based on remarks made by the author at the American Swiss Foundation Forum, Harvard Faculty Club, May 26, 1999.

[106] Ibid.

[107] Peter F. Weibel, interview with author, Zürich, August 19, 2009.

sponsors recognized the Young Leaders Conference as an important vehicle for presenting a more realistic view of Switzerland's interaction with the United States and the global economy.

Whittlesey's role as a balanced voice for Switzerland proved critical in promoting the bilateral relationship during these difficult times, according to Steven Bernard, director of the Geneva Financial Center. Bernard describes Whittlesey as one of Switzerland's "most dedicated and consistent friends" in the United States. In Bernard's view, she is the most effective advocate for maintaining the sometimes awkward relationship between a small country such as Switzerland and a colossus such as the United States. While Whittlesey had built an impressive list of contacts within the United States and Switzerland during her political career in the 1970s and ambassadorial years in the 1980s, she bridged her networks to leverage the Young Leaders Conference to create a unique corps of mutual friends of America and Switzerland, across multiple professional backgrounds and generations.[108]

Faith ensured that these connections proved lasting and durable. Doug Sears, who served in the U.S. embassy with Whittlesey in the late 1980s and who later became vice president and chief of staff at Boston University, explained this newfound Swiss appreciation for Whittlesey as a testimony to the depth of commitment she demonstrated in political and personal relationships. "Faith isn't a fair-weather friend—she's a foul-weather friend. So, when the Swiss were being unfairly attacked for the 'Holocaust accounts'—so-called—and that whole controversy brewed up, everybody in Washington was running from them."[109] But not Faith.

Prior to that period, in Sears' view, the Swiss government and banking center had misplaced their trust in the basic fairness of the American system. Leaders in Switzerland, Sears believes, mistakenly assumed that individuals in the U.S. government and media establishment would treat the issue in a rational and logical manner. Yet, such contentious political disagreements more often expose raw emotion and crude power relationships, according to Sears. "It's really more about who your friends are and who has backbone at the end of the day."[110] Sears believed that the Swiss benefited from Whittlesey's core commitment to those American and Swiss

---

[108] Steven Bernard, interview by author, telephone, August 17, 2009.
[109] Doug Sears, interview with author, Boston, July 9, 2009.
[110] Ibid.

citizens who wanted to maintain mutually positive connections between the two nations. "Anybody who gets on the list of loyal … she goes way out of her way for."[111]

Whittlesey believed that subsequent events supported her call for the United States to exercise caution when confronting the Swiss on this issue. She cited an October 13, 2001, *The Times* of London report that few of the unclaimed "dormant" accounts under question actually belonged to Holocaust survivors or heirs of those who died. After publishing a list of dormant accounts and processing about 10,000 claims, the international Claims Resolution Tribunal for Dormant Accounts in Switzerland, headed by former Chairman of the U.S. Federal Reserve System Paul Volcker, could trace only 200 accounts—amounting to approximately $16 million—to victims of Nazi Germany's mass murder campaign. This figure paled in comparison to the $1.25 billion paid by the Swiss banks to resolve the class-action suit. *The Times* headline for the story read "Swiss Holocaust Cash Revealed to Be Myth."[112] Faith recalled that many Swiss citizens cited this revelation as evidence that the United States had treated their country unfairly, but that this news was not widely reported in the United States, if at all.[113]

ANOTHER STRAIN ON U.S.-SWISS RELATIONS: THE POST-SEPTEMBER 11 WORLD

In the early 21st century, U.S. military interventions overseas dominated European perceptions of America. Switzerland in particular maintained a long-standing aversion to expanding empires. The Swiss had resisted imperial powers from the days of the legendary William Tell, who defied the Habsburg empire in the 14th century, to Napoleonic France and Hitler's Germany. America's unilateral efforts to dictate global norms and standards regarding democracy, terrorism, and banking practices, among other things, appeared overreaching and counterproductive, from the Swiss perspective.

Cleveland Democratic Councilman Zachary Reed, who attended the conference in 2004, recalled listening intently to Whittlesey's first formal address to the U.S. participants prior to meeting their Swiss coparticipants. Faith provided a detailed briefing on the Europeans' skepticism toward the 2003 U.S. invasion of Iraq. In Reed's view, "It was not an antiwar speech, but

---

[111] Ibid.

[112] Adam Sage and Roger Boyes, "Swiss Holocaust Cash Revealed to Be Myth," *The Times* (London), October 13, 2001. Copy in Faith Whittlesey's possession.

[113] Faith Whittlesey, discussion with author, telephone, July 11, 2011.

she wanted us to appreciate some of the Swiss people's reasons for opposing the war. You could understand she was motivated by her love for the USA." This background briefing prepared the Americans for Swiss questions and comments at the conference which might otherwise spark defensive and impulsive retorts. With his lack of prior knowledge about Switzerland, in particular, and Europeans, in general, Reed believed that Whittlesey had helped him—and his colleagues—avoid tense emotional exchanges with the Swiss participants. "I felt she wanted to look out for us—she was showing that she 'had our back.' "[114]

Swiss accounts suggest that Whittlesey was not overestimating Swiss hostility to the 2003 U.S. invasion. Most Swiss express strong reservations about America's projection of military power abroad and its fortress-like posture in response to the September 11, 2001, terrorist attacks in the United States. Banking executive Jean Pierre Cuoni described a shift in the Swiss images of the United States from "the friendly American" to "the ugly American" during the period 2003–2008. Cuoni's treatment by border officials upon arrival in U.S. airports persuaded him to consider not returning to the United States, although he noted an improvement in the greeting he received in 2009.[115]

Gabriela Lippe-Holst recalled many people in Switzerland, especially young people, turning against the United States during the first decade of the 21st century. When she worked for Swiss Re in New York City, Lippe-Holst was surprised that some Swiss began to ask incredulously, "How could you even live in America—and you would like to go *back?*"[116] In Lippe-Holst's experience, however, she and other Swiss participants in the Young Leaders Conference defended the United States when they encountered anti-Americanism at private and public events. Lippe-Holst credited Whittlesey's initiatives for cultivating a more favorable view of Americans among the Swiss. "The American Swiss Foundation—and Ambassador Whittlesey—was continuously repeating a positive message and helping support the Young Leaders," she noted.[117] Faith's willingness to listen to thoughtful Swiss critiques of U.S. foreign policy also reinforced her credibility in Switzerland.

---

[114] Zachary Reed, interview by author, telephone, August 20, 2010.
[115] Jean Pierre Cuoni, interview with author, telephone, November 21, 2009.
[116] Gabriela Lippe-Holst, interview by author, Zürich, August 20, 2009.
[117] Ibid.

Several Americans also appreciated how Whittlesey went the extra mile to allow the Swiss to see beyond a monolithic view of the United States. Writer and television commentator and 2009 Young Leader Keli Goff, who regularly expresses commentary at the *Huffington Post* website as well as through several cable television news outlets, admired Whittlesey for creating conditions conducive to discussing genuine and honest differences of opinion. Despite the enormous personal effort required to create, personally monitor, and sustain the conference each year, Whittlesey never used the Young Leaders Conference as a platform for advancing a particular policy agenda, in Goff's view. "Ambassador Whittlesey reaches out to people that she doesn't agree with on every issue," Goff stated, "because she wants to reflect the best of America."[118]

Beyond political diversity, Faith also strived for cultural and ethnic diversity at the conference. According to Goff, "As an African American woman, I respect her for recognizing that everyone in the program can't look like her and think like her."[119] Niger Innis, national spokesman for the Congress of Racial Equality (CORE) and a 2000 Young Leader, praised Whittlesey for ensuring that the U.S. delegation represented "the entire cross section of America." On August 29, 2004, CORE held an event at the Museum of the City of New York, in Harlem, to recognize Whittlesey's friendship and support for the organization.[120]

U.S. DEMANDS FOR CLIENT INFORMATION
FROM UBS AND OTHER SWISS BANKS

Whittlesey continued to speak about the importance of the U.S.-Swiss relationship when, more recently, U.S. government officials and media reports suddenly delivered torrents of accusations against Swiss banks.

In 2008, a U.S. Senate panel accused UBS and other Swiss banks of helping Americans evade taxes. The bank, a global financial giant following its merger with, first, Swiss Bank Corporation (1997) and then U.S.-based Paine Webber (2000), agreed in February 2009 to pay $780 million and provide information on roughly 250 U.S. customers in a settlement of a criminal lawsuit with the United States.

---

[118] Keli Goff, interview by author, telephone, February 9, 2012.
[119] Ibid.
[120] Niger Innis, interview by author, telephone, July 2, 2012.

The Internal Revenue Service (IRS) of the United States, almost immediately following this agreement, sued UBS in a civil claim for the release of
52,000 client names of U.S. citizens whom government authorities wanted
to investigate for potential evasion of taxes. Since Swiss law protected the
privacy of account holders, UBS was faced with the prospect of defying
either the U.S. or Swiss government.[121]

Many in Switzerland viewed the United States as having exceeded the
bounds of international cooperation by demanding an immediate transfer of
private client data from UBS to the IRS. The Swiss perceived such demands
as "extra-territorial application of U.S. law," according to Whittlesey. "The
Justice Department and the U.S. Treasury Department are determined to
make U.S. tax cheats pay," Whittlesey noted, "but they seek to force Swiss
banks to reveal names of U.S. clients in violation of the long-established
banking privacy laws of Switzerland." Whittlesey doubted that the United
States would permit such demands on its own domestic banks "by South
American governments, for example, seeking to identify undeclared funds
of account holders deposited in the banks of Florida, Delaware, Wyoming,
or Nevada, which have similar privacy policies."[122]

Just as during the earlier dormant accounts controversy, Faith
Whittlesey's was almost the only voice from the U.S. political class which
suggested that the U.S. government seek a discreet, diplomatic solution
between two friendly, commercially interdependent nations rather than
engage in a contentious and coercive court battle. In a March 1, 2009, op-ed
article titled "America Must Treat Its Swiss Friend with Care," published in
the London-based *Financial Times*, Whittlesey called on President Barack
Obama's administration to exhibit the "partnership" model in foreign
policy upon which the newly elected president had campaigned.[123] Many
Swiss from diverse ideological backgrounds, Whittlesey noted, strongly
opposed the U.S. government's demands for client information because
such data transfers would violate Swiss financial privacy laws and national
sovereignty as well as bilateral agreements between the United States and
Switzerland. In Whittlesey's view, such enforcement actions on the part of

---

[121] Lynnley Browning, "U.S. Ends Inquiry of UBS over Offshore Tax Evasion," *New York Times*, November 16, 2010; accessed on March 15, 2012, at *www.nytimes.com/2010/11/17/business/17tax.html*. See also Haig Simonian, "UBS in Fresh DoJ Deal Delay," *Financial Times*, August 9, 2009, p. 9.

[122] Faith Whittlesey, discussion with author, telephone, January 19, 2012.

[123] Faith Whittlesey, "America Must Treat Its Swiss Friend with Care," accessed on March 15, 2012, at *www.ft.com/intl/cms/s/0/74a51894-0694-11de-ab0f-000077b07658.html*.

the U.S. authorities contradicted Obama's election-year pledge to establish "multilateral co-operation" with foreign countries.[124]

Whittlesey warned that bullying of a fellow democracy had diplomatic and economic consequences, among other considerations. Switzerland helped the United States resist drug trafficking and terrorism, and Swiss investment in the United States created about 500,000 American jobs. These political and economic relationships, Whittlesey noted, relied on trust that the United States would deal in a manner consistent with the principles of Swiss law. By acting as "a superpower exerting raw Goliath power" to pressure Switzerland's banks to violate Swiss law, however, "the U.S. ignored formal, negotiated understandings with a long-time friend, a constitutional federal republic where rule of law is enshrined."[125] Furthermore, Whittlesey warned that such disregard for Swiss law might easily offend "a nation that was prepared to work with U.S. authorities in, among other activities, the repatriation of Guantánamo inmates, in line with its role as a high contracting party and depository of the human rights convention."[126] These practical considerations should counsel caution to U.S. officials, in Whittlesey's view.

Faith's article accurately and probably more temperately expressed the sense of indignation which many Swiss held about America's casual dismissal of their national laws, sovereignty, and existing tax treaties. Former Swiss Re COO Andreas Beerli appreciated Whittlesey's *Financial Times* op-ed piece—"I distributed it to all my colleagues and friends here." But he lamented the absence of additional supportive voices in the English-language media.[127] U.S. ignorance and general disinterest in Swiss views suggested that Americans little appreciated or even respected Switzerland's right to autonomy, self-government, and its long-established democratic system of law and justice.

Many Swiss seemed to have concluded that benign neglect best characterized America's relationship toward their nation. As the U.S. government applied heavy legal pressure on UBS, many Swiss sympathized with the ends—but not the means—of America's claims. In Jean Pierre Cuoni's view, "We don't blame the United States for going after UBS; this is absolutely normal and has to be that way."[128] America seemed to be asking the bank to

---

[124] Ibid.
[125] Ibid.
[126] Ibid.
[127] Andreas Beerli, interview by author, Zürich, August 20, 2010.
[128] Jean Pierre Cuoni, interview by author, telephone, November 21, 2009.

flout Swiss national law, however, by requesting information about *so many* accounts without probable cause in what resembled a "fishing expedition."

Former Credit Suisse executive Peter Weibel agreed that Switzerland's legislators and judges should make the determinations about criminal activity within Swiss borders. "We see that some UBS staff members did wrong. We also would like to punish them ourselves, here in Switzerland, rather than being pushed from the U.S." Yet, in Weibel's view, the U.S. and Swiss motivations for pursuing client information differed widely. "We think that the IRS only wants to get more money out of these UBS clients. For us, it is not primarily a financial topic. For us, it is an ethical topic. And for the U.S., we have a perception that it is more of a financial topic."[129]

Switzerland had much to lose from assaults on their financial center as well. Many Swiss even believed they had the obligation to protect their financial sector as a matter of national security. As a *Bloomberg Markets* article noted in 2010, "If the attack on bank secrecy results in foreigners doing their banking in some other country, that could be dire news for Switzerland, which derives almost 10 percent of its gross domestic product from the industry."[130] A natural response of Swiss managers of capital, noted Whittlesey, would be to redeploy these monies from Wall Street to such other banking centers as Hong Kong, Singapore, or London. The potential for quiet Swiss disinvestment in the United States continued to worry Whittlesey in 2012.[131]

BLUEGRASS MUSIC AND CULTURAL DIPLOMACY

Rather than despair about such acrimonious bilateral disagreements, Faith continued to pursue various creative means of constructing connections between the two nations. Even during her period as chairman emeritus since 2008, Whittlesey actively organized events to generate mutual appreciation of the two distinct cultures of the United States and Switzerland.

For just one example, circumstances in 2003 led Whittlesey to initiate a simple yet unique connection between the two countries which developed into a series of events to foster goodwill between the United States in Switzerland. That year, driving along Florida's long, straight, and flat route 60 in the central part of the state, she and her daughter Amy—a talented singer

---

[129] Peter F. Weibel, interview by author, Zürich, August 19, 2009.
[130] Stephane Baker and Warren Giles, "Geneva Banks: Against the Wind," *Bloomberg Markets*, August 2009, p. 45.
[131] Faith Whittlesey, discussion with author, telephone, January 19, 2012.

and songwriter herself—had spotted occasional roadside signs announcing a large bluegrass festival. Whittlesey would not have stopped in Yee Haw Junction on this cool January evening except for Amy's pleas to her mother to "just take a look for a few minutes." Hours later, after listening to Amy's beautiful singing in one of the festival's "side jams," Whittlesey remained seated on a metal outdoor chair wrapped in a blanket. She and Amy now watched and listened to the evening's featured group, Doyle Lawson and Quicksilver, which had received several nominations for the music industry's highest honor, the Grammy Award. The group's formal attire—coats and ties—and practiced stage presence impressed Whittlesey. Young lead tenor Jamie Dailey made the strongest impact.[132]

After waiting in line outside the tent to purchase the band's CDs, Whittlesey asked Dailey if he would consider attending the Young Leaders Conference. The young singer seemed unsure. "After all, I was wearing jeans and casual clothes, and it did sound like a most unlikely proposition right in the middle of a cow pasture in remote Yee Haw Junction," Whittlesey recalled. Dailey's busy travel schedule limited his ability to commit. Nonetheless, Whittlesey's unusual offer intrigued Jamie, and he soon agreed to attend the 2005 conference.[133]

Whittlesey asked Dailey to bring his guitar and to perform during the annual alumni dinner in Bern. This occasion brought the first-time conference participants together with previous Young Leaders as well as many high-powered sponsors for a formal meal at the elegant Bellevue Palace Hotel in Bern, with some brief remarks by American Swiss Foundation representatives. Although she knew that the highly cultivated Swiss bankers and heads of multinational corporations might have chosen Bach or Mozart as the musical accompaniment to their evening, Whittlesey asked Dailey to sing and play, and his performance did not disappoint.[134]

Dailey seemed a very appropriate cultural diplomat for the United States. His boyish good looks, respectful and unassuming demeanor, comedic skills, and extraordinary musical talents immediately charmed audiences. Furthermore, bluegrass music could claim authentic American roots in the Appalachian Mountains of the eastern United States. Many Americans—and even Swiss—increasingly listened to bluegrass. Whittlesey also realized that

---

[132] Faith Whittlesey, email to author, August 9, 2011.
[133] Ibid.
[134] Ibid.

bluegrass music's roots in remote mountain regions produced characteristics and themes similar to Switzerland's own musical traditions. Like many Americans, the contemporary Swiss citizenry descended predominantly from "a rural, isolated, mountainous people who sing, yodel, and play the alphorn."[135]

Whittlesey continued to support Dailey as he teamed up with Darrin Vincent to form a new group—Dailey and Vincent—in 2008, and she addressed the audience of 2,000 prior to the newly formed band's first concert in Dailey's small Tennessee hometown of Cookeville. In November 2010, she met with Donald S. Beyer, Jr., the U.S. ambassador in Bern, and proposed an idea. Dailey and Vincent would visit Switzerland in 2011, and the group would be available to play at the U.S. ambassador's residence in Bern. Beyer agreed enthusiastically. He and his wife Megan themselves hailed from Virginia and had long enjoyed listening to bluegrass music, especially the native Virginian Statler brothers.

Despite Whittlesey's background as a Republican, she worked well with and very much admired Ambassador Beyer, whom Democratic President Barack Obama appointed in 2009. The two ambassadors had cooperated in the past, as Beyer had continued the tradition of hosting a reception for the Young Leaders in the ambassador's official residence at Rainmattstrasse 21. Ambassador Beyer asked her to cohost the event officially with him. Whittlesey's committed participation included counseling Dailey and Vincent about their press release for the event, questions for a televised interview the group would conduct with the U.S. ambassador, and background information about the venue where they would perform so that they might address the Swiss audience in an informed and respectful manner.

Whittlesey believed that the U.S. embassy event on September 8, 2011, and the two concerts in Gstaad which followed proved to be successful in helping improve Swiss perceptions of the United States at a critical time. Dailey could comment in a humorous manner about Switzerland, and his responsible personal conduct contrasted with the image of Americans as reckless and dismissive of the Swiss. She was pleased that both American and Swiss attendees, including many Young Leaders, found the performance "joyful and uplifting." The group performed—to many standing ovations—on September 9 and 10 in front of sold-out audiences of 3,000 as part of "Country Night

---

[135] Ibid.

Gstaad," in one of Switzerland's most fashionable resort destinations.[136] Along with Young Leader Jamie Dailey and his partner Darrin Vincent (the three-time international Bluegrass Music Association entertainer of the year team), Whittlesey had achieved another objective in preserving the bonds between U.S. and Swiss citizens.

MAINTAINING RELATIONSHIPS

Whittlesey's personal commitment to individuals has long formed the foundation of the Young Leaders Conference's unique success. Her close attention to each participant helps create a sense of community. With currently more than 900 Young Leader alumni, this large network has the ability to strengthen person-to-person relations across national borders.

Many Swiss suggest that Whittlesey's person-to-person relationships best explain her success in improving dialogue and understanding between the United States and Switzerland. Jürg Hauswirth, chief operating officer of EGI Direct, recalled that Whittlesey formed personal bonds with all the Young Leaders. "Even after many years she still knows our names and remembers some discussions. She takes care of the [Young Leaders]." In Hauswirth's view, Whittlesey appears to view the Young Leaders as a "huge family."[137] Andreas Beerli, a former member of Swiss Re's executive committee and chairman of the Swiss Advisory Council of the American Swiss Foundation in 2009, agreed with this assessment. During my travels through Switzerland to hear Swiss perspectives on her legacy, Beerli told me: "She cares about individuals. She knows all the people that you are interviewing now; she knows them very well. She knows the whole family, the children, their career, their problems."[138] Geneva banker Jean-Vital de Muralt noted that "one of the most faithful friends, in the case of our country, has certainly been Madam Whittlesey."[139]

Whittlesey's creativity in bilateral political and cultural exchange was not limited to Switzerland. During her long career in the public and private sectors, she had quietly cultivated relationships with high-level ministers in—one of the most unlikely countries for such a committed anticommunist as she—China. Once again, she was acting "under the radar."

---

[136] Ibid.
[137] Jürg Hauswirth, email to author, August 17, 2010.
[138] Andreas Beerli, interview by author, Zürich, August 20, 2010.
[139] Jean-Vital de Muralt, interview by author, Geneva, August 15, 2009.

CHAPTER 9

Enlarging U.S.-China Connections
Private Diplomacy (part 2)

Traffic slowed to a standstill as Faith Whittlesey sat with four other Americans and Chinese officials in the rear seats of a Chinese government limousine in May 1994. China's red flag in miniature extended upward from each of the front headlights of the long black sedan. Liao Dong, a Chinese Communist Party official whom Whittlesey had befriended in 1979, had offered her (along with several Republican colleagues of her choice) the opportunity to visit and meet with important Chinese officials. Now they headed along a highway to experience the Great Wall, one of the world's most celebrated landmarks. Before anyone was able to even remark on the delay, however, the driver pulled into the lane for oncoming traffic and sped along at breakneck speed. Bicycles, rickshaws, and the much smaller Chinese cars dutifully pulled over to the side of the road and allowed free passage to this imposing state vehicle.[1]

"Visiting China with Faith Whittlesey was like traveling with the Queen of England," recalled more than one American whom she invited to accompany her.[2] Although Whittlesey never represented the U.S. government in her travels to China, leaders of the People's Republic of China (PRC) treated her with the highest respect as a former Pennsylvania-state elected official, U.S. ambassador, and member of President Ronald Reagan's

---

[1] Michael Farris, interview by author, telephone, March 29, 2012.
[2] Jeanne Marie Cella, discussion with author, New York, May 9, 2012. Michael Farris, interview by author, telephone, March 29, 2012.

senior White House staff. Several of Whittlesey's American companions on these visits to China were invariably surprised at the great deference accorded her by the Chinese.

Switzerland had occupied the bulk of Faith's attention outside of the United States ever since her first appointment as ambassador in 1981, but she simultaneously had begun establishing inconspicuous durable relationships with high-level officials of the Chinese Communist Party (CCP), starting in 1979. By leading the first delegation of high-profile Republicans to China in 1994, Faith was recognized by Chinese officials as a pioneer in creating bilateral ties between the two nations.

Despite her clear abhorrence of that government's totalitarian rule—with hundreds of thousands of prisoners of conscience as well as coercive population-control policies—she demonstrated a constructive attitude by cultivating positive and productive relationships in China. Whittlesey had defined herself as a fully committed "Cold Warrior" as U.S. ambassador to Switzerland and senior staff member in Reagan's White House during the 1980s. Nonetheless, she believed it was vitally important for U.S. security to cultivate connections with the CCP—the real power in China—in order to seek better understanding with this emerging world power. Through extending venues of contact and consultation, Faith hoped the United States could decrease the likelihood of military confrontation in Asia and achieve a better case scenario.

As a direct consequence of her efforts at engagement, China's leaders held her in high esteem, thus providing her with the unique capability of being able to advocate for her policy views. Many friends in the conservative movement did not agree with her approach and remained consistent "hawks" on the People's Republic of China, avoiding contact with Chinese officials altogether. But Whittlesey had always greeted the most contentious disagreements as opportunities for dialogue and improved understanding. As a politician, diplomat, and private citizen, she chose to engage with a potential adversary, if they posed no imminent threat to U.S. security.

FAITH WHITTLESEY'S MULTIPLE CONNECTIONS TO CHINA
Whittlesey first traveled to the PRC in 1979. Invited by the American Council of Young Political Leaders,[3] she brought with her a much more extensive knowledge of that country than most Americans had at the time. Very few

---

[3]   A project of the now-defunct United States International Communications Agency.

U.S. citizens had ventured behind the bamboo curtain since the beginning of communist rule in 1949. In fact, when the United States established formal relations with this communist government on January 1, 1979, only one member of President Jimmy Carter's administration had visited China.[4]

Whittlesey arrived in Beijing in 1979 with a basic familiarity with the Chinese language, culture, and history. Faith's exposure to China came most directly from her brother, Thomas M. Ryan, who had completed years of study at Yale and the University of Michigan in Chinese literature and language, subsequently teaching Chinese at the University of Alabama, Birmingham. He and his wife Joan had lived in Taiwan for 2 years as part of a U.S. government-sponsored academic program.[5]

In addition, there were multiple Whittlesey connections to China. Albert W. Whittlesey, her late husband Roger's father, had been born in China to Presbyterian missionary parents. Faith fondly recalled Albert's riveting accounts of, among other places, Chongqing (Chungking)—China's major southwestern economic center and transportation hub upstream of the vast Yangtze River (China's longest river and the world's third-longest).[6] Her older son Henry would later marry Ellen Zhang, a Chinese woman who had come to Massachusetts at age 17 from Shanghai for her college education and later became a U.S. citizen.[7]

From the perspective of China's power elite, another important bond between Faith Whittlesey and the PRC existed. Her deceased husband's uncle was U.S. Army Captain Henry Clark Whittlesey, whom the CCP leadership regarded as a hero and martyr. In the later years of World War II, Captain Whittlesey served on a secret mission in Japanese-occupied Shannxi (Shensi) province in northwest China. As one of the six children born to Roger and Annie Withey Whittlesey (both China Inland missionaries), Henry had learned Chinese as a boy growing up in the Chongqing region.

When the United States battled Japan in the China-Burma-India (CBI) theater, Henry (then working as a journalist in Philadelphia) volunteered late in the war for a secret, dangerous mission behind enemy lines in the

---

4   According to the American Council of Young Political Leaders website, "In 1979, when President Carter normalized relations with the People's Republic of China, then special White House advisor Sarah Weddington was the only person working in the administration who had actually been to China, as a young Texas state representative on the first ACYPL delegation in 1977." Accessed on April 3, 2012, at *www.acypl.org/about/our-story/*.
5   Faith Whittlesey, discussion with author, telephone, April 12, 2012.
6   Faith Whittlesey, email to author, April 8, 2012.
7   Faith Whittlesey, discussion with author, telephone, April 10, 2012.

Shannxi region of China. The 17-man mission's special instructions were to pursue possible cooperation and coordination with the Chinese communist leader Mao Tse-tung in defeating the Japanese. Having established their headquarters in 1936 in remote Yan'an (Yenan), a small town in an impoverished mountain region, Mao and the communists had impressed various American observers with their effective resistance to the Japanese military.

After taking a short course at Yale to refresh his Mandarin language skills, newly commissioned First Lieutenant Whittlesey embarked on his top-secret assignment to Yan'an as part of what is now known as the "Dixie Mission."[8]

"A ROAD NOT TAKEN": CAPTAIN WHITTLESEY AND THE DIXIE MISSION

First Lieutenant (soon to be Captain) Whittlesey's mission to connect with the communist insurgents had the potential to prove vitally significant to U.S. interests in China. President Franklin Roosevelt's administration had grown frustrated with the Chinese Nationalist government, through which the United States coordinated all resistance to the Japanese occupation of China. Inefficiency and corruption seemed pervasive among the Nationalists, while the communists—bitter adversaries of the Nationalists for control of China's interior regions—frequently fought more effectively against the Japanese.[9]

Therefore, beginning in July 1944 the U.S. government sent Henry Whittlesey and 16 other military and diplomatic personnel—formally known as the United States Army Observer Group—to Yan'an. One of their primary initial goals would be to engage and coordinate rescue operations for downed American pilots with the communists.[10] Some of Henry's colleagues in this group were, like he, also the children of missionaries. They all served under the command of the famous U.S. General Joseph Stilwell, commander of the American army in the CBI theater.

Henry Whittlesey had accepted a dangerous assignment. Working with army officers, technicians, U.S. Foreign Service political officers, and OSS (Office of Strategic Services, predecessor to the CIA) operatives, First Lt. Whittlesey lived about a half-mile from Yan'an, with tunnels dug into a

8   Faith Whittlesey, email to author, April 8, 2012.
9   June Grasso, Jay Corrin, and Michael Kort, *Modernization and Revolution in China: From the Opium Wars to World Power*, 3rd ed. (Armonk, NY: M. E. Sharpe, 2004), p. 134.
10 Carolle J. Carter, *Mission to Yenan: American Liaison with the Chinese Communists, 1944–1947* (Lexington: University Press of Kentucky, 1997), pp. 11, 13. Michael Schaller, *The U.S. Crusade in China, 1938–1945* (New York: Columbia University Press, 1979), pp. 181–182.

hillside serving as their initial residence. Lacking running water and with windows covered with paper rather than glass, they struggled to heat their humble residence with charcoal—although this method often sickened and threatened to asphyxiate them.[11] Someone coined the code name "Dixie" for the unit, in reference to their vulnerable geographic position within enemy territory.[12]

The Dixie Mission in China suffered only one casualty—Henry Whittlesey—in its 3 years of existence, and the circumstances of his death are somewhat unclear. Assigned as a representative of the Air Ground Aid Service, Whittlesey was responsible for arranging for the escape of U.S. prisoners of war held in Japanese-occupied areas. Soon promoted to captain, Whittlesey endeavored to establish safe houses for U.S. pilots whose planes were forced down behind enemy lines in Japanese-occupied China. During one of these operations, Captain Whittlesey (in civilian clothes) and a communist photographer-guide visited a village close to enemy-controlled territory. Although the Chinese had assured them that the Japanese had abandoned the village, Japanese snipers remained in hiding. The gunmen mortally wounded Captain Whittlesey and the photographer. Many CCP soldiers were killed in efforts to retrieve the bodies.[13] According to historian Carolle Carter, "The Chinese were extremely distressed, not only because of their own loss and their high regard for Whittlesey, but also because they had lost face, since Whittlesey had entered the village after they had assured him there were no Japanese in it."[14] After Faith's husband Roger died in 1974, she consistently cultivated pride among her three children, and later her 10 grandchildren, about the heroism of their great uncle, Captain Henry C. Whittlesey, the only U.S. casualty of the historic Dixie Mission to war-torn China.

Even though the Dixie Mission was considered a failure in U.S. military circles, the Communist Party valued Captain Whittlesey's sacrifice as a significant symbol—"a road not taken," in the words of Swarthmore College political science professor James Kurth—of U.S.-Chinese solidarity against a common foe. In the Robert Frost poem "The Road Not Taken," a

---

[11]   Jonathan Fenby, *Modern China: The Fall and Rise of a Great Power, 1850 to the Present* (New York: Ecco, 2008), p. 311.

[12]   Comparable to the Union soldiers who ventured behind enemy lines in Confederate states during the U.S. Civil War.

[13]   Carter, *Mission to Yenan*, pp. 60–61.

[14]   Ibid., p. 61.

traveler chooses a path which has multiple unforeseen consequences. Kurth noted that the U.S. government and communist insurgents parted ways soon after the end of World War II. In 1949, the United States refused to recognize the newly established "People's Republic of China" in the wake of the communists' victory over the Nationalists on the mainland, and it was another 30 years before the United States ultimately acknowledged the Chinese communist authority as a sovereign state, on January 1, 1979.[15]

Despite this rebuff from the United States, CCP leaders continued to recall the Dixie Mission as a moment of harmony of purpose with America. For the Chinese, who had suffered invasion and brutal atrocities (including mass rape and the murder of some 300,000 people in Nanjing) at the hands of the Japanese military,[16] Captain Whittlesey particularly deserved admiration as an American who deeply respected their commitment to the all-out war effort to defeat imperial Japan.

China's government thus granted the Dixie Mission an important place in the PRC's institutional history. The Dixie Mission's story was recounted in documentaries which were aired repeatedly on Chinese state television. The PRC preserved General Stilwell's Chongqing headquarters—still intact—as a museum, which even today (2012) displays photographs of Captain Whittlesey and other Dixie Mission members.[17] Out front, a large statue of General Stilwell dominates the entrance. The museum's photo gallery also prominently displays a photograph of Jane Barnard Whittlesey, the captain's widow (and a beloved aunt to Faith and Roger), who later traveled to China as an honored guest, with other wives and children from this mission's members. After the war another museum, in Yan'an, preserved the quarters where the members of the Dixie Mission actually lived. The Chinese communists designated the dining hall in this group of buildings as "Whittlesey Hall," in honor of Henry.[18]

"THE KING IS EVERYWHERE": FIRST VISIT TO CHINA IN 1979

In 1979, representatives of the American Council of Young Political Leaders invited Faith to accompany other rising American politicians to China. Whittlesey's prominence as the highest-ranking female elected official in

---

[15] James Kurth, interview by author, telephone, April 2, 2012.
[16] See, for example, Iris Chang, *The Rape of Nanking: The Forgotten Holocaust of World War II* (New York: Basic Books, 1997).
[17] Nancy Price, interview by author, telephone, April 26, 2012.
[18] Faith Whittlesey, email to author, April 8, 2012.

Pennsylvania at that time earned her this privilege of being one among the first group of Americans to visit the newly recognized PRC. Chuck Robb and Kit Bond, who later became U.S. senators, were also members of the small delegation, as was Peter McPherson, later director of USAID[19] under Reagan, and Bernard Aronson, a Democrat who later served as an assistant secretary of state in the George H. W. Bush administration.[20]

Whittlesey traveled to China as a committed anti-communist in 1979, but she engaged politely with her hosts. She assiduously recorded her impressions in a small wirebound reporter's notebook. Perhaps reflecting the government's strict control over the Americans' activities, she paraphrased a quotation from 17th-century English political philosopher Thomas Hobbes, " 'Freedom is the place where the King is not looking.' In China—King is everywhere."[21]

Despite this fundamental aversion to the CCP's Marxist-Leninist core, however, Whittlesey's pleasant disposition and her family connections with China provided her with singular opportunities to engage actively with Chinese communist officials. PRC officials soon learned of Faith's relation, by marriage, to Captain Henry Clark Whittlesey, and her status perceptibly improved. "I noticed as the trip went on, I was moved closer and closer to the guests of honor in the seating arrangements," she later recalled.

A young Chinese translator, Liao Dong, retained her contact information, and they soon developed a correspondence that has lasted down to the present day. By the 1990s, Liao had risen to a high-ranking post in the International Department of the Chinese Communist Party.[22]

RETURNING TO CHINA IN 1994

This continuing communications link between Whittlesey and Liao resulted—a decade later—in several invitations for Whittlesey to bring a delegation of Republicans to China. Initially Whittlesey declined these offers, not wishing to provide any implicit support for the PRC in the wake of the infamous June 1989 Tiananmen Square massacre. But by 1994, she resolved to witness, firsthand, ongoing changes behind the bamboo curtain.

---

[19] United States Agency for International Development.
[20] Faith Whittlesey, discussion with author, telephone, April 10, 2012.
[21] From the Faith Whittlesey Collection, Howard Gotlieb Archival Research Center at Boston University (hereafter referred to as FW), Box 1, Folder 2.
[22] Faith Whittlesey, email to author, April 8, 2012. Liao later served in a high-ranking position in the Chinese embassy in Washington, DC.

The Republican Party looked askance at the PRC, especially following Tiananmen Square in 1989. After months-long Chinese student protests for greater personal freedoms, an overnight media blackout and violent military action struck early on the morning of June 4. Reports estimated that the army killed hundreds of Chinese college-age youths.[23] President George H. W. Bush suffered public embarrassment when the PRC released photographs of the president's national security advisor, Brent Scowcroft, in China formally toasting that country's leaders only months following the killings.[24] Many U.S. conservatives in particular believed that the United States should contain and resist China in a manner similar to U.S. policy toward the Soviet Union during the Cold War.

Whittlesey did not deny that the PRC sought to disguise "totalitarian practice" through the pretext of communism's vaunted "idealized principles." The Soviet Union, however, had never demonstrated an inclination to compete in the global economy, as China was then undertaking to do. "The Soviets practiced military expansion. Chinese expansion is by trade and economic development," she noted.[25]

In 1994, moreover, Whittlesey perceived China as a country with which the United States should have more direct and open dialogue. "It was becoming clear to me and others," she later remembered, "that the Chinese would be increasingly important to the U.S.—and in world events—and that communication and better understanding were desirable, despite our continued strong disapproval of their oppressive governing system."[26] Whittlesey now viewed Liao's invitation as a valuable opportunity to learn more about China's rich culture, economy, and foreign policy perspectives, as well as to advocate firsthand for greater PRC respect for religious liberties and human dignity.

RAISING THE SUBJECT OF RELIGIOUS FREEDOM

Powerful government indoctrination, even in fashion, made an impression on Whittlesey in 1994. Mass-produced tunic-style jackets, in imitation of the iconic CCP Chairman Mao, appeared on most Chinese torsos, and Whittlesey witnessed few signs of Western styles or prosperity. "I remember

---

[23] David C. Wright, *The History of China* (Westport, CT: Greenwood Press, 2001), p. 174.
[24] Timothy Naftali, *George H. W. Bush* (New York: Times Books, 2007), p. 81.
[25] Faith Whittlesey, discussion with author, telephone, April 12, 2012.
[26] Faith Whittlesey, email to author, April 8, 2012.

seeing Chinese of both sexes in the cities wearing uniforms of dark 'Mao suits' and a sea of such brigades on bicycles as far as the eye could see."[27]

Faith wondered if Christian churches in China might prove islands of freedom in this vast ocean of government-enforced conformity. At each town on the 1994 visit, Whittlesey requested to visit a Protestant church. She had not yet converted to Catholicism, which she would do in 2000. The PRC allowed only government-authorized hymnals, she realized. When she asked her government-assigned liaison, Zhang Zhijun, why no children were visible in the services and why the government permitted no Sunday school, he replied, "with ever-so-slight hardness in his voice," that "the education of children is the responsibility of the state." In Whittlesey's view, "They were trying to prevent the faith being transmitted from one generation to the next."[28]

Faith understood the reality and impact of religious repression in China. She had served for several years on the board of directors and for 3 years as chairman of Christian Freedom International (CFI; which was founded during the Cold War as Christian Solidarity International [CSI] by Reverend Hans Stückelberger, a prominent Reformed pastor from Zürich).[29] Whittlesey invited another CSI board member, Michael Farris, to join her in traveling to China in 1994. Whittlesey and Farris raised questions with PRC officials about several policy issues, including government suppression of individual liberties through its one-child limitation, coerced abortions (sometimes in the eighth month of pregnancy) and the wholesale infanticide resulting from this rigid state security-enforced family planning regime.[30]

Farris recalled a friendly though intense exchange between the two sides. The discussions split about 50–50 on competing agendas, which Whittlesey

---

[27] Ibid.

[28] Ibid.

[29] CSI organized trips to the communist Soviet Union and other nations to prevent the persecution of Christians and Jews. For example, CSI negotiated for the importation of Bibles and the release of Christians imprisoned and forced into psychiatric institutions. See *www. christianfreedom.org.*

[30] Whittlesey's voice (along with those of many others) may well have helped in persuading PRC health officials ultimately to announce, in November 1994, a ban on permitting parents to identify a fetus' gender in order to ensure, through abortion, that their next child might be male. David B. H. Denoon, ed., *China: Contemporary Political, Economic, and International Affairs* (New York: New York University Press, 2007), p. 221. However, as late as 2007, National Public Radio correspondent Rob Gifford described interviews with Chinese citizens about the practice of such late-term abortions and the drowning of newborns who survived this procedure. Rob Gifford, *China Road: A Journey into the Future of a Rising Power* (New York: Random House, 2007), p. 20.

had negotiated in advance with the Chinese hosts. "Faith and I wanted to open dialogue on Christian freedom and the dignity of human life in China, and the Chinese wanted to talk about business opportunities."[31] In a similar way, as director of the White House Office of Public Liaison from 1983 to 1985, Whittlesey had specialized in arranging for such balanced discussions with visiting interest groups.

This evenhanded treatment of contentious policy disagreements may partially explain why Chinese government officials demonstrated genuine respect for Whittlesey. Farris, who later founded Patrick Henry College in Virginia (of which he became chancellor) and the Home School Legal Defense Association, recognized that Faith's personal charm and gentility earned the respect of the leaders they met.

In Farris' words, "She wraps a firm set of convictions inside a cocoon of grace. Everybody loves Faith." Thus, even while raising questions at every meeting about the one-child policy, imprisonment of pastors and priests, and restrictions on Christian worship, Whittlesey maintained a polite decorum with Chinese officials.[32]

When they traveled to China in 1994, Whittlesey and Farris had no misplaced illusions that the senior CCP officials would listen to and seriously consider their arguments. These party members, typically older than 60 (sometimes 70) years of age, had advanced their careers through years of submitting themselves to thoroughgoing ideological indoctrination. But Whittlesey and Farris hoped that their younger assistants (rising members of the CCP power structure) might listen to, process, and consider their arguments. As Farris recalled, "I was talking to the 30- and 40-year-olds who were sitting around with the notebooks. They were the senior officials of the future. In my mind, I was planting seeds."[33]

As one example of how these junior officials would later rise to top-level decision-making status in China, Farris cited their highly engaging official liaison, Zhang Zhijun. When they returned in 2006, Zhang had advanced to the position of vice minister of the International Department of the Central Committee of the Communist Party. By 2009, he had become vice minister

[31] Michael Farris, interview by author, telephone, March 28, 2012.
[32] Ibid.
[33] Ibid.

of foreign affairs, the second-ranking position in that important ministry (comparable to the State Department in the United States).[34]

Faith left China in 1994 totally convinced that her decision to visit the country had been the right one. "All of our discussions were intense and, I believe, productive." In Whittlesey's view, the PRC elevated young "highly educated and polished Communist Party members" to leadership roles. She concluded that engagement with these leaders would benefit the United States in many ways. Chinese authorities clearly admired U.S. organization, technology, and prosperity. This approval and respect "were apparent in every meeting," she recalled. But Faith noted that "they also had many inaccurate impressions," which bilateral dialogue had helped to correct.[35]

VISITING CHINA'S CATHOLIC CHURCHES IN 2005

During the subsequent decade, China's affluence continued to surge, and Whittlesey eventually returned to a much changed China in 2005. Chinese economic growth consistently approached or exceeded 10 percent from 1995 to 2005. Faith's decision to engage with the CCP seemed to make sense, especially as the PRC began to accumulate U.S. dollars and treasury bonds.

As the PRC prepared to celebrate the 60th anniversary of China's 1945 victory against Japan in lavish fashion, Whittlesey received a high-level invitation to a series of events. The PRC provided her a five-city tour in grandeur resembling a formal "state visit," which concluded with a theatrical World War II victory commemoration and ceremonial dinner for thousands of guests hosted by China's President Hu Jintao at Beijing's Great Hall of the People.

While the Chinese had prepared a detailed formal program for the 2005 trip, Whittlesey also asked to visit a church in each city included in the itinerary. In 1994, she had asked to see Protestant churches. Having converted to Catholicism in 2000—and accompanied by another observant Catholic, her friend and assistant Nancy Price—Whittlesey now inquired about the Catholic church in every city they visited. In Whittlesey's recollection, these requests made their Chinese guides and translators very

---

[34] Accessed on March 29, 2012, at *www.fmprc.gov.cn/eng/wjb/zygy/gyjl/ZhangZhijun*. In later years, Whittlesey organized a dinner discussion for Zhang in Boston with Boston University scholars. She also took him to visit her friends Cosmo and Cathi Cremaldi of Cambridge, Massachusetts, so that he could meet typical Americans in a typical American home. Cosmo Cremaldi, discussion with author, telephone, July 26, 2012.

[35] Faith Whittlesey, email to author, April 8, 2012.

nervous. As loyal members of the Communist Party, they knew their bosses' aversion and fear of Christianity as a potential source of subversive Western ideas. The Chinese guides frequently mentioned the example of the fall of communism in Eastern Europe, which they appeared to attribute to the churches. Whittlesey was often told that the Catholic churches were closed or in dangerous sections of the town. "But we politely insisted. They were so eager to please us—as their honored guests—that they relented."[36]

Whittlesey described a variety of unexpected and moving experiences at the Catholic churches in Chinese cities. Although Westerners came much more frequently to China than in earlier years, very few U.S. and European citizens visited Chinese churches. In Chongqing, the largest municipality in China, Whittlesey recalled, "The people were dumbstruck and overjoyed that two Americans had come there." At this city's Catholic Cathedral, where they attended Sunday mass, Whittlesey and Price were greeted enthusiastically. "When we entered," Price recalled, "the parishioners wanted to take our hand, and they brought us immediately to the front pew."[37] In Whittlesey's recollection, "I was somewhat embarrassed that Nancy and I were treated like rock stars."[38] Price was moved to tears, aware that attending religious ceremonies meant risking one's job in China: "I felt completely unworthy of this reverential greeting."[39] Few guests from outside China visited the cathedral, which may have explained the parishioners' earnest efforts to show gratitude and appreciation to these surprise guests, Whittlesey surmised.

The poverty and hardship Faith witnessed in the vicinity of the churches likely explained the absence of Western visitors. Tourists or commercial travelers did not seek out this impoverished side of China. In Whittlesey's recollection, "We walked around the muddy exterior of the church, saw extreme poverty and people with deformities." The grateful response of the Chinese Christians to their presence inspired her to perceive the "spirit of Christ" in their suffering. Whittlesey and Price distributed Christian literature in English which they had brought with them.[40]

On the final leg of their 5-day visit, Whittlesey and Price visited a Catholic church in Beijing for tea, where they met the "Patriotic" (approved

---

36 Faith Whittlesey, discussion with author, telephone, April 12, 2012.
37 Nancy Price, interview by author, telephone, April 26, 2012.
38 Faith Whittlesey, discussion with author, telephone, April 12, 2012.
39 Nancy Price, interview by author, telephone, April 26, 2012.
40 Faith Whittlesey, discussion with author, telephone, April 12, 2012; Nancy Price, interview by author, telephone, April 26, 2012.

by the Communist Party) priests and nuns assigned to it. "They looked frightened, as we were always accompanied by Communist Party officials," in Whittlesey's recollection.[41] Yet, Whittlesey recalled one priest's smiling, excited reception of them. He had visited New York City for several months at the invitation of that city's archbishop, John Cardinal O'Connor. Whittlesey knew that some Catholics had criticized the cardinal at the time because the PRC would only allow priests from the "Patriotic Church" to visit. This Chinese priest's positive impression of the United States, however, persuaded Whittlesey to credit O'Connor's "private diplomacy—looking forward, as he did, to a time of greater freedom for the church in China."

The lesson which Whittlesey took from this experience was that the American people have a knack for cultivating positive responses in visitors to the United States. In her view, America "generally makes a very good impression on all those who visit and disarms those inclined to be critical and hostile."[42]

AN HONORED GUEST IN THE GREAT HALL OF THE PEOPLE, 2005

The tour concluded with a lavish celebration and formal dinner with the entire diplomatic corps and thousands of other guests in Beijing's Great Hall of the People. Displays of China's strong nationalist pride predominated. Faith witnessed a spectacle which symbolized the recent return of the Middle Kingdom to global prominence.

Immediately before the victory dinner in the Great Hall of the People, there was a majestic theatrical performance in the Grand Auditorium (which seats 10,000). "Tall Chinese soldiers in dress uniform with fixed bayonets stood at attention, shoulder to shoulder, flanking each side of the stage and across the rear as the backdrop," Whittlesey remembered. Amid this military-tinged setting, the actors and dancers on stage recounted the tale of China's resistance to Japanese aggression from 1931 to 1945. "It was a truly heart-wrenching and yet frightening sight, a mixture of overwhelming military power and drama."[43] In Whittlesey's view, PRC officials conveyed a calculated message, namely, that China would not permit any repetition of

---

[41] Faith Whittlesey, discussion with author, telephone, April 12, 2012.
[42] Faith Whittlesey, email to author, April 8, 2012.
[43] Ibid.

the humiliations which the Chinese had suffered at the hands of the West and Japan in the late-19th and 20th centuries.[44]

Even prior to her 2005 visit to China, Whittlesey had developed a special sensitivity to anti-American sentiments. Her many friends in Switzerland had made clear their disapproval of the U.S. invasion of Iraq. In China, Whittlesey found similar attitudes. "In long conversations with Communist Party officials in every city, I became alarmed at the level of hostility to what were perceived as the double standards of the U.S. in preaching democracy but engaging at the same time in military intervention and policies which they believed were imperialistic," Whittlesey recalled. "I asked various of our hosts one on one if they had a 'colonial grievance' from the historical past. The answer was always in the affirmative."[45] Foreign powers had seized Chinese ports and forced China to grant favorable trade conditions, especially during the 19th century. China's officials also perceived U.S. actions in the post–World War II Korean and Vietnam wars as unjustified invasions.

Somewhat alarmed, Whittlesey viewed this strident criticism on the part of young Chinese intellectuals as requiring a more concerted U.S. response. She had advocated Ronald Reagan's foreign and economic policy to often skeptical audiences during the 1980s. In Whittlesey's view, the PRC needed to know that not all Americans, or even conservatives, shared then President George W. Bush's foreign policy positions. "I tried to explain to them that many Americans, and even many Republicans, did not agree with current policies of military interventionism and were in favor of a more prudent and cautious foreign policy protective of U.S. interests more narrowly defined."[46] In her mind, Whittlesey resolved to expose the Chinese to a variety of U.S. viewpoints.

An opportunity soon presented itself. Her longtime contact Liao Dong invited Whittlesey to bring a much larger delegation to China the following year. Liao had risen to director general of the U.S. and British section of the International Department of the Central Committee of the Communist Party.

The 2005 celebrations in China had provided Faith with a unique American access to understand that country's deeply felt emotions regarding

---

[44]   Ibid. Whittlesey noted the commemoration of many past wrongdoings by Japan and the West. "I was shocked by the repetition on numerous channels of Chinese television of stories about Japanese atrocities committed during the long Japanese occupation of China," she recalled. In her own conversations, Whittlesey heard most of the Chinese she encountered express very strong anti-Japanese opinions. Ibid.

[45]   Ibid.

[46]   Faith Whittlesey, discussion with author, telephone, April 12, 2012.

their history and also allowed her to communicate American respect for their ancient civilization. Faith's connections (if only by marriage) to a revered American hero in China (even if perhaps a forgotten one in the United States) had given her a special status. Her own cultivation of personal contacts with Chinese officials further expanded her influence.

High-level U.S. representatives were few at the victory dinner in the Great Hall of the People. PRC officials had placed Whittlesey next to General Stilwell's grandson, Lt. Col. John Easterbrook. Hu Jintao, president of China, personally walked over to greet them both and chat from the nearby table where he had been seated. The only other Americans in attendance at the head tables were U.S. Congressman Joe Wilson, Republican of South Carolina, and U.S. Congresswoman Madeleine Bordallo, Democrat of Guam, members of the China caucus in the House.[47]

2006: "A FORCED MARCH THROUGH PARADISE"

In her week-long August 2006 visit to China, Whittlesey brought several foreign policy scholars, a journalist, a radio and TV commentator, a lawyer, a businessman, and Henry Whittlesey Barnard (Captain Henry Whittlesey's nephew) with her. Officially designated as the U.S. Bipartisan Opinion Leaders Delegation, the group traveled to Shanghai, Beijing, and Tianjin, among other places. The group engaged with Chinese officials and scholars on such subjects as trade, currency issues, the status of Tibet, and the upcoming 2008 Olympic Games in China as well as the issue of religious and political liberty (which Whittlesey always raised).

Jeanne Marie Cella, Whittlesey's confidante from her Pennsylvania political days, also attended and remembered the dialogues as highly substantive. When they disembarked from the plane, the Chinese officials greeted Whittlesey on a red carpet with a larger-than-life bouquet of flowers. "Faith was treated as a [highly esteemed] dignitary," Cella recalled.[48]

Patrick Henry College founder and President Michael Farris, who had made the earlier trip with Whittlesey in 1994, recognized dramatic changes in China since his previous visit. Bicycles, rickshaws, and smaller automobiles shared the small rustic roadways in Farris' earlier visit, but in 2006 he had to scramble a bit to avoid being hit by a Maserati that raced

---

[47] Faith Whittlesey, email to author, April 8, 2012. On the China caucus, see *www.forbes.house.gov/ChinaCaucus.*
[48] Jeanne Marie Cella, email to author, April 12, 2012.

by him as he emerged from the Shanghai airport. In slightly more than a decade, that city had been transformed from a "dirty, smelly" metropolis to "one of the most beautiful cities in the modern world." Farris recalled staying in lavish hotels and enjoying sumptuous culinary fare every night, although he did not find himself able to consume one particular "Chinese delicacy"—small birds presented with their heads still intact.[49]

Another U.S. representative, Swarthmore College political science Professor James Kurth, similarly recalled the Communist Party's concerted efforts to host Whittlesey's delegation in the most generous manner possible. They dined at Beijing's most prestigious restaurant, where portraits of U.S. Presidents Richard Nixon and Gerald Ford hung on the walls.[50] Georgetown University's Joshua Mitchell remembered "continually marveling at the Chinese hospitality." He characterized the 7-day tour somewhat whimsically as "a forced march through paradise."[51] The Americans met the most senior PRC officials (known as vice ministers) from several key ministries responsible for economic development, social and religious affairs, culture, and higher education. "The Chinese organizers brought out 'heavy hitters' on the most sensitive topics of government policy," Kurth observed.[52] Members of the Chinese planning committee for the 2008 Olympic Games, hosted in Beijing, also addressed the U.S. visitors. The delegation, however, was pointedly not invited to any Chinese universities.[53]

As the U.S. invasion and occupation of Iraq—which began in 2003—continued to accumulate international and domestic critics, Whittlesey hoped to present the PRC's leadership with a more traditional conservative analysis of America's role in the world. Republican President George W. Bush was facing the looming prospect of a sweeping defeat for his party in the approaching congressional elections of November 2006 (and a national defeat again in 2008). In Whittlesey's view, the Chinese leaders would benefit from hearing a range of U.S. viewpoints. Professors Kurth and Andrew Bacevich of Boston University articulated a narrower and more cautious definition of U.S. national interests. Whittlesey found these intellectuals' foreign policy vision "consistent with the ideas of the Founding Fathers,

---

[49] Michael Farris, interview by author, telephone, March 29, 2012.
[50] James Kurth, interview by author, telephone, April 2, 2012.
[51] Joshua Mitchell, interview by author, telephone, April 2, 2012.
[52] James Kurth, interview by author, telephone, April 2, 2012.
[53] Ibid.

such as John Quincy Adams, who warned against 'going abroad in search of monsters to destroy'."[54]

WHITTLESEY'S DIPLOMATIC DIALOGUE

Chinese and other human rights activists continued to complain that the CCP—the only route to political and other forms of leadership in China—did not permit its elite membership to express religious beliefs.[55] The PRC also required Christian churches to register with the government, which appointed church administration and clergy and rigidly controlled the publication of religious materials. Many Protestant and Catholic Christians chose to join underground, or "house," churches in defiance of the "Patriotic Church" system.[56] These issues were regularly raised by Whittlesey with the Chinese.[57]

Faith also raised the subjects of Tibet and Taiwan with the officials who represented the PRC. "I tried on every occasion not to hector or preach to them, but to listen, draw them out as best I could, and make reasonable contrary arguments in the spirit of goodwill."[58]

The Chinese "thoroughly dismissed" these topics, but Whittlesey did not avoid these disagreements. She spent a lot of time with the "rising stars" of the Communist Party assigned to their group as guides and translators. "I found their young party intellectuals truly impressive—well spoken, polished to a high gloss, very well read and informed."[59]

Each of Whittlesey's companions credited her with articulating a persuasive critique of the PRC's government in an inoffensive manner. "The preeminent concern of Faith is the responsible use of liberty in the world," opined Georgetown University Professor Joshua Mitchell.[60] In Mitchell's view, Whittlesey endeavored to encourage Americans to balance freedom and order through consistent dialogue, negotiation, and a more thoroughgoing understanding of Chinese history and culture.[61] James Kurth believed that

---

[54] Faith Whittlesey, "Seeking 'Monsters' to Kill Abroad," *Washington Times*, October 14, 2009.

[55] See Ka Lun Leung, "Cultural Christians and Contemporary Christianity in China," in *Challenging China: Struggle and Hope in an Era of Change*, eds. Sharon Hom and Stacy Mosher (New York: The New Press, 2007), p. 256.

[56] Liu Xiaobo, "The Rise of Civil Society in China," in *Challenging China*, p. 114.

[57] Michael Farris, interview by author, telephone, March 29, 2012; James Kurth, interview by author, telephone, April 2, 2012.

[58] Faith Whittlesey, discussion with author, telephone, April 12, 2012.

[59] Joshua Mitchell, interview by author, telephone, April 2, 2012.

[60] Ibid.

[61] Ibid.

the U.S. questioning of China's one-child policy ultimately persuaded PRC officials to acknowledge the value of individual choice in these matters. The Chinese made an effort to present the government's policy as "nuanced and subtle with exceptions that made the one-child policy look less onerous." While the argument did not persuade Kurth, the Chinese had not dismissed the premise that individual freedom deserved respect.[62]

The professors who accompanied Whittlesey appreciated her awareness of the proper protocols within China. U.S. foreign policy scholars often have a highly developed sensitivity to non-American cultures through their research and travel experiences, and Faith did not disappoint them in those terms. In Kurth's recollection, Whittlesey demonstrated an "unfailing sensibility and sensitivity to doing and saying the right thing at the right time—she represented herself impeccably. There were no 'cringe moments' when the American does something that appears—from the point of view of the foreign host—appalling or '*gauche.*'"[63] Boston University's Andrew Bacevich agreed, saying, "There was a certain modesty in her demeanor that was attractive. She did not come across as 'the Ugly American'—pushy, arrogant." In Joshua Mitchell's recollection, "She had more energy than all of us, and she always 'turned on' the diplomat, smiled, and was engaging." Whittlesey's behavior served as a model for the other Americans, added Mitchell, who described Faith as a "gentle shepherd" whose example "makes you want to step up to the next level."[64]

PROFESSIONAL DEVELOPMENT

Members of the U.S. Bipartisan Opinion Leaders Delegation reported immense personal and professional benefits from their partaking in the meetings and excursions. They expressed their opinions, but they also listened and learned from the Chinese. Several participants provided concrete examples of how the visit affected their careers.

April Ryan, White House correspondent for American Urban Radio Networks, reported that the experience gave her a more practical real-world understanding of the many issues related to China in her day-to-day work. Whittlesey served as a valuable mentor who helped deepen Ryan's understanding of a country she would have otherwise known only obliquely.

---

[62] James Kurth, interview by author, telephone, April 2, 2012.
[63] Ibid.
[64] Joshua Mitchell, interview by author, telephone, April 2, 2012.

Ryan kept in contact with some of the Chinese leaders she met, and she greatly appreciated Whittlesey's including her in the delegation.[65] Faith, in turn, complimented Ryan's respectful but insistent questioning of Chinese officials.[66]

The scholars also credited the visit with improving their writing and speaking about China, and global politics in general. In Kurth's frequent lectures and writings since that experience, he noted an ability to articulate ideas about the Chinese in a less remote and mechanistic way.[67] Mitchell developed a course on political economy in which he considers China's hybrid model of state capitalism. Bacevich concurred with the general consensus: "My conception of China derives largely from that trip. That trip was formative. For example, I am now very skeptical of the view that the United States and China are somehow destined to be in a competitive relationship."[68] Bacevich suggested that "U.S. and China interests are compatible, because when I visited it seemed to me that the Chinese approach to matters is exceedingly pragmatic."[69]

NEW AND OLD ROSES: 'FAITH WHITTLESEY'™
AND THE CHINA ROSE (*ROSA CHINENSIS*)

While Faith certainly participated in sophisticated and sometimes contentious policy discussions with the Chinese, she also enjoyed cultural exchanges. She played a Chinese guitar and sang American folk songs on the American Council of Young Political Leaders trip in 1979 to China. In U.S. Embassy Bern, Whittlesey had commonly used American music as a means of sharing U.S. culture with the Swiss. In the 21st century, she discovered another way of promoting cooperation with China—through voluntary rose organizations.

Roses might seem an unlikely tool of diplomacy with China, but this flower symbolizes love, loyalty, and friendship around the world. Millions of Americans appreciated roses, and Whittlesey herself had developed a particular fondness for this flower. Shortly after her departure from the White House, President Ronald Reagan signed a proclamation which made the rose America's national floral emblem in 1986.

---

[65] April Ryan, interview by author, telephone, April 24, 2012.
[66] Faith Whittlesey, discussion with author, April 12, 2012.
[67] James Kurth, interview by author, telephone, April 2, 2012.
[68] Joshua Mitchell, interview by author, telephone, April 2, 2012.
[69] Andrew Bacevich, interview by author, telephone, March 29, 2012.

This act had more significance to her nearly two decades later when Gene Waering—then executive director of the American Swiss Foundation, a longtime member of the American Rose Society and president of the Jacksonville Rose Society in Florida—asked if she would consider agreeing to a new tea rose being named for her.[70] He wanted to attract attention to a particular novel rose which was the first new tea rose to be introduced into the United States in decades.[71] Whittlesey consented and quickly adopted a high-profile leadership role among rosarians. In 2006, she attended the New York Metropolitan Rose Council Dinner, which brought together rose lovers from all over the country at the Union League Club in New York. At this dinner, Scot D. Medbury, president and chief executive officer of Brooklyn Botanic Garden, one of America's premier cultural institutions, and American Rose Society President Marilyn Wellan (one of only two female presidents in that organization's more than 100 years of existence) presented Whittlesey with the 'Faith Whittlesey'™ rose. In 2010, she wrote a foreword for *The Sustainable Rose Garden: Exploring 21st Century Environmental Rose Gardening.* Whittlesey also began cultivating an expanded rose garden at her Winter Haven, Florida, home.[72]

As Whittlesey became active in the American Rose Society, she began to pursue means of using this flower to create cultural cooperation between the United States and China. Starting in 2005, Faith invited Chinese diplomats to accompany her to the annual New York Metropolitan Rose Council dinner. In 2009, Whittlesey arranged for the council to present a China rose (*Rosa chinensis*) to Kuang Weilin, minister-counselor and head of the political section at China's embassy in Washington.[73] Whittlesey intended this species rose—which was rediscovered in China some years ago—as a gift for the garden of the large new chancery building of the People's Republic of China embassy in the United States. The following year, she helped organize another event with the Chinese to present the same China rose to the New York Botanical Garden.[74]

[70] Pat Shanley, Peter Kukielski, and Gene Waering, eds., *The Sustainable Rose Garden: A Reader in Rose Culture* (Philadelphia: Newbury Books, 2010), p. 90.
[71] Gene Waering, email to author, May 24, 2011.
[72] Faith Whittlesey, discussion with author, telephone, April 12, 2012.
[73] This "species rose," *R. chinensis* var. spontanea, had proven useful for breeding those modern roses which could bloom more than once. *Sustainable Rose Garden*, insert following page 128. On Kuang, see *www.icasinc.org/bios/kuang_wl.html.*
[74] Faith Whittlesey, discussion with author, telephone, April 12, 2012.

Whittlesey's intervention proved important in overcoming Chinese suspicions that contact with the U.S. rose community might have ulterior motives. Lingering tensions deriving from centuries of conflict with the West in part explained why representatives of China's government initially balked at Whittlesey's invitation. "The Chinese were skittish and skeptical at first," recalled Waering.[75] According to Clair Martin, III, who served as the Shannon curator of roses at the Huntington Botanical Garden in San Marino, California, "There is always a possibility—in a diplomatic mind—that somebody is trying to use them for other reasons than you're saying."[76] Through her long-standing reputation and networks of trust with PRC officials, however, Whittlesey assured them that this offer had mutually beneficial possibilities. "Mrs. Whittlesey convinced them of the Americans' goodwill," Pat Shanley, president-elect of the American Rose Society, recalled, "and the Chinese sent the high-level representative requested in due course." Later, the Chinese followed up by sending Dr. Wang Guoliang, China's greatest expert on the species roses of China, on a tour to visit U.S. rose groups. The old "China rose" soon took its place in the Chinese embassy garden and the New York Botanical Garden as gifts of the American Rose Society.[77]

Whittlesey received acknowledgment from rose growers for her outreach to China, and she continued to support the joint U.S.-Chinese rose community's voluntary associations. In 2010 in New York, Clair Martin presented Whittlesey with the International Friend of the Rose Award in recognition of her role in reestablishing high-level connections between the United States and China on issues of importance to the rose-growing community.[78]

"UNDERSTAND YOUR ADVERSARIES"

Whittlesey remained personally engaged with Chinese diplomats even though she no longer felt comfortable making the long trans-Pacific flight to China after 2006. China's government frequently invited her to their Washington events, such as the dedication of the new Chinese embassy

---

[75] Gene Waering, email to author, May 24, 2011.
[76] Clair Martin, interview by author, telephone, February 18, 2012.
[77] Faith Whittlesey, discussion with author, telephone, April 12, 2012.
[78] Shanley et al., *The Sustainable Rose Garden*, insert following p. 128. During the following year, on June 10, 2011, Whittlesey hosted a luncheon at the Union League Club in New York in honor of American Rose Society Executive Director Jeff Ware. Faith Whittlesey, discussion with author, telephone, April 12, 2012.

in Washington. Her longtime Chinese friend and high-level diplomat Liao Dong has worked with her brother Tom on translating some of Liao's poems into English. Liao's twin children Ruylin and Rupeng had occasion to spend 6 weeks with Faith, her daughter Amy, and grandsons Paul Whittlesey O'Neill and Joseph Ryan Whittlesey in their Boynton Beach, Florida, home, in 2011.[79]

"I do not believe we can afford to reduce our relationship with China to trade, military and intelligence components," Whittlesey has argued. "The Soviets never played such a pivotal role in the world economy as China does today." Most significantly, Whittlesey notes that the Chinese own a substantial amount of U.S. treasury bonds and thus fund the U.S. government's monumental debt. "We cannot afford to make the Chinese our enemy. They're our major creditors."[80]

Some analysts interpret China's behavior as part of a long-range plan for global domination, but Whittlesey believes that such assumptions can create unnecessary confrontation and risk. "Some of my good conservative friends note that China is engaged in relentless intelligence gathering against U.S. targets, including computer hacking which they believe confirms Chinese intent to displace us as the dominant world power." Faith respects this point of view but in the end believes that engagement and dialogue will prove most likely to guarantee long-term U.S. security without war. "I am aware of the worst-case scenario with China and the United States. I believe, however, we should work hard to create the best case scenario."[81]

Whittlesey's visits to China allowed for the same kind of person-to-person diplomacy which had strengthened her own commitment to preserving the U.S.-Swiss relationship. She concluded, "Our political elites need to study more extensively and know the full spectrum of past events, not just the most recent 10 years, in order to understand both our friends' and our adversaries' motivations and goals."[82]

---

[79] Faith Whittlesey, discussion with author, telephone, April 12, 2012.
[80] Ibid.
[81] Ibid.
[82] Ibid.

CONCLUSION

In the Introduction of this book, I proposed that scholars and the public should incorporate Faith Whittlesey within the historical political narrative of U.S. women pioneers. Why has so little been written to chronicle Whittlesey's extraordinary career? Some political analysts and scholars may have perhaps overlooked Whittlesey because she is prolife and avoids the "feminist" label. She also does not fit into a perfectly neat box of the orthodoxy of the current Republican Party. She has championed decentralized, limited government, anticommunism, and the rights of the unborn.

The quotation Faith popularized about Ginger Rogers "entered common speech decades ago," noted the historian of gender and women Linda Kerber, but Whittlesey herself remains unknown among most academics who study women's issues.[1] Even though Faith's name frequently appears associated with "backwards, in high heels" when academics address women in politics and feminism,[2] her previously untold story surpasses the mere phrase in significance.

Whittlesey made a unique mark as a woman in the public and private sector. She defied the odds by entering law school when only 3 percent of American women earned graduate degrees, and she worked as a lawyer during a period when a similarly small percentage of women accomplished that feat in the United States.[3] In the most recent decades, she served on boards of directors for several multinational corporations. Although more females than males graduated from law school by the 21st century, as late as

---

[1]   Linda Kerber, email to author, June 16, 2011.
[2]   E.g. Linda Kerber, "Foreword," in Gerda Lerner, *The Majority Finds Its Past: Placing Women in History* (Chapel Hill: University of North Carolina Press, 2005), p. xiv. Joan Ferrante, *Sociology: A Global Perspective*, 8th ed. (New York: Cenage, 2012), p. 263.
[3]   Rochelle Gatlin, *American Women Since 1945* (Jackson: University Press of Mississippi, 1987), p. 204.

2012, women made up only 16 percent of all board members in the United States.[4]

Her work ethic and courage were exceptional if not unique. Faith was often an outsider, first as the highest-ranking woman politician in Pennsylvania (the one Republican female "boss"), later as the only woman on the White House senior staff and as one of the few female ambassadors to serve her country in the tumultuous final days of the Cold War. And of course, she balanced these high-pressure jobs with her heavy responsibilities as a widowed, single mother of three.

This illustrious career speaks volumes about her professional achievements. She also helped other women who benefited from her example and mentoring. Alexandra Preate, a longtime family friend who founded CapitalHQ, a New York public relations firm, identifies Whittlesey as a mentor to many women. By extending herself so willingly to help others, Whittlesey has become a "collector of people," Preate believes. The high value Faith places on personal relationships particularly impresses her.[5] Darla Romfo, president and chief operating officer of the Children's Scholarship Fund and an American Swiss Foundation Young Leader alumna, also admires and learned from Whittlesey's seriousness of purpose.[6] In the many interviews I conducted for this project, several other women echoed this high regard for Whittlesey's accomplishments, particularly as she rose to prominence within a generation in which few women engaged so widely in politics and business.

Whittlesey has opposed wars of choice and military overextension. She points out that Reagan won the Cold War with public diplomacy and ideas, not by force of arms in a hot war. Jeane Kirkpatrick, another Reagan ambassador, also expressed reservations about U.S. military intervention in Iraq during the George W. Bush administration. Faith adopted her prolife opinion not as a political ploy, but as a convert through the witness of leading Catholic politicians and her close friends with whom she worked in Pennsylvania. As this book has explained, however, Faith's conservatism came to her from deliberate and thoughtful consideration about the proper role of government in society and the role of individual responsibility.

---

4   Insert, "Female Representation," *Wall Street Journal*, June 6, 2012, p. B1.
5   Alexandra Preate, interview by author, telephone, June 12, 2012.
6   Darla Romfo, interview by author, telephone, May 21, 2012.

Another critique of Whittlesey's career may derive from her reputation for organizing and hosting lectures, publications, and social events. Some observers could have mistakenly concluded that Faith did not deserve consideration as a serious decision maker and policy expert. But such an assumption would exhibit an underestimation of her intellectual gifts and powers of persuasion. Without drawing attention to herself, Whittlesey's flair for behind-the-scenes activities has allowed her to promote honest discussion of difficult domestic issues and generate bipartisan agreement at home and bilateral cooperation abroad. As these pages have illustrated, Faith discovered novel ways of publicizing Reagan's ideas from her White House West Wing office several years prior to the proliferation of Internet and cable media outlets. Through her public diplomacy initiatives, she also created strong relationships with private-sector opinion makers in Switzerland and with emerging world leaders in China.

Whittlesey mobilized individuals in such creative ways that one might most aptly describe her as a true American political entrepreneur. She constantly questioned the established way of running the government, seeking to improve the system and make public servants more accountable. Motivated by her curiosity about people and ideas, she approached every interaction as an opportunity to learn—and teach. As a student of personalities, she constantly strategized about effective ways of finding common ground between people.

In this book, I have sought to recognize Whittlesey's achievements in context, as well as how her story might instruct 21st-century citizens of a rapidly changing world. Her career encourages us to remain open to dialogue, even with people who might appear idiosyncratic and who might disagree strongly with our point of view. In her recent years especially, she has encouraged U.S. citizens to learn more about the motivations of potential adversaries. "Americans have often held an incomplete, and in many cases flawed, understanding of Switzerland and China," Faith asserts. Ultimately, her legacy may be persistence in engaging with others about the most important policy questions of the day.

———

In July 2012, as this narrative concludes, Faith Whittlesey continues to balance her private family and public commitments. Living in Florida, where she has purchased property to be near her daughter Amy and several of her grandchildren, she frequently visits her two sons and their families living in and around Cambridge, Massachusetts. These trips, too, enable her to receive continued treatments for her cancer in remission at the Beth Israel Deaconess Medical Center, a teaching hospital of Harvard Medical School in Boston, while also providing her time to spend with her 10 grandchildren, a circumstance she especially cherishes. She also continues to serve as an active member of two corporate boards.

Switzerland remains at the forefront of Whittlesey's ever busy schedule. She annually contributes to the organization of—and attends—each American Swiss Foundation Young Leaders Conference as well as acting in support of other foundation events as chairman emeritus. The Boston-based Friends of Switzerland awarded her the 2003 Stratton Prize for Intercultural Achievement at the Harvard Club in Boston. In 2011, the ambassador of Switzerland to the United States presented her with the Tell Award, and in October 2012 the American Swiss Foundation plans to honor her again with a lifetime achievement award to be presented in Washington, DC, at a dinner at the National Air and Space Museum. And the 'Faith Whittlesey' tea rose will grace the cover of the September–October 2012 cover of the American Rose Society's national magazine, *American Rose*.

AFTERWORD

In Michael Reagan's Foreword to this book, the former president's son underscored Faith Whittlesey's role in the "triumph of the free world led by the United States over the Soviet Empire." The evidence presented in these pages supports that sentiment. Even beyond the struggle against communism, furthermore, she has consistently defended a core of ideas which empower individuals rather than impersonal bureaucracies.

Some (but certainly not all) scholars have rightly noted the power of ideas within the Reagan administration. Political scientist Fred Greenstein specifically spotlighted the importance of vision in making the "difference" between Reagan's effective presidency and other, less successful, administrations.[1] Historian Robert Dallek similarly has credited vision and the leader's credibility for "making" a presidency.[2] Other accounts, however, attribute President Ronald Reagan's popularity to sheer dumb luck or "mass patriotic fervor."[3] But I have argued that Faith's consistent and resourceful advocacy for the Reagan administration did not merely, or even primarily, reflect slick marketing techniques or media savvy. Neither did Reagan win public support only as a by-product of economic good times.

Whittlesey, as both ambassador and member of President Reagan's senior staff, worked to realize the president's vision and to maintain his credibility among the public. She waged public diplomacy campaigns in

---

[1]   Fred Greenstein, *The Presidential Difference: Leadership Style from FDR to Barack Obama,* 3rd ed. (Princeton, NJ: Princeton University Press, 2009), p. 187.

[2]   Robert Dallek, *Hail to the Chief: The Making and Unmaking of American Presidents* (New York: Hyperion, 1996).

[3]   For example, one historian suggested that the Grenada invasion in 1983 combined with Reagan's speeches to celebrate the 40th anniversary of D-Day, as well as the Los Angeles Olympic Games, in 1984 to create this "mass patriotic fervor" and a "wave of American jingoism." Sean Wilentz, *The Age of Reagan: A History, 1974–2008* (New York: Harper Perennial, 2009), p. 167.

Switzerland to explain the president's foreign policy agenda during her two tours there. And from the White House she launched creative efforts to publicize and spread the administration's core ideas—especially Reagan's confident message that U.S. values would ultimately defeat the communist experiment.

As Michael Reagan also mentioned, many critics of his father labeled the president (and he might have included Whittlesey herself) as extremist and militant. But the president and Faith both resisted communism and other challenges to individual freedom by means other than war. Rather than rely primarily on sending U.S. troops abroad, President Reagan empowered Whittlesey and other proponents of public diplomacy to mobilize members of America's "chattering class" for the "Reagan revolution" at home and abroad. These advocates of Reagan's vision would provide the most effective armies against the Soviet empire, the president believed.

In summary, Faith enhanced Reagan's effectiveness as a leader of the nation. Several years prior to the 1980 election which brought Reagan to power, she had recognized and energized suburban Americans—previously known as the "silent majority" or Reagan Democrats—behind a permanent vision which would soon make conservatives more popular than liberals in the late-20th-century United States. From the prime real estate of the White House's West Wing, Faith engaged with multiple segments of the Reagan governing coalition and encouraged these groups to support a common mission. Most notably, her emphasis on assisting anticommunist forces in Central America saw concrete results in November 1983 when Congress (temporarily) voted to continue funding El Salvador's government and covert aid to the Contras.[4] A year later, Reagan won an overwhelming victory in the 1984 presidential election.

As ambassador prior to and following her years in the White House, Whittlesey improved America's prestige in Switzerland. In an articulate way, she explained Reagan's innovative agenda to Swiss citizens who had often viewed the new president as brash and unsophisticated. Faith cultivated a friendship with Switzerland, an important friend and sister republic, even when many Americans ignored Swiss protestations that the powerful U.S. government was bullying this smaller nation. She thus encouraged a diplomatic relationship based on shared understanding and mutual respect.

[4]   Helen Dewar, "Congress Slows, Doesn't Halt, Reagan Changes," *New York Times*, November 20, 1983, p. A6.

Within the limits of Switzerland's neutrality, the Swiss responded favorably, as they cherished many of the same values, such as individual liberty and the rule of law, which the Reagan administration advanced. This continuing friendship brought economic and security benefits to the United States in the final years of the Cold War and beyond.

Perhaps most impressively, Faith provided a model for women in general. As Faith struggled to raise her three children as a widowed single mother, she certainly received no special accommodations in a work-driven White House. To the contrary, a few members of the White House staff, Congress, State Department, and the media appeared more than willing to exploit her vulnerability. As she noted without acrimony, she had to "work harder and run faster" than her male colleagues. President Reagan appeared to appreciate the particular challenge she faced. In a March 26, 1985, letter from the president to Faith as she departed the White House, he began with the following line: "I have formed a strong impression during the past four years that in Washington, criticism of public figures is the favorite blood sport."[5]

Whittlesey refused to be relegated to participate only in "women's issues" and insisted on her right to offer analysis on a broad range of topics. During the 1970s and 1980s, few women succeeded in this regard. But as this book has shown, rather than accept the role of token woman in order to ascend the party's bureaucratic machinery, she persisted, as she had done for years, in seeking to address the full portfolio of public policy questions by sometimes unconventional ways. As a result, she developed a broad range of skills, which she proved able to utilize in the private sector as a member of multiple boards of directors and president and chairman of the American Swiss Foundation.

Whittlesey's most lasting legacy may be her translation of President Reagan's principles, as well as the administration's public diplomacy initiatives, into her active private-sector career. Several institutions, especially the American Swiss Foundation and the Institute of World Politics, prospered and thrived under her leadership and with her active participation. In particular, the American Swiss Foundation's Young Leaders Conference brought many of today's most important American decision makers into contact with the Swiss people and political culture. While hard to measure or quantify, these relationships may prove lasting and important for the

---

5   Ronald Reagan to Faith Whittlesey, March 26, 1985, letter in Faith Whittlesey's possession.

21st century as both nations confront the economic, security, and other challenges of an increasingly complex and interdependent world.

Ultimately, Whittlesey's life demonstrates what a single person can accomplish despite the seemingly omnipotent and impersonal forces of social and bureaucratic norms.

ABOUT THE AUTHOR

Thomas J. Carty is chairman of the social sciences department and associate professor of history and American studies at Springfield College in Massachusetts. His 2004 book *A Catholic in the White House? Religion, Politics, and John Kennedy's Presidential Campaign* was reprinted in paperback in 2008. Professor Carty has written widely on religion and politics for several edited books, encyclopedias, and journals, and he has presented his research findings at academic conferences in the United States and United Kingdom as well as in local New England and national media outlets, including Bloomberg News and C-SPAN. He earned a B.A. from the College of the Holy Cross, and the University of Connecticut awarded him an M.A. and Ph.D. Professor Carty currently lives in Connecticut with his wife and two children.

INDEX

m